PSYCHOLOGY AND SPORT BEHAVIOR

PSYCHOLOGY AND SPORT BEHAVIOR

ANNE MARIE BIRD, Ph.D.

Professor
Department of Health, Physical Education and Recreation
California State University, Fullerton
Fullerton, California

BERNETTE K. CRIPE, M.S.

Formerly Assistant Professor and Chair
Department of Physical Education and Recreation
Whittier College
Whittier, California

with 60 illustrations

Photographs by
Dr. Ann Stutts and Dr. Judith Brame

TIMES MIRROR/MOSBY
COLLEGE PUBLISHING

ST. LOUIS • TORONTO • SANTA CLARA   1986

Editor: Nancy K. Roberson
Developmental editor: Kathy Sedovic
Editing supervisor: Judi Wolken
Manuscript editor: Mark Spann, Melissa Neves
Designer: Diane M. Beasley
Production: Kathleen L. Teal

Library of Congress Cataloging in Publication Data

Bird, Anne Marie.
    Psychology and sport behavior.

    Includes bibliographies and index.
    1. Sports—Psychological aspects. I. Cripe,
Bernette K. II. Title.
GV706.4.B57 1986   796'.01   85-10538
ISBN 0-8016-0600-4

GW/VH/VH 9 8 7 6 5 4 3 2 1   01/B/045

We finally found a way
to say a special thanks to two dear friends.
This book is dedicated to
Barbara and Lou.

PREFACE

During the past decade the field of sport psychology has experienced an explosion of knowledge. This advancement can be seen in both the expansion of the scientific basis and the increase in clinical applications. *Psychology and Sport Behavior* is the first text to fully cover the topics of most contemporary concern in an integrated fashion. It is designed for undergraduate major classes and introductory graduate courses in sport psychology. Its reliance on a strong research base coupled with a very readable writing style should make it appealing to both students and professors. Listed below are some reasons why we think this book is unique and innovative.

A Personal Approach

Anyone who has participated in sport competition, whether it be a weekend athlete, a little league player, or a varsity athlete, has some personal understanding of why sport psychology is so important to athletic success. We have attempted to capitalize on the personal experiences of the reader by using a writing style that personalizes the information presented and allows the student to relate to the examples provided. Such an approach should help to stimulate student interest and understanding.

Practical Orientation

Incorporated into every chapter are multiple practical examples and applications. This strategy further personalizes the information presented, since students can actually implement sport psychology principles within their own activities or when working with others.

Up-To-Date Presentation of Topics

This book represents the most current thinking and research evidence in the field. Similarly, the topics covered are those currently receiving the widest research and clinical attention.

Comprehensive Coverage of Topics

We believe that a student's initial exposure to sport psychology should be one that emphasizes breadth without ignoring the necessary scientific and theoretical frameworks. It is this contemporary blend of the scientific and the practical that contributes so much to the uniqueness of this book. Also we cover topics never systematically offered in previous texts (intervention strategies, imagery, attentional style), as well as the more traditional issues.

Organization

No previous text in sport psychology reflects the timely and comprehensive approach taken in this book. The book is organized into four sections. Section I initially introduces the student to the field of sport psychology and the basic concepts and vocabulary of scientific inquiry. Some professors may want to skip over that preliminary material in favor of getting directly to the "meat" of sport psychology such as the overview of the traditional perspectives used to describe sport behavior, which is presented in the following chapter. Traditional perspectives include behaviorism, trait psychology, and interactionism. Section II first discusses the important and interesting topics of arousal and anxiety in sport situations. Then intervention strategies that can be used to help people learn to cope with competitive stress are introduced. Section III presents the most current issues in the emerging field of cognitive sport psychology. Chapters address the processes of attentional style, observational learning, imagery, and motivation. Section IV discusses sport aggression, group performance, and the coach's leadership style. Taken together, the content of the book provides a conceptual framework for understanding and changing the behaviors of performers, teams, and coaches. Chapter organization should facilitate understanding not only by systematically developing a particular concept, but also by going one step further and illustrating its application.

Pedagogical and Design Features

The appeal and uniqueness of this book are enhanced through the systematic incorporation of several innovative and useful pedagogical and design features.

Unifying model. The unifying model is presented in eight of the twelve chapters. It was developed specifically for this text to facilitate understanding of individual difference variables such as anxiety and cognitive processes such as observational learning and imagery. Its explicit purpose is to assist the student in the formulation of a unified conceptualization of important concepts and processes. It provides students with a visual representation that summarizes the written text. Having used this approach with undergraduate students ourselves, we can say with some real enthusiasm that *it works!*

Chapter openers. The introduction to each chapter is designed to alert the reader to the content to follow. Whenever possible, questions are posed to draw the student's interest and stimulate the desire to learn the answers.

Case studies. Each chapter includes one or more case studies. These are realistic situations that motivate the student to apply the principles identified in the chapter. The case studies present actual, practical situations with which the reader can easily identify.

Chapter summaries. At the end of each chapter a summary is provided. It highlights the most important concepts and issues. The summary should also serve as a valuable review before examinations.

Figures and tables. Specially selected photographs are used at the opening of each chapter. Each should help to focus the student's attention on the topic to follow. Multiple figures and tables are used throughout the text. They highlight, summarize, and illustrate important concepts.

Implications for sport sections. Every chapter presents a specific section on how the student can apply the chapter content in sport settings. Implications are drawn in regard to athletes, teams, and coaching behaviors.

Glossaries. Key terms are presented in boldface in the text and reemphasized and defined in the chapter glossary. These key terms are presented once again in a comprehensive glossary located at the end of the book for easy accessibility to the student.

Review questions. At the end of each chapter thought-provoking questions are posed. They provide a vehicle for both review and further analysis of the material presented earlier in the chapter.

Annotated readings. The annotated readings are primarily designed to direct the student to sources for additional reading or study. Generally, the selections either extend or apply the material presented in the text. The annotations provide useful synopses to promote student interest.

References. The reference list at the end of the text mirrors both the foremost traditional sources and the most current studies, reflecting the "cutting edge" of the field.

Acknowledgments

A book of this import is never really the work of only the authors. Many individuals contribute either through their own research efforts, their technical expertise, or their personal encouragement. Although we cannot express our appreciation to each person individually, several deserve particular recognition.

We wish to express our sincere appreciation to the publisher's reviewers for their significant contributions to the quality of this book:

Steven Houseworth, Ph.D., University of Kansas
Sharon A. Mathes, Ph.D., Iowa State University
Gerald DeMers, Ph.D., Washington State University
David B. Wardell, Ph.D., University of Colorado-Boulder
Dean Ryan, Ed.D., University of California-Davis
William Kozar, Ph.D., Texas Tech University
Evelyn Hall, Ph.D., Louisiana State University-Baton Rouge
David P. Yukelson, Ph.D., University of Houston
Julius Gundershiem, Ph.D., University of Massachusetts-Amherst
Margaret Faulkner, Ph.D., Towson State University
Sherman Button, Ph.D., Boise State University

We are both impressed by and indebted to the very fine editorial staff of our publisher. In particular we appreciate the excellent work done by Nancy K. Roberson, Kathy Sedovic, and Mark Spann.

We are very appreciative of the sensitive and creative photography done by Dr. Judith Brame and Dr. Ann Stutts. We would also like to thank Steve Boaz for his initial assistance with the indexing of this book.

Finally, we would like to express our appreciation to the many friends, students, and colleagues who expressed both interest in and encouragement for our project.

Anne Marie Bird
Bernette K. Cripe

CONTENTS

SECTION III

COGNITIVE PROCESSES AND SPORT BEHAVIOR

SECTION IV

AGGRESSION, GROUP PERFORMANCE, AND COACHING BEHAVIOR

PSYCHOLOGY AND SPORT BEHAVIOR

I

THE SCIENTIFIC BASIS OF
SPORT PSYCHOLOGY

1
Scientific Dimensions of
Sport Behavior

2
Perspectives on Understanding
Sport Behavior

SCIENTIFIC DIMENSIONS OF SPORT BEHAVIOR

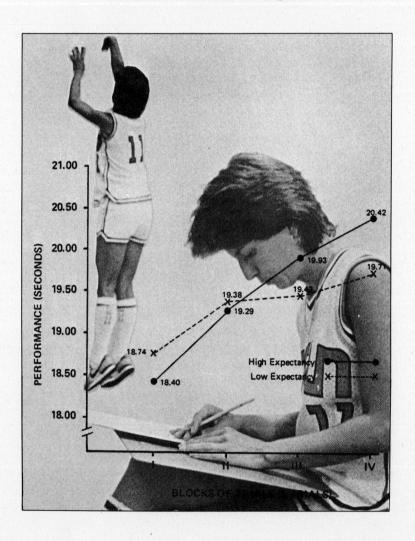

Comparatively speaking, the field of sport psychology is quite young; although some studies on athletes were conducted from the 1920s through the 1960s, they were mostly done on a "one shot" basis. Systematic programs of research did not take place until about 1970. Today, however, the field is an exciting, multidimensional one for researchers, coaches, teachers, and athletes alike. Sport psychology research efforts address questions about individual behavior as it occurs in sport and other movement settings: "How do psychological factors affect sport behavior?" "How do sport experiences influence psychological variables?"

In pursuit of answers to such questions, sport psychologists use research methods common to all behavioral sciences. They follow a series of steps to describe, explain, predict, and ultimately change behavior in the hope of developing theories that can further our understanding of individual behavior in sport and movement settings. That knowledge can then be applied to modify negative psychological influences or enhance skilled performance. Without a solid grounding in both the method of science and current knowledge in aspects of sport psychology research, it is not possible to have a clear understanding of how individual sport behavior can be improved.

This chapter introduces you to the historical development of the field of sport psychology and to several aspects of the scientific process. A discussion of the concepts and vocabulary associated with scientific inquiry is included because this knowledge is crucial to a full appreciation of the nature of contemporary sport psychology.

DEVELOPMENT OF SPORT PSYCHOLOGY

Most of the early sport psychology research focused on attempts to link personality or character with participation in athletics. As such, the majority of those early investigations were designed to compare the personalities of athletes with those of nonathletes.

When few definitive trends emerged from personality-based research, sport psychologists became disheartened with that approach and began to argue that a better avenue for understanding psychological aspects of individual sport behavior might be theory testing. Throughout most of the 1970s sport psychologists searched the literature for theories in the parent discipline of psychology that might also be applicable to motor skills. A good example of such theory borrowing is the use of social facilitation theory, which provided testable predictions of how the presence of other people should affect both initial skill acquisition and later skill performance. The most fundamental prediction was that the presence of other persons should be disruptive to early skill acquisition but facilitative to later (more highly skilled) performance. Much of this theory testing took place in laboratory settings, and the early laboratory-based results were promising in terms of developing sport psychology as a scientific field. Unfortunately, when those same predictions were taken to field settings for reality testing, little was uncovered in terms of practical applications to sport behavior.

As a result of the difficulties in applying theories such as social facilitation to sport, theory testing of this nature was almost totally abandoned by sport psychologists in the late 1970s and early 1980s (Landers, 1983). Researchers began to ask more clinical questions such as "How should the coach intervene to enhance athletic performance?" "How does mental practice or imagery affect sport performance?" "How can relaxation or biofeedback assist in the management of sport-related stress?" Many researchers also studied coach-athlete compatibility and the relationship between team cohesion and team outcome.

As a consequence of this more clinical approach to sport psychology, the field has moved closer to answering the questions posed most frequently by coaches. This is certainly desirable; however, a distinct vacuum in sport psychology theory still exists. When sport psychologists rejected theory testing in favor of more humanistic concerns they also almost eliminated any systematic attempts at building theoretical understandings of sport-related behavior. Such theory building is critical to providing a sound basis on which to draw the methods and strategies used to intervene or change behavior within sport settings.

On the other hand, many of today's leading researchers in the field are again arguing for and actively engaging in research that can lead to development of new theories that are unique to individual sport behavior. Research is taking place on the playing field, in the gymnasium, and in the laboratory. Questions are being answered for both practical and theoretical reasons. It is hoped that the next decade will continue to see much more sport-specific theory building as the discipline of sport psychology matures as a science in its own right, ultimately complete with its own theories and its own sound clinical principles.

PRINCIPLES OF SCIENTIFIC INQUIRY

To more clearly understand how a science develops and why theory development is so important, it is necessary to understand certain aspects of science and scientific inquiry. If sport psychology is to be considered a legitimate science, then it must use the methods and vocabulary common to all sciences. Throughout the text you will encounter common scientific vocabulary. We hope that by explaining the vocabulary, methods, and strategies of scientific inquiry in this chapter, you will be free to concentrate on the pertinent topics and issues presented in the rest of this text.

The unit of analysis in sport psychology is *individual behavior as it occurs in sport situations*. To achieve an understanding of that behavior, four steps must be followed.

Description and Explanation

First, you must attempt to *describe* exactly how a person behaves in an identifiable situation. For instance, you might observe that when other people are watching, the strokes of a particular tennis player become stiff and erratic. Once you see that this behavior is rather consistent, the second step is to try to *explain* why such effects occur. Therefore, once you are able to describe behavior, you then try to explain the causes underlying that behavior. Although the latter may seem relatively easy, in reality it is often most difficult. In our tennis example it is not enough to say that the presence of spectators causes the negative effects on the tennis player's strokes. That merely describes what takes place. To explain such effects, you have to determine what is happening inside the player to cause the stiffness that you observed. How can you do this?

One way is to attach electrodes to the various muscle groups involved in stroking the ball. You can then measure muscle activity patterns under conditions of hitting the ball when alone and stroking the ball with others watching. If you find different muscle activity patterns under those two conditions, you then have at least a partial explanation of how the presence of other persons affects the athlete internally and thus one explanation for why motor performance is hindered under the conditions described.

To explain more fully the relationship between the presence of spectators and negative effects on tennis performance, you can then test other hypotheses. For instance, instead of measuring the patterns of muscle activity, you can assess what is happening to the person's processing of environmental cues. Perhaps the tennis player is distracted by the presence of other persons and therefore splits his or her attention between watching the tennis ball and assessing what is happening among the spectators. It seems reasonable that such attentional scanning or switching can cause performance problems. Perhaps the player cannot see the oncoming ball soon enough and therefore hurries the stroke. It is through this process of testing alternative hypotheses to determine their "fit" that you can ultimately construct a sound explanation of the relationship between the presence of other persons and its effects on one person's tennis strokes.

Prediction and Intervention

The third step is a *prediction*. A primary goal of the science of sport psychology is the ability to predict individual sport behavior under identifiable conditions. Returning to our tennis example, if nothing changes, you can reasonably predict that any time this tennis player attempts to play in the presence of spectators, his or her performance will be hindered.

Should you simply stop at that point? Certainly not! Once you are able to make fairly definitive predictions, you can then apply principles of psychology so that behavior can be changed or controlled. This is the process of *intervention,* the use of psychological principles to enhance individual sport performance. In the case of the tennis player, performance can be enhanced by applying any one of several intervention strategies. For example, the athlete can be instructed in the use of relaxation procedures so that control over muscular tension is increased. Or attentional control can be gained by teaching the performer to use verbal cues such as "bounce" and "hit" at the appropriate time.

Sport psychology has the same goals as does any other behavioral science—the description, explanation, prediction, and change of individual behavior. Its uniqueness lies in its attempt to achieve those goals within the framework of sport and motor performance situations. The attainment of those goals allows you to apply strategies to assist the performer in enhancing sport performance.

BASIC SCIENTIFIC CONCEPTS AND VOCABULARY

Ways of Knowing

To more fully understand sport psychology as a science, it is necessary to understand the basic concepts and vocabulary of scientific inquiry. In this first section we will discuss various ways in which scientists answer questions such as "How do we know what is truth?" "What is reality or fact?"

Phenomenology

How does a scientist know that something is true, that an observed event is real and factual? One way is to call on personal experience, or **phenomenology.** Many of the beliefs we all hold are based on our own experiences. In the field of sport psychology, much of what takes place when coaches attempt to apply psychological principles to improve the performance of athletes is based on their own past experiences. They reason that "if it worked for me, then it should work for the other person." However, this is not necessarily true; people differ too much from one another. Therefore the phenomenological method is not considered adequate in a scientific sense. For a method to be adequate scientifically, it must allow for the generation of cause-and-effect relationships or laws that can be applied to large numbers of persons or events (i.e., **generalizability).**

Authority

Another method of "knowing" that is used with great frequency in sport psychology is that of authority. From this perspective, one looks to a major **authority** in the field to provide the answers or facts. For instance, many basketball coaches have looked to John Wooden, former UCLA basketball coach, for advice on how to best coach basketball. What's wrong with this approach? On the surface it seems logical to look to outstanding coaches for ideas on how to coach. But think for a moment: would Wooden's approach work equally well with high school students in a small Iowa town? Would Pat Head Summitt, coach of the U.S. Women's Olympic basketball team, be as successful as she was with the 1984 Olympic team if she used the same methods with a junior varsity basketball team? Is there a single, best approach to the coaching of all basketball teams, regardless of factors such as skill level, personality of the head coach, or gender of the players? Probably not. Thus the method of authority lacks sufficient scientific credibility because it fails to provide principles that can be generally applied.

Empiricism

The third approach to knowing is **empiricism,** which simple means "based on observation." Thus it is similar to the phenomenological method, which is based on personal experience. However, it differs from phenomenology in that empiricism refers to observations that are made under strictly controlled experimental conditions. From this perspective, a "fact" is generated by following the steps of the *scientific method.* The scientific method is common to all scientific inquiries, regardless of whether the question concerns physics, biology, sociology, or sport psychology. There are four basic steps in the scientific method.

First, a *statement of the problem* must be formulated. This simply means that the scientist must state exactly what the question is that he or she is attempting to answer, such as "What are the effects of failure on future task persistence?" or "Is there any cause-and-effect relationship between the coach's leadership style and team success?"

Second, one or more *hypotheses* must be posed. A **hypothesis** is a prediction of the answer to a previously identified question. In the first question above, the hypothesis might state that failure will cause a decrease in duration of task persistence. The hypothesis posed for the second question might be that a task-oriented coach should be more successful as compared with a socioemotionally oriented coach.

Third, an experiment is designed in which *data are collected and analyzed*. The method of data collection varies according to the nature of the question asked. If, as in the first question above, task persistence was to be observed, then time of duration at the task would be measured. However, if the study were designed to determine differences between leadership styles of coaches, then the data would most likely be collected through the assessment of personality by means of a standardized (paper and pencil) instrument. In sport psychology research, data are collected in a wide variety of settings, ranging from the playing field to the ski slopes to the laboratory situation. However, the analysis of those data is almost always accomplished by the use of statistical procedures. Given that the data must eventually be subjected to statistical analysis, it must be capable of taking on numerical values; it must be **quantifiable.** For instance, task persistence could be quantified on the basis of some unit of time such as seconds or minutes, whereas personality would take on some numerical value associated with a person's score on a particular personality scale.

Fourth, after the data are collected and analyzed, the scientist draws a **conclusion** on the basis of what the data analysis has shown. Recall that the purpose of the third step is to design an investigation that will allow the scientist to test the hypothesis that was posited in the second step. Therefore the conclusions derived on the basis of the data analysis tell the experimenter whether the hypothesis can be accepted or must be rejected. In our examples, the data analysis would indicate whether a failure outcome did indeed have a negative effect on subsequent task persistence and whether differences in coaching style had any measurable effect on team outcome.

The scientific method is elegant in its simplicity, yet rigorous in a scientific sense because of its inherent checks and balances. Given the latter, and given that the scientific method is the method of empiricism, you might reasonably conclude that the method of empiricism is the best or should be the only acceptable method of "scientifically" knowing. What could be lacking?

One difficulty is that the method of empiricism has as its goal only the identification of facts. More specifically, it generates facts for their own sake, regardless of any connection or relationship to other existing facts. In the early stages of scientific inquiry the identification of such facts is crucial. However, as more and more facts are generated, if they are allowed to remain in isolation from one another, adequate understanding of a **phenomenon** becomes almost impossible.

Look at this problem from the point of view of a coach and consider the array of seemingly unrelated information that a coach would need to know about psychology to work effectively with just one athlete in a single event. The coach would need to understand why some athletes are anxious in competitive settings whereas others are not; why people with different levels of anxiety perform differently within competitive sport settings; and how an athlete's anxiety reaction can be raised or lowered. Certainly it would be inefficient to require that every coach attempt to identify and synthesize all of the known facts about each of the notions just mentioned. What is the alternative?

Theory Building

The fourth method of knowing is theory building. A **theory** is developed by pulling together the known facts relative to a certain phenomenon and establishing predictions concerning how each may be related to the others. Those predictions are then subjected to testing through studies that follow the steps of the scientific method. Therefore, although the basic scientific procedures are identical to those followed by the empirical method, the purpose differs. In theory testing the hypothesis is derived directly from the theory, and the conclusion derived from the data analysis feeds back to the theory. In other words the conclusion indicates whether the prediction made by the theory was accurate. Therefore both the development and the eventual testing of theories is an efficient, ongoing process.

Developing a field of scientific inquiry requires both the method of empiricism and the method of theory building. Obviously, empirically based investigations must precede theoretically founded studies. A researcher needs a collection of facts before he or she can speculate on the interrelationships among those facts. Without empiricism there would be less possibility of generating fresh and innovative ideas. As you saw earlier in our example of what a coach would need to know about anxiety and athletic performance, without attempts at theory building a researcher would have only a cumbersome group of facts.

Variables

A **variable** is an entity capable of being measured, or quantified; that is, it can be assigned numerical value. In the early stages of the development of a science, much energy is put into identifying and measuring variables thought to be important to that particular domain. However, the individual variables themselves provide little information of real value; it is the *interrelationships* that occur between the variables that are of most concern. For instance, it is of small value to be able to say that it is possible to measure whether an athlete tends to be an extrovert or an introvert. Of more importance is the ability to specify exactly how the level of introversion or extroversion relates to successful performance on a team sport such as water polo. Thus in the first case one variable, the degree of extroversion versus introversion, was measured. In the second case the interrelationship between the psychological variable of introversion versus extroversion and sport team performance was identified. Clearly, the second case provides more valuable information.

At its most fundamental level, research in the area of sport psychology consists of the study of two variables in an effort to establish if any relationship exists between those variables. These important relationships are called **causal relationships** because a change in one of the variables causes a systematic change in the other. These cause-and-effect relationships relative to individual behavior in sport or movement settings formulate the research domain of sport psychology.

Independent variables are those thought to be the cause of an observed effect. They are the variables that are usually manipulated across experimental groups in a study. For instance, suppose that you designed an investigation in which you predicted that athletes who mentally practiced (practiced imaginally) would perform better than similarly skilled athletes who did not. The study was then designed so that one group mentally practiced basketball free throws and the other group did not. If you then measured the actual free throw performance of both groups and found that the group that had practiced mentally had better free throw performance than the group that did not, you could conclude that practicing mentally caused the effect of enhancing basketball free throw performance. In this example the causative, or independent, variable was mental practice.

Dependent variables are those variables that are affected systematically by a change in the independent variable. The dependent variable is measured or assessed during the collection of data. In the basketball free throw example described above, the dependent variable would be free throw performance.

Control variables are any other variables that could effect changes in the dependent variable. In the example above, because you obviously wanted to establish a cause-and-effect relationship between mental practice and effectiveness of basketball free throw shooting, you would not want a situation in which you could not be sure that the observed effect was a result of mental practice alone. Therefore when designing your study you must eliminate or control any variable, other than the independent variable, that could effect changes in the dependent variable. In our basketball example, control variables might be variables such as initial differences in skill level or initial differences in free throw percentages between the two groups of free throw shooters.

Theories, Models, and Paradigms

Frequently the three terms *theory, model,* and *paradigm* are used synonymously. Actually they are quite different. A **theory** attempts to synthesize what is known about a collection of facts and to make predictions concerning the relationships among those facts. A theory can be conceived of as a collection of hypotheses that attempts to predict or explain the relationships between multiple independent and dependent variables. Therefore a theoretical framework provides testable predictions concerning the interrelationships among the variables associated with a particular phenomenon. Although we realize that such a description of theory may leave you puzzled at this point, the concept will become clearer as we discuss several theories later in the text, such as theories concerning how anxiety should affect motor performance in predictable ways and conflicting theories concerning phenomena such as observational learning (imitation), imagery effects, and personality. As you will see, all these theories have certain commonalities. They all identify independent and dependent variables of interest and they all propose specific hypotheses concerning the interrelationships among those variables.

A **model** is an analogy that is devised to help you conceptualize something about the interrelationships between a set of variables. It is usually visual or graphic. When coaches use *X*s and *O*s to diagram a play on a chalkboard, that is a model of the play to be executed. The *X*s and *O*s represent, or are analogous to, the actual players. When architects develop blueprints to represent the structure of a building or when pharmaceutical companies design plastic human figures to show how certain drugs such as aspirin move through the body, they have constructed models. Scientists interested in the relationship between psychology and sport and motor behavior have developed several models of their own. One of the earliest of those models was developed by Lewin (1935). As shown below

$$B = f (P \times S)$$

this model simply indicates that behavior (B) is a function of the interaction between some characteristic of the person (P) and some event in the situation (S). From this perspective, behavior is seen as being determined by the interrelationships among elements contained within a certain person and the circumstances that are observable in the social situation.

An alternative explanation for human behavior is that proposed by the **external causation model:**

Stimulus → Response → Positive Reinforcement

It states that a human response is caused by some observable, antecedent environmental condition called a **stimulus.** If such a response is followed by some pleasurable consequence labeled positive reinforcement, then that same or a highly similar response will tend to recur under those same stimulus conditions. The underlying notions of this model are that responses are generated on the basis of some external factor (set of stimulus conditions) in the first place and are maintained by some other external factor (positive reinforcement). We will discuss this model at length in Chapter 2.

To better understand the external causation model, suppose that a Little League player is at bat with a single runner on third base (stimulus). With no previous instructions or experience, the player bunts the ball (response). The coach is ecstatic and praises the athlete profusely (positive reinforcement). The external causation model would predict that the next time this player is at bat under those same stimulus conditions, the same response (that is, an attempt to bunt) will most likely recur.

Another commonly used model is the **internal mediational model:**

Stimulus → Cognition → Response

In this model the term *stimulus* is used to describe the sensory input into the human system, whereas *cognition* is used to describe how information is processed before eliciting a response. Therefore this model portrays humans as thinking beings who process environmental information before deciding on an appropriate behavioral response. For instance, this model would predict that an athlete would mentally process feedback or information from a coach before attempting to change a particular skill execution.

The three models discussed above all provide visual representations concerning how persons are said to learn skills and to make changes in those skills. Once a model is developed, it influences how a research experiment is designed.

The manner in which such an investigation is carried out is called a **paradigm.** A paradigm describes the experimental protocol or methodological procedures used in a particular investigation. These procedures are drawn logically from the theoretical framework, or model, on which the study is based. We will use the external causation model (stimulus → response → positive reinforcement) and the internal mediational model (stimulus → cognition → response) to help clarify this definition. Suppose that two scholars were both interested in understanding how a person learns motor skills. If you were to walk unannounced into each of their laboratories, you would probably not find the same experiment underway because they probably would not have selected the same motor task or the same subjects. However, for the sake of our argument, assume that they were both assessing motor skill acquisition on the same task by highly similar subjects. Would they be following identical procedures? Probably not. However, it is certain that each would be setting up an experimental arrangement that would be consistent with the theoretical model that each experimenter believed best explains the acquisition of motor skills. If the first experimenter believed that such behaviors are acquired as a function of some external factor (the external causation model), he or she would then logically design an experiment in which some factor in the environment was varied, such as whether positive reinforcement was provided after each response. On the other hand, if the second scientist took the perspective that motor skills are learned primarily through cognitive processing (the internal mediational model), then it would follow that he or she would construct an experimental protocol in which some aspect of cognition (for example, mental practice) was varied. Thus it is clear that the paradigm employed by each of the two scientists is drawn logically from the different theoretical perspectives they hold.

Teachers and coaches follow the same pattern as scientists. If coach A believes that players can improve athletic performance primarily through means such as awarding letters or posting track times, then that coach is following the principles of the external causation model. If Coach B attempts to improve athletes' sport performance by pointing out errors and videotaping plays, then Coach B is trying to enhance performance by providing information to the players and is therefore applying the principles of the internal mediational model.

Although the examples of experiments cited earlier both took place in a laboratory setting, there is no reason why similar studies cannot be conducted in field situations. The type and location of research studies in sport psychology are quite flexible.

FUNDAMENTAL TYPES OF RESEARCH

The research undertaken in the field of sport psychology involves (1) the relative applicability of the findings and (2) the origin of the hypothesis.

Applied Research versus Basic Research

Research that is completed with an eye toward directly applying the results to a real-life situation is called **applied research.** Evidence obtained from such investigations is applicable to athletes in actual sport settings. Obviously, this is the type of research that most coaches and teachers want sport psychologists to do. They want answers to questions about psychological aspects of athlete behavior. Thus applied research holds an extremely important position within the research efforts of many sport psychologists.

Other researchers are more interested in **basic research,** in which they gather information concerning individual psychology in movement settings simply for the sake of increasing knowledge; they are not interested in the immediate application of their results. Often students, teachers, and coaches do not understand why basic research is important because it has no clear-cut relationship to real-life behaviors or situations. Perhaps a contemporary example will help you understand why basic research is necessary.

Few of us could deny the impact that contemporary high-technology information and applications have on our daily life. What many persons do not realize, however, is that the fundamental mathematical principles and theoretical notions associated with those technological advances were generated from basic research; that is, the information was generated simply for the sake of the information itself. It was only later that other researchers took the basic information and applied it for various technological purposes. For instance, in the field of biomechanics, much of the research uses computer-assisted techniques. However, when those techniques were first developed, no thought was given to their application to movement analysis.

Empirical Research versus Theoretical Research

The second dimension along which research in sport psychology can be conceptualized is the origin of the hypothesis to be tested. We used the term *empiricism* earlier to refer to the method of observation. Many research hypotheses are generated on the basis of the observations or experiences of the scientist. For example, a scientist might observe that there appears to be something different about the personalities of athletes who prefer team sports to individual sports. This observation could lead to the development of a study designed to test the validity of that empirically based hypothesis.

At the other end of the empirical dimension lies the element of the theoretically based hypothesis. In that instance, the hypothesis is derived directly from an existing theory. Figure 1-1 depicts the two dimensions along which research can be classified.

To better understand the interrelationships among the elements of applied, basic, empirical, and theoretical research, suppose that a particular scientist was interested in the question of how images are stored in memory. Suppose further this interest was purely to gain new knowledge and that there was no available theory to guide the investigator. This investigation would be classified as being from the basic-empirical perspective. If, on the other hand, there was a theory available that predicted that images are stored in analog form (that is, in the form of pictures and words), then the same study should be categorized as being within the domain of basic-theoretical research.

From a different point of view, suppose that a teacher observed that some students

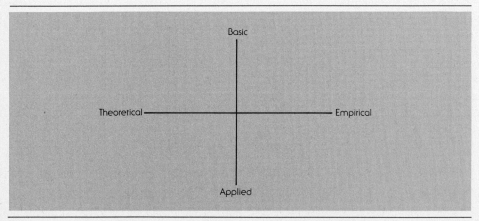

FIGURE 1-1   Classification of research approaches.

seem to prefer and to excel in competitive situations and others seem to prefer and to perform better in cooperative situations. A study could then be designed to ascertain exactly how the two groups of students might differ in terms of some psychological characteristic. The purpose of such an investigation might be to apply the results in a manner capable of changing the behavior of one or the other of the groups. In this case the researcher would be operating within the framework of applied-empirical research.

It is interesting to note, however, that if that same teacher had been aware of achievement motivation theory, he or she would have known that that theory would predict that persons characterized as being high in achievement motivation should prefer and perform well in competitive settings. On the other hand, persons who are assessed as being low in achievement motivation should prefer and perform best in cooperative situations. Therefore if a hypothesis were derived from the perspective of achievement motivation, and if the results were to be applied in a real-life situation, such as a class in physical education, then that investigation would be considered to fall within the category of applied-theoretical research.

Quasi-Experimental Research versus True Experimental Research

To conclude our discussion of the scientific dimensions of the psychology of sport behavior, one final notion needs to be addressed: the distinction between quasi-experimental research and true experimental research. Earlier we said that the independent variable in an investigation was considered to be the cause of some effect on a dependent variable. One example was the possible effect of failure on subsequent persistence behavior at the same task (see p. 7). In that example, failure would be categorized as the independent variable and persistence would be classified as the dependent variable. The distinction between quasi- and true experimental research rests on two criteria. The first is whether an independent variable is actually varied or manipulated in that particular study. The second criterion is whether there is a **control group.** A control group is a group of subjects who are not exposed to the independent variable. If the independent variable is not manipulated and there is no control group, the study is called a **quasi-experiment.** If an independent variable is manipulated and there is a control group, then the study is considered a **true experiment.** It is important to note that in either case some measurement is made on the dependent variable.

Consider a situation in which an experimenter notices that highly skilled gymnasts appear to exhibit lower degrees of anxiety as compared with less-skilled participants. An anxiety test is then administered to both groups of gymnasts, and the data analysis reveals that the experimenter's hypothesis was correct. On the average, the more highly skilled athletes had lower levels of anxiety as compared with the less-skilled gymnasts. In this example a dependent variable was assessed (anxiety). However, the independent variable (skill in gymnastics) was not actually varied by the investigator; the athletes possessed that skill before the study. In addition, there was no control group, such as a comparison group of nonathletes. Therefore even though the study proposed a hypothesis, systematically collected data, and used appropriate statistical analysis, it would not be considered a true experimental design but rather a quasi-experiment.

Suppose that another person observed that beginning tennis players seemed to perform better or worse as a consequence of the information that was provided to them after a response. In terms of the content of the feedback, it appeared that beginners performed better after positive feedback and worse after negative feedback. An experiment was then designed in which half of the players performed and always received negative feedback, whereas the other half performed an identical task but always received positive feedback. After the collection and analysis of the data, no differences between the groups were shown. Was this a true or a quasi-experiment? Could it be considered to be a true experiment in that the independent variable was manipulated? Half the players were provided with negative feedback, whereas the other half received positive feedback. However, something is missing from the experiment: the design did not include a control group. In this case, to be a true experiment, a third group should have been included, one to which no feedback was provided.

There are some very real advantages to designing true experiments. The inclusion of a manipulated independent variable and a control group allows researchers to show cause-and-effect relationships. Those cause-and-effect relationships allow a science to move toward adequate explanations and eventually to the point at which genuine theory building can begin. However, good quasi-experiments or descriptions of variables must usually precede the design and implementation of true experiments.

The science of sport psychology is young and exciting. It is not limited to one experimental site or to a single research approach. It is equally appropriate to conduct studies in locations such as a swimming pool, a baseball diamond, or an experimental laboratory. Scientific inquiries are limited only by the creativity and imagination of the researcher, who can be a full-time researcher, a teacher, a coach, or an athlete.

IMPLICATIONS FOR SPORT

- An effective coach or teacher must take a philosophical position on how people acquire, maintain, and improve their motor skills. This chapter presents three models of somewhat differing views of that process. By adopting one of them, you can then gear your instructional strategies accordingly. For instance, if you adopt the external causation model, then you should concentrate on varying external factors such as stimulus conditions present before movement and the nature of the reinforcements provided after a response. If you favor the internal mediational model, then you should concentrate on the amount and content of the feedback you provide performers.
- The steps of the scientific method provide a logical basis on which any teacher or coach can obtain the information needed to solve a problem. Use those steps to gather the information you need as a teacher or coach. In addition to getting the answers you want, you may also find that you have become more effective as a problem solver.

You should now have a fairly good grasp of many of the concepts and variables associated with undertaking scientific investigations in sport psychology. To help your comprehension of those notions and to help you apply your understanding, we have constructed two hypothetical case studies. After reading them, try to answer the questions at the end of each case study.*

*The answers to the questions for Case Study 1 and Case Study 2 can be found on p. 19.

CASE STUDY 1

A baseball coach is interested in finding out if ballet training will improve the playing ability of athletes. All the players' names are placed in a baseball cap and are then drawn randomly; equal numbers of players are then assigned randomly either to participate in ballet training or to read a book on the rules of baseball. Each group performs the assigned activity for 6 weeks, after which time the coach assesses the playing ability of all the participants.
1. Is the origin of the hypothesis empirical or theoretical?
2. Is this a quasi- or true experiment?
3. Is this research applied or basic?
4. What is the independent variable?
5. What is the dependent variable?

CASE STUDY 2

A teacher reads a book on a social psychological theory of sport participation. The theory proposes that boys participate in sports for purposes of achievement striving, whereas girls tend to participate for reasons of affiliation. The teacher then designs a survey to assess whether that hypothesis is valid. One hundred boys and one hundred girls are surveyed, and the findings contradict the hypothesis: boys tended to join sport groups to be with their friends, and girls participated to achieve goals such as better skill. The teacher is shocked at the results and decides after the termination of the experiment to design a behavior-modification program capable of changing the motivation patterns of both the boys and the girls. The boys will be reinforced only for achievement-oriented responses and the girls will be reinforced only for affiliative behaviors.
1. Is the origin of the hypothesis empirical or theoretical?
2. Is this a quasi- or true experiment?
3. Is this research applied or basic?
4. What is the independent variable?
5. What is the dependent variable?

SUMMARY

- The field of sport psychology began with an interest in studying the personalities and characters of sport participants. Subsequently it focused most of its research attention on testing theories that were borrowed from the parent discipline of psychology. Today, research interests are multifaceted, encompassing questions of both applied and theoretical research.
- The uniqueness of sport psychology is its focus on studying individual behavior in movement settings. It has as its goals the description, explanation, prediction, and change of such behavior within the framework of sport and motor performance situations.

- Of the four ways of knowing (phenomenology, authority, empiricism, and theory building), the methods of empiricism and theory building are most capable of providing adequate answers to sport psychology questions.
- Variables are classified as being independent, dependent, or control.
- Hypotheses are generally based on either empirical observations or theoretical predictions.
- The process of conceptualizing relationships among variables is facilitated by the use of theories, models, and paradigms.
- Research investigations can be classified along the two dimensions of applied versus basic and empirical versus theoretical.
- In terms of research designs, quasi-experiments usually involve only the measurement of selected dependent variables, whereas true experiments require that an independent variable be manipulated, a dependent variable measured, and a control group used.
- Research in sport psychology is not restricted by either the origin of the hypothesis or the location of the data collection.

DISCUSSION QUESTIONS

1 Can you explain how a research question might be tested differently within the framework of two different paradigmatic approaches?
2 Based on your own sport experiences (the phenomenological way of knowing), identify a testable research question. Indicate the independent and dependent variables. What would your hypothesis be concerning the predicted outcome of your study?
3 Can you identify examples of models in addition to the ones mentioned in this chapter?
4 What are some variables that might have to be controlled in a study designed to test the superiority of two methods of teaching beginning swimming?
5 How does the origin of a hypothesis (that is, empirical versus theoretical) relate to the probability of finding differences between two experimental groups? In which case would you be most likely to find differences between the groups? Provide an argument to support your position.

GLOSSARY

antecedent   An event or set of circumstances that occurs before another event
applied research   Research undertaken for purposes of immediate and practical application
authority   A person with vast knowledge or experience in a particular field
basic research   Research conducted for the purpose of gathering information simply to increase knowledge; it usually has no immediate application and may have no future application
causal relationship   A relationship in which one variable has an identifiable effect on a second variable
conclusion   A summary statement or judgment based on the outcome of an experiment
control group   The group in an experiment that is not exposed to the independent variable
control variable   A variable that could affect the dependent variable or the independent variable; therefore it must be controlled either experimentally or statistically or it must be eliminated before the study

dependent variable   The variable thought to be affected in an experiment and therefore measured during data collection

empiricism   A scientific method using observations made concerning a particular event or phenomenon

external causation model   A model in which human behavior is said to be determined by environmental effects

generalizability   In science, the degree of applicability of the results of a particular investigation to larger samples or populations or different situations

hypothesis   A prediction or educated guess that an investigator makes before beginning a study

independent variable   The variable that is said to be the cause underlying some observed effect and is often manipulated or varied during an experiment

internal mediational model   A model in which human behavior is said to be based on cognitive activities, during which information is processed and rational decisions are made

mediation   Pertaining to one element or event occurring between two other elements or events; for example, an arbitrator is often called in to mediate between labor and management during a dispute

model   A visual or graphic representation of the relationships between identifiable variables; for example, X's and O's drawn on a coach's blackboard represent athletes' positions or movements

paradigm   The experimental protocol used in a particular investigation and usually drawn logically from either a theoretical or hypothetical framework

phenomenology   As used in this text, a scientific method based on personal, subjective experience

phenomenon   Any observation, experience, or circumstance that can be described and measured scientifically

quantifiable   The ability to represent an entity numerically

quasi-experiment   An experiment in which only a dependent variable is assessed

stimulus   An observable event in the environment that precedes a response

theory   A constellation of hypothesized relationships used to describe the interrelationships between multiple variables or phenomena

true experiment   An experiment that contains at least one independent variable, one dependent variable, and a control group

variable   An entity that can be quantified; that is, it can be assigned a numeric value

SUGGESTED READINGS

Bird, A.M., & Ross, D. (1984). Current methodological problems and future directions for theory development in the psychology of sport and motor behavior. *Quest, 36,* 1-6.

This article first identifies several reasons why theory development in sport psychology has faltered in the past. The processes of anxiety and observational learning are then used as examples of how systematic research can lead to theory development.

Henry, F.M. (1964). Physical education: An academic discipline. *Proceedings of the 67th Annual Conference of the National College Physical Education Association for Men,* Dallas, Texas, 6-9.

This is the landmark paper defining physical education as an academic discipline. It argues for an interdisciplinary approach to the study of individual behavior in motor performance settings.

Martens, R. (1979). About smocks and jocks. *Journal of Sport Psychology, 1,* 94-99.

This controversial paper formed the basis for much discussion within the field of sport psychology. It emphasizes the inadequacies of experimental research and the desirability of long-term field research.

Platt, J.R. (1964). Strong inference. *Science, 146,* 347-352.

This article explains why research productivity has moved so rapidly within the field of molecular biology. Although it represents the strategies used in a discipline other than sport psychology, the method of strong inference appears equally applicable to both disciplines.

Ryan, E.D. (1981). The emergence of psychological research as related to performance in physical activity. In G.A. Brooks (Ed.), *Perspectives on the academic discipline of physical education.* Champaign, IL: Human Kinetics.

This article traces the development of psychological studies in the field of physical education. It identifies a chronology of topics studied and discusses several of the more prominent researchers in the field.

Answers to case study questions: Case Study One, 1., empirical; 2., true; 3., applied; 4., ballet training; 5., playing ability. Case Study Two, 1., theoretical; 2., quasi-experimental; 3., applied; 4., motivation (that is, achievement and affiliation); 5., sport participation.

2

PERSPECTIVES ON UNDERSTANDING SPORT BEHAVIOR

A variety of perspectives have been used in an effort to understand and account for differences in individual behavior in sport settings. Why do some persons persist at developing their athletic skills whereas others drop out? Why do Olympic hopefuls persist in a rigorous and continued training program that may or may not pay off after 4 years? Why has there been such a dramatic increase in the number of women participating in sports? In this chapter we will briefly introduce you to the three major perspectives—behaviorism, trait psychology, and interactionism—that can provide some insights to the answers to these questions.

BEHAVIORISM AND SPORT

The primary focus of all behavioristic theories are factors that are external to the person; behavior is seen as being acquired, maintained, and changed as a function of external or environmental causes. This would apply equally to social behaviors, such as aggression, or motor behaviors, such as shooting a free throw.

Sport behaviorists explore questions such as "What are the external rewards that maintain a professional's versus an amateur's persistence in an athletic event?" "What recent changes have occurred in available reinforcements for female athletes?" or "Why do black athletes seem to prefer certain sports over others?" In all of these questions the behaviorist is focusing on external factors such as reinforcement or punishment as opposed to internal constructs such as personality.

The model of human behavior associated with the behavioristic school of thought is the external causation model (S → R → Re). The letters *S, R,* and *Re* refer to stimulus, response, and reinforcement, respectively. A stimulus pertains to a set of observable, antecedent conditions in the environment. A response is defined as the observable act, whereas reinforcement pertains to the observable consequences of emitting a response. Notice that the word *observable* appears in connection with each of the three terms. From the behavioristic point of view, all elements associated with the learning process must be observable; they must be measurable.

The interrelationships that occur among the three elements of stimulus, response, and reinforcement are called the *contingencies of reinforcement*. It is through those interrelationships that the learning of behaviors is explained.

Thorndike's Law of Effect

During the 1920s, Thorndike proposed a simple law concerning how stimulus, response, and reinforcement are interrelated (Figure 2-1). His **law of effect** stated that if the consequences of a response were positive (favorable, pleasant), then the probability should increase that the same or a similar response would recur under the same set of stimulus

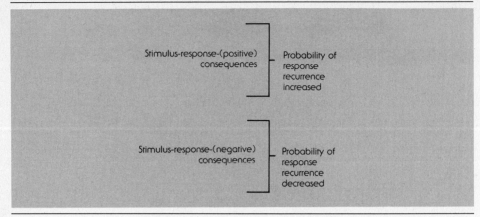

FIGURE 2-1   Thorndike's law of effect.

conditions at some future date. Conversely, if the consequences of a response were negative (adverse, unpleasant), then the probability of the same response recurring under the same stimulus conditions should decrease. For example, suppose that you change your grip in golf (new response) to accommodate a "dog leg" to the left. (A dog leg left means the fairway is bent markedly to the left.) You have changed your grip in an attempt to make the ball hook. You execute your usual great swing and the ball does exactly what you want it to do; it hooks to the left and lands in the center of the fairway. According to Thorndike's law of effect, the probability is high that the next time you are faced with the same or a similar "dog leg" to the left, you will adjust your grip in the same way that you did on the first occasion. The consequences of your initial response were most pleasant. Suppose on another occasion that you are about to tee off and there is water to the right. You decide to adjust your grip so that you will definitely avoid the water. You are confident and secure. You again swing your usual great swing. You look up with great expectation of landing in the center of the fairway, but before you can see your ball, you hear the much-dreaded "splash." The law of effect predicts that, given the negative consequences associated with your response, the next time you are faced with the same or a similar stimulus condition (water on the right) the probability would be low that you would emit the identical response.

Skinner's Operant Reinforcement Theory

Similar to other behavioristic theorists, Skinner's *operant reinforcement theory* rejected internal, mentalistic causes of behavior. Instead, it proposed that behavior is a function of external, observable elements. Skinner identified three major factors that affect human behavior: (1) reinforcement, (2) stimuli, and (3) deprivation.

Reinforcement

The term *reinforcement* is used to refer to any factor or incident that occurs after a response and increases the probability that the response will recur. There are two types of reinforcement: positive and negative.

Positive reinforcement occurs when a stimulus is applied after a response, which increases the probability that the same or a similar response will recur. The prestige associated with making a team, the praise received from a coach, or the awarding of an Olympic medal would all be classified as positive reinforcements.

Negative reinforcement refers to the withdrawal or removal of an unpleasant or aversive element or stimulus. However, that withdrawal must serve to increase the probability of the response recurring. For example, suppose you were a basketball player who was constantly criticized by your coach. Then during one game you really tried to hustle more by passing off more than shooting and by going for the boards with as much effort as possible. As a consequence, your coach voiced no criticisms of your performance after the game. The coach's unpleasant behavior has now been withdrawn, and the result would probably be that you would attempt to duplicate your effective responses in the next game.

As opposed to negative reinforcement, **punishment** refers to the application of some unpleasant or aversive condition subsequent to a response. This situation should result in a decrease in response probability. In sport, punishment often takes the form of actions such as benching an athlete, giving verbal criticism, or even suspending a performer from the team.

To test your understanding of behaviorism so far, answer the following question. Which two of the three elements of positive reinforcement, negative reinforcement, and punishment are incorporated within Thorndike's law of effect? If your answer was positive reinforcement and punishment, you were correct.

Another distinction in terms of reinforcement is that of primary versus secondary reinforcement. *Primary reinforcers* do not need to be learned. Their effectiveness is inherent. Eating when hungry or drinking when thirsty are both primary reinforcers. *Secondary reinforcers* acquire their meaning and effectiveness either through association with primary reinforcers or through learning. In sport and athletics, the most important secondary reinforcers are those that are learned. For instance, money does not reinforce an infant's responses; however, it is a reinforcer to most professional athletes. Medals, trophies, and even the applause of fans are initially of no importance. They become secondary reinforcers only after their value has been learned by the performer.

Stimuli

When referring to stimuli, we are still concerned with observable, external elements in the environment. However, it is important to stress that from Skinner's point of view the presentation of a stimulus does not trigger a particular response. After a response is emitted in a set of stimulus conditions, it is the *consequences* of that response that determine whether the connection between the stimulus and the response will be strengthened. In operant reinforcement theory, the primary focus is always on the response.

Deprivation

Because the focus of Skinner's perspective is on external determinants, much of the research conducted used animals such as rats or pigeons rather than human beings. This approach was more practical and avoided the problem of human consent. Throughout much of this research, deprivation was used as a means of studying animal behavior. For instance, rats might be deprived of food or water for a certain number of hours. It was noted that after that period of deprivation the food or water took on reinforcing value.

In regard to sport, it may be that the promoters of the new United States Football

League (USFL) are aware of Skinner's notion of deprivation. It seems that many fans experience "football deprivation" immediately following the Super Bowl. It could be speculated that the promoters of the USFL have launched a new league to cash in on this feeling of deprivation. It remains to be seen, however, if those same fans experience the opposite emotion, "football satiation," which might occur if the fans have seen too much football and become weary of watching another game or the contests of another league. If they do, there is little hope of success for the new league.

Shaping of Behavior

Shaping of behavior is the phrase used to describe Skinner's approach to the teaching of new skills or behaviors. First, the teacher must know exactly what the goal of the skill is; that is, the teacher must be aware of the precise terminal behavior that is desired. The major way that behavior is "shaped" is through the application of reinforcements. From this perspective, a response must be emitted before the presentation of the reinforcement.

A second component of behavior-shaping is the **principle of contingency.** This principle means that reinforcement should only be applied if a desired response is emitted because the application of reinforcement is said to increase the probability of that same response recurring under the same stimulus conditions. If an undesired response is reinforced, its probability of recurrence is increased. Obviously, this would not lead to skill development in terms of reaching the identified terminal goal.

If we think in terms of a complex motor skill such as a "kip" (coming to a stand from a rolled-back position) in gymnastics or a half-gainer (reverse dive), how likely is it that the terminal behavior (the actual kip or half-gainer) will occur on the first try? Not very likely. To account for this problem, Skinner proposed the notion of *successive approximations. Successive* refers to a series of responses; *approximations* denotes responses that progressively come closer to the desired (terminal) response.

Much of Skinner's research was conducted on pigeons in a laboratory setting, so let's speculate on how he might have shaped the behavior of a pigeon so that the terminal behavior of pecking at a particular disc would be acquired. Figure 2-2 presents our hypothetical series of events leading to the final goal of pecking behavior. Recall that the first step requires that a desired response (successive approximation) occur. In Figure 2-2, *2,* the bird has by chance made the response of turning her head toward the disc. That is the first approximation, and a reinforcer (a food pellet) would be given right away. To receive another pellet, however, the pigeon must make a response that is a closer approximation to the act of pecking. In Figure 2-2, *3,* the pigeon has made a bending response toward the disc. She is reinforced again with a pellet. This procedure continues until the final goal of continued pecking takes place (Figure 2-2, *4*).

The shaping of behavior procedure discussed above is used quite frequently in teaching complex motor skills. Consider the traditional approach to teaching the front dive. For the first attempt at entering the pool headfirst, the learner hooks the toes of one foot over the edge of the pool and assumes a kneeling position with that leg while the other leg is extended backward. Usually, the teacher supports the back and guides the direction of the head. This is the first response in a series of successive approximations. The successful completion of the desired approximation is followed by the application of a reinforcer such as verbal praise. Once the learner is capable of emitting the first approximation, practice at the next approximation begins. The second step usually entails a bent-over position followed by a headfirst entry. Positive reinforcement should follow the successful

FIGURE 2-2   Shaping of pecking response.

execution of the response. Eventually the learner is able to attempt the terminal response. The learner's behavior has been shaped through the process of successive approximations followed by positive reinforcement.

Stimulus Generalization

Once a response has been learned relative to one stimulus, in a sense it has been learned in regard to other similar stimuli; that is, once a response has been systematically associated with one stimulus, that response will tend to be emitted on presentation of another, highly similar, stimulus. Usually, however, the magnitude or intensity of the second response is decreased. This phenomenon is called **stimulus generalization.** Stimulus generalization can be more easily understood by grasping the notion of the *gradient of stimulus generalization.*

Gradient of stimulus generalization. The gradient of stimulus generalization is a graphical representation of how the magnitude of a response is systematically affected by a decreasing similarity between a new stimulus and the original stimulus. This relationship is shown in Figure 2-3. The diagonal line indicates that the magnitude of the response decreases as a stimulus becomes more dissimilar to the original stimulus.

Let's return to Skinner's pigeon experiments to take a closer look at the notions of stimulus generalization and the gradient of stimulus generalization. For instance, suppose that the original disc was blue; the pigeon's response therefore was shaped specifically in terms of pecking at a blue disc. If new discs were presented that varied over the wavelength spectrum of colors, then we would expect to see the pigeon generalize, or transfer, the pecking behavior to the new stimuli. The closer the new stimulus is to the original blue disc, the more similar would the response be in terms of both magnitude and intensity. However, as the color of the newly presented stimulus deviated more from the original stimulus, the rate of pecking would decrease. The less the amount of stimulus generalization, the greater the *stimulus discrimination.* Therefore the relationship between stimulus generalization and stimulus discrimination is **inverse;** the more there is of one process, the less there is of the other.

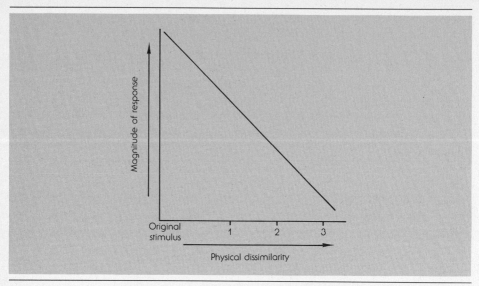

FIGURE 2-3   Gradient of stimulus generalization.

In terms of sport skills, during the early stages of learning much stimulus generalization takes place. However, with practice and accompanying skill development, more stimulus discrimination can be observed. The stance taken on the fairway in golf provides a good example of how stimulus generalization and stimulus discrimination may operate as a function of increased skill and knowledge. A novice golfer often assumes a similar stance regardless of club selection or desired flight of the ball. Therefore the beginner generalizes a similar response to all clubs and terrains, regardless of varying stimulus conditions. With experience and increased knowledge, however, a good golfer modifies the stance so that either an open or closed stance is assumed, depending on the lay of the land or selection of a particular club. Thus the experienced golfer is able to discriminate between different stimulus conditions.

This same relationship is also seen in other sports such as softball or baseball. The novice hitter tends to swing about the same way regardless of the nature of the pitch. More advanced players are able to discriminate rather well between pitches such as a fastball or a curve and modify the swing according to the pitch.

Current Status and Future Directions of Behaviorism

Although not nearly as popular as they once were, behavioristic approaches to the learning and modification of sport skills are still held in favor by some sport psychologists. Particularly in the early stages of skill development, it would be difficult to argue against the merits of understanding the notions associated with the law of effect, the principle of contingency, and the practice of behavior shaping. However, most contemporary thinking and theorizing in the field of sport psychology are based on the idea that cognitive processes play a significant role in the learning and refinement of sport skills. Therefore, although many of the principles derived from behaviorism can assist us in understanding aspects of sport behavior, most sport psychologists do not find that point of view to be comprehensive enough.

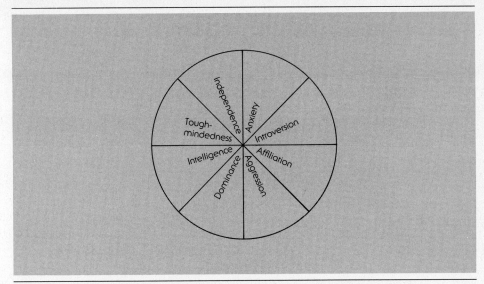

FIGURE 2-4   Hypothetical constellation of personality factors.

Two alternatives to the behavioristic interpretation of human behavior are trait psychology and interactionism. In the next two sections we will first discuss the fundamental premises of trait theory and then turn our attention to interactionism.

TRAIT PSYCHOLOGY AND PERSONALITY IN SPORT

Trait theory takes the position that stable factors or characteristics exist in persons, and those traits can allow us to describe personality. This perspective places primary emphasis on these aspects of the person. Typical questions posed within this framework are "Do athletes differ from nonathletes?" "Are there unique personality characteristics associated with the female athlete versus either the female nonathlete or the male athlete?" "Do athletes in one sport differ from athletes in another sport?" "Does the skill of the athlete relate to certain personality traits?" "Does sport participation affect personality?"

Trait theory proposes that individual behavior is primarily, although not exclusively, a function of personality. There is no universal agreement on a definition of personality; however, there is little argument against the position that personality can be conceived of as a collection of factors, or traits, that are used to describe a person's predisposition to behave in predictable ways. It should be noted that *traits* are characterized by their stable nature, whereas *states* refer to transitory, or changeable, behaviors. In a sense then, the term *personality* is used to describe the enduring (stable) set of traits that make one person different from another.

Because the typical trait approach views personality as consisting of a collection of traits, or factors, these factors are used to identify differences between various persons. Figure 2-4 depicts a hypothetical constellation of personality factors. In this hypothetical configuration, personality is defined as a person's degree or amount of each of eight traits. Therefore, from this perspective, researchers must be able to measure each trait.

This is usually accomplished after a lengthy and difficult period of test development and validation. Once test development is completed, hypotheses are made concerning how people who differ in these traits might vary in their sport behavior. For instance, how might a person who is high in introversion differ from another person who is low in this factor? Think about sport preference. Do you think that introverts might differ from extroverts in terms of the type of sport they prefer? Who should prefer team sports as opposed to individual sports?

From another perspective, is it possible that participation in certain sports can affect the development of identifiable personality characteristics? For example, is it not possible that as a consequence of *continued* playing on the defensive line in football, the player's relative degree of aggression might increase?

It is clear that personality can affect the type of sport selected for participation, and participation in a particular sport may in turn influence personality. Therefore the study of how personality may relate to individual sport behavior is important. However, before presenting specific research evidence on the relationship between personality and sport behavior, it is important to consider two of the most popular theoretical approaches to trait psychology that have been used to study athletes. Although scholars such as Guilford, Allport, and Jackson have made significant contributions to trait psychology, the work of Cattell and Eysenck have had the greatest impact on sport psychology research.

Cattell's Approach

Cattell views personality as a complex set of multiple traits that are identified or inferred on the basis of observed behavior. The trait name is then used as a means by which the observed behavior (usually of an enduring or consistent nature) is labeled. In the process of developing both the structure of his theory and the content of his assessment instrument (Cattell's 16 PF Questionnaire), he went through a lengthy process of first identifying possible traits and then reducing them in number. His questionnaire contains the 16 factors that he felt composed the psychological foundation underlying personality. The box on the facing page presents these 16 primary *(first-order)* factors.

Of more importance to the study of individual sport behavior was Cattell's reduction of the initial 16 primary factors into four *second-order factors*. The second-order factors were identified on the basis of objective test data that indicated that the behavioral tendencies measured by the 16 primary factors could be described efficiently by a reduced number of second-order factors. The box on the facing page lists the four-second order factors and their corresponding relationship to the initial 16 primary factors.

Because there have been only a few scientific attempts to directly study the relationship between Cattell's second-order factors and athletic performance, much caution should be used in attempting to generalize the results to different sports or athletes. With this warning in mind, we will briefly discuss one well-designed study.

Schurr, Ashley, and Joy (1977) addressed the question of sport specificity and Cattell's second-order factors. They used a three-way classification system to categorize the nature of the sport. As can be seen in the box on the facing page, the three-way classification system was based on the variables of team versus individual, direct versus parallel, and the long versus short category used within the individual sport classification. The category

Primary Factors of the 16 PF Questionnaire

A	Warm, sociable vs aloof, stiff
B	Mentally bright vs mentally dull
C	Mature, calm vs emotional, immature
E	Aggressive, competitive vs mild, submissive
F	Enthusiastic vs prudent, serious
G	Conscientious vs casual, undependable
H	Adventurous vs shy, timid
I	Sensitive, effeminate vs tough, realistic
L	Suspecting, jealous vs accepting, adaptable
M	Imaginative vs practical
N	Sophisticated vs simple, unpretentious
O	Timid, insecure vs confident, self-secure
Q1	Radicalism vs conservatism
Q2	Self-sufficiency vs group adherence
Q3	Uncontrolled, lax vs controlled
Q4	Phlegmatic, relaxed vs tense, excitable

Adapted from Carron, A.V. (1980). Social *psychology of sport.* Ithaca, NY: Mouvement Publications.

Cattell's Four Second-Order Factors

SECOND-ORDER FACTOR	PRIMARY FACTOR COMPONENTS
Anxiety (high vs low)	C, H, L, O, Q3, Q4
Introversion vs extroversion	A, E, F, H, Q2
Tough minded vs tender minded	A, C, E, F, I, M, N
Independence vs subduedness	A, E, G, M, I, Q2

Adapted from Carron, A.V. (1980). *Social psychology of sport.* Ithaca, NY: Mouvement Publications.

Three-Way Classification of Sports

	DIRECT	PARALLEL	
TEAM	Basketball Football Soccer	Volleyball Baseball	
INDIVIDUAL	Wrestling	**LONG** Golf Tennis Cross-country	**SHORT** Gymnastics Swimming Track

Adapted from Schurr, K.T., Ashley, M.A., & Joy, K.L. (1977). A multivariate analysis of male athlete characteristics: Sport type and success. *Multivariate Experimental Clinical Research, 3,* 53-68.

TABLE 2-1   Summary of Schurr and Associates' Findings

Sport Group	Comparison Group	Secondary Factors
Direct	Nonathlete	Higher extroversion More independent
Parallel	Nonathlete	Lower anxiety Less independent More tough minded
Team	Nonathlete	Higher extroversion More dependent Less tough minded
Individual	Nonathlete	Lower anxiety More dependent
Team	Individual	More dependent Higher anxiety Higher extroversion

Adapted from Schurr, K.T., Ashley, M.A., & Joy, K.L. (1977). A multivariate analysis of male athlete characteristics: Sport type and success. *Multivariate Experimental Clinical Research, 3,* 53-68.

of long versus short was used to separate the sports on the basis of the time required to complete the event. The notion of direct versus parallel was used to differentiate between sports in which direct physical contact is usual. For example, in football, physical contact is part of the sport, whereas in volleyball it is not.

In addition to the classification system used to specify sport type, Schurr and his associates further categorized subjects as being either athletes or nonathletes. Athletes were then subdivided into groups of letter winners versus non–letter winners. A summary of the major findings are located in Table 2-1. Several salient differences emerged on the basis of their analysis.

First, in comparison to individual sport participants, team sport participants tended to be more dependent and extroverted, with accompanying higher anxiety.

Second, in comparison to nonathletes, both team and individual sport participants tended to be more dependent. However, the team-oriented athletes had higher degrees of extroversion and were less tough minded, whereas the individually oriented athletes demonstrated lower anxiety.

Third, in sports that entail direct physical contact, the athletes tended to be both extroverted and more independent than nonathletes. Athletes who took part in parallel sports demonstrated lower anxiety, less independence, and more tough-mindedness as compared with nonathletes.

Although based only on a single investigation, these results are interesting and important. They argue for the importance of using reasonable classification systems to understand the relationships between personality and sport performance and provide some substantiation for the use of Cattell's second-order factors for sport personality analysis. The latter point is warranted in that much of the early research using the full 16 scales of Cattell's PF Questionnaire did not yield consistently meaningful results, whereas the use of the four second-order factors has generated more comprehensible results.

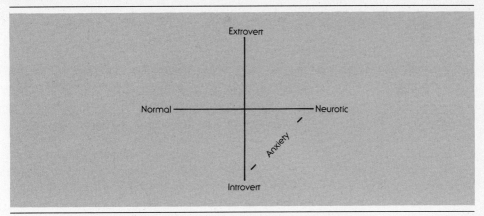

FIGURE 2-5   Eysenck's three-factor theory.

Eysenck's Approach

As we saw from Cattell's work, the second-order factors of anxiety and introversion versus extroversion may be somewhat related to sport behavior. Although Eysenck's perspective differs from that of Cattell, Eysenck's three-factor theory predicts a similar relationship. The three important factors identified by Eysenck are (1) neuroticism, (2) introversion versus extroversion, and (3) anxiety. Figure 2-5 shows the interrelationships among those factors.

With few exceptions, the three-factor theory has received little research attention in the field of sport psychology. However, in 1980 Morgan synthesized the findings of the available studies that used successful male athletes and demonstrated a systematic relationship regarding the introversion versus extroversion scale. For example, Morgan (1968) found that wrestling tournament success correlated moderately with higher degrees of extroversion. Similarly, Kane (1964) reported that a correlation existed between athletic ability and degree of extroversion. More specifically, higher ability was found to be related to extroversion, whereas lower ability was correlated with introversion.

However, in his more recent work, Morgan (1980) has favored what he calls a *mental health* model. This model proposes that there is an inverse relationship between **psychopathy** and athletic success. It predicts that an athlete who suffers from psychological disorders such as neuroticism, anxiety, depression, introversion, and low physical vigor should not experience success equal to an athlete who is not afflicted by such conditions.

Research Evidence on Personality and Sport

The Mental Health Model

Nagle, Morgan, Hellickson, Serfass, and Alexander (1975) used an instrument called the Profile of Mood States (POMS) to assess 40 aspiring wrestling team members for the 1972 U.S. Olympic team. The POMS incorporates a five-point adjective scale that measures six moods or affective states: tension-anxiety, depression-dejection, anger-hostility, vigor-activity, fatigue-inertia, and confusion-bewilderment (Demers, 1983). Measurements were made the evening before the final tournament. Similar assessments were again conducted before the 1976 Olympic tryouts. Notice in Figure 2-6 the similarity of the two profiles. Morgan has coined the term *iceberg profile* to describe these wrestlers. The solid line at T score 50 indicates an average score. All of the negatively based scores (namely, tension, *TEN*; depression, *DEP*; anger, *ANG*; fatigue, *FAT*; and confusion, *CON*) fall below average. The positive quality of vigor *(VIG)* is well above average. It should be noted that the wrestlers who did not make the team generally socred at about T score 50 (average score) on the six scales of POMS.

Subsequently, Morgan and his associates (see Morgan, 1980; Morgan & Johnson, 1977; Morgan & Pollock, 1977) investigated elite (world-class) athletes such as rowers, oarsmen, and distance runners. Figure 2-7 summarizes the findings concerning the relative mood states of the three athletic groups. These data demonstrate a remarkable amount of similarity among successful participants in different sport groups. In terms of traits rather than states, the elite, male athletes also were found to be lower in trait anxiety as compared with the population as a whole. This lower anxiety may help to explain why the elite athletes demonstrated low levels of tension under highly stressful conditions. Also, in regard to extroversion, both the elite runners and the elite wrestlers were highly similar. This finding is not in agreement with earlier evidence (Morgan, 1968; Morgan & Costill, 1972), which used the same measure, Eysenck's Personality Inventory (EPI), and found that long-distance runners tended to be introverted. As Morgan (1980) has speculated, that change may well be a function of a change in the personalities of long-distance runners over the past decade. His idea appears reasonable, given the vast number of people who have begun running programs during that time period. Such a large increase in the number of runners has most likely increased the diversity of the pool of participants in running.

The results of the data collected on the basis of the mental health model are promising in terms of telling researchers something about the personalities of elite male performers. Recent evidence (Demers, 1983) has also suggested that the ''iceberg'' profile associated with the mental health model is also characteristic of both male and female national-caliber divers. Taken together, the available evidence indicates that the emotional state of the athlete before competition may have an effect on athletic accomplishments during competition. What is needed in the future is the application of more theoretically sound **multivariate** (having multiple variables) models, such as the mental health model. Such models should then be used to compare elite and other levels of both male and female sport groups. Then perhaps researchers will know whether all successful athletes, regardless of gender, are indeed less anxious, extroverted, and ''icebergs''!

Female Athletes

In reviewing the available literature on female athletes, the first fact that becomes apparent is that there is very little of it. Instead, the vast majority of the literature focuses directly on men. If it were true that differences in gender had no relationship to aspects of personality, then perhaps the solution would be to simply generalize what we know about men to women. However, that solution hardly seems tenable.

Through the process of socialization and sex-role stereotyping, gender-related differences in predominant needs and preferred personality characteristics do exist (whether or not they should is another question). For instance, Garai and Scheinfeld (1970) studied

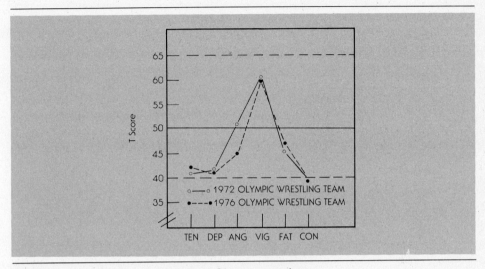

FIGURE 2-6   Profile of mood states of Olympic wrestlers.
From Morgan, W.P. (1980). The trait psychology controversy. *Research Quarterly for Exercise and Sport, 51,* 50-76.

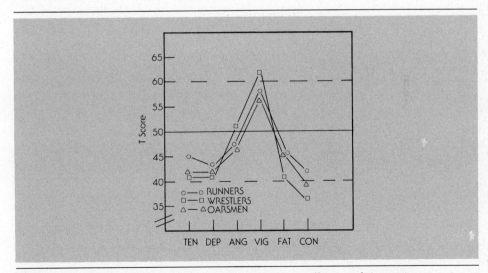

FIGURE 2-7   Profile of mood states of elite runners, wrestlers, and oarsmen.
Adapted from Morgan, W.P. (1980). The trait psychology controversy. *Research Quarterly for Exercise and Sport, 51,* 50-76.

gender-related needs and found needs associated with women to include safety-orient-edness, passivity, defensiveness, submissiveness, and the need to be sedentary. On the other hand, men's needs included vigorous physical exertion, aggression, achievement, motor activity, independence, and dominance. There is a wealth of evidence to support this dualistic model of male characteristics and needs versus female characteristics and needs. In fact, this "separation on the basis of gender" phenomenon is subtly reinforced by the fact that most personality tests include separate norms for men and women. Therefore they indirectly propose that there is some difference between the ideal or even the average man and his female counterpart.

Recently, however, social and behavioral scientists have begun to question the tradi-tional, bipolar distinction between the psychological attributes linked to biological gender. This school of thought proposed the notion of **androgyny.** Basically, the androgynous position says that desirable characteristics need not be gender-linked. Instead, the an-drogynous person would possess the most desirable attributes previously associated with both genders. For instance, the androgynous person would be aggressive when the situation called for it and warm, caring, and gentle when those characteristics were most appro-priate.

From this perspective, Helmreich and Spence (1977) studied male and female college students, male and female scientists, and female athletes. Table 2-2 presents the results of their comparisons. Notice in particular the similarity between the female scientists and the female athletes and furthermore how those two groups differ from the female students in general.

The female scientists and athletes had the largest percentages in the masculine and androgynous categories, whereas the general female students fell mostly in the feminine classification. Now compare the relative percentages of female athletes and scientists in the androgynous block to their male counterparts. The data are encouraging in terms of the female achiever. As Helmreich and Spence (1977) explain the findings:

> The joint distribution also suggests that those women (both athletes and scientists) who
> succeed in those areas of endeavor defined as stereotypically masculine do not do this at the
> expense of their femininity. Indeed, these data suggest that rather than suffering a deficit of
> femininity, the high-achieving women (at least in athletics and science) are more likely than
> their male counterparts to possess both masculine and feminine attributes. At the least, these
> data suggest that our stereotypic conceptions of masculinity and femininity in relation to
> achieving women may have been overly simplistic. (p. 42)

TABLE 2-2 Distribution of Percentages by Category and Respondent

	Category			
Respondent	Undifferentiated	Feminine	Masculine	Androgynous
Male students	31	13	27	29
Female students	21	39	11	29
Male scientists	20	5	43	32
Female scientists	8	23	23	46
Female athletes	20	10	31	39

Adapted from Helmreich, R., & Spence, J.T. (1977). Sex roles and achievement. In R.W. Christina & D.M. Lan-ders (Eds.), *Psychology of motor behavior and sport*. Champaign, IL: Human Kinetics.

Coming more from the usual trait perspective, Williams (1978) reviewed literature that met two criteria: (1) the investigation focused on the more highly skilled female athlete, and (2) personality was assessed by either Cattell's 16 PF Questionnaire or the Edwards' Personal Preference Schedule (EPPS). Studying women who participated in several sports (fencers, ice hockey players, track athletes, swimmers, lacrosse players, and race-car drivers), she was able to identify several trends:

1. There was a low degree of personality variability or personality differences within a particular sport activity.
2. This low variability, or "sameness," was evident regardless of age or experience.
3. Certain characteristics appear to be related to highly skilled female athletes. These athletes appear to be more "assertive, dominant, self-sufficient, independent, aggressive, intelligent, reserved, achievement oriented, and to have average to low emotionality" (p. 253).

Taken together, Williams (1978) data appear to agree both with Helmreich and Spence's (1977) androgynous position and Morgan's analysis of male elite athletes. In addition, although there have not been a large number of well-designed studies, the results are encouraging in terms of positive psychological attributes associated with highly skilled female sport participants. Obviously, caution needs to be exercised in overgeneralizing these findings until long-term investigations are conducted.

Now that you have some idea about the personalities of both highly skilled male and female athletes, let's examine another question concerning how personality may relate to sport participation: Do athletes really differ from nonathletes?

Athletes versus Nonathletes

Morgan (1980) reviewed 15 studies that addressed the question of personality differences between athletes and nonathletes. Although some differences were found in each of the studies, no meaningful conclusions could be drawn. There was no consistency in either the nature of the sample selected or in the assessment procedure employed. Samples ranged from athletes involved in sport clubs at Tokyo University to junior high school boys in the United States. Assessment techniques were just as diverse. Therefore, instead of arguing in favor of a trait approach to sport personality research, the data analyzed by Morgan simply reflected a state of confusion relative to the trait explanation underlying sport behavior. As a consequence, no meaningful conclusions can be drawn on the basis of investigations that approach the study of the personality of athletes versus nonathletes by merely selecting an available instrument and measuring people. The lack of a theoretical framework apparent in these investigations hinders any attempt to interpret their results. Furthermore, it should be clearer at this point why the approach taken by Schurr and others (1977), wherein the investigation is housed within an appropriate theoretical framework and a sport classification system is employed, is the more desirable approach to understanding the relationship between sport participation and personality.

The Credulous-Skeptical Controversy

Taken as a whole, the synthesis of the research evidence using the trait approach to sport personality research appears to show some trends for both skilled male and female athletes. However, there is still some controversy among sport psychologists regarding the value of the trait approach. This is called the credulous-skeptical controversy. The credulous-skeptical controversy provides valuable insights into both the strengths and weaknesses of trait psychology in sport psychology research.

From about 1950 through the mid-1960s, most of the research conducted in an effort to understand what, if any, relationship existed between personality traits and sport behavior used an empirical approach. Theories such as those proposed by Cattell and Eysenck were generally ignored. Instead, the usual strategy was to simply secure and administer a standardized personality inventory to a group of subjects who were readily available. Not surprisingly, the results tended to be unimpressive. Sometimes differences were observed; sometimes they were not. Because no single test was used, sometimes the results of one study could be compared with that of another; other times they could not. These problems led many sport psychologists to take a *skeptical perspective* on the relationship between personality and sport behavior (Martens, 1975; Rushall, 1970). Many called for the abandonment of such attempts and argued in favor of other avenues of research such as laboratory-based studies.

Others took a *credulous perspective* and argued that the reason why the research evidence was in such a shambles was the lack of any supporting theoretical framework (see Morgan, 1978, 1980). Even when existing personality theories, such as those developed by Cattell and Eysenck, were employed, they were done in an atheoretical fashion. Second-order factors were usually ignored in favor of primary factors. In addition, it was proposed that if psychological states (immediate, transitory measures) as well as traits were incorporated into the experimental protocol, then better prediction would result.

The controversy still exists to a certain degree; however, it is somewhat difficult to accept the skeptical position, given that its basis appears to be primarily the atheoretical, empirical early work in sport personality research. As we discussed in Chapter 1, for a field to develop adequately in a scientific sense, some attempt at theoretically based investigations is imperative. If researchers do begin systematic programs of theoretically founded personality research such as that enacted by Morgan and his associates, then perhaps there will be a resolution of the credulous-skeptical argument.

Current Status and Future Directions in Trait Psychology

Traditionally, most of the assessment instruments used to measure personality within sport settings were general or broad in nature rather than sport-specific. They were also designed to measure traits rather than states. In terms of contemporary approaches to personality assessment in sport settings, two issues appear to be most important: (1) whether the test is broad or narrow and (2) whether the test measures traits or states. Figure 2-8 depicts these two dimensions. As we mentioned earlier, *traits* are enduring predispositions to behave in predictable ways. *States,* on the other hand, refer to transitory or momentary occurrences. For instance, the emotions you feel just before athletic competition would be classified as a state. Your predisposition to consistently seek out competitive sport situations would be classified as a trait. State measures are generally better predictors of subsequent performance than are trait measures (Zuckerman, 1979).

The second dimension refers to the scope of the assessment instrument. A *narrow* inventory usually measures a single variable such as anxiety or introversion, whereas a *broad* measure includes multiple variables such as the 16 factors measured by the Cattell

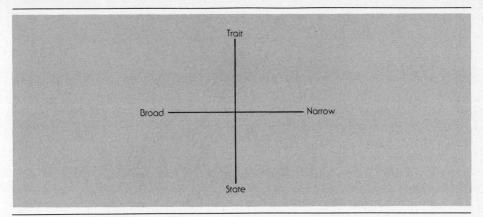

FIGURE 2-8   Dimensions of broad-narrow and trait-state.

16 PF Questionnaire. Zuckerman (1979) has shown that narrow measures are more effective in predicting behavior than are broad assessment instruments.

Until recently sport psychologists did not have access to sport-specific measures that were narrow in scope. However, in 1977 Martens published *The Sport Competitive Anxiety Test* (SCAT). This is a narrow trait measure designed specifically to assess the anxiety a person generally feels in competitive sport settings. The introduction of this assessment technique was certainly a much-needed addition to the field of sport psychology. However, all of the assessment problems were not solved. Recall that state measures are thought to be superior to trait measures in terms of accuracy of prediction. Martens (1981) has again come to the rescue! He has recently developed and validated a state assessment of sport competitive anxiety called the Sport Competitive Anxiety Test–2. It is hoped that the next decade will see the introduction of similar narrow state and trait measures of other sport-related personality variables.

In addition to the nature and structure of assessment instruments, two other current trends in the future direction of the trait approach to sport personality research can be identified. First, recently there has been a marked increase in the number of investigations that have examined cognitive or perceptual characteristics as opposed to the traditional personality variables associated with trait psychology. Later in the text we will discuss some of those variables, such as attentional style and imagery. The cognitive approach to sport psychology is highly promising in terms of providing us with better insights into individual sport behavior. The second new direction in sport psychology is that of inter-actionism.

INTERACTIONISM AND SPORT BEHAVIOR

According to the interactionist position, aspects of both the person and the situation (that is, person × situation) must be studied simultaneously. Researchers in interactionism ask questions such as "Will extroverts perform better in a team sport situation as compared with introverts?" "Will low-anxious persons excel more in competitive sport settings as compared with high-anxious performers?'' The interactionist position is the most popular one used today. It appears capable of accounting for more variations in behavior than either behavioristic or trait theory.

With some notable exceptions, the trait psychology approach does not appear to be adequate in terms of allowing sport psychologists to describe or explain individual sport behavior. As a result, many scholars became highly dissatisfied with the trait approach and abandoned that framework in favor of one called the **individual difference framework.** Its roots are in the tradition of trait psychology, but instead of simultaneously testing many personality traits to see if some relationship to sport behavior exists, the individual difference strategy selects one or two variables that are thought to be related to sport behavior. Thus it is clear that the individual difference framework differs from the usual approach of trait psychology in two important ways. The variables that are selected for study have some theoretical reason for being chosen, and only one or two variables are studied at a time.

The Interactionist Paradigm

The paradigm derived from the individual difference perspective is called the **interactionist paradigm.** The interactionist paradigm (person × situation) assesses one or two theoretically based variables as they are thought to operate in a clearly defined social situation.

In sport psychology studies the social situations of interest would be sport-related. For example, the experimenter might select persons who differ in levels of anxiety. It would then be predicted that high-anxious persons should differ from low-anxious persons when performing a complex motor task under conditions of either competition or cooperation. From this perspective, anxiety (an individual difference variable) is said to interact with a particular social situation (either competition or cooperation).

Another sport example is one in which a researcher would identify persons who tend to be extroverted or introverted and then observe differences in their preference for either individual or team sports. In this person × situation study, it would be predicted that extroverts would prefer team sports whereas introverts would tend to select individual sports.

Current Status and Future Directions of Interactionism

The person × situation framework has been able to provide much better descriptions of individual behavior in sport and motor performance settings. However, if you recall the goals of science, you know that description is not sufficient in and of itself. Researchers need to move to the next level, explanation. Is it possible to modify the person × situation paradigm in such a way that explanation would be possible? Yes; all that a researcher would have to do is to include measures of meaningful cognitive or physiological processes within the experimental procedures. When we say meaningful, we mean that the process or mechanism that is measured must be linked intimately with sport or motor performance. For example, when studying high- versus low-anxious performers, one physiological variable known to vary between the two groups is the pattern of muscular activity exhibited by the two groups. By including such measures within a research design, the researcher is then able to highlight one process that can help to explain why the motor performance of low-anxious persons is usually better than that of high-anxious persons. When the usual interactive paradigm (that is, person × situation) is modified so that cognitive or physiological processes are also included in the experimental procedures, it is called the *interactional-mediational paradigm* (Bird, 1979). It is possible that the use of both the usual interactive approach and the interactional-mediational paradigm will allow faster progress than ever before in understanding the causes underlying differences in individual behavior in various sport settings.

Therefore it is imperative that you gain a clearer understanding of these paradigms. To do this, it is necessary to understand the structure of the unifying model of sport behavior. An appreciation of this unifying model is also important to your understanding of most of the material presented in the remainder of this text.

The Unifying Model and Sport Behavior

In Chapter 1 we discussed the notion that paradigms are related to research strategies and are derived from theoretical frameworks, or models. The development of the interactional-mediational paradigm was based on what we refer to as the unifying model of individual sport behavior (Figure 2-9).

Input

Beginning at the left side of Figure 2-9, you can see that first the human system must receive sensory *input* from the environment; that is, some input must come into the system from the stimulus conditions present at a particular time.

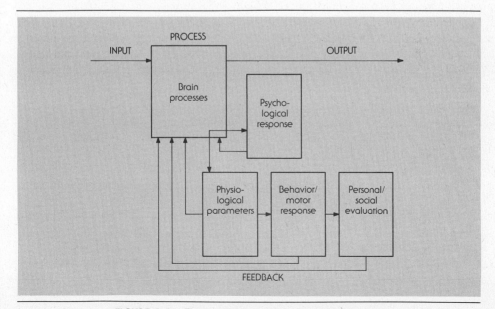

FIGURE 2-9   The unifying model of sport behavior.

Process

The input is then translated and interpreted *(processed)* in the brain. It is put into a form that is meaningful to the person.

Output

From Figure 2-9 you can see that *output* can be viewed on at least four levels: psychological, physiological, behavior or motor response, and the social or personal evaluation of the response outcome.

The psychological response refers to the affective, or emotional, reactions that are experienced as a consequence of the result of the brain processing. A person may feel apprehensive, anxious, or elated.

We have already discussed some aspects of physiological response (physiological response refers to any changes in activation, such as heart rate or respiration); however, throughout this text we will present a great deal more information about the interrelationships among sensory input, brain processes, and physiological responses. These interrelationships form the backbone of our approach to sport psychology. The behavioral response is the one that actually can be observed.

A performer can evaluate the motor response on the basis of internally based information (such as kinesthetic information) and on externally based information (such as auditory information and visual evaluation of success or failure). In addition, because most participation in sport is public in nature, the quality of the behavioral response is usually evaluated by both the participant and other persons. Do you perform in an identical fashion when you are alone as opposed to when there are other persons present? Not necessarily. Therefore both an athlete's own evaluation and those of others may affect future performance.

Feedback

The unifying model is characterized by four feedback loops. Notice that information is fed back to the brain from all four levels of output (that is, psychological, physiological, motor, and evaluation). After a response is made, a person receives information about the quality of that response from both internal and external sources. This feedback information affects future perceptions of input information and therefore can affect how well or poorly a person performs in the future.

To understand individual sport behavior, you must first understand the psychophysiological nature of human beings. You must realize that the athlete is not simply a physical being; it is the interactions that occur at several levels and among several systems that ultimately determine how effective a sport or motor response will be. Once this is accomplished, you must learn how feedback information and cognitive processing can be used to enhance future performance. We will try to facilitate this understanding through the re-introduction of the unifying model throughout this text.

Let's put the unifying model into a real-life sport situation. It's the first day of swimming practice. Your specialty is the breast stroke. You're new at school and want to make a good impression. You're changed and on the deck. The coach has everyone practice at the same time, and she wants all the swimmers to warm up with four laps of freestyle. This is the input in terms of what you should be doing. What about the other information you would be processing? Psychologically, you feel highly motivated but apprehensive. Physiologically, your heart is racing and your breathing is rapid. Behaviorally, you dive into the pool and try to break away from the crowd in your lane. You feel yourself surging ahead; you speculate about your performance when you actually make the team. You fantasize about the roar of the crowd as you pull away from the pack. You forecast the positive reactions your future swimming victories will bring.

IMPLICATIONS FOR SPORT

- Because there is no such thing as a "typical" athlete in terms of personality, each individual should be treated somewhat differently. To be an effective coach or teacher you must "know your athletes."
- Athletes' personalities are rather stable; do not expect them to change. Instead, try to adopt a coaching or teaching style that is flexible enough to be effective with different individuals.
- Apply positive reinforcements based on the principle of contingency; that is, only reward an athlete after you observe a desired response. That response can be either the ideal skill execution or a close approximation. Noncontingent reinforcement will not assist the player in making a connection between an identifiable stimulus and the correct response.
- Rewards for each athlete vary according to individual motivations; therefore an effective coach should attempt to understand each athlete's reason for participating. For some it is the glory of winning; for others it is the coach's approval.
- Use the idea of successive approximations. Schedule conferences to discuss the degree to which each athlete is progressing in relation to the established goal.
- Effective coaching is characterized by positive reinforcement, not punishment. Be positive, not punitive.
- Make practices as gamelike as possible. Because the social situation interacts with the athlete's personality, optimal performance requires a realistic setting.

CASE STUDY 1

Applied Behavioral Coaching

In this case study we describe a practice regimen designed to improve specific volleyball skills of a beginning player. The athlete demonstrates inconsistent and inaccurate passing skills. The coach observes that the performer tends to attempt passing with both straight legs and bent elbows.

Practice Regimen

Goal 1: Pass execution using correct leg position

    1. Coach identifies cues to observe for legs

        a. Lowered center of gravity

        b. Bent knees

    2. Coach tells player which cues to observe

    3. Player observes a correct model

    4. Player attempts to pass tossed ball back to the tosser using correct leg position

    5. Correct responses are reinforced by coach, appropriate cues are repeated after incorrect responses

Goal 2: Pass execution using correct arm position

    1. Coach identifies cues to observe for arms

        a. Locked elbows

        b. Flat forearm surface

    2. Coach tells player which cues to observe

    3. Player observes a correct model

    4. Player attempts to pass tossed ball back to the tosser using correct arm position

    5. Correct responses are reinforced by coach, appropriate cues are repeated after incorrect responses

Goal 3: Pass execution using correct positions for both arms and legs

    1. Coach identifies cues to observe for both arms and legs

        a. Lowered center of gravity

        b. Bent knees

        c. Locked elbows

        d. Flat forearm surface

    2. Coach tells player which cues to observe

    3. Player observes a correct model

    4. Player attempts to pass tossed ball back to the tosser using correct leg and arm positions

    5. Correct responses are reinforced by coach, appropriate cues are repeated after incorrect responses

Goal 4: Increase in consistency and accuracy of passing skill

    1. Identification of desired terminal behavior: the consistent reception and accurate return of at least eight out of ten passes

    2. Correct responses are reinforced by the coach, appropriate cues are repeated after incorrect responses

    3. On attainment of the desired terminal behavior (at least eight out of ten consistent receptions and accurate returns), the player's name is posted on the sheet showing individual goals for skill development

    4. A new terminal goal is established (for example, 16 out of 20 consistent receptions and accurate returns)

CASE STUDY 2
Low Basketball Free Throw Performance and the Unifying Model

Suppose that you were the coach of a center on a basketball team who carried a field goal percentage of 70% and a free throw percentage of 28%. Based on the player's field goal percentage, you would certainly conclude that the skill was there. If that is the case, why should the free throw percentage be so low? Is it simply the fixed distance from the basket to the free throw line? No, your statistics indicate that the center consistently scores very well from the same distance when the team is on offense. If it is not a problem associated with skill execution at that distance, then what is left to consider? Most likely there is something about the change in social situation that occurs during free throws.

From the perspective of the unifying model, we see a poor behavioral or motor response under specific environmental conditions. The player's observation of these conditions (input) is processed by the brain. The player might then think that "everyone is watching me" or "I always miss this shot." What should be the accompanying emotional response? Most likely an anxiety response occurs. There are probably increased physiological responses (rapid heart rate, profuse sweating) and more negative thoughts. What should be the content and future consequences of both the player's and the spectators' evaluation of the missed basket? Is it likely that performance will change for the better in the future? Not unless some other factor changes.

What can you do to improve the player's free throw percentage?

1. The skill is there, so additional practice is probably not the only answer.
2. The environmental conditions during free throws are somewhat fixed; therefore it is impossible to change the stimulus conditions.
3. The major elements that remain are emotions, cognitions, physiological parameters, and response evaluation. Emotions function as a consequence of cognitions, whereas the response evaluation follows the skill execution. That leaves cognitions and physiological parameters as the likely candidates.
4. A person cannot think two separate thoughts simultaneously; therefore one approach would be to give the player a specific, positively based script to rehearse before the shot. Or, depending on the individual athlete, positive self-statements such as "I feel good" or "I know I can make this shot" can work with equal effectiveness.
5. Positive thoughts should not usually result in adverse physiological reactions. However, as insurance, the player should perform a relaxing maneuver just before the shot such as bouncing the ball twice or taking a deep breath. Many players find this to be relaxing. Furthermore, it is not possible to be relaxed and anxious simultaneously.

If (4) and (5) are practiced sufficiently, the probability is increased that free throw percentage will go up. With successful shots, positive evaluations occur and ultimately the environmental conditions associated with free throw shooting will not produce as much anxiety. The negative cycle will then be broken.

SUMMARY

- Thorndike's law of effect was an early explanation of how stimulus, response, and reinforcement were said to be related in terms of affecting the acquisition, maintenance, and change of human behavior.
- A more recent behavioristic approach is that of Skinner's operant reinforcement theory. It is based on the factors of reinforcement, stimuli, and deprivation. He uses the principles of successive approximations and response contingency to explain how behavior is shaped.
- In trait psychology, when theoretical frameworks such as those proposed by Cattell and Eysenck are employed, more consistent personality differences appear to exist in regard to highly skilled men and women athletes as compared with their less successful counterparts. However, it is currently not possible to directly compare men and women relative to the presence of identical personality characteristics.
- Any time personality assessments are made, it would appear that narrow state measures are better predictors than broad trait measures.
- The most current and most popular approach to understanding individual sport behavior is called interactionism. Interactionism is a person × situation paradigm that studies individual difference variables in identifiable sport situations.
- Based on the framework of the unifying model, the original interactionist paradigm can be modified into what is referred to as the interactional-mediational paradigm. Cognitive and physiological variables can now be evaluated regarding the development of explanations underlying variations in individual sport-motor performance.

DISCUSSION QUESTIONS

1 What principle would a coach be violating if he or she praised an athlete for trying even though the skill was performed incorrectly?
2 In terms of learning and improving sport skills, what important process or mechanism is ignored by the behavioristic perspective?
3 What two characteristics should personality assessment instruments have to yield the best predictions of athlete behavior?
4 Using the framework of the unifying model, can you identify sport situations that systematically affect you differently in terms of your thoughts (cognitions), emotions (positive and negative), and physiological responses (increased or decreased)? Taken together, how do these responses affect your sport performance?
5 Can you trace the development and changes in sport personality research from its beginnings to current approaches? Based on that analysis, would you argue in support of the credulous or skeptical perspective?

GLOSSARY

androgyny In terms of personality, the simultaneous possession of the healthiest psychological characteristics usually associated with feminine and masculine personality profiles

approximation In sport performance, any skill performance that closely resembles the desired skill performance

deprivation A state in which a person is deprived or denied something

individual difference framework The study of either one or two variables on which persons are known to vary

interactionist paradigm The simultaneous study of some aspect of the person and the social situation

inverse relationship A relationship between variables wherein as one increases the other decreases

law of effect If the consequences of a response are positive, then the probability increases that the same or a similar response will recur under the same set of stimulus conditions; if the consequences of a response are negative, then the probability of response recurrence decreases

multivariate More than one variable

negative reinforcement Withdrawal or removal of an unpleasant stimulus

operant Something, such as reinforcement, that acts on a person in a manner that then produces an effect

perception Process through which information is received through the senses and translated into conscious meaning in the brain

positive reinforcement Application of a pleasant stimulus after the emission of a response

principle of contingency The application of reinforcement should be dependent on the enactment of a desired response

psychopathy A state of psychological disorder, disease, or abnormality

punishment Application of an unpleasant stimulus after a response

stimulus generalization The transfer of a response to a new similar stimulus

terminal objective The end or desired objective

trait theory A theory that views human behavior as primarily determined by stable personality characteristics

SUGGESTED READINGS

Donahue, J.A., Gillis, J.H., & King, K. (1980). Behavior modification in sport and physical education: A review. *Journal of Sport Psychology, 2,* 311-328.

    The authors review the major research on behavior modification in sport and physical education settings. Specific topics covered are behavior modification and coaching or teaching behavior, behavior modification in physical education and sport environments, and behavior modification and skill development.

Highlen, P.S., & Bennett, B.B. (1979). Psychological characteristics of successful and nonsuccessful elite wrestlers: An exploratory study. *Journal of Sport Psychology, 1,* 123-137.

    Highlen and Bennett used a questionnaire approach to study the psychological factors affecting the training and competition of Canadian World Wrestling teams. In particular, their focus was an attempt to identify psychological characteristics of qualifiers versus nonqualifiers.

Lanning, W. (1979). Coach and athlete personality interaction: A critical variable in athletic success. *Journal of Sport Psychology, 1,* 262-267.

   Lanning presents a discussion of the importance of the interaction between the personalities of athletes and coaches. He identifies implications for coaching, recruiting, hiring assistant coaches, and the selection of coaches and athletes for elite teams.

Martens, R. (1975). The paradigmatic crisis in American sport personology. *Sportwissenschaft, 5,* 9-24.

   In this article, Martens focuses on the study of personality in sport. He identifies the problem associated with using either personal observations or personality research methods and theories and traces the direction that sport personality research has taken in the United States. Martens concludes that the interactional paradigm is the direction that sport personality research should take.

Martin, G., & Hrycaiko, D. (1983). Effective behavioral coaching: What's it all about? *Journal of Sport Psychology, 5,* 8-20.

   This article presents six factors that appear to have considerable potential for the use of behavior modification techniques for the improvement of performance in sport and physical education settings. Emphasis is placed on careful application and continuous evaluation of coaching strategies.

Morgan, W.P. (1979). Prediction of performance in athletics. In P. Klavora & J.V. Daniels (Eds.), *Coach, athlete, and the sport psychologist*. Champaign, IL: Human Kinetics.

   Morgan addresses the usefulness of personality research in sport settings. He cautions that the current state of the art does not support the notion of selecting athletes on the basis of psychological data alone.

Morgan, W.P. (1980). The trait psychology controversy. *Research Quarterly for Exercise and Sport, 51*, 50-76.

   In this article, Morgan traces the development and controversy surrounding the trait approach to personality research. He addresses the skeptical and credulous arguments relative to sport personality research and explains long-term methodological problems and exciting avenues for future research.

Silva, J.M., Shultz, B.B., Haslam, R.W., & Murray, D.A. (1981). A psychophysiological assessment of elite wrestlers. *Research Quarterly for Exercise and Sport, 52*, 348-358.

   The authors used a psychophysiological model to assess both psychological and physiological variables of athletes participating in the 1979 United States Junior World Wrestling Camp. Qualifiers could be distinguished from nonqualifiers on the basis of both psychological and physiological factors.

II

AROUSAL, ANXIETY, AND INTERVENTIONS IN SPORT

3
Arousal and Sport Behavior

4
Anxiety, Motor Performance,
Sport, and Exercise

5
Intervention Strategies and
Sport Behavior

3

AROUSAL AND SPORT BEHAVIOR

Arousal pertains to your level of physiological **activation.** As you read this chapter your arousal level is probably low, and unless you make a concerted effort to monitor physiological responses such as heart or respiration rate, you are unaware of those indices of arousal. Suppose, however, that the next time you went to class, your professor unexpectedly asked you to stand up in front of the room and summarize the major points of this chapter. More than likely you would become very aware of changes in your level of physiological activation. Similar increases in level of arousal frequently take place in sport situations and can have a direct effect on the quality of performance. This chapter explores the relationship between arousal and sport performance.

THE NATURE OF AROUSAL

Arousal can be viewed as the intensity underlying behavior; it is the physiological activation that instigates or activates behavior. The simplest way to conceptualize arousal is along the continuum proposed by Duffy (1957) and Malmo (1959). From their perspective, arousal varies along a continuum that ranges from deep sleep to intense excitement. *Arousal* is a neutral term in that it does not take into account aspects of accompanying emotions or thoughts. Two persons may have equal amounts of arousal or physiological activation but experience different emotions or thoughts. For example, before a soccer match, one player may be "psyched up" and in a positive emotional state, whereas a teammate might be scared to death. Both would have high degrees of physiological activation (arousal) but dissimilar affect (emotions).

There have been two predominant explanations of how level of arousal is related to the performance of motor skills, the earliest being drive theory. More recently, optimal level theory has produced a second explanation, called the inverted-U hypothesis.

CONFLICTING THEORETICAL EXPLANATIONS

Drive Theory

Although many theorists have examined behavior from the framework of drive theory, the major theorists associated with this perspective are Clark L. Hull and Kenneth W. Spence. Both had origins in the behavioristic tradition, so notions relating to aspects of consciousness or cognitive processes were not emphasized in their explanations of the causes underlying human behavior. The basic prediction that can be derived from drive theory is

$$\text{Performance} = \text{Drive} \times \text{Habit}$$

Thus two crucial variables are said to underlie behavior or performance: drive and habit.

Drive

Drive is the motivational force that activates or elicits behavior. As used here, drive is synonymous with arousal. Therefore, although drive acts to initiate behavior, it does not direct it toward a specific goal. There are several characteristics associated with drive states:

1. There is fairly strong physiological evidence to support the assertion that arousal and drive are synonymous (Berlyne, 1966). Therefore it can be assumed that what is known about drive and drive states can be applied to arousal or varying levels of arousal.
2. If a stimulus, whether it be internal or external in origin, is strong enough, it can evoke a drive state and thus impel action.
3. Drives are not equal in strength. The stronger the drive, the more powerful or vigorous the response. This relates to Duffy's (1957) and Malmo's (1959) notion of a continuum ranging from deep sleep to high excitation.
4. Drive (arousal) is not constant; it varies from moment to moment.
5. High levels of drive (arousal) cause high levels of activation within the body's physiological systems. The effects can be evidenced in the electrical activity that takes place in the brain, changes in heart rate or respiration, and changes in the diameter of the pupil in the eye.
6. The response produced by a high drive level is intimately associated with the nature of the stimulus that elicited the increased drive. For example, if a person is deprived of food, the expected response is food-seeking.
7. Increases in drive are said to facilitate learning by making a person receptive to reinforcement. This notion is directly associated with *habit*.

Habit

We said earlier that drives were related to the intensity of behavior. They are thought of in terms of general energy mobilization or physiological activation. However, if you think of performance in terms of both the intensity and direction of behavior, then you must also address the way in which behavior is directed toward a particular goal. Within the framework of drive theory, the direction of behavior is accounted for by the inclusion of habit. **Habit strength** refers to the degree of association between a stimulus and a response. Therefore the stronger the link or association between a stimulus and a response, the stronger the habit. Think of the observable difference in the behaviors of a novice versus an advanced tennis player. The novice performer only has a weak connection between a particular stimulus, such as a lob, and the most appropriate response, a smash. An advanced player has a much stronger habit strength, and the response to a lob appears to be almost automatic. How does such automaticity develop?

Habits are learned behaviors. If they are learned, and if drive theory is coming from the framework of the behavioristic tradition, then how do you think habits are learned? Think back to the contingencies of reinforcement discussed in Chapter 1. If your answer is reinforcement, you are correct.

From Hull's perspective, for habit strength to develop, the response must be followed by reinforcement, and the application of such reinforcers must follow the response closely in terms of both time and space. This is called the **principle of contiguity.** Keep this principle in mind: it is fundamental to Hull's conceptualization of drive theory, and we will return to it later in this chapter. Hull also said that the development of habit strength was dependent on the *frequency* with which the response was reinforced.

Habit hierarchy. Habit hierarchy pertains to the idea that responses can be conceptualized in a hierarchic order; that is, they can be thought of as being ''stacked'' from high to low or from incorrect to correct. According to the notion of habit hierarchy, each person has within himself or herself a range of possible responses from the most incorrect to the most correct.

For example, early in learning, persons tend to emit more incorrect than correct responses; at this point they are operating low on the habit hierarchy. With practice and reinforcement there should be improvement, resulting with the emission of more correct responses. In that case, the person has moved up on the hierarchy of habit.

Dominant responses. At any particular time, there is a tendency for correct responses to compete with incorrect responses. This is the notion of **competing response tendencies.** As we mentioned earlier, during the early stages of practice at a new skill, usually more incorrect than correct responses occur; however, with practice and reinforcement, correct responses become dominant over incorrect responses.

How does drive fit into this picture? Within the framework of the habit hierarchy, a basic prediction is that as drive increases, the probability of the emission of the dominant response also increases. How should this affect performance? Think about what you have experienced when you first began practicing a new motor skill. Assume that it is a fairly complex skill. What should happen to the quality of your skill execution if you are highly aroused (high drive)? You will probably make more mistakes than accurate executions, which is exactly what drive theory would predict. During the early stages of practice (learning), high levels of drive should cause a decrease or disruption in skill quality. That decrease occurs because the increase in drive caused the emission of the dominant (incorrect) response.

Now think of yourself as you practice your favorite sport, one in which you are highly skilled. What should happen to the quality of your skill execution under conditions of increased arousal or drive? In this situation you will most likely perform well. According to drive theory, the increase in drive caused the emission of the dominant response. Recall that when a person is highly skilled, the correct response should be dominant.

Basic Prediction Concerning Motor Performance

Strictly speaking, the prediction of what should happen during early learning is not as clear-cut as we have presented it. For instance, a **flooring effect** could exist wherein the performance is so bad that increases in drive cannot serve to hinder it any more; that is, performance cannot get any worse. However, in the case of later skill development, in which the dominant response is correct, drive theory makes a straightforward prediction about the relationship between increases in drive and quality of motor performance. Figure 3-1 portrays that prediction. Notice that the relationship shown is a positive linear function. Quite simply, it predicts that when the dominant response is correct and the performer is highly skilled, increases in drive (arousal) should result in increases in performance. As one variable increases, so should the other. It is important to point out that, taken to its extreme, drive theory predicts that increasingly higher levels of drive should result in

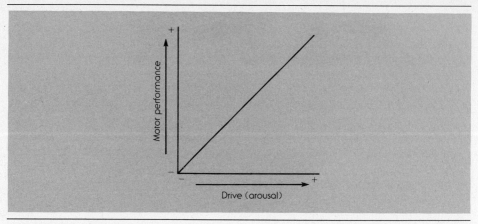

FIGURE 3-1 Predicted relationship between level of drive (arousal) and quality of motor performance.

increasingly better performance. We will discuss the validity of that prediction later within our presentation of the inverted-U hypothesis. For now we will turn our attention to the validity of other dimensions of drive theory.

Current Status of Drive Theory

A significant number of researchers have argued against drive theory as a viable theoretical framework for the study of motor skills. Martens (1974) has pointed out several flaws within a drive interpretation of motor behavior. The primary basis of his argument rests on the fact that

> At the present time no one has been able to determine clearly the habit hierarchies for the motor responses on various motor tasks. If it is impossible to predict clearly whether the correct or incorrect response is dominant, then it is impossible to test the equation: performance = habit × drive and its derivatives. (p. 173)

Obviously, if researchers cannot test the basic prediction associated with a theory, then it is difficult to argue that the theory is capable of producing adequate explanations. In addition to the problems associated with identifying a habit hierarchy for motor skills, other evidence calls into question the **principle of contiguity,** which states that reinforcement must follow a response closely in time. Some cognitively based research has shown that reinforcement is effective even after the passage of several hours, whereas other evidence shows that a person can learn in the absence of any form of reinforcement (Landers & Landers, 1973). Therefore these data argue against both the necessity of reinforcement and the necessity for a contiguous relationship between a response and the application of reinforcement. Taken together, there appears to be some evidence that questions the validity of drive theory as the best interpretation of human behavior.

Social Facilitation Theory

We would be remiss if we did not mention social facilitation theory, one of the most popular theoretical frameworks in the early days of sport psychology. Its origin was in the tradition of drive theory, although later a cognitive interpretation was proposed. Basically, social facilitation theory makes predictions regarding how the presence of other people, in the form of either a passive audience or other coactors, should affect performance. A passive audience is one in which no manifestation of approval or disapproval is evidenced. The usual elements associated with an audience in a competitive situation, such as clapping or expressing emotions, is absent. Usually the audience consists of two or more persons who observe another person perform.

Coactors are two or more persons who perform the same task at the same time in view of all the other coactors. For example, if you and a friend face each other and both perform as many push-ups as possible, you are performing in a coactive situation.

Conflicting Hypotheses

Zajonc (1965) proposed what is called the *mere physical presence hypothesis*. He attempted to explain social facilitation effects within the framework of drive theory and proposed that persons have an innate tendency toward increased drive under conditions of social facilitation. More specifically, when other persons are merely physically present in the form of either a passive audience or other coactors, there should be an increase in drive. As we discussed earlier, such increased drive should cause the emission of the dominant response. Whether the emission of the dominant response facilitates or hinders skill execution is directly related to stage of skill development.

Drive theorists divide skill development into two stages, learning and performance. The early stage of practice, wherein the dominant response is incorrect, is called learning. The later stage of practice, wherein the dominant response is correct, is called performance. The major prediction made by Zajonc was that the social situation of either the mere physical presence of a passive audience or other coactors (cause) should hinder skill execution in the early stages and facilitate it in the later stages (effect). The cause of these effects was the mere physical presence of others and the resultant increase in drive (arousal), which then impelled the emission of the dominant response.

Recall, however, that Zajonc proposed that the reason why these effects would be predicted rested on some **innate** tendency. The question then becomes that of the validity of explaining human behavior on the basis of innate tendencies. Do you agree that there is an innate, inborn tendency for all persons, regardless of age or experience, to respond in the predicted direction when other people are merely present physically? Let us say that you tend to respond with increased drive, or arousal, when others are present while you are learning or performing a skill. Why does this happen? Is it some quality or tendency with which you were born? Can you think of an alternative explanation underlying the cause of that effect?

In 1968 Cottrell and his associates (Cottrell, Wack, Sekerak, & Rittle, 1968) advanced the argument that the effects observed under conditions of social facilitation were mediated not by some innately based tendency but instead by the *evaluation potential* that is present when others witness a person's performance. Thus their hypothesis was called the *evaluation apprehension hypothesis* and was based on a cognitive interpretation.

In the realm of science it is not sufficient to propose a counterargument to an existing theoretical explanation. In addition to positing an alternative explanation, the scientist must design an experiment that can simultaneously test both theoretical explanations and subsequently show support for one and nonsupport for the other. Such an investigation is called a **crucial experiment**.

Let's see what kind of scientist you are. In the case of social facilitation, the first hypothesis proposed that the effects are caused by an innate tendency to respond in a predictable fashion under the conditions specified in the social facilitation paradigm (Zajonc's mere physical presence hypothesis). The second hypothesis is a cognitively based one that suggests that the causes underlying the effects are that people learn that others are evaluating them when they are present as spectators (the evaluation apprehension hypothesis). How would you design an investigation that could simultaneously test both hypotheses? The outcome of your study would have to show that one hypothesis was clearly a better explanation than the other. Let's say the motor task involved was a free throw in basketball. Because it is going to be a social facilitation paradigm, you must use the presence of a passive audience or other coactors as the independent variable. The dependent variable will be free throw accuracy. It would seem more reasonable to use the presence of an audience in the situation of free throws because this skill is executed that way in the game. How could you manipulate the audience so that they were physically present in each condition, but in one condition evaluation potential was operating and in the other it was not? If you said that you could either have the audience turn their backs or wear blindfolds in one condition and have the audience able to see the performance in the other condition, you would be thinking in a fashion similar to Cottrell and his associates.

In their crucial experiment, Cottrell and others (1968) used three different conditions. Subjects either performed alone, in the presence of two blindfolded audience members, or in the presence of two audience members who were not blindfolded. If they were to obtain different performance effects under the two audience conditions, then the mere physical presence hypothesis would be called into question. That is exactly what happened. The "alone" and the "blindfolded audience" groups performed similarly, whereas the "nonblindfolded audience" group performed best. On the basis of these results, they argued in favor of the evaluation apprehension hypothesis. Other researchers (Carment & Hodkins, 1973) have shown further support for the cognitive rather than the innate drive position based on cross-cultural research. When members of the same species do not exhibit identical behaviors under similar conditions, then it is difficult, if not erroneous, to propose an innate source of drive.

Although the cognitive interpretation of social facilitation effects appears to have the most merit, testing for social facilitation effects in sport and motor performance settings has declined sharply over the last decade. One reason for this decline was evidence that questioned whether the presence of a passive audience and other coactors should provide identical effects. For instance, using two different motor tasks, Bird (1973) found that subjects in a coaction condition performed better than subjects who performed under audience conditions. These data call into question a fundamental aspect of social facilitation theory. They also argue that performers most likely interpret the two social settings differently. They most probably make a cognitive appraisal of the amount of evaluation potential present in each situation. Such differential appraisals then lead to dissimilar levels of arousal and thus differential task performance.

Of even greater importance were the problems that occurred when investigators took their social facilitation studies out of the laboratory and into field settings. Although many of the highly controlled laboratory investigations substantiated the predictions derived from social facilitation theory, those same effects did not generally emerge in real-life sport situations. Because individual behavior in sport settings is of primary interest to the field of sport psychology, the study of social facilitation effects fell into disfavor.

The Inverted-U Hypothesis

With the criticisms associated with both drive theory and social facilitation theory came the emergence of an alternative position concerning the relationship between arousal and motor performance: the **inverted-U hypothesis.**

Recall that Duffy (1957) proposed that arousal can vary along a continuum from deep sleep to high excitation. For well-learned skills, drive theory proposes a positive, linear relationship between level of arousal and quality of motor performance. Coming from optimal level theory, the inverted-U hypothesis proposes instead that the relationship between level of arousal and quality of skilled motor performance is curvilinear. Figure 3-2 portrays the predictions connected with both drive theory and the inverted-U hypothesis. Drive theory predicts that as increases occur in arousal, increases in motor performance will also take place. However, the inverted-U hypothesis predicts that, although performance increases with arousal up to a certain point, with further increases in arousal, performance will decrease. Look closely at Figure 3-2. At what point should predicted differences become most apparent? Notice that at the point of high level of arousal that drive theory predicts excellent performance, whereas at that same point the inverted-U hypothesis predicts that performance will decrease. These conflicting predictions are frequently observed in sport. For instance, a coach who says that an athlete can never be too psyched-up is adhering to drive theory, whereas a performer such as Dwight Stones, who mentally visualizes his high jump, waiting for the perfect image before he jumps, may be subscribing to the inverted-U hypothesis.

Origin of the Hypothesis

The origin of the inverted-U hypothesis can be traced back to the work of Yerkes and Dodson in 1908. Using data from their experiments with mice, they proposed a principle

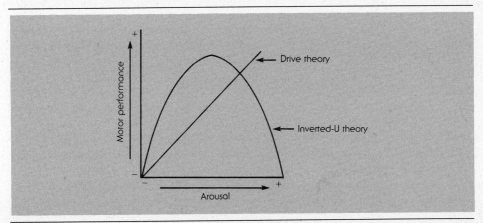

FIGURE 3-2 The conflicting predictions of drive theory versus the inverted-U hypothesis.

that became known as the **Yerkes-Dodson law.** This law proposed that an optimal level of arousal exists for best performance of a particular task. This law is represented in Figure 3-3, which shows the ideal level of arousal for best performance of three tasks that are either complex, moderate, or simple in nature. The figure indicates that complex tasks require low levels of arousal for best performance; moderate tasks require moderate levels of arousal; and simple tasks are performed better under conditions of high arousal.

The inverted-U hypothesis is a generalization. It does not predict a single person's actual performance on a specific task. Several factors or mediating variables must be taken into account before speculating on the relationship between arousal and motor performance.

Mediating variables. *Task difficulty* affects the desired level of arousal, as demonstrated in Figure 3-3. Why should this be? Suppose you were asked to perform a boring, simple task for about 20 minutes. Let's say you had to place round pegs in round holes and square pegs in square holes. You would get bored rapidly. However, if you were motivated by being paid $5 per peg, you would most likely fit more pegs in the appropriate holes over the given time period. On the other hand, if the task were very complex, the high pay might result in a large number of errors caused by overarousal.

On an intuitive level, the notion that task difficulty or the nature of the task itself interacts with optimal levels of arousal seems reasonable. However, on a more scientific level, the precise delineation of the relationship between task type and desired level of arousal is not that easy. What criterion should be employed to make such decisions? Some writers (Carron, 1980; Oxendine, 1970) have suggested the following relationships:

- High arousal is desired for optimal performance of gross motor tasks that demand endurance, strength, and speed, such as weight lifting and the 100-yard dash.

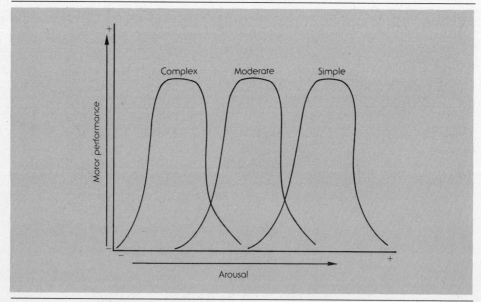

FIGURE 3-3   Yerkes-Dodson law and task complexity.

- High arousal is detrimental to performance of complex tasks, fine motor tasks, and tasks that require coordination and steadiness, such as playing a piano or performing intricate ice-skating routines.
- Slightly higher-than-moderate levels of arousal are more desirable than moderate or low levels of arousal for almost all motor tasks.

Although these suggested relationships may have some merit, they have not been without criticism. For instance, what might be an easy task for one person might be a difficult task for another person. Therefore, when looking at task difficulty as a mediating variable, we must also address the nature of the performer or athlete.

A second mediating variable associated with the interpretation of the inverted-U hypothesis is that of *individual differences*. Factors such as the performer's base level of arousal before actual performance, level of skill, and ability to inhibit the effects of arousal all play a role in determining performance.

A third mediating variable is *the social situation* present when the performance takes place. Characteristics of the social situation, such as the presence of an audience are capable of affecting degree of arousal.

Current Status of the Hypothesis

Although several mediating factors must be looked at when attempting to apply the inverted-U hypothesis, today it is considered to be the most useful perspective for understanding how arousal affects motor performance. Much current research in sport psychology is being conducted in an effort to uncover more precisely what processes or factors underlie the inverted-U hypothesis. If the inverted-U function is the best explanation for the relationship between arousal and sport-motor performance, why is this so? What happens to a person under conditions of high arousal so that performance is disrupted?

One way to understand the manner in which arousal operates within a person is to understand how arousal is ordinarily measured. Obviously, the physiological parameters selected for measurement are the ones that scientists feel reflect the manifestations of differing levels of arousal. We will use the unifying model to assist us in discussing the physiologically based methods of arousal measurement.

THE UNIFYING MODEL AND THE MEASUREMENT OF AROUSAL

Figure 3-4 presents the arousal process within the framework of the unifying model. The following sections are focused on brain processes and physiological parameters.

Brain Processes

A primary, or direct, measure of physiological activation or arousal is the assessment of the electrical activity in the brain, which is ordinarily done through the use of an electroencephalogram (EEG). The EEG records the brain's electrical activity in terms of alpha waves. Under conditions of a relaxed, wakeful state the brain produces alpha waves at a frequency of about 10 cycles per second. Under conditions of increased arousal those waves take on a more flattened appearance, become more irregular, and yield a desynchronized pattern (Berlyne, 1966). Although the EEG has the advantage of being a direct measure of arousal, it has not been the most frequently used measure in sport psychology

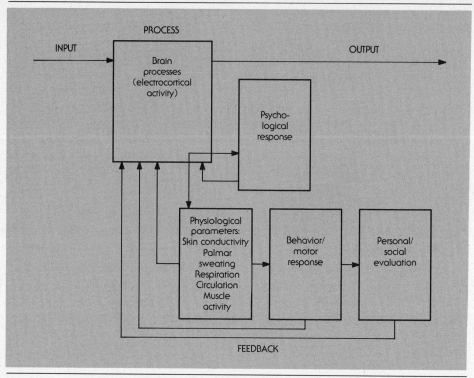

FIGURE 3-4   The unifying model and the measurement of arousal.

research because of its cost and the training needed in order to accurately interpret the recordings. Instead, generally one or more peripheral assessments are made. These are measures of physiological parameters that lie outside the brain or spinal cord and are frequently associated with the autonomic nervous system.

Peripheral Measures

Skin conductivity refers to the electrical properties of the skin. Measures such as the galvanic skin response (GSR) assess the resistance or conductivity of the skin to electrical current, which increases with increases in arousal.

Palmar sweating pertains to the amount of perspiration present on the palm of the hand. An instrument called a sudorimeter is usually used in making such assessments. As arousal increases, there should be increased palmar sweating. Most likely at one time or another you have experienced sweaty palms under conditions of high arousal.

Respiration can be measured in a number of ways. One method compares differences between the temperature of the air taken into the lungs (inspired) as compared with the temperature of the air that is exhaled. Because body temperature usually rises under conditions of high arousal, the exhaled air should have a higher temperature. Another method measures the rate of respiration, which usually increases with increases in arousal.

Circulatory effects are also associated with increased arousal. As Martens (1974) points out, there can be changes in the pumping action of the heart and also in the degree of

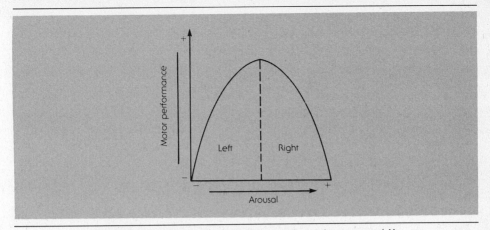

FIGURE 3-5   Errors on the left and right of the inverted-U.

dilation or constriction of the blood vessels. In past research the most frequently used assessment was heart rate. Today many scientists believe that heart rate variability is a more valid measure. The degree of dilation or constriction of the blood vessels is called blood pressure. When blood pressure is measured in current research it is generally done through sophisticated computer-assisted techniques.

Muscle activity is measured through a technique called electromyography (EMG). By means of surface electrodes placed at crucial muscles or muscle groups, the degree of tension present in the muscles can be assessed. Increased muscle tension generally accompanies high degrees of arousal.

Other measures include changes in the dilation of the pupil of the eye, body temperature, metabolic rate, and biochemical properties of the urine.

In terms of the unifying model, how do these physiological parameters and the electrical activity of the brain interrelate with motor performance? First, they provide evidence to support the notion that high degrees of arousal are associated with overexcitability or "overmotivation." Under such a state several factors may affect the quality of motor performance. High rates of heart beat and respiration are inefficient; if an activity requires endurance, duration of persistence could be adversely affected. High physiological activation could also have a negative effect on skills requiring hand steadiness or fine motor control. In addition, when high activation occurs, it is likely that the performer will focus attention on some aspect of the physiological responses rather than the sport or motor task to be performed. If attention is focused internally, it cannot be simultaneously focused externally; therefore performance decrements should take place. Perhaps the most important physiological parameter affected by increased arousal is the level of tension in the muscles. When high levels of tension exist, muscles tend to work against one another rather than in sequence. This tension causes the stiff or awkward motor patterns characteristic of someone who is experiencing a high level of arousal.

Collectively, the processes and parameters discussed above can provide some insights into why arousal may have a deleterious effect on motor performance. The behavioral-motor response shown in Figure 3-4 should be impaired under conditions in which the level of arousal exceeds the level most appropriate for the best performance of a particular skill. We will now turn our attention to more specific evidence concerning applications to motor, sport, and exercise behavior.

APPLICATIONS TO MOTOR, SPORT, AND EXERCISE BEHAVIOR

Errors on the Left versus Errors on the Right

If we divide the pictorial representation of the inverted-U hypothesis into halves as shown in Figure 3-5, you can see that under conditions of both too little arousal and too much arousal performance decrements occur. Are the causes of the errors the same under both conditions? Put another way, if you observed a performer operating under a very low level of arousal, would you see the same behaviors as those portrayed by another person operating under excessive arousal? Probably not. As such, it follows that the reasons why errors occur "on the left" are quite different from the reasons why errors occur "on the right." In the first case there is too little arousal or motivation; in the second case there is excess arousal or overmotivation.

When arousal is too low, at least two behaviors are generally evident. First, the athlete tends to have low task persistence. The athlete is lethargic and appears unmotivated and disinterested. Second, attention tends to wander from the task. If attention shifts away from the task, then the athlete may be unaware of the cues that are required for good performance to take place. Because task-relevant cues will not be processed, performance will suffer.

The strategies that a teacher or coach might use to increase arousal and thus diminish "errors of insufficient arousal" are called **psyching-up strategies.** Although little research has been done in this area, some preliminary evidence is available. One question concerns the nature of the psyching-up strategies that athletes use on their own. Weinberg, Gould, and Jackson (1980) used an open-ended inventory in an attempt to find out exactly what strategies performers generally use. Athletes in their survey responded with statements such as "I just tried to concentrate on the task and eliminate all irrelevant information," "I told myself I could do it," "I pictured myself in perfect balance," "I tried to get mad, aroused, and psyched-up," and "I just tried to relax all of my muscles and think about something else" (Weinberg, 1982). Notice that the strategies employed by these athletes varied considerably in both the nature of the strategy and the predicted relationship to level of arousal. One athlete is trying to relax (an arousal reducer); another athlete is trying to raise arousal by getting mad; and two athletes are trying to control attentional focus. The most important point is that the nature of the task most likely affects the strategy selected. This agrees with the inverted-U hypothesis and the Yerkes-Dodson law.

Earlier in the chapter we mentioned that high levels of arousal should be beneficial to the performance of motor tasks that demand strength. If so, then techniques designed to augment the level of arousal or psych-up the athlete should enhance performance of strength-related skills. Shelton and Mahoney (1980) found that when weightlifters were told to psych themselves up, they performed much better than a control group. Subsequently, Weinberg, Gould, and Jackson (1980) found similar results for a task that required leg strength. In a related study, Gould, Weinberg, and Jackson (1980) found that both preparatory arousal (psyching-up) and imagery enhanced performance. In discussing the results of these investigations, Weinberg (1982) concluded that

(1). Psyching-up effects appear to be task specific, being especially effective on tasks requiring predominantly strength and endurance. (2). Preparatory arousal and imagery were the most effective techniques for enhancing strength performance. (p. 209)

The findings of Weinberg and his associates agree with the proposition presented earlier (Carron, 1980; Oxendine, 1970) concerning the predicted relationship between tasks requiring strength and a high level of arousal. It is difficult to speculate any further on the relative effectiveness of various psyching-up strategies because there is little empirical evidence on which to base a discussion. However, one word of caution is mandatory.

Many coaches make a major error in attempting to psych up the whole team, regardless of the baseline arousal levels of the individual athletes or the nature of the task each athlete is expected to perform. They take the position that the more arousal, the better; thus without realizing it, these coaches are following the tenets of drive theory. From what we know about the inverted-U hypothesis, attempting unilateral psyching-up is simply poor coaching practice.

A few years ago I was explaining to an undergraduate class in sport psychology why unilateral psyching up is poor coaching practice. One of the students, who was also an assistant football coach at a local high school, raised loud and emotional objections to this position. To keep peace and allow the class to finish on time, I suggested that the student spend some time the following week observing football practice to learn how the players attempted to control their own level of arousal. This was a pretty safe suggestion because the student had said that the head coach used strong psyching-up strategies with all of the players and that the team was in first place in their high school division. In theory it seemed reasonable that some of the players, such as the first-string quarterback, would have to be doing something on their own to regulate their level of arousal.

The result of the student's observations were interesting. When the team had an away game, they always rode in two buses; one bus was for the first-string players and the other was reserved for the benchwarmers. The protocol on the first bus required that the players be very quiet and that any conversation be specifically related to the game. On the second bus, there was no mandate regarding conversation or joking around. The student observed that the first-string quarterback chose to ride on the second bus. Still not accepting any implications relative to the inverted-U hypothesis, the student observer assumed that the quarterback chose to ride on the second bus because he had friends on that bus. However, when he questioned the quarterback about his bus selection, the quarterback said that he rode on the second bus so he could calm himself before the game. The quarterback had found that if he rode on the first bus, he felt tense and anxious before the game and his performance reflected those emotions. Although the coach may have thought that relaxing on a quiet bus would help performance, obviously all the athletes didn't feel the same way. Score one for the inverted-U hypothesis and the athlete; score zero for drive theory and the coach!

To apply psyching-up strategies effectively, a coach must be confident that the athlete really is too low in arousal or motivation. Although it might seem that some assessment of an athlete's level of arousal can be made simply by observing overt behavior, this technique can be misleading at times.

Athletes manifest the effects of arousal in unique ways, and each must be assessed individually. For example, a member of a women's intercollegiate basketball team indicated that just before an important game she usually became very psyched-up and overly aroused; however, she exhibited that state through an uncontrollable series of yawns. What do you think the coach's immediate response might be if he or she observed such behavior? Certainly the coach would be inclined to employ some sort of motivating or psyching-up technique. What should be the result? That's correct: excess arousal leading to performance decrements. This is just one example that leads us to argue that behavioral observation alone is not sufficient. To use psyching-up strategies effectively, the coach should also talk to the athlete and have the athlete fill out a questionnaire regarding level of activation. Through such conversations and assessments the coach can gain better insights into the athlete's actual level of arousal.

Sport psychologists are generally more concerned with errors that can be attributed to excess arousal as opposed to errors that can be ascribed to too little arousal. Because of the competitive settings in which sport performance takes place, athletes often have more problems in dealing with overarousal than they do with experiencing too little arousal. We will be focusing a great deal of attention on possible explanations underlying the high arousal–motor performance decrement in Chapter 4. For now, we will simply say that evidence exists that relates disruptions in both the sequence of muscle firing and perceptual processing to high levels of arousal. Such evidence can lead to explanations of why high levels of arousal have a negative effect on the performance of certain motor and sport skills. For now, let us turn our attention to other factors that seem to be intimately related to varying levels of arousal.

Task Requirements

Task Difficulty and Energy Requirements

As we discussed earlier, the Yerkes-Dodson law and the inverted-U hypothesis together provide a conceptual framework for understanding the relationship that appears to exist between task difficulty and level of arousal. In addition to the difficulty of the task, the physiological demands of the task (the energy required to complete the task successfully) must also be considered (Fiske & Maddi, 1961; Martens, 1974). The successful execution of tasks that are difficult and require large amounts of energy expenditure most likely occurs within a very limited range of optimal arousal. As Martens (1974) has said:

> High-energy requirements with high task difficulty are the precise task conditions that exist in many well-known sports such as tennis, basketball, and wrestling. Thus, because these activities have such a narrow range for optimal performance, it is easy to understand why it is so difficult to achieve and maintain an optimal arousal level when performing these tasks. (p. 179)

From this same perspective, it can also be argued that as the task becomes easier and the energy demands decrease, the range of optimal arousal broadens; that is, there is greater leniency in terms of the preciseness of the best or optimal level of arousal.

Power and Control

As we saw in terms of tasks that required either strength or endurance, similarly tasks that require high degrees of powerful, rapid movements also benefit from higher degrees   •

of arousal. For example, when football players practice blocking against sleds, they need to perform rapid and powerful movements and thus need high degrees of arousal. In boxing, the performer also needs rapid and powerful movements, but precise control is also required. Because the optimal level of arousal decreases as the control demands of the task increase, the boxer should be operating at a lower level of arousal as compared with the football player.

Attentional and Cue Processing Demands

It has also been observed that as arousal increases, the breadth of the visual field tends to decrease. Therefore if a person must process multiple environmental cues, that processing will be affected negatively under conditions of high arousal. (This principle is discussed in more detail in Chapters 4 and 6.)

One schema used to classify motor and sport skills is that of *open* versus *closed* skills. Open skills, such as soccer and volleyball, require that the performer deal with a changing game environment. In the performance of closed skills, such as diving and gymnastics, the environment is usually stable. Based on the open-closed skill classification, we can see that open skills require more cue-processing ability; therefore the desired level of arousal is lower for open versus closed skills.

Also in terms of attentional demands, many complex tasks are classified as such because they require the processing of more cues than do simple skills. This is one important reason that the performance of such complex skills may be hindered by high levels of arousal.

Task Performance Outcome

The task performance outcome for most sport and motor skills is usually clear success or clear failure. In addition, that outcome is usually public in nature. If you attempt to clear a high jump bar or a high hurdle, your success or failure is usually obvious to all present. For this reason, the quality of your outcome usually affects subsequent degrees of arousal. Failure ordinarily generates increased arousal, which may be debilitating. Success, on the other hand, does not usually result in excess levels of arousal. Therefore the outcome of one motor response may have a direct effect on the next response. A failure outcome may result in a tendency for the athlete to try even harder; this "pressing" may then increase errors.

Novelty and Change

Until now, we have addressed aspects of task requirements from the perspective of how a person's level of arousal can affect performance. From another perspective, it can be shown that the nature of the task or the environment can also affect level of arousal. Berlyne (1966) has shown that moderate amounts of change and task novelty can be arousing because change or novelty can make a task more interesting, thus inspiring a person to want to learn more. This is fundamental to the thinking that underlies movement education. Exploratory behavior and arousal are seen to increase when the environment contains complex, novel, and ambiguous stimuli because they evoke curiosity and encourage learning. Novelty also increases an athlete's motivation and interest during practice; therefore practice sessions should be carefully designed with the idea of novelty in mind.

Individual Variability

Skill Level

Fitts and Posner (1967) have identified three stages in the learning of skills.

The cognitive stage involves instruction concerning the nature of the skill and how the skill components are related to one another. This is an internal stage in which the potential performer tries to grasp the information necessary to perform the skill. A coach's demonstrations and verbal instructions to the beginner are attempts to provide information sufficient to understand the skill.

The associative stage occurs during practice, wherein both the detection and elimination of initial errors and the strengthening of the connections among the elements needed for successful performance take place (Anderson, 1980).

The autonomous stage allows for the skill execution to become more automatic. As automatization progresses, the need for cognitive mediation and attention decreases. When automatization is present, the skill can be executed rapidly and with little interference with other skills. After much practice and overlearning, skilled athletes can perform an automated response while at the same time thinking about their next response. A skilled tennis player can execute a serve and at the same time decide whether or not to rush the net. The serve is automated and thus does not require attention; therefore, available attention can be placed on questions of strategy.

How does Fitts and Posner's (1967) conceptualization of the stages of skill learning relate to level of arousal? From our previous discussion of the relationship between attentional demands and arousal (see p. 65) it should be clear that high degrees of arousal in the early stages of skill development should be detrimental. During the cognitive and associative stages, cognitive and attentional demand is high; therefore, high arousal should hinder performance.

This position is similar to that discussed by Schmidt (1982), who specifically addressed the relationship between amount of practice and level of arousal. Figure 3-6 portrays the predicted association between degree of practice and optimal level of arousal. Two principles can be seen. First, less practice will result in worse motor performance as compared with more practice. Second, lower arousal is more desirable during early skill development (low practice), whereas higher arousal is more desirable during later skill development (high practice). Thus, whether from the skill-development perspective of Fitts and Posner or from the degree-of-practice perspective of Schmidt, arousal has a systematic effect on motor performance that varies as a function of degree of skill or practice.

Personal Characteristics

Earlier we discussed aspects of individual characteristics that may influence level of arousal. These included a person's baseline measure of arousal before task performance and ability to inhibit the effects of an arousal-producing situation. In addition, enduring personality characteristics such as need to achieve, perceived ability, and leadership tendencies may affect the arousal-performance relationship. Nideffer (1980) has indicated that the athlete's need for control and self-esteem seem to be most important.

Conflict is a known generator of increased arousal (Berlyne, 1966). For an athlete who has a very high **need for control,** conflict arises when that control is taken away. Control can be threatened by the removal or challenge of leadership roles or by the questioning of the athlete's beliefs or decisions (Nideffer, 1980). On the other hand, persons who are characterized by low levels of need to control should experience conflict and resultant

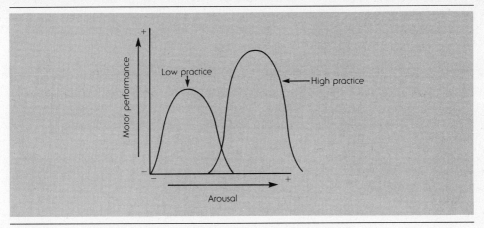

FIGURE 3-6   Level of practice, arousal, and motor performance.
Adapted from Schmidt, R.A. (1982). *Motor control and learning.* Champaign, IL: Human Kinetics.

increases in arousal under any condition in which they are thrust into a controlling or leadership role.

The second personal factor identified by Nideffer (1980) as interrelating with fluctuations in level of arousal is that of **self-esteem.** In terms of sport performance, self-esteem is most likely directly associated with the performer's perception of his or her ability. The higher the perceived ability, the higher the level of self-esteem. From Nideffer's (1980) point of view, athletes who have high self-esteem should tend to act independently and also tend to be aroused by criticism; however, they should use the criticism and the enhanced arousal to improve performance. On the contrary, persons characterized by low levels of self-esteem, and, therefore probably low levels of perceived ability, tend to perform worse as a result of criticism.

Sport Specific Evidence

Underwater Divers

Bowen, Andersen, and Promisel (1966) conducted a field study of divers' performance during the SEALAB II project. A strong correlation was shown between level of arousal and number of dives undertaken. However, the correlation was negative in direction in that the higher the arousal, the fewer dives attempted. In terms of quality of task performance, simple, short-term tasks were performed well underwater. However, the stress or arousal experienced while underwater had a severely detrimental effect on performance of complex tasks. More than likely attention was shifted to aspects of surviving underwater rather than to the task at hand. This is reflected in the commentary made by one of the divers.

> So much of your mental capacity is devoted to listening to your exhaust, wondering whether it's working, keeping in mind how far you are from the laboratory and taking care of your tools. You're spread pretty thin and you don't have much of your mental capacity to devote to the performance of your task.*

*From *Human Factors,* 1966, *8,* p. 196. Copyright 1966 by The Human Factors Society, Inc., and reproduced by permission.

The effects of underwater diving on attentional processing was also studied by Weltman and Egstrom (1966). Their subjects were college-age novice divers. Using a visual monitoring task, they found that the divers exhibited differences in response times in three different situations. In particular, the novice divers demonstrated increased response time when diving as compared with being on land. In addition, the response times for the ocean dives were greater than the response times measured in the tank. Weltman and Egstrom attributed the results to the increased stress (arousal) that the divers experienced in the two diving conditions. This increased stress or arousal was then proposed to cause perceptual (peripheral) narrowing. We have referred to this relationship before (see p. 65). Generalizing their findings to other skills, it would be predicted that increased arousal should hinder the performance of any task that requires processing of cues in the visual periphery.

Parachutists

Fenz and his associates (Fenz, 1964; Fenz & Epstein, 1967; Fenz & Epstein, 1968; Fenz & Epstein, 1969; Fenz & Jones, 1972; Fenz, Kluck, & Bankart, 1969) have conducted an impressive series of investigations into aspects of arousal and the performance of parachutists. The data from Fenz and Jones' (1972) study nicely illustrates their approach and findings. Their purpose was to evaluate relationships between aspects of autonomic arousal and performance during the jump sequence. More specifically, first they assessed both respiration rate and heart rate of experienced versus novice jumpers during the jump sequence, which began with the jumper's arrival at the airport and finished with an assessment after landing. Their next question concerned the effects that the quality of the previous jump (good versus bad) would have on autonomic responding during the next jump sequence.

Subjects consisted of 14 novice (only one previous jump) and 16 experienced sport parachutists. A polygraph was used to assess heart and respiration rate. Recordings were made at each of eight points within the jump sequence. The novice jumpers were evaluated by a jumpmaster during the jump in which the physiological readings were recorded. Subsequently, he was asked to rank order the 14 novice jumpers according to the quality of the jump. Two experienced jumpers rated the quality of the jump of the experienced parachutists. Criteria were performance compared with other jumpers of equal experience and the consistency of performance. Because the patterns of respiration rate and heart rate were highly reliable, for the sake of brevity we will only present the data concerning heart rate.

Figure 3-7 shows the patterns of heart rate of the experienced and novice jumpers over the duration of the jump sequence. Notice that both groups exhibited similar increases in heart rate up until point 4 (engine warmup) in the jump sequence. Once the plane took off and gained altitude, the novice jumpers continued to increase their heart rates until they reached the jump run. However, after the takeoff the experienced jumpers showed a leveling off that was followed by a decrease in heart rate at the jump run. Thus at the time of the actual jump there were obvious differences in the physiological activation (arousal) between the novice and the experienced jumpers.

A second question explored by Fenz and Jones (1972) was how the quality of the first jump might be related to physiological activation during the jump sequence leading up

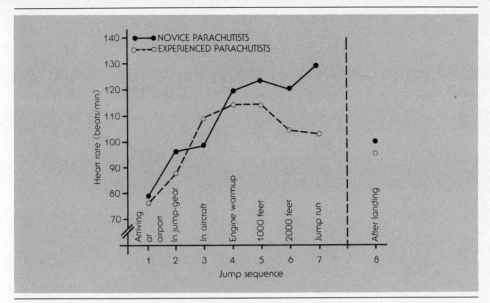

FIGURE 3-7   Heart rate of experienced and novice parachutists as a function of events leading up to and following a jump.

Reprinted by permission of the publisher from Individual differences in physiologic arousal and performance in sport parachutists, by Fenz, W.D., & Jones, G.B. *Psychosomatic Medicine, 34,* pp. 1-8. Copyright 1972 by The American Psychosomatic Society, Inc.

to the next jump; that is, they looked specifically at the heart rates of jumpers who had their previous jump rated as good versus poor. Because it is apparent that experienced jumpers would, on the whole, perform in a superior manner to the novice jumpers, the data for the two groups were analyzed separately.

Figure 3-8 contains the heart rate data for the novice jumpers, including persons with both good and poor previous jump evaluations. Notice the great disparity between the heart rate patterns of the good and poor performers. From what you know about the inverted-U hypothesis, what should be the effect of such high levels of physiological activation on the next jump?

Figure 3-9 presents the results of the heart rate analysis for the experienced parachutists during the jump sequence. Notice in particular the U-shaped function associated with the pattern of the good jumpers. Heart rate increased up to the time an altitude of about 1000 feet was achieved, then a marked decrease was evidenced until the exodus from the plane. The experienced, poor performers, however, showed a pattern that was quite similar to the novice parachutists. This similarily was demonstrated both in their overall heart rate responses and in their pattern of responding.

The data on parachutists produced by Fenz and his associates have some very important implications. First, in a skill in which there is a certain degree of fear and complexity, it appears that novices, as a group, experience higher degrees of physiological activation as compared with experienced performers. Second, some substantiation for the inverted-

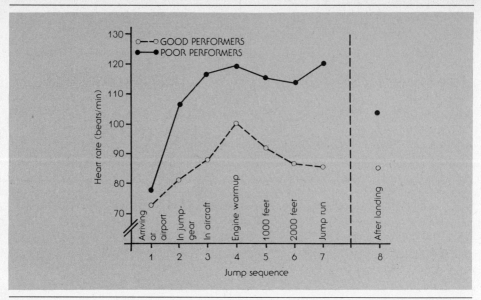

FIGURE 3-8 Heart rate of good and poor performers from among novice parachutists as a function of events leading up to the jump.

Reprinted by permission of the publisher from Individual differences in physiologic arousal and performance in sport parachutists, by Fenz, W.D., & Jones, G.B. *Psychosomatic Medicine, 34*, pp. 1-8. Copyright 1972 by the American Psychosomatic Society, Inc.

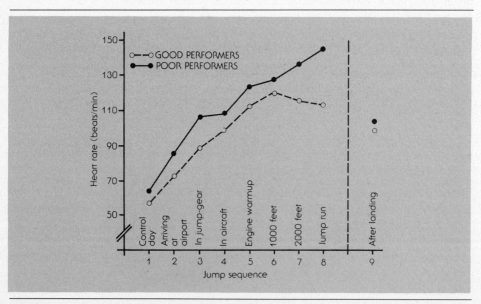

FIGURE 3-9 Heart rate of good and poor performers from among experienced parachutists as a function of events leading up to the jump.

Reprinted by permission of the publisher from Individual differences in physiologic arousal and performance in sport parachutists, by Fenz, W.D., & Jones, G.B. *Psychosomatic Medicine, 34*, pp. 1-8. Copyright 1972 by The American Psychosomatic Society, Inc.

U hypothesis can be gleaned from the fact that the good jumpers tended to have lower levels of arousal just before the jump as compared with the poor jumpers. This was true whether the jumper was a novice or experienced jumper. Third, although we did not present the respiration rate data, the patterns associated with those assessments paralleled those of heart rate. This further supports the role that physiological activation plays in terms of quality of motor and sport performance. In Chapter 5 we will present several intervention strategies that could be used to assist performers such as novice parachutists in learning to cope with and control excessive arousal. Now, however, we will look at how vigorous exercise is related to level of arousal.

Exercise

As early as 1936, Jacobson studied aspects of muscle tension and relaxation. He was one of the first researchers to use electromyographic (EMG) techniques to measure muscle tension and extended his investigations specifically to athletes. He proposed that athletes should be more capable of relaxing their muscles as compared with nonathletes (Jacobson, 1936) because of their more fully developed musculature and better coordination. His data supported his assertion but did not provide clear insights into exactly why the effects were observed.

More recently, deVries and his associates (deVries, 1968; deVries, 1981; deVries & Adams, 1972; deVries, Wiswell, Bulbulian, & Moritani, 1981) have systematically attempted to investigate what they have called the *tranquilizer effect* of exercise. In a series of studies using EMG techniques to measure muscle tension (deVries, 1968; deVries & Adams, 1972), their results have indeed supported the notion that both long-term (chronic) and short-term (acute) exercise bouts can result in reduced muscular tension.

deVries (1981) summarizes the results of this work:

> Although more corroborative evidence is needed, we should draw a cautious conclusion that appropriate types, intensities, and durations of exercise can bring about a significant tranquilizer effect. We have shown a chronic as well as an immediate effect in young, middle-aged, and elderly subjects. On the basis of our data, rhythmic exercise such as walking, jogging, cycling, and bench stepping from 5 to 30 minutes at 30% to 60% of maximum intensities was effective. (p. 53)*

These data argue that exercise can be beneficial not only in terms of positive physical effects but also as a means of lowering arousal and inducing relaxation. Certainly it is wiser to embark on a well-designed, scientifically based program of vigorous physical activity to reduce stress or arousal than to be dependent on a pharmaceutical approach to the problem. However, more research is needed to determine if there is an optimal level of exercise most effective for achieving the tranquilizer effect. This is because it may be that extremely strenuous exercise could serve as a stressor rather than a relaxer.

These findings also support the idea that human beings are indeed psychophysiological in nature. To fully understand the principles of sport psychology, you must be aware of both dimensions and how they interrelate.

*Reprinted by permission of *The Physician and Sportsmedicine,* A McGraw-Hill publication.

IMPLICATIONS FOR SPORT

- Before attempting to "psych-up" athletes, both the complexity of the task and the characteristics of the individual athlete need to be taken into account.
- Individual coach-athlete conferences will yield more information about how arousal operates within a particular athlete than will merely observing behavior because athletes manifest the effects of increased arousal differently.
- When task performance requires strength or endurance, moderately high levels of arousal appear to be the most desirable. This is true also for skills that require powerful and rapid movements.
- Most successful performers have learned how to control their own level of arousal; however, less skilled performers will benefit from some assistance from the coach. Three techniques the coach might try are relaxation training, the use of more positive feedback, and attempting to decrease the amount of evaluation potential in the environment. In addition, Case Study 1 below describes how cue reduction feedback can help.
- When skills are not well-learned, try to avoid situations such as public skills tests; such situations will most likely have a negative effect on behavior.
- Because complex skills require the athlete to process many cues and because high levels of arousal tend to hinder that ability, at least two coaching strategies should be avoided: (1) do not provide complicated feedback that will "overload" the athlete even more and (2) do not use sarcasm or excessive criticism.
- Because success tends to lower arousal and failure tends to increase it, always choose a goal or standard at which the performer has at least some chance of success.
- Over an extended period of time, practice regimens tend to lower arousal or motivation, which then leads to reduced persistence, boredom, and lowered performance. To avoid this situation, incorporate novel but gamelike activities or drills into the practice session. (See Case Study 2 on the facing page for some examples in basketball.)
- Use various "psyching-up" techniques with more highly skilled performers.
- Always consider individual characteristics, such as self-esteem and need for control, when making coaching decisions such as selecting a team leader.

CASE STUDY 1

Using Cue Reduction Feedback to Reduce Arousal

As we mentioned earlier in this chapter, coaches often must work with athletes who are both low in self-esteem and highly sensitive to criticism. If such an athlete makes an error during game play and if the coach's reaction is critical, the probability is high that the athlete's response will be an increase in arousal. What should then happen to the athlete's next skill execution? Most likely, performance will deteriorate even further.

The critical nature of the coach's reaction to an athlete's performance error ordinarily takes one of two forms. Either too much error information is provided and the athlete becomes confused and "overloaded," or the coach loudly yells something vague such as "concentrate" or "try harder." What does the coach really mean by using the latter remarks? The coach conveys to all present that the athlete has failed. In addition, those remarks do not provide any concrete information concerning what must be done in order to eliminate the performance error.

An effective alternative is to provide what is called **cue-reduction feedback.** Cue-reduction feedback consists of a limited number of cues the athlete can attend to in order to enhance the probability of success. Generally, cue-reduction feedback takes the form of a few "if, then" statements. This case study uses the situation of a corner kick in soccer to demonstrate how a coach might effectively use cue-reduction feedback.

The corner kick is usually executed by the wing (forward) on the side of the field where the ball was kicked out of bounds. Because a quick shot at the goal can be expected from a forward on the attacking team, the goalie must be able to anticipate the location and angle of the kick. This becomes particularly crucial as no member of the defending team can be within 5 yards of the ball, and the area in front of the goal is usually "flooded" with players from the attacking team.

Assuming that the corner kick is to be taken from a point on the goalie's right, the coach needs to identify one or two key moves on the part of the goalie in a restricted area. It seems plausible to anticipate that the backs to the goalie's right will cover attacking forwards who are well within the penalty area. Therefore two cue-reduction "if, then" statements the coach could give to the goalie before a corner kick are:
1. If the corner kick is directed to the right uppermost portion of the penalty area, then look for an open attacker in front of the goal.
2. If the corner kick is sent in front of the goal and to the left, then face the opponent immediately in front of and to the left of the goal.

Such cue-reduction statements are positive, rather than negative, in content. They specifically direct the athlete's attention to the most likely events and therefore they increase the probability of successful skill execution. Taken together, the positive thrust of the cue-reduction information and the successful skill outcome should reduce excess arousal. When the level of arousal is no longer excessive, subsequent success is more likely.

Although we have used the technique of cue reduction feedback specifically in regard to an athlete who is low in self-esteem, its use is by no means limited to such persons. It can be a highly effective and positive method to impart skill-related information and to help prevent errors caused by excessive arousal in all sport participants. One word of caution: to use this method successfully, the coach must be extremely knowledgable about the sport and the associated characteristics and skills of the athlete in question. The coach must be a good analyzer of both the sport and the particular athlete.

CASE STUDY 2
Novelty Drills for Increased Motivation in Basketball

Often, as the number and length of team practices increase, players tend to become bored, to lose motivation, and to have low levels of arousal. One way to increase player interest and motivation is to introduce new and challenging drills. It is important, however, that such drills mimic the skills and techniques used in the actual game. This case study presents ideas that could be used to increase the novelty of basketball practice sessions.

Two-Ball Basketball

In this drill the goal is to play basketball using two balls. The rules remain the same as in a regular basketball game. After some initial hesitancy and possible confusion, the game will open up and move rapidly. At any time a player can choose to be on offense, defense, or transition. This drill is excellent for conditioning, uses all basketball skills, and increases motivation. In addition to all of those benefits, it is fun.

Flag Basketball

This drill emphasizes both ball control and body control. To begin, one third of the players are designated as dribblers. Each is given a ball and then lines up on the baseline opposite the remaining two thirds of the players. The latter are each given a flag football flag and then line up at midcourt. The flagholders must then tuck the flag into the waistband of their shorts, with the major portion of the flag showing. At a signal, the dribblers must chase the flagholders and attempt to remove all of the flags while simultaneously keeping the ball under control. When a player's flag is removed, that player is eliminated. The drill is over when the dribblers have captured all the flags.

Shrink and Dribble

Again in this drill the focus is on ball and body control. A fairly large area is initially designated as fair territory for dribbling. Players each have a ball and dribble continuously. At the sound of a whistle, two things happen. The area shrinks (you can have other players act as boundaries) and all dribblers must change direction and dribbling hand. This drill teaches ball protection and control.

SUMMARY

- Arousal is perceived to be the intensity dimension underlying behavior and can be conceptualized along a continuum ranging from deep sleep to extreme excitation.
- The term *arousal* can be used interchangeably with physiological activation, energy mobilization, and drive.
- The two major explanations of the relationship between arousal and performance are drive theory and the inverted-U hypothesis.
- Drive theory predicts a linear relationship between increases in drive and increases in motor performance.
- Currently, the more favored explanation of the relationship between arousal and motor performance is the curvilinear function proposed by the inverted-U hypothesis; however, the inverted-U prediction is mediated by variables such as task difficulty, individual differences, and social or environmental factors.
- The unifying model can be used to demonstrate the strong relationship that exists between arousal and physiological activation. Indeed, level of arousal is generally assessed through selected physiological indicators.
- Motor performance errors can result from either too little or too much arousal. The goal is to attain an optimal level of arousal.
- In addition to task difficulty, the demands for power, control, and cue processing also affect the desirable level of arousal.

- Success tends to lower arousal, whereas change and novelty can raise the level of arousal.
- High levels of arousal should be most detrimental in the early as compared with the later stages of learning.
- In terms of enduring personality characteristics, both need for control and self-esteem appear to interact with optimal level of arousal.
- Research on underwater divers and parachutists has shown definite effects concerning level of arousal and quality of sport performance. In addition, studies on the role of exercise on reducing arousal have demonstrated a tranquilizer effect that is associated with vigorous physical activity.

DISCUSSION QUESTIONS

1 Identify the major weaknesses associated with a drive theory interpretation of motor performance.
2 What are the primary mediating variables associated with the inverted-U hypothesis?
3 Generally speaking, would a sport psychologist usually be more interested in the construct of drive or of habit? Why?
4 Discuss the cycle that apparently exists between a failure outcome at a task and effects on arousal level.
5 Why is *arousal* said to be a neutral term?

GLOSSARY

activation A neuropsychological term that can be used interchangeably with arousal and refers to the intensity of behavior; it is generally measured through central assessments (such as brain activity) or peripheral assessments (for example, heart rate, muscle tension, and respiration)

arousal The degree of physiological activation present at a particular time

competing response tendencies The notion that correct responses compete with incorrect responses

contiguity Refers to at least two events that occur closely together in time

crucial experiment An experiment in which two conflicting hypotheses are tested simultaneously

cue-reduction feedback Feedback that presents a limited number of task-related cues

drive The motivational component of drive theory

flooring effect A situation in which a performance or score cannot become any lower or worse than it already is

habit strength The degree of association between a stimulus and a response

innate Inborn or instinctual

inverted-U hypothesis A proposed curvilinear relationship between level of arousal and quality of motor performance

linear A relationship between two variables that tend to vary in the same direction; for instance, there should be a linear relationship between IQ score and grades in school—as the value of the first variable increases, the value of the second variable should also increase

need for control Relative need to be in a decision-making or leadership role

principle of contiguity Principle that reinforcement must follow a response closely in time

psyching-up strategies Techniques designed to increase arousal or motivation

self-esteem A feeling of competence or self-worth

temporal   As used here, this term refers to an association between two variables that exists on the basis of time, as opposed to a relationship between two variables that exists as a function of space or physical location

Yerkes-Dodson law   Proposal that there is an optimal level of arousal for best performance of a particular task; for example, simple tasks are facilitated by higher arousal, whereas complex tasks are facilitated by lower arousal

SUGGESTED READINGS

Harris, D. (1980). On the brink of catastrophe. In R.M. Suinn (Ed.), *Psychology in sports.* Minneapolis, MN: Burgess.

   Harris identifies the concept of eustress, which is associated with adventure and excitement and is considered to be a pleasant type of stress. The article presents several factors thought to influence eustress-seeking and also describes vicarious eustress.

Klavora, P. (1979). Customary arousal for peak athletic performance. In P. Klavora & J.V. Daniel (Eds.), *Coach, athlete, and the sport psychologist.* University of Toronto, Toronto, Canada.

   This study presents some of the relationships shown between an athlete's customary level of arousal and sports performance. Klavora proposes that both appropriate assessment instruments and coaches' observations can be used to determine customary arousal. He argues that various motivation techniques can be used to bring an athlete to within his or her customary level of arousal.

Ness, R.G. (1977). Stress perception among novice divers: A comparison by age, sex, and height of dive attempt. In D.M. Landers & R.M. Christina (Eds.), *Psychology of motor behavior and sport,* Champaign, IL: Human Kinetics.

Ness measured three types of responses to stress as a function of facing a diving task: stress felt physiologically, stress as measured by performance, and stress revealed by a self-report. Differences in level of stress were shown for gender and the relative height of the dive.

Oxendine, J.B. (1980). Emotional arousal and motor performance. In R.M. Suinn (Ed.), *Psychology in sports,* Minneapolis, MN: Burgess.

In this study, Oxendine uses the Yerkes-Dodson law to explain the proposed relationship between level of arousal and task performance. Based on the available research evidence, three generalizations are presented regarding the arousal-performance relationship. The article makes applications to specific sport skills and concludes with a discussion of how to change arousal state.

4

ANXIETY, MOTOR PERFORMANCE, SPORT, AND EXERCISE

Anxiety differs from arousal in that it encompasses both some degree of activation and an unpleasant emotional state. Thus the term *anxiety* is used to describe the combination of intensity of behavior and direction of **affect,** or emotion. The direction of affect characteristic of anxiety is negative in that it describes subjective feelings that are unpleasant (Spielberger, 1977).

In this chapter we identify and define various types of anxiety and briefly discuss their interpretation within the framework of the unifying model and the inverted-U hypothesis. However, the focus of this chapter is on current evidence concerning the relationship between competitive anxiety and sport behavior, emphasizing field studies involving real-life sport participation.

TYPES OF ANXIETY

State Anxiety

State anxiety is transitory in nature; it changes or varies over time. It is commonly referred to as A-state, which is the degree of anxiety a person experiences at a given moment. Spielberger (1966) was the first anxiety theorist to distinguish between such transitory fluctuations in level of anxiety and the concept of anxiety as a stable personality variable.

Trait Anxiety

When we talk about anxiety as an enduring personality characteristic, it is labeled trait anxiety (A-trait). Trait anxiety relates to both the frequency and intensity of a person's elevations in A-state. More specifically, high trait-anxious persons perceive more situations as being threatening and tend to respond to such situations with higher degrees of physiological intensity.

Competitive Anxiety

Competitive anxiety is the anxiety generated in a sport competitive situation. Thus it is a specific form of anxiety that occurs as a function of the competitive situation. As we discussed previously in regard to anxiety responses in general, competitive anxiety can also be classified as being either trait or state in nature.

Competitive Trait Anxiety

Based on Spielberger's (1966) conception of trait anxiety, Martens (1977) derived the notion of **competitive trait anxiety** as a situation-specific or sport-specific construct. He defined competitive trait anxiety "as a tendency to perceive competitive situations as threatening and to respond to these situations with feelings of apprehension or tension'' (p. 23). Therefore persons characterized by high degrees of competitive trait anxiety would be predicted to perceive more competitive situations as threatening and should experience higher degrees of anxiety in those situations as compared with persons who have low levels of competitive trait anxiety.

Competitive State Anxiety

The anxiety reaction triggered by a particular competitive situation is called **competitive state anxiety.** It is the same as general state anxiety except that the stimulus instigating the anxiety reaction is always a sport situation.

Obviously, certain factors strongly influence a person's appraisal of a situation in terms of its potential for ego threat. A highly skilled athlete with a long history of success in that or similar situations would not be predicted to demonstrate the same degree of state anxiety as compared with a poorly skilled or beginning performer. Similarly, a person with a high degree of trait anxiety will more likely, but not necessarily, perceive a highly evaluative sport setting as threatening and therefore respond with elevated state anxiety. This would be predicted because, by definition, high trait-anxious persons tend to perceive many situations as threatening and subsequently tend to respond with increased activation or intensity. Whether or not a specific situation is perceived as being threatening to the high trait-anxious person depends on several factors, such as skill, experience, and ability to inhibit the anxiety response.

Suppose, for example, that two college students both had equally high levels of trait anxiety. One was a varsity football player and a physical education major. The other was on the debating team and a speech communications major. If both were faced with a public-speaking situation, one would most likely experience high degrees of state anxiety whereas the other would not. Both, however, should exhibit increased activation. In the physical education major's case that activation would most likely be accompanied by a high degree of negative affect, whereas the increased activation of the communications major would be a result of being ''psyched-up'' or highly motivated. The latter situation is precisely why sport psychologists cannot adequately distinguish between arousal and anxiety on the basis of physiological measures alone. To measure anxiety validly we must also assess the degree of unpleasantness inherent in the emotional state.

THE COMPETITIVE PROCESS AND PRECOMPETITIVE ANXIETY

Martens (1975, 1977) proposes that competition is a process that includes four highly interrelated elements: the objective competitive situation, the subjective competitive situation, the response, and the consequences of the response.

The Objective Competitive Situation

The objective competitive situation is in actuality Martens' operational definition of competition. An **operational definition** specifies exactly how a variable is manipulated or measured. In the case of the objective competitive situation, the definition specifies the factors or variables that must be operational in the environment for a situation to be classified as competitive. More specifically, three factors must be present: (1) a standard of evaluation or excellence, (2) the presence of an evaluator who is aware of the standard, and (3) the comparison of the performance outcome against the standard. The standard of evaluation or the criterion of comparison can vary from a personal best performance to an established record. What is important in the definition is that the evaluator must be aware of the exact nature of the evaluation criterion.

Therefore if, just before running the 100-yard dash, you turned to the runner on your left and said "My goal today is to beat my time on last Friday," then that would be classified as a competitive situation. On the other hand, if you were by yourself shooting free throws in your backyard, no matter how well you did, that would not be considered to be a competitive situation.

The Subjective Competitive Situation

Obviously, all persons do not react identically when faced with an objective competitive situation. Depending on the standard of comparison and the evaluator, both can cause the same person to perceive two competitive situations quite differently. In addition, persons who freely enter a competitive situation will most likely have different perceptions of that situation as compared with other persons who are forced or coerced into the same situation. In addition, a performer's past history of success or failure at that same or a similar task can influence the perception of the situation.

Therefore Martens uses the step within the competitive process termed the **subjective competitive situation** to refer to a particular person's unique cognitive appraisal of that situation. A person's subjective evaluation of the competitive situation is the causative process that determines whether or not a precompetitive anxiety response will occur. If the competitive situation results in worries, feelings of uneasiness, and heightened physiological activation, an anxiety response should follow.

The Response

If the outcome of the cognitive appraisal is negative, such as the perception of probable failure, then the obvious response would be to get out of the situation. However, that option is not always available. If the situation cannot be avoided, a response must be executed. The nature or quality of the response can be assessed at three different levels. Psychological and physiological responses relate most directly to anxiety, whereas the behavioral response is most observable and is the one that is evaluated.

The Consequences

Evaluation of the response is the fourth stage of Martens' (1977) competitive process. In most sport situations the consequences of the response are clear; either success or failure is evidenced. This public display of the consequences of a sport-related response is most likely a major reason why such situations have the potential to generate strong anxiety responses. However, whether the consequences of a response are successful or unsuccessful, that outcome is remembered and should affect future subjective appraisals of similar situations.

Specific Factors Producing Precompetitive Anxiety

Kroll (1979) proposed five factors that underlie the precompetitive anxiety response: somatic complaints, fear of failure, feelings of inadequacy, loss of control, and guilt.

Somatic Complaints

Increased physiological activation is tied intimately to potentially stressful situations such as competition. Examples of somatic complaints identified by Kroll include upset stomach, urge to urinate, ringing in the ears (tinnitus), trembling, and excessive yawning. (See p. 63 for an example of excessive yawning by a highly anxious athlete.)

Fear of Failure

When an athlete's subjective evaluation results in a perception of probable failure, an anxiety response is almost sure to follow. Several perceptions appear to be associated with a performer's concern about failure: making a foolish mistake, losing, choking up, and living up to the coach's expectations.

Feelings of Inadequacy

Although somewhat similar to the items found in the fear of failure category, according to Kroll (1979), feelings of inadequacy are characterized by the athlete's perception that something is wrong with himself or herself. Such personal dissatisfaction should then result in feelings of weakness, fatigue, or inability to concentrate.

Loss of Control

Loss of control is characterized by the perception that the performer is not in control of what happens. Events are seen as being controlled by some external determinant such as luck. This anxiety factor is represented by thoughts of being jinxed, having poor or unfair officials, or performing on a poor playing surface.

Guilt

Feelings of guilt appear to be most closely associated with issues of morality and aggression (Kroll, 1979). Concerns about hurting an opponent, playing dirty, or swearing too much are reflective of thoughts about guilt.

After identifying those five clusters of factors that appear to cause precompetitive anxiety responses, Kroll has begun preliminary work on developing an assessment instrument (namely, the Competitive Athletic Stress Scale) that could be used to gain insights into probable causes of precompetitive anxiety.

Measurement of Anxiety

The measurement of anxiety has received much recent research interest. A major thrust toward significant progress in anxiety measurement approaches came with Spielberger's (1966) conceptualization regarding the dual nature of anxiety in regard to the state and trait dimensions. Before Spielberger's reconceptualization, anxiety was thought of in general terms; no clear distinction was made between its transitory (state) versus its enduring (trait) qualities.

Based on the notion of the dual nature of the anxiety construct, Spielberger and his associates (Spielberger, Gorsuch, & Lushene, 1970) developed the State-Trait Anxiety Inventory (STAI). Currently, this is the most frequently used assessment instrument in general anxiety research. Using a 4-point rating scale, responses are recorded to statements such as ''I feel calm'' or ''I feel nervous.''

In regard to sport research, however, Martens and his associates (Martens, 1977; Martens, 1983; Martens, Burton, Rivkin, & Simon, 1980) have developed sport-specific assessment instruments for measuring competitive anxiety. The Sport Competitive Anxiety Test (SCAT) is a trait measure, whereas the Competitive State Anxiety Inventory (CSAI) is a state measure of competitive anxiety. In addition, Martens has recently produced the Competitive State Anxiety Inventory–2 (CSAI–2), which more precisely reflects the multidimensionality of anxiety by assessing aspects of both cognitive (thoughts, feelings) and somatic (physiological) responses. These sport-specific instruments should be of great help to future research endeavors.

Because the unpleasant nature of the emotional state and the degree of physiological activation interact to affect motor performance, it is important to gain an understanding of their interrelationship within the anxiety process. Take the situation of a relatively inexperienced young basketball player with a strong desire to make the junior high school squad. He has practiced every day after school and on weekends. Finally, the day of tryouts arrives. On entering the gym the athlete sees the coach, clipboard in hand, watching the other boys practice. The other boys all seem to be highly skilled. The coach looks stern and distant; he calls everyone together and selects players for the opposing sides. Our player is chosen. Suddenly he feels his heart racing; his mouth is dry and he can't hear what his teammates are saying. The scrimmage begins and the ball is passed to him. He can't think clearly; he can only hear his heart pounding. He shoots. The ball falls far short of the basket and the opposing team recovers it. His teammates and the coach look at him with annoyance. He feels awful and decides that he is not really very good at playing basketball.

This situation should be familiar to you; most of us have experienced a similar situation in which our high state of anxiety interfered with our performance. The following section describes the temporal sequence of our player's responses and their consequences from the perspective of the unifying model.

THE UNIFYING MODEL AND THE ANXIETY PROCESS

Figure 4-1 reflects the various dimensions of the anxiety process as it operates within the competitive sport situation described above. This unifying model is composed of four parts: input, process, output, and feedback.

Input

Anxiety is triggered by a potentially psychologically threatening set of circumstances. In our basketball player's case, the environmental conditions he faced in the gym were extremely potent in terms of evaluation potential.

Process

The basketball player's cognitive appraisal resulted in the perception of threat. That perception of psychological threat triggered a state anxiety response.

Output

On the psychological side of this process, the perception of threat should result in feelings of apprehension that could generate disruptions in cognitive processes such as cue processing. The player's physiological activation was also increased, as reflected by his rapid heart rate. The consequence of all of these effects on the behavioral level of the basketball player was a missed shot. Recall that the evaluation of that shot was rather negative.

Feedback

Notice in Figure 4-1 that all levels of the output (that is, psychological, physiological, behavioral, and evaluative) are fed back to the brain and thus can affect future performance. The negative outcome accompanied by negative evaluation should increase the probability of the perception of threat in future situations of the same or similar nature. Such an experience strengthens the tendency to perceive similar environmental conditions as being psychologically threatening and therefore increases the probability of an intense state anxiety reaction in the future.

Because at least a partial explanation for poor motor response is high physiological activation accompanied by cognitive disruptions in cue processing, it is reasonable to assume that if these effects are reduced, minimized, then motor performance will be more effective. We will discuss ways that this can be accomplished in Chapter 5. For now, however, let's examine how anxiety is studied in sport and motor skills settings.

CONTEMPORARY PERSPECTIVES ON ANXIETY AND MOTOR SKILLS

Most of the early research concerning anxiety and motor performance was housed within the theoretical framework of drive theory. As we discussed in Chapter 3, the drive theory interpretation of arousal did not adequately explain effects on motor performance. This was also found to occur in regard to anxiety (Martens, 1971). However, progress in anxiety research advanced appreciably with the change in thinking along two related avenues. First, the state-trait approach to anxiety measurement was adopted. Second, the theoretical interpretation of the relationship between level of arousal and quality of motor performance was reconceptualized into the framework of the inverted-U hypothesis.

Recall from our discussion of arousal in Chapter 3 that the basic prediction from drive theory was that the relationship that should exist between arousal and quality of motor performance is linear. Subsequently, theorists (for example, Duffy, 1962; Malmo, 1959) argued that a better explanation for the proposed relationship was represented by an inverted-U function. The relationship was then predicted to be curvilinear in nature. As such, performance was said to increase systematically with increases in arousal up to a certain point. Increases beyond that point would hinder or lower performance. Recent evidence relative to motor performance and anxiety has demonstrated support for the

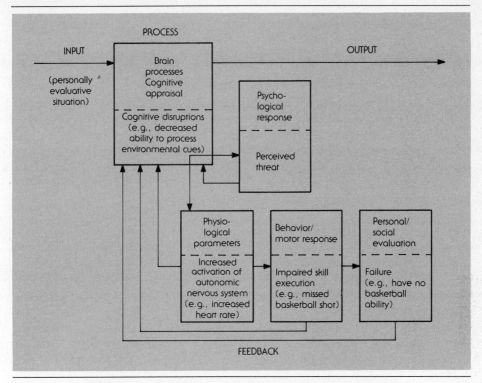

FIGURE 4-1   The unifying model and psychological threat.

inverted-U interpretation of that relationship (for example, Martens & Landers, 1970; Weinberg, 1978; Weinberg & Hunt, 1976; Weinberg & Ragan, 1978).

Anxiety and the Inverted-U Hypothesis

One of the earliest attempts to test the "fit" of the inverted-U hypothesis in regard to motor performance was a study of junior high school boys conducted by Martens and Landers (1970). Using Taylor's (1953) Manifest Anxiety Scale (MAS), over 1000 boys were tested initially. Based on those scores, three different groups were selected to be included in the actual experiment. The high-anxious group were those scoring in the upper 10%, and the low-anxious group comprised boys scoring in the lower 10%. The moderately anxious group all scored exactly at the mean (average).

In addition to including three levels of anxiety in the experiment, the investigators also manipulated experimental stress at three levels of intensity. In the low-stress condition an attempt was made to relax the subject and no emphasis was placed on the quality of the subject's motor performance. In the moderate-stress treatment, emphasis was placed on performing well, especially because the subjects were threatened with electrical shock if they performed poorly. The high-stress group was threatened with severely painful shock, and electrodes were placed on their foreheads to reinforce the potential of the threat. (You might be interested to know that no shocks were actually administered!) Looking at the experimental design as a whole one third of the subjects from each of the three anxiety groups (low, moderate, high) were exposed to each of the three levels of stress (low, moderate, high).

The motor task involved tracking a ring along a tube that somewhat resembled an inverted-U shape. The frequency of contacts of the ring with the tube was counted electrically and served as the dependent measure. In addition to the motor task performance, two physiological measures (heart rate and palmar sweat) were recorded. Support for an inverted-U interpretation was found for both anxiety and stress. These effects are displayed in Figure 4-2 and show that subjects who were selected on the basis of having low, moderate, or high anxiety performed according to the prediction of the inverted-U hypothesis. Similarly, the manipulation of low, moderate, or high stress resulted in poorer performances by the low and high stress groups as compared with the group under moderate stress.

More recently, Weinberg and others (Weinberg, 1978; Weinberg & Hunt, 1976; Weinberg & Ragan, 1978) have conducted a series of studies using the state-trait approach for testing the inverted-U hypothesis. Weinberg and Hunt (1976) used the Trait Anxiety Inventory (TAI) to select 10 high-anxious and 10 low-anxious subjects from an initial pool of 175 college men. Their experimental paradigm also involved the use of electromyography. Surface electrodes were placed on two antagonistic muscles (muscles performing opposing movements) from the upper arm (extensor carpi radialis and flexor carpi ulnaris).

After arriving at the experimental site, the electrodes were put in place and state anxiety was measured. The task was to throw a ball at a target containing three concentric circles. Each subject had 10 throws, with the scoring as follows: 5 points for hitting the red area, 3 for the yellow area, and 1 for the blue area. Before performance, the experimenter gave instructions designed to emphasize personal evaluation. After completing the 10 throws, all subjects received negative, false feedback that indicated they had performed poorly compared with other college students. Subjects then completed 10 more throws, followed by a second measure of A-state. The findings indicated that:

- Significantly more A-state was evidenced in the high A-trait group as compared with the low A-trait group.
- The low A-trait group had better motor performance than the high A-trait group.
- The high A-trait group demonstrated inefficient use of muscle energy as compared with the low A-trait group. The high A-trait group exhibited cocontraction of **agonists** and **antagonists,** whereas the low A-trait subjects showed a sequential pattern of muscle firing.

Figure 4-3 presents hypothetical patterns of muscle activity that would be expected on the basis of the Weinberg and Hunt (1976) study. The relationships shown do not represent their actual data. The vertical lines in Figure 4-3 represent three phases in the throwing of a tennis ball: before, during, and after the throw. For this example, think of the muscles in the upper arm only; the biceps should act as flexors and the triceps as extensors. Now notice the hypothesized difference in the patterns of muscle firing of the low- versus high-anxious groups. During the movement itself (middle phase) we see that the high-anxious group is simultaneously contracting both agonists and antagonists. This is called **cocontraction** and results in inefficient, tense movements. The low-anxious group, on the other hand, shows a pattern of sequential firing of antagonists and agonists. This should produce fluid movement and more efficient use of energy. You have probably observed these differences when watching various persons in sport settings. Think of the

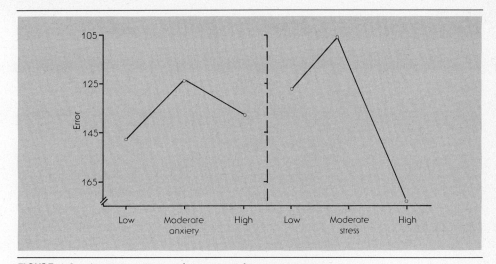

FIGURE 4-2 Anxiety, stress and motor performance errors.
Adapted from Martens, R., & Landers, D.M. (1970). Motor performance under stress: A test of the inverted-U hypothesis. *Journal of Personality and Social Psychology, 16,* 29-37.

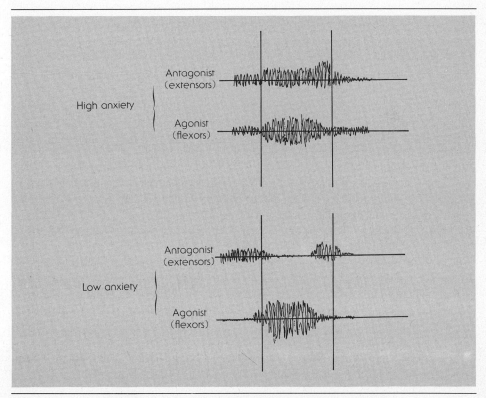

FIGURE 4-3 Hypothesized patterns of muscle activity.

"jerky," awkward patterns exhibited by a novice as compared with the smooth, flowing movements of a professional athlete.

The major contribution of the Weinberg and Hunt (1976) study was the insight it provided in terms of the qualitative aspects of movement as exhibited by high- versus low-anxious persons. However, it did not actually test the inverted-U hypothesis because it failed to include a moderately anxious group. It was also weakened somewhat by not looking at any type of false feedback (manipulated stress) other than negative feedback.

Cognitively Based Interpretations of the Inverted-U Hypothesis

As opposed to the muscle activity orientation of Weinberg and his associates, other theorists have been more interested in cognitively based explanations of the inverted-U prediction. The common theme of the many cognitively based explanations underlying the inverted-U hypothesis is that increases in anxiety (or arousal) cause disruptions or biases in the information the performer receives from the environment. The focus is on input, or reception of information, rather than on aspects of incorrect output (that is, the motor response). The latter process was the central question addressed in drive theory, wherein emphasis was placed on "response dominance" (Landers, 1980) or the notion of competing responses (habit hierarchy). Drive theory explains lower performance as being caused by selection errors associated with the response; that is, as drive (anxiety) increases, the dominant response is emitted. If the dominant response in the habit hierarchy is incorrect, motor performance should be hindered. Cognitive theories attempt to explain impaired performance under conditions of elevated anxiety on the basis of selection errors before information processing. They focus on the processes underlying the input of information into the system. Two explanations that cognitive theorists use to explain differences between the processing of environmental information by high- versus low-anxious persons are (1) peripheral, or perceptual, narrowing and (2) "distractability" or attentional shifts.

Peripheral, or perceptual, narrowing. The classic explanation of peripheral narrowing and its relationship to anxiety level was proposed by Easterbrook (1959). He based his hypothesis on the idea that every task has cues associated with it that may be either relevant or irrelevant to better performance. Relevant cues are associated with correct or successful performance; irrelevant cues have no direct bearing on task performance. After an extensive review of the available research literature, Easterbrook argued that as anxiety increases, the number of cues to which a person can attend decreases. Under conditions of increasing anxiety, task-irrelevant cues are at first eliminated and performance is enhanced. With further increases in anxiety, task-relevant cues are eliminated and performance is hindered.

Figure 4-4 depicts Easterbrook's (1959) *cue utilization hypothesis* graphically. The term *utilization* refers to the use or processing of cues during task performance. The fundamental idea underlying the perceptual narrowing explanation is that increased anxiety reduces the number of cues that can be attended to in the environment. As anxiety increases up to a certain point, attention is directed to task-relevant or meaningful cues. Beyond that optimal point, however, attentional disruptions occur; either irrelevant cues are processed or sufficient relevant cues are not processed. Obviously, as with all generalizations, the degree to which a particular person is affected by peripheral narrowing depends on several mediating factors such as skill level, ability to inhibit anxiety effects, and ability to control attentional focus.

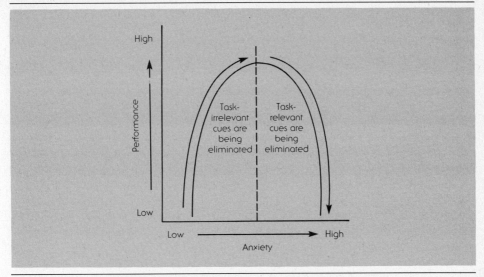

FIGURE 4-4   Easterbrook's cue utilization hypothesis.

"Distractability," or attentional shifts. A concept closely allied to the peripheral narrowing idea is that of "distractability," or attentional shifts. Kahneman (1973) has suggested that as anxiety level rises, people tend to increasingly shift their attention to various environmental stimuli. He labeled this switching phenomenon "distractability." Under conditions of high anxiety, attentional scanning could occur wherein the person swiftly shifts from one input cue (stimulus) to another. Some cues would probably be task-relevant whereas others would be task-irrelevant. As Schmidt (1982) suggests, the performer would then be forced to discriminate between relevant and irrelevant cues. However, one effect of increased anxiety (arousal) appears to be an impairment in the ability to make such discriminations. Therefore, under conditions of "distractability," motor performance should decline because the performer cannot adequately determine which cues are important for successful performance and which ones are not.

Taken together, both the peripheral narrowing and the "distractability" explanations propose that increases in anxiety should result in problems associated with the input of environmental information into the information processing system. Use of such inappropriate or task-irrelevant information should then result in motor performance decrements. Currently, both explanations appear to have merit.

In summary, it is clear that evidence exists to support the inverted-U hypothesis on both a physiological and a cognitive basis. Another issue of more practical concern is the relationship between anxiety and performance in sport competitive situations.

COMPETITIVE ANXIETY AND SPORT BEHAVIOR

Most persons have experienced some degree of anxiety in a sport situation. Sometimes a small amount of state anxiety is facilitative and allows a person to perform extremely well. At other times too much state anxiety has most likely hindered performance.

Therefore, each of us has our own inverted-U function wherein some increase in state anxiety, up to a certain point, is facilitative and any further increases become hinderances to good sport performance. The following studies involve the inverted-U hypothesis as applied to the performance of various basketball players.

Basketball Performance and the Inverted-U Hypothesis

Klavora (1978) used Spielberger and others' (1970) State-Trait Anxiety Inventory (STAI) to assess the state and trait anxiety scores of boys in a high school basketball league. The scores on the STAI can range from a low of 20 to a high of 80. The A-state scale was administered before each game. The A-trait scale was administered once before the start of the season and again either during the playing season or immediately after the end of the season. In addition, throughout the season, each player's coach evaluated his performance after every game. The evaluation scale contained three possible ratings of individual performance: "poor or below his performance ability, average or close to his performance ability, and outstanding performance" (p. 372).

The major purpose of the study was to explore the relationship between basketball playing performance and the athletes' precompetitive state anxiety. More specifically, an attempt was made to derive inverted-U functions on the basis of precompetitive state anxiety and player performance. Figure 4-5 depicts the theoretical relationship that should exist between precompetitive state anxiety and basketball playing performance.

Recall that the coach could evaluate the player in one of three ways: poor performance (PP), average or expected performance (AP), or outstanding performance (OP). These evaluation points are indicated on the vertical axis shown in Figure 4-5. If the predictions associated with the inverted-U hypothesis have merit, then there should be a specific relationship evidenced between identifiable points on the performance curve and level of precompetitive state anxiety as presented on the horizontal axis. For instance, outstanding performance should be related to optimal state anxiety; average performance should be related to either moderately low or moderately high state anxiety; and poor performance should be related to either extremely low or extremely high levels of precompetitive anxiety. In the latter two cases, impaired sport performance can be caused by either too much or too little state anxiety. Thus in the case of average and poor performances the cause of the impairment can be either apathy or too much anxiety.

Klavora's findings indicated that overall ratings of poor performance were associated with either too little state anxiety or excessive anxiety. Average performances were related to moderately low or moderately high state anxiety levels. It is interesting to note that more players performed poorly or about average as a result of low rather than high levels of anxiety. However, outstanding performances were associated with the theoretically predicted optimal level of state anxiety. These data provide support for the hypothesized relationships contained within the inverted-U function.

As mentioned previously, elevations in A-state reactions are not only caused by the perception of ego-threat in competitive situations but also may vary as a function of the level of A-trait. Persons with higher degrees of A-trait are predicted to perceive more situations as threatening and to respond to threatening situations with greater degrees of intensity. To look at this question in an applied setting, Klavora also analyzed differences in precompetitive state anxiety and basketball performance of high versus low A-trait players. Figure 4-6 illustrates the two curves that resulted from the analysis of differences

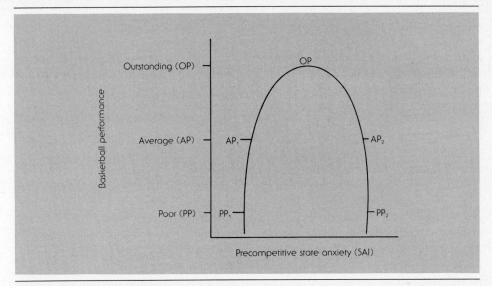

FIGURE 4-5   The predicted theoretical relationship between precompetitive A-state and basketball performance.
Adapted from Klavora, P. (1978). An attempt to derive inverted-U curves based on the relationship between anxiety and athletic performance. In D.M. Landers, & R.W. Christina, (Eds.), *Psychology of motor behavior and sport.* Champaign, IL: Human Kinetics.

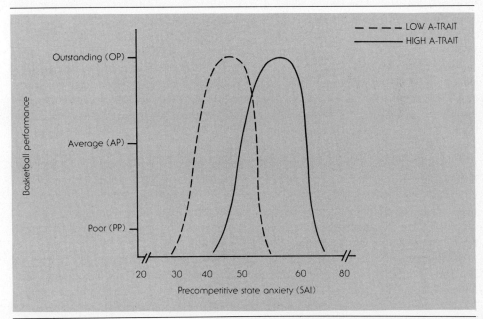

FIGURE 4-6   Precompetitive A-state scores and basketball performance of high versus low A-trait players.
Adapted from Klavora, P. (1978). An attempt to derive inverted-U curves based on the relationship between anxiety and athletic performance. In D.M. Landers, & R.W. Christina, (Eds.), *Psychology of motor behavior and sport.* Champaign, IL: Human Kinetics.

between high and low A-trait persons. Notice that both curves strongly resemble the proposed inverted-U function; however, the curve for the low A-trait players is shifted to the left in comparison with the curve for the high A-trait performers. This would indicate that low A-trait players experienced lower levels of precompetitive A-state as compared with high A-trait athletes. In addition, on the average, outstanding performances for low A-trait persons were associated with an A-state score of 42.5, whereas outstanding performances by high A-trait persons were generated at a value of 50.8. In terms of enhancing the sport performance of all players, regardless of initial level of A-trait, these findings indicate that all players need a relative amount of psyching-up to achieve optimal performance. However, that level differs as a function of degree of A-trait. In either case, too much or too little state anxiety will impair performance.

Also studying basketball players, Sonstroem and Bernardo (1982) tested the fit of the inverted-U hypothesis of female collegiate performers. Competitive trait anxiety was assessed before the season through the Sport Competition Anxiety Test (SCAT), and competitive state anxiety was measured through the use of the Competitive State Anxiety Inventory (CSAI). The CSAI was administered to all athletes between 20 to 30 minutes before each game in a basketball tournament. The state anxiety scores used in any subsequent analysis were the lowest, median, and highest pregame state anxiety scores for each particular performer. Quality of basketball performance was evaluated by a composite score that combined various aspects of players' participation such as rebounds, assists, and steals, and another measure that simply represented total points in a game.

The first question asked whether or not the predicted relationship between A-trait and A-state would emerge; that is, would there be observable differences between the low, moderate, and high state anxiety scores of low, moderate, and high trait-anxious players? Recall that according to the Klavora (1978) data, it would be predicted that systematic differences in intensity of A-state responses should occur as a direct result of differences in level of A-trait. Figure 4-7 presents the results of the Sonstroem and Bernardo investigation. Their results show a strong linear relationship between persons characterized by differences in A-trait and scores on the A-state measure. High trait-anxious persons showed consistently higher levels of state anxiety as compared with both the moderate and low groups. Furthermore, consistent with prediction, the moderate group was systematically higher as compared with the low group.

The next question addressed the relationship between level of anxiety and quality of performance. Figure 4-8 shows the relationship of players' performances, taking into account the level of both A-state and A-trait. Notice that all the players had their best performance under conditions of moderate anxiety. Their next best performance was under conditions of low anxiety, whereas under high state-anxiety conditions severe decrements in performance occurred. This performance decrease was particularly apparent for the high trait-anxious athletes.

By observing the functions contained in Figure 4-8, you can see that within each of the three separate trait anxiety classifications the hypothesized inverted-U appears. This observation should lead to some implications for coaching. It would appear that moderate levels of precompetitive state anxiety are most desirable for purposes of enhancing game performance. In addition, in congruence with current theory, high trait-anxious athletes appear to be most adversely affected by high degrees of state anxiety. Therefore some type of "psyching-down" strategy, such as a relaxation technique, might be most effective for facilitating the performance of such players.

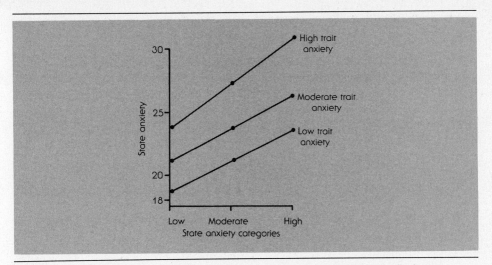

FIGURE 4-7   A-state scores of high, moderate, and low A-trait basketball players.
From Sonstroem, R.J., & Bernardo, P. (1982). Intraindividual pregame state anxiety and basketball performance: A re-examination of the inverted-U curve. *Journal of Sport Psychology, 4,* 235-245.

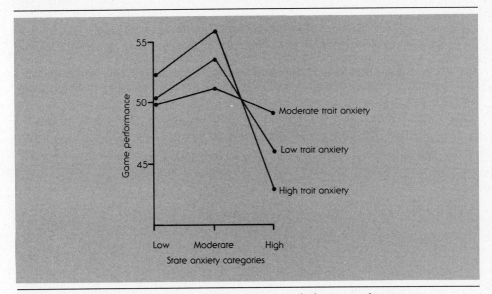

FIGURE 4-8   Relationships among A-state, A-trait, and playing performance.
From Sonstroem, R.J., & Bernardo, P. (1982). Intraindividual pregame state anxiety and basketball performance: A re-examination of the inverted-U curve. *Journal of Sport Psychology, 4,* 235-245.

Field Research with Youth Sports

Soccer

In one of the earliest studies designed specifically to investigate aspects of social and psychological dimensions of youth sports, Scanlan and Passer (1977) studied the effects of competitive trait anxiety and game win or loss on children's perception of threat to self-esteem. Subjects were 11- and 12-year-old boys participating in two divisions of the American Youth Soccer Organization (AYSO). The assessment instruments were Martens' (1977) Sport Competitive Anxiety Test (SCAT) and Spielberger's (1973) State-Trait Anxiety Inventory for Children (SAIC).

Hypotheses predicted that competitive A-trait would be positively related to pregame A-state and that success or failure during the soccer match would affect the level of postgame A-state. The findings indicated that there was indeed a relationship between level of competitive A-trait and the state anxiety the players demonstrated just before the match. It was also shown that players on losing teams exhibited elevated levels of postgame A-state as compared with players on winning teams. This would indicate that the outcome of the match in terms of success or failure can affect postgame psychological states such as anxiety.

In a subsequent investigation, Scanlan and Passer (1979) studied various sources of competitive stress evidenced by young women participating in two divisions of the AYSO. Competitive stress was again measured by Spielberger's SAIC. Assessments were made before and immediately after a soccer match. Although they made other comparisons, team outcome was again shown to be the predominant variable associated with the level of postcompetitive anxiety. Consistent with their previous study, players on losing teams exhibited higher degrees of state anxiety as compared with players on winning teams.

However, the player's perceptions concerning the amount of fun experienced during the game also affected the postgame level of state anxiety. Players who indicated that they had experienced less fun during the game showed higher degrees of postgame state anxiety as compared with players who perceived themselves as having experienced more enjoyment.

At least two implications can be drawn from the Scanlan and Passer (1977, 1979) studies. First, it appears that there is a great deal of similarity between the manner in which boys and girls experience competitive stress; a failure outcome tends to produce elevations in postcompetitive state anxiety. Second, there appears to be a relationship between perception of fun within the sport experience and magnitude of postgame state anxiety. Therefore it seems reasonable that an increased emphasis on aspects of fun and satisfaction associated with sport performance would help reduce the emphasis on winning versus losing. This would be particularly important considering the consistent evidence that a failure outcome produces increases in state anxiety. If sport participation can be perceived as being a vehicle for fun rather than stress, then it can have psychological merit. If, on the other hand, sport participation merely provides a potential vehicle for elevated stress under conditions in which obviously at least half of the youth participants are going to lose, then its contribution to the psychological welfare of its participants is questionable at best. It also appears that the potential negative effects inherent in soccer participation may be even greater for players who are characterized by high levels of competitive trait anxiety.

In a recent study, Passer (1983) used the SCAT to investigate several potential sources of perceived threat among male youth soccer players who were classified as being either high or low in competitive trait anxiety. His findings indicated that the high trait-anxious athletes expected to play less well and experience greater shame, upset, and more frequent criticism from parents and coaches in the event of poor performance. Even when these expectancies were controlled, high-anxious players worried more frequently than low-anxious players about not playing well, losing, and being evaluated by parents, coaches, and teammates. (p. 172)

It is also of importance to note that in terms of the expectation of criticism, it was the anticipation of more frequent *parental* disapproval that most clearly showed differences between the high versus low competitive trait-anxious athletes.

As a whole, Passer's (1983) results support the position that the cognitive dimension of competitive anxiety includes aspects of both performance-related worry and concerns regarding evaluation. Given that the current study as well as other research (Passer, 1984; Passer & Scanlan, 1980) have shown that low and high competitive-anxious persons have similar evaluations of their ability in sport, it cannot be said that the differences in evaluation apprehension and worry evidenced by the two groups is based on any real differences attributable to actual or perceived sport ability. If that is so, then it is apparent that more study concerning the personal and social factors influencing the development of high versus low competitive anxiety is needed.

Wrestling

Gould, Horn, and Spreemann (1983a) studied the competitive anxiety of approximately 1000 junior elite wrestlers who were participating in the United States Wrestling Federation (USWF) Junior National Greco-Roman or Free-Style championships. A questionnaire was designed to assess wrestler anxiety and anxiety-related responses. As part of their data analyses, Gould, Horn, and Spreeman looked at differences in the anxiety responses of high versus low SCAT participants. Figure 4-9 shows the anxiety response differences

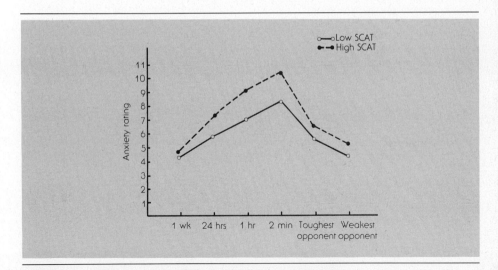

FIGURE 4-9   High versus low SCAT wrestler anxiety responses.
From Gould, D., Horn, T., & Spreeman, J. (1983). Competitive anxiety in junior elite wrestlers. *Journal of Sport Psychology, 5,* 58-71.

as a function of being either high or low on SCAT. Notice that in all cases the low SCAT wrestlers had lower anxiety responses as compared with the high SCAT wrestlers. Gould, Horn, and Spreeman also found that

> low SCAT wrestlers compared to high SCAT wrestlers rated themselves higher in ability, predicted that they would finish higher in the tournament, were more confident in their tournament prediction, worried in a fewer number of all matches, felt their nervousness less often hurt their performance, had less trouble sleeping, and thought it was more important to their parents that they wrestle well. (p. 66)

TABLE 4-1 Sources of Stress, Rankings, and Percent of Respondents Summed Over All Wrestlers

Sources of Stress	Rank	Percentage of Sample*
Concern about performing up to my level of ability	1	53.2
Improving on my last performance	2	46.8
Participating in championship meets	3	44.4
Not wrestling well	4	42.4
Losing	5	44.4
Not making weight	6	43.0
Being able to get mentally ready to wrestle	7	40.7
Making mistakes	8	29.7
My physical condition before matches (e.g., yawning too much, always going to the bathroom, tightness in neck, sore muscles)	9	30.2
Feeling weak	10	25.3
Running out of gas—my physical condition	11	29.2
My physical appearance	12	30.4
What my parents will think or say	13	32.0
What my teammates will think or say	14	26.5
What my coach will think or say	15	24.8
Choking up	16	19.4
Not being able to concentrate	17	19.4
My friends or relatives are watching	18	19.2
Not being mean enough	19	21.2
Falling for a sucker move	20	21.1
Not feeling right (such as, upset stomach, throwing up)	21	18.5
Bad (unfair/inconsistent) calls by officials	22	15.0
Going stale	23	12.2
Remembering instructions	24	15.1
Not getting enough rest	25	22.3
Getting hurt or injured	26	7.3
Losing my temper	27	6.6
Because my sibling is a successful athlete	28	10.2
Being outcoached	29	6.4
Hurting my opponent	30	7.5
Having bad luck—being jinxed	31	4.8
Spectators getting on me	32	3.8
Making my opponent look foolish	33	4.8

*Percent respondents refers to the percentage of the sample who indicated a lot, almost always, or always experienced this type of stress
(Adapted from Gould, D., Horn, T., & Spreeman, J. (1983b). Sources of stress in junior elite wrestlers. *Journal of Sport Psychology, 5,* 159-171.)

One difference that had been predicted on the basis of previous research (Fenz 1975; Higlen & Bennett 1979; Mahoney & Avener, 1977; Meyers, Cooke, Cullen, & Liles, 1979) but was not found was any difference between either successful versus unsuccessful or experienced versus inexperienced wrestlers. Also of interest was the fact that they found no difference in anxiety patterns as a function of the age of the wrestler.

In a subsequent investigation, Gould, Horn, and Spreemann (1983b) addressed the question of the causes or sources of stress in young elite wrestlers. Table 4-1 contains their list of sources of stress, the ranking of those stress sources, and the percentage of the sample who indicated that they were bothered by the source. One interesting aspect of the information contained in Table 4-1 is that there is no single cause of stress experienced by all of the wrestlers. The highest ranked source of stress was the concern about performing up to ability level. Although 53.2% of the wrestlers indicated that this was a stress factor, 46.8% did not concur. Therefore these findings, along with those of Kroll (1979), indicate that there is a large degree of individual variability in the potential sources of stress for individual wrestling participants.

The evidence concerning the relationship between participation in activities such as youth sports and level of anxiety lead to two apparent trends. First, such participation can indeed generate increased levels of competitive anxiety. Second, apparently two variables associated with elevations in anxiety are concerns about being evaluated and about losing or failing. However, there also appears to be much individual variation in the factors related to stress reactions in sport settings. At present it seems wise to exercise caution when attempting to make general applications to specific individual participants or in different sport settings. Although increased research has been focused on studying aspects of youth sport, at the present time this field of inquiry is in its infancy.

Field Research with Collegiate Activities

Golf

Using scores from SCAT, Weinberg and Genuchi (1980) classified male intercollegiate golfers as being high, moderate, or low in trait anxiety. All golfers were involved in a tournament that included a practice round and three consecutive rounds of competition. Using Spielberger and others' (1970) SAI, state anxiety was assessed for the low, moderate, and high SCAT groups.

Table 4-2 presents the average scores for state anxiety and the golf scores achieved

TABLE 4-2   State Anxiety and Golf Performance

Practice		First Day Competition		Last Day Competition	
A-state	Golf Score	A-state	Golf Score	A-state	Golf Score
High SCAT 33.6	76.4	39.1	78.2	36.2	81.7
Moderate SCAT 29.3	77.0	34.6	74.7	34.3	79.3
Low SCAT 26.1	73.6	29.5	73.3	27.5	74.9

Adapted from Weinberg, R.S., & Genuchi, M. (1980). Relationship between competitive trait anxiety, state anxiety, and golf performance: A field study. *Journal of Sport Psychology, 2,* 148-154.

by each of the groups of golfers during practice, the first day of competition, and the last day of competition. It should be noted that when interpreting the golf scores, the higher the score, the poorer the performance. With the anxiety scores, a higher score represents a higher degree of state anxiety. In looking at the high trait-anxious performers, we see that they exhibited higher degrees of state anxiety as compared with both the moderate and low trait-anxious groups. This would be in agreement with Martens' (1977) conceptualization that persons characterized by higher degrees of competitive A-trait should demonstrate higher degrees of A-state when placed in a competitive situation.

If we view the practice round as a noncompetitive situation and the first day of competition as a competitive situation, we also see that level of A-state increased from the noncompetitive to the competitive situation. However, this same effect was not evidenced on the last day of competition. The failure of this effect to emerge could be the result of several factors, such as the ability of the golfers to habituate (get used to) the competitive setting or the fact that by the second day all the golfers had a much clearer idea of where they stood in the competition. Once they knew their relative standing, much of the ambiguity or uncertainty was removed from the competitive setting.

Only one significant effect was shown in regard to performance. The low trait-anxious golfers performed significantly better than either the moderate or high trait-anxious performers. Because golf is a sport that requires smooth execution of complex skills, it is reasonable to expect that persons characterized by low levels of anxiety should perform in a superior fashion to persons prone to higher levels of anxiety. This would also be in agreement with Oxendine's (1970) prediction that optimal performance of tasks requiring fine muscle movements, coordination, precision, steadiness, and concentration should be facilitated by low levels of arousal (anxiety).

Bowling

Hall and Purvis (1981) studied both the competitive bowling performance and the A-state scores of students who were initially classified as being either high or low in A-trait. Consistent with theoretical prediction, they found that lower precompetitive and competitive averages were related to higher levels of A-state. In addition, high A-trait subjects tended to have higher levels of A-state under competitive conditions.

Gymnastics

Mahoney and Avener (1977) conducted an exploratory study to gather information on various psychological factors and cognitive strategies used by elite gymnasts. They studied the six athletes who qualified for the 1976 U.S. Olympic team versus the six contenders who did not qualify. Their statistical procedure determined correlations among a large number of possible variables. This type of statistic reveals nothing about what causes differences between groups; however, it can provide some initial and tentative insights into possible reasons why one group was able to qualify whereas the other was not. Their findings regarding patterns of anxiety exhibited by qualifiers versus nonqualifiers was similar to that which Fenz and his associates (Fenz, 1975) showed for experienced versus inexperienced sky divers. Mahoney and Avener found relatively small differences between the two groups before the actual competition, but those differences indicated that the qualifiers tended to be more anxious. Of more importance is the pattern of anxiety demonstrated by the two groups during actual performance. Although both groups reported being anxious, the qualifiers were relatively less anxious as compared with the nonqualifiers. Based on later interviews, Mahoney and Avener suggested that the more successful athletes tended to 'use' their anxiety as a stimulant to better performance. The less successful gymnasts seemed to arouse themselves into near-panic states by self-verbalizations and images which belied self-doubts and impending tragedies. (p. 140)

Wrestling. Using an adaptation of the Mahoney and Avener (1977) questionnaire, Highlen and Bennett (1979) studied psychological aspects of elite wrestlers. The wrestlers represented the most skilled 10% in terms of skill of all Canadian wrestlers. Similar to the Mahoney and Avener study, comparisons were made between qualifiers and non-qualifiers for selected wrestling tournaments. Their results concerning general anxiety conflicted with those obtained by Mahoney and Avener on elite gymnasts. Highlen and Bennett found that the qualifiers reported less stress during both the precompetitive period and the competition. This inconsistency could be caused by several factors, including dissimilar statistical procedures used in the studies or the nature of the two sports. Of more importance, however, is the pattern of anxiety exhibited by both the qualifiers and nonqualifiers before and during competition.

Although the qualifiers were consistently lower in anxiety before and during wrestling competition, both groups exhibited extremely high levels of anxiety during anticipation of competing against a tough opponent as compared with level of anxiety during actual performance against that opponent. This trend was evidenced again during anticipation and actual performance against a weak opponent but not to nearly the same extent. Also, during the week before and the day before actual competition, anxiety levels were higher than they were during actual performance. Such findings support the position that focus should be placed on anticipatory anxiety rather than on performance anxiety. In keeping with this perspective, Highlen and Bennett note

that *1 hour* prior to competition, qualifiers withdrew more from others, were able to more effectively block their anxiety, and had fewer negative self-thoughts than nonqualifiers. Based on these results, specific training strategies could be devised and experimentally tested to ascertain their efficacy for helping wrestlers deal with anxiety. (p. 135)

Although the results of the Highlen and Bennett (1979) and the Mahoney and Avener (1977) investigations show much consistency, other evidence is somewhat contradictory. Gould, Weiss, and Weinberg (1981) used most of the same items employed in the Highlen and Bennett investigation to study psychological characteristics of collegiate wrestlers who were participating in the Big Ten Conference Wrestling Championships. In contrast to previous studies, Gould, Weiss, and Weinberg found few significant differences in terms of the anxiety responses of successful and unsuccessful athletes.

Each of the above studies discussed (Gould and others, 1981; Highlen & Bennett, 1979; Mahoney & Avener, 1979) was exploratory in nature. What is currently needed is the design of investigations capable of identifying causal relationships between independent and dependent variables.

Changes in A-State Occurring within the Competitive Process

Before, During, and After Competition

Since the development of sport-specific measures of competitive anxiety (namely, SCAT, SCAI, and SCAI—2), several researchers have investigated differences in anxiety as a function of varying levels of potential threat in the competitive situation.

One approach is the study of A-state changes that occur as a result of both the nature of the competitive situation itself and the temporal location (time) of that situation, which can be at any time before, during, or after competition. Simon and Martens (1977) used such a strategy to study the A-state scores of high-school female basketball players. Twelve situations that could occur as a consequence of playing basketball were rank-ordered, and the A-state the players experienced in each of those situations was assessed. The box on the facing page contains those situations, and the average A-state value is presented after each of the situations. Notice the low value associated with the first situation; because this situation does not contain any threat to self, it should not generate any elevation in A-state. However, situations 2 through 12 contain increasing amounts of potential threat and, as such, elevations in A-state are shown in a generally increasing fashion. Their findings show strong support for the predicted relationship between the perception of threat in competitive situations and systematic changes in state anxiety.

Taking a different approach, Gruber and Beauchamp (1979) studied the A-state re-actions of female collegiate basketball players as a result of both the importance and outcome of the game. Games were classified by the players as being either easy (wherein they felt that their opponents could be easily defeated) or difficult (wherein they believed the game was crucial). All of the easy games were won and all of the crucial games were lost. Their findings showed a strong relationship between the degree of threat in the social situation and level of state anxiety. The players were significantly more anxious before the crucial games than before the easy games. In addition, A-state was lower after all the games that were won as compared with the games that were lost.

Huddleston and Gill (1981) were interested in the patterns of state anxiety exhibited by female track and field participants during both practice and actual competition. They measured A-state at four different times, prepractice, postpractice, premeet, and pre-event. The last measurement is important because it takes into account the anxiety level exhibited by each performer just before her own event. However, it should also be noted that the study was weakened somewhat by a failure to assess postevent anxiety. Figure 4-10 presents the levels of state anxiety for each of the four measurement times. A few implications appear to be warranted. Notice the drop in anxiety level after practice; this probably occurred because any potential threat is no longer present. The relatively similar levels in anxiety during both practice and before the meet appear to indicate that both situations contain a potential threat to self-esteem. Finally, the highest degree of anxiety is shown just before the event.

Changes in A-State Occurring Before and After the Season

Klavora (1975) studied changes in A-state of high school football and basketball players using Spielberger & others' STAI. Figure 4-11 shows the patterns of A-state for 1 week before a game, 30 minutes before a regular season game, and 30 minutes before tournament playoffs. High A-trait participants in both football and basketball were higher in A-state across all three measurement times. However, both high and low A-trait players dem-onstrated increases in A-state before both competitive situations as compared with the practice period. There was no difference in state anxiety level between the regular season game and the tournament playoff game.

Although the Klavora (1975) study was hindered somewhat by some methodological

Basketball Situations and Average A-State Reactions

SITUATION	A-STATE*
1. You are watching a basketball game between two schools with whom you will *not* be competing. How do you feel when watching this game?	15.27
2. You are getting dressed in the locker room for a practice session. How do you feel while you are getting dressed?	19.04
3. You have just scored the winning basket and the game is over. How do you feel at this moment?	21.69
4. Your team is about to play a very weak opponent. They have won only one of eight games all season. How do you feel just before the game?	22.04
5. You are five minutes into the game and the other team calls a time-out. You are playing very well and your team has a big lead. The other team appears to be disorganized and unmotivated. How do you feel during this time-out?	22.18
6. You have traveled out of town for an important basketball game. You arrive at the motel the night before your game. How do you feel just before you prepare for bed that evening?	24.86
7. The coach, team, and you are watching a film of last week's basketball game. Your team won, but you did not play well, committing numerous mistakes. How do you feel as you watch the film with the coach and other members of the team?	26.68
8. In the practice sessions all week you have been battling for a starting position on the team. You are quite uncertain whether you will be in the starting line-up. It is the end of the last practice session prior to an important game and the coach is about to announce the starting line-up. How do you feel as you are waiting to hear the line-up?	31.21
9. Your team is about to play the most important game of the season. You are at center court waiting for the tip-off. How do you feel just before beginning this game?	31.48
10. It is 5 minutes before your game with the defending state champions who are visiting your school. They have not lost a game this year. How do you feel as you wait to play this team?	32.57
11. With 10 seconds remaining in the game and your team ahead by 1 point, you double dribble. In your anger you throw the ball down in disgust and the official calls a technical foul. The other team not only makes the free throw, but when they get the ball out of bounds, they score a basket and as a result win the game. How do you feel immediately after this loss?	33.04
12. You are in the midst of a very close game. There are only 2 seconds left in the game and your team is behind by *1* point. You were fouled while getting off a shot and have been awarded two free throws. The other team calls a time out at this point. How do you feel during the time out?	34.15

*Higher A-state scores indicate higher levels of anxiety.

Adapted from Simon, J.A., & Martens, R. (1977). SCAT as a predictor of A-states in varying competitive situations. In D.M. Landers & R.W. Christina (Eds.), *Psychology of motor behavior and sport*. Champaign, IL: Human Kinetics.

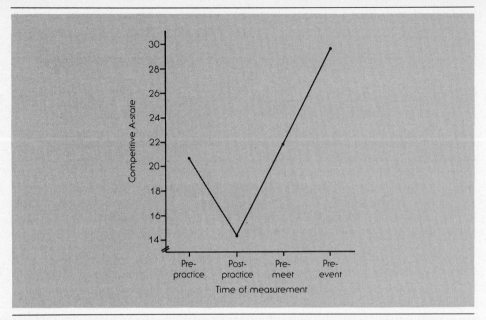

FIGURE 4-10   A-state of track and field participants across four measurement times.
Data from Huddleston, S., and Gill, D.L. (1981). State anxiety as a function of skill level and proximity to competition. *Research Quarterly for Exercise and Sport, 52,* 31-34.

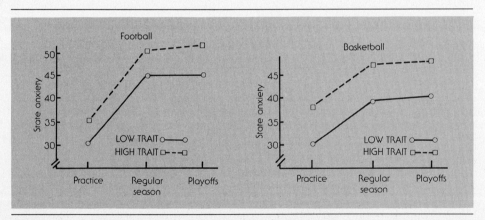

FIGURE 4-11   Changes in A-state occurring before and throughout the season.
From Klavora, P. (1975). Application of the Spielberger trait-state anxiety model and STAI in precompetitive anxiety research. In D.M. Landers, D.V. Harris, & R.W. Christina, (Eds.), *Psychology of sport and motor behavior II.* University Park, PA.: The Pennsylvania State University.

problems, it provided some insights into the relationship between state anxiety, trait anxiety, and sport participation. For instance, the fact that there were differences in state anxiety between high and low A-trait players is in agreement with the Huddleston and Gill (1981) data, which indicated that anticipation of competition can generate increases in state anxiety responses. However, Klavora's findings are in disagreement with those of Morgan (1970), who found decreases in state anxiety of college wrestlers before both an easy and a difficult match. Also, Morgan and Hammer (1974) found no differences in state anxiety from early season to the weigh-in before a wrestling match. Furthermore, in contradiction to his earlier study (Morgan, 1970), Morgan and Hammer found elevated levels of state anxiety just before competition.

Given the conflicts in the available literature and the nonsimilarity of the methods used in those studies, at the present time it is difficult to draw any firm conclusions regarding the relationship between seasonal competition and changes in state anxiety. Again, what is necessary is the design of studies that are methodologically sound and capable of testing relationships between the variables of state anxiety and aspects of the competitive process.

Anxiety and Exercise

A question of critical concern for physical educators and sport psychologists involves the relationship between exercise and anxiety. What effect, if any, does exercise have on anxiety? Few of us would question the physiological benefits of vigorous, **aerobic** exercise; however, until recently, little was documented about the psychological benefits of exercise. In the previous chapter we discussed studies that explored how vigorous exercise regimens could reduce resting neuromuscular tension (deVries, 1968; deVries & Adams, 1972). The studies presented below have directly assessed psychological aspects of anxiety within the experimental protocol. This is important because earlier we distinguished between the constructs of arousal and anxiety and argued that to assess anxiety adequately, we must investigate both the arousal or activation dimensions and the degree of unpleasantness in the emotional state.

Acute Effects

The primary researcher in the domain of the acute effects of exercise on anxiety is William Morgan, who is affiliated with the University of Wisconsin. His program of research has been in existence for over a decade. Morgan's interest in the relationship of exercise and anxiety was triggered by the Pitts-McClure hypothesis (see Pitts, 1969; Pitts & McClure, 1967). This hypothesis proposed that because exercise increases blood lactate the consequences of exercise could be undesirable psychological effects. It was based on Pitts and McClure's data, which showed that after subjects had been infused with lactate, anxiety symptoms were evidenced. Thus they argued that if vigorous exercise increases lactation, it can produce anxiety symptoms.

Since 1973, Morgan has generally measured state anxiety through the use of the SAI (Spielberger & others, 1970). He has replicated evidence in several investigations (Morgan, 1973, 1976). Overall, his evidence indicates that vigorous physical activity of short duration (acute exercise) can decrease state anxiety for both normal and high-anxious persons. Figure 4-12 is based on Morgan's 1973 study, which investigated the state

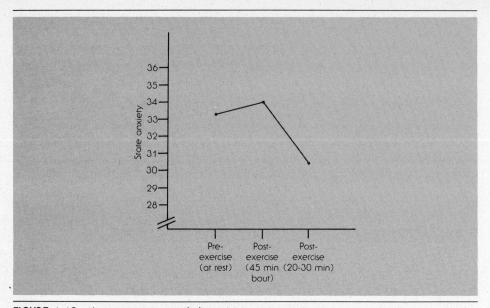

FIGURE 4-12   Acute exercise and changes in state anxiety.
Adapted from Morgan, W.P. (1973). Influence of acute physical activity on state anxiety. *Proceedings of the National College Physical Education Association for Men.*

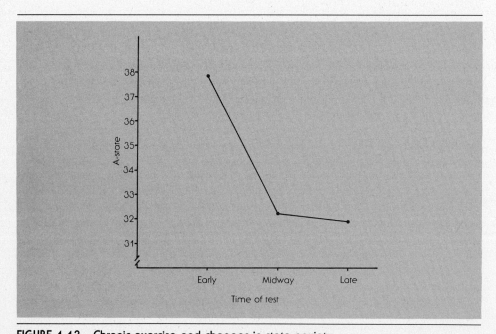

FIGURE 4-13   Chronic exercise and changes in state anxiety.
From Bird, A.M., Ravizza, K.H., & Reis, J.A. (1983). Physical activity, anxiety, and attentional style. Unpublished manuscript.

anxiety of 40 adult men before exercise, immediately after exercise, and after 30 minutes of recovery. These data, along with subsequent studies (such as Morgan & Horstman, 1976) indicate that vigorous exercise does produce increases in both lactate and state anxiety. However, after a very short period of time, anxiety is lower than it was at rest.

Morgan's results are consistent with other recent evidence generated by deVries, Wiswell, Bulbulian, & Moritani (1981). Taken together, the work of Morgan and deVries refutes the validity of the Pitts-McClure hypothesis and supports the validity of the tranquilizing effect of acute, vigorous exercise.

Chronic Effects

Few studies have attempted to measure long-term or chronic effects of exercise or physical activity on anxiety. Recently, Bird, Ravizza, and Reis (1983) contrasted anxiety reduction effects for college students enrolled in either tennis or Hatha yoga classes. Their findings showed that participation in either activity had similar effects. State anxiety was systematically reduced across time, regardless of the nature of the physical activity (Figure 4-13). Notice in Figure 4-13 the sharp drop initially, followed by a less noticeable decline. This study needs to be replicated before researchers can determine whether or not the effect is consistent; however, the results of the investigation argue strongly for the psychological benefits that can be gained through participation in physical activity courses.

The Bird, Ravizza, and Reis (1983) results are also in agreement with deVries' 1968 study. He found a 25% decrease in electrical activity in the muscles of adult men as a consequence of a 5- to 10-week program of exercise training. Similarly, Morgan, Roberts, Brand, and Feinerman (1970) reported a ''feeling better'' effect that resulted from a program of chronic exercise. These combined results are encouraging.

The current status concerning the beneficial psychological effects of both acute and chronic exercise and physical activity indicate that participation in such activities is of value above and beyond any physiological effects. Although little supporting evidence has been made available, apparently physicians share this viewpoint. Byrd (1963) has reported that out of 439 doctors he surveyed, 93% indicated that they had prescribed some form of exercise for the relief of tension in their patients.

IMPLICATIONS FOR SPORT

- When coaches publicly criticize athletes, they run the risk of creating feelings of psychological threat and thus high levels of anxiety. The consequence will most likely be more mistakes by the athlete.
- Player feedback should be positive in nature and should highlight a *few* relevant cues concerning future performance.
- ''Jerky,'' awkward motor patterns may be an indication of elevated state anxiety. Under such conditions, a player conference is needed. Talk to the athlete!
- In addition to designing drills that are as nearly gamelike as possible, try to structure the environment so that players can get used to the competitive anxiety they might feel during a game. One way to do this is to schedule as many scrimmages as possible.
- Because each person manifests the effects of anxiety differently, schedule individual conferences to identify how each performer experiences and attempts to cope with anxiety.

- DO NOT stress that winning is everything. Sport participation should be fun.
- Instructing an athlete to ''concentrate'' without directing attention to important cues only serves to frustrate the performer and can heighten anxiety.
- Do not assume that all highly skilled athletes are capable of controlling their own arousal or anxiety.
- Both acute and chronic vigorous exercise can be used to reduce anxiety.
- Carefully observe the athlete's behavior just before competition. Look for signs of nervousness and tension.

CASE STUDY 1

Gymnastics and Precompetitive Practice

Evidence from the Klavora (1975) study of high school football and basketball players indicated a significant rise in state anxiety from practice to regular season competition for both low and high trait-anxiety groups. Subsequent research by Huddleston and Gill (1981) reported similar levels of state anxiety for track and field participants during practice and competitive meet conditions. The Huddleston and Gill protocol included specific attempts to mimic meet conditions during practice, but the Klavora investigation did not.

Intuitively, coaches have believed in the merits of structuring the practice environment so that it mirrors as much as possible the conditions found during competition. By increasing the amount of evaluation potential in the practice regimen, perception of threat should be increased and level of state anxiety should be elevated. Athletes can learn to execute their skills effectively under such conditions and, in the long run, should be able to practice the techniques and defenses necessary to control or eliminate the anxiety response.

Given that individual differences in anxiety responsiveness do exist, keep in mind that the process of structuring the precompetitive practice session for purposes of increasing evaluation potential must be somewhat individualized. The following suggested practice conditions are general in nature and would therefore have to be modified by a coach to best meet the needs of each performer.

Gymnastics Practice Sessions

Preseason gymnastic practices should strongly emphasize conditioning, flexibility, and skill development and refinement. As we discussed in Chapter 2, correct responses should be reinforced, and selected appropriate cues should be presented after an incorrect response.

As the physical properties associated with a person's skill performance reach the established goal, meetlike ratings of performers should take place during the practice session. The benefits of this strategy are twofold. It allows the coach to observe athletes in a competitive environment, and it affords performers an opportunity to experience conditions highly similar to those they will face in a meet.

Before the competitive season, practice sessions should be interspersed with intrasquad competition and, if possible, practice meets against other local teams. Emphasis should be placed on the evaluation of performance outcome. Intrasquad competition ordinarily means having each performer attempt to better the score of the preceding performer in that event. All performances and scores should be visible to all participants.

Throughout the season, refinement of individual skills and routines should be accompanied by frequent evaluation in the form of judges' ratings and in an environment that resembles a gymnastic meet. Depending on the behaviors observed under these conditions, the coach may need to raise or lower the athlete's state anxiety reactions. Specific intervention techniques designed to lower anxiety (psyching-down) are presented in Chapter 5, and a brief discussion of psyching-up strategies appears in Chapter 3.

CASE STUDY 2

Competitive Stress and Youth Soccer

Passer's (1983) investigation regarding the identification of possible sources of perceived threat among male participants in youth soccer indicated that anticipation of parental disapproval or criticism was one factor that appeared to differentiate high versus low competitive trait–anxious athletes. This cognitive dimension of competitive anxiety is but one of many variables attracting research interest in the expanding realm of youth sport. As more and more youngsters become involved in organized sports such as T-ball, soccer, Pop Warner football, Little League baseball, and Ponytail softball, the need for techniques to help volunteer coaches combat negative player expectations and affect is becoming more important.

The beginning of each new youth soccer season is generally "kicked-off" by an organizational meeting attended by coaches, sponsors, potential participants, and parents. This is an opportune time to set the tone for the upcoming sport season. Based on the current evidence, we have listed below several factors that appear to be related to high levels of competitive stress in young soccer players. An open discussion by all in attendance could serve to raise awareness and perhaps change the perceptions and behaviors that are the potentially triggering stimuli for elevations in anxiety reactions.

Sources of Competitive Stress

Worries about making mistakes, not playing well, and losing
Feelings of being ashamed and upset about failure
Expectations concerning parental criticism
Worries about evaluation by parents and teammates

Of the sources listed above, worries about making mistakes and parental evaluation appear to be the most potent factors in producing elevations in competitive stress (Passer, 1983). Therefore the greatest amount of discussion should probably center on techniques and strategies designed to reduce or eliminate these variables.

CASE STUDY 3

Anxiety and Evaluation Potential in Discus Performance

The field events coach of a collegiate track team observed a significant decrease in the distance thrown by one of his athletes in the discus during meets as compared with practice throws. Although the discus performer was able to throw near the qualifying standard during practice, she was unable to meet even her poorest practice throws during meets.

The coach believed the discus thrower was experiencing elevated state anxiety during meets. He also believed that the athlete's anxiety reaction might be a result of the increased amount of psychological or ego threat present during meet conditions.

Based on those observations and analyses, the coach conferred with the athlete to find out exactly what the athlete's thoughts were under both practice and meet conditions. The athlete revealed that she was very concerned about letting her teammates down during a meet. She was bothered by how the other athletes were evaluating her performance.

The coach realized that a change in practice regimen was in order. Instead of allowing her to practice throwing the discus in almost virtual isolation, he constructed a systemized program based on increasing amounts of evaluation potential. The first change he made was to have all of the discus throwers practice together, using alternating throws. This allowed both the continued presence of other observers and the continued comparison of performance outcomes. He then arranged to have systematically increasing numbers of her teammates assemble as an informal audience during discus practice. Also, during this process the crucial variables of positive encouragement and feedback were employed by both the coach and the fellow competitors.

The systematic increase in evaluation potential was continued up until the final practice before the next scheduled meet. By the final practice, conditions were as similar to the actual meet as was possible. At the time of the meet, several teammates gathered at the discus site to provide support and encouragement.

After the meet (which was successful for the discus thrower), the coach again conferred with the athlete. She indicated that the change in practice regimen had allowed her to gradually get used to coping with feelings of anxiety. By the time of the meet she felt comfortable with the environmental conditions and could therefore focus solely on her throw rather than being concerned about what others were thinking about her and her performance. Not only had she learned to control her anxiety, but also she had not let her teammates down when it counted.

SUMMARY

- Anxiety differs from arousal in that it encompasses the dimensions of intensity and direction.
- Anxiety has both state and trait components.
- The anxiety experienced in sport situations is called competitive anxiety; it too has both state and trait dimensions.
- A major triggering stimulus causing elevation in state anxiety appears to be the perception of psychological threat.
- Anxiety is a psychophysiological construct in that it has both cognitive and physiological aspects.
- The major theoretical explanations of the anxiety process have been those of drive theory and the inverted-U hypothesis; currently, more of the available research evidence appears to support the inverted-U explanation.
- Klavora (1977) showed a systematic relationship between playing performance and state anxiety level in basketball players. He also demonstrated that high trait-anxious players had higher degrees of state anxiety as compared with low trait-anxious athletes.
- Sonstroem and Bernardo (1982) found higher levels of A-state for high as compared with low A-trait female collegiate basketball players. They found partial support for the predictions of the inverted-U hypothesis in that all of the players had their best performances under conditions of either moderate or low state anxiety.

- Research on youth soccer players showed the relationship between level of A-trait and predicted levels of A-state. Players on losing teams had higher state anxiety as compared with players on winning teams; these findings were shown for both boys and girls. In addition, a later investigation (Passer, 1983) found that the concerns about not playing well, losing, and evaluations by parents, coaches, and teammates were related to high anxiety.
- Studies of wrestlers (Gould, Horn, & Spreeman, 1983a, 1983b) showed both the predicted relationship between competitive A-trait and A-state and also the large degree of variability within individual participants.
- In terms of changes in anxiety occurring either before and after a single competition or during the competitive season, the current evidence appears to be somewhat contradictory. This is most likely because of the nonsimilarity in the assessment instruments employed and the paradigmatic approaches used in these studies.
- One means of reducing state anxiety is through vigorous exercise. Both acute and chronic exercise regimens appear capable of significantly reducing anxiety states.

DISCUSSION QUESTIONS

1 What are some of the major factors that appear to mediate between participation in youth sports and elevations in state anxiety?
2 On the basis of what you have read, identify as many explanations as possible of how elevated levels of anxiety may adversely affect motor performance.
3 What is the tranquilizer effect of exercise?
4 Compare and contrast the constructs of arousal and anxiety.
5 What would be predicted to happen to a high trait-anxious person's state anxiety when faced with a competitive sport setting? Would that person more likely make "errors on the right" or "errors on the left" of the inverted-U?

GLOSSARY

affect Positive or negative emotional state
aerobic Submaximal cardiovascular exercise, such as jogging or bicycling over long distances
agonist muscles Muscles that perform a specific movement; for example, the biceps are the agonist muscles for arm flexion
antagonist muscles Muscles that oppose a specific movement if they are not relaxed; for example, the triceps of the upper arm are the antagonist muscles for arm flexion
competitive state anxiety The level of anxiety that a particular sport situation generates in a performer
competitive trait anxiety The anxiety a performer generally experiences in sport situations
cocontraction The simultaneous contraction of two opposing muscle groups
idiosyncratic Uniquely characteristic of a particular person
lactate A metabolic waste product
operational definition A definition that specifies how something should be manipulated or measured
psychophysiology The application of physiological methods to the understanding of individual behavior
subjective competitive situation How a competitive situation is cognitively appraised by a performer

SUGGESTED READINGS

Bird, A.M., Cripe, B.K., & Morrison, N.L. (1980). Children and stress. *Journal of Physical Education and Recreation, 51,* 28-29, 62.

   The authors initially argue that the traditional approach to the teaching of physical education may induce stress while ignoring any responsibility for providing children with ways of reducing or coping with anxiety reactions. Subsequently, an alternative psychophysiological approach is presented.

Cook, D., Gansneder, B., Rotella, R., Malone, C., Bunker, L., & Owens, D. (1983). Relationship among competitive state anxiety, ability, and golf performance. *Journal of Sport Psychology, 5,* 460-465.

   The authors investigated the potential interaction between ability and anxiety. Several interesting findings were evidenced, including the notion that lower anxiety appeared to enhance the performance of low handicappers and detract from the performance of high handicappers.

Gould, D., Petlichkoff, L., & Weinberg, R.S. (1984). Antecedents of, temporal changes in, and relationships between CSAI-2 subcomponents. *Journal of Sport Psychology, 6,* 289-304.

   Two investigations were conducted to look at various aspects of the cognitive, somatic, and self-confidence components of the CSAI-2. In addition to supporting the independence of the three components of the instrument, several other pertinent findings were shown between aspects of anxiety and competition.

Kroll, W. (1979). The stress of high performance athletics. In P. Klavora & J.V. Daniels (Eds.), *Coach, athlete and the sport psychologist.* Champaign, IL: Human Kinetics.

   Kroll discusses the many causes of anxiety in sport competitive situations and suggests training and coaching practices that can be used to reduce excessive performer anxiety.

Landers, D.M. (1980). The arousal-performance relationship revisited. *Research Quarterly for Exercise and Sport, 51,* 77-90.

Landers presents a reexamination of the traditional arousal-performance relationship. The article emphasizes the role that attention plays in the anxiety process and the multidimensionality of the anxiety construct.

Martens, R. (1971). Anxiety and motor behavior: A review. *Journal of Motor Behavior, 3,* 151-179.

This is a classic review of literature concerning the relationship between anxiety and motor behavior. It traces the accumulated evidence concerning drive theory and then proposes two alternative approaches to the study of anxiety within motor skills settings.

Scanlan, T.K. (1984). Competitive stress and the child athlete. In J.M. Silva & R.S. Weinberg (Eds.), *Psychological foundations of sport.* Champaign, IL: Human Kinetics.

This article looks at the nature of competitive stress, the factors associated with competition that can induce stress, and the role that adults sometimes play in influencing stress reactions. Scanlan draws implications relative to reducing stress and making sport participation a positive experience.

Sonstroem, R.J. (1984). An overview of anxiety in sport. In J.M. Silva & R.S. Weinberg (Eds.), *Psychological foundations of sport.* Champaign, IL: Human Kinetics.

This review presents an overview of anxiety and sport, including definitions and opposing theoretical interpretations. It also addresses issues such as individual differences, aspects of measurement, and approaches to anxiety reduction.

5

INTERVENTION STRATEGIES AND SPORT BEHAVIOR

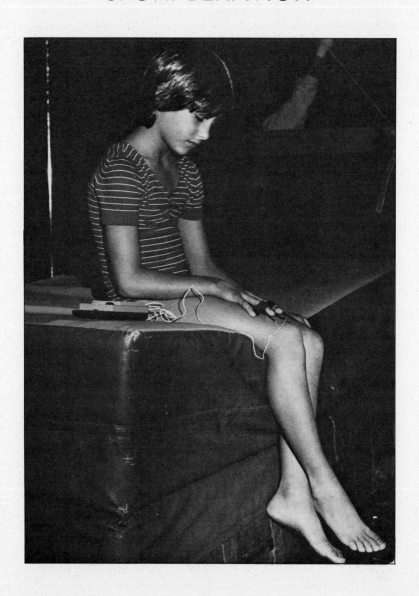

Intervention strategies provide the performer with skills to cope with competitive anxiety or stress. Although some people try to make a distinction between the terms *anxiety* and *stress,* we prefer to use them interchangeably. In this chapter we discuss several strategies based on physiological, cognitive, and affective approaches to stress management. These strategies appear to work best when presented in an integrated fashion.

The rationale underlying the integrated approach to the teaching of coping skills is based on the notion of every performer's idiosyncratic reactions to competitive stress situations. Remember from our discussion of anxiety that individual athletes vary in the manner in which they experience stress. By learning several coping skills, performers can select the approaches that work best for them.

SELECTING AND DESIGNING INTERVENTION APPROACHES

How do you know when an athlete is experiencing sport-related stress? The best indicator is the observation of performance decrements that cannot be attributed to obvious factors such as injury, change in coaching strategy, or lack of skill. If a performer demonstrates reduced skill execution, or what coaches generally refer to as a "slump," then the underlying cause is frequently elevated stress associated with sport performance.

Because people tend to be idiosyncratic in manifesting the effects of stress, a coach or teacher must find out whether those effects are being experienced primarily in the cognitive or the physiological domain. Although this is not always possible, two techniques can help. The first technique is to interview the athlete to determine how he or she perceives the effects of stress. What does the athlete think just before performance? Does the athlete make negative self-statements such as "I know I'm going to mess up in this game" or "I know I'm going to strike out?" This part of the interview assesses the degree to which negative self-statements might produce stress-related performance decrements. To assess potential physiological activation problems, similar questions could be asked about what is happening physiologically before competition. It is important to identify any negative physiologically oriented self-statements such as "I have butterflies in my stomach" or "I feel tension in all my muscles."

Although the personal interview approach may work with some athletes, it has two potential weaknesses. First, it may not be possible to spend the necessary amount of time with each athlete. Second, many performers have difficulty in precisely monitoring or expressing what is actually occurring cognitively or physiologically. A second approach would be to use appropriate assessment instruments to measure cognitive or physiological reactions to sport competitive situations. Two useful instruments are the Competitive State Anxiety Inventory—2 (CSAI—2) or the Autonomic Perception Questionnaire (APQ). Martens' (1983) CSAI—2 may be more useful because it assesses competitive state anxiety responses along both the cognitive and somatic dimensions, whereas the APQ (Mandler, Mandler, & Uviller, 1958) measures only perceived physiological or autonomic arousal.

If such standardized instruments are not available, then have the athletes write personal essays about what they are thinking or feeling just before competition. Have them imagine themselves in the competitive setting right before their event. What are they thinking about? What are they apprehensive about? How do they feel? Try to get them to tap both the cognitive and physiological domains.

Given the overall difficulties in terms of both time and assessment of the manner in which different persons manifest stress reactions, the approach taken by many sport psychologists is to design stress management programs that include both cognitive and physiological techniques. These can be taught and practiced on a group basis. After sufficient practice, most athletes learn which intervention strategies work most effectively for them and they should no longer need the assistance of the sport psychologist or coach to use coping skills. Those skills should become part of the athlete's own repertoire of sport-related skills.

This raises another important issue. Most coaches turn to sport psychologists for assistance with athletes who are experiencing performance problems; however, instruction in the use of intervention strategies can be beneficial for other reasons. For example, techniques such as relaxation and imaginal rehearsal can be used for *performance enhancement* as well as stress management. Many world-class athletes use such techniques not to reduce precompetitive stress reactions but instead to mentally practice until they reach a ''perfect'' mental replica of the skill to be performed. Basically, they mentally run through the skill execution, reducing performance errors as they proceed. When they have eliminated all the potential errors, they have achieved a ''perfect'' mental execution. This procedure is most effective when the performer has sufficient skill so that a perfect physical execution has been achieved in the past.

Another important reason for teaching intervention strategies as an integral part of any athletic coaching plan has to do with the notion of **lifetime stress.** The intervention strategies discussed in this chapter were not originally designed for specific application to sport settings; instead they have their origins in clinical psychology. They were designed to help people cope with stressful events encountered in everyday life. By teaching athletes to use such techniques, you are providing them with more generalized, lifetime psychological coping skills rather than short-term coping skills that are only specific to sport situations.

SELECTED INTERVENTION STRATEGIES

Relaxation Procedures

Perception of threat elicits a diversified response with cognitive, physiological, and behavioral components. However, responses within the physiological domain most clearly demonstrate how perception of threat tends to systematically affect certain parameters. Cannon (1941) popularized the phrase ''fight or flight'' to describe the integrated physiological responses that occur when threatening stimuli are present in the environment.

TABLE 5-1   Physiological Manifestations of High Anxiety and the Relaxation Response and the Elements Needed to Induce a Relaxation Response

Physiological Manifestations of High Anxiety	Physiological Manifestations of Relaxation Response	Elements Needed to Induce Relaxation Response
High oxygen consumption and carbon dioxide elimination	Low oxygen consumption and carbon dioxide elimination	Mental device
High heart rate	Low heart rate	Passive attitude
High respiration rate	Low respiration rate	Decreased muscle tension
Low skin resistance	High skin resistance	Quiet environment
Low alpha brain wave	High alpha brain wave	
High skeletal muscle tension	Low skeletal muscle tension	

As shown in Table 5-1, the physiological responses associated with high anxiety (the fight or flight response) include high oxygen consumption and high elimination of carbon dioxide, high heart and respiration rates, low skin resistance, low levels of alpha brain wave activity, and high skeletal muscle tension.

In earlier times, the physiological responses associated with the fight or flight response were viewed as being positive in that these physiological changes prepared the person to meet and conquer environmental threat. In contemporary life most of us only rarely face objective, life-threatening dangers; most of the threats we face are psychological. In sport, frequently perceived threat is based on anticipation of a negative evaluation of performance outcome. As such, the physiological manifestations associated with the fight or flight response do not necessarily function in an adaptive fashion.

The *relaxation response* is characterized by a physiological pattern of responses in direct opposition to the fight or flight response. As Benson, Beary, and Carol (1974) indicate, the relaxation response in humans is characterized by low oxygen consumption and low carbon dioxide elimination, low heart rate, low respiration rate, high skin resistance, high alpha brain wave activity, and low levels of skeletal muscle tension (see Table 5-1).

As we stated in our earlier discussions of the inverted-U hypothesis, either extremely high (fight or flight response) or extremely low (relaxation response) levels of physiological activation can be detrimental to motor or sport performance. However, there is a fundamental difference between the origin of the two integrated physiological responses. The fight or flight response occurs without conscious direction or awareness, whereas the relaxation response takes place only when the performer consciously follows certain procedures. As indicated in Table 5-1, four basic elements are needed: a mental device, a passive attitude, decreased muscle tension **(tonus),** and a quiet environment. These elements were originally identified and described by Benson and others (1974):

(1) *Mental device*—There should be a constant stimulus—e.g., a sound, word, or phrase repeated silently or audibly, or fixed gazing at an object. The purpose of these procedures is to shift from logical, externally oriented thought.

(2) *Passive attitude*—If distracting thoughts do occur during the repetition or gazing, they should be disregarded and one's attention should be redirected to the technique. One should not worry about how well he is performing the technique.

(3) *Decreased muscle tonus*—The subject should be in a comfortable posture so that minimal muscular work is required.

(4) *Quiet environment*—A quiet environment with decreased environmental stimuli should be chosen. Most techniques instruct the practitioner to close his eyes. A place of worship is often suitable, as is a quiet room. (p. 38)

Benson and others (1974) have identified several intervention techniques that after much practice should help the performer achieve the relaxation response: progressive relaxation, autogenic training, hypnosis, and transcendental meditation.

Progressive Relaxation

The originator of the progressive relaxation technique was Edmond Jacobson (1938). His fundamental premise was that states of muscle tension are incompatible with states of muscle relaxation; that is, it is not possible to be tense and relaxed at the same time. Although many forms of relaxation procedures exist, the uniqueness of the progressive relaxation approach is its use of muscle tension before muscle relaxation. Jacobson believed that this process would help a person recognize the difference between the two states.

He then suggested that the initial portion of the progressive relaxation session be devoted to the systematic tensing and relaxing of various muscle groups. Once this is accomplished, the person should focus on complete relaxation in muscle groups. Relaxation of a muscle group is complete when there is an absence of any muscular contraction in that group.

Because Jacobson's original program was rather lengthy, we will present a modified progressive relaxation program designed by Borkovec and his associates (Borkovec, 1981; Bernstein & Borkovec, 1973). The **modified progressive relaxation training** approach involves systematically tensing and relaxing 16 muscle groups. During this procedure, the performer concentrates on the sensations generated during the relaxation process. Muscle groups such as each hand and forearm, the abdomen, and each upper leg are tensed for 5 to 7 seconds, then relaxed for 30 to 45 seconds. The tensing and relaxing procedure is repeated two or more times until total relaxation of that muscle group is achieved. Once a particular muscle group becomes fully relaxed, the procedure begins with a new muscle group until the entire body is relaxed. The performer should passively attend to the sensations that arise during the relaxation process. The performer shouldn't worry or try to concentrate too much. He or she should simply let the feelings associated with being relaxed enter consciousness.

The full procedure should be practiced at least twice a day for 15 to 20 minutes. With sufficient practice, a person can become adept at identifying even minimal amounts of tension present in the muscles. This ability to identify muscle tension is critical because it is a cue that relaxation procedures should be instigated before muscle tension levels become detrimental to performance.

With sufficient practice the original 16 muscle groups can be combined into larger units until ultimately only four major groups are used. This reduction in the number of muscle groups makes the use of the procedure more efficient because complete relaxation can be achieved more rapidly (see p. 140 for a similar muscle relaxation exercise that was developed by Suinn, 1980). As a person becomes more skilled at the relaxation process, the tension-relaxation portion of the procedure can be eliminated. Eventually a state of relaxation can be achieved simply through the recall of sensations associated with previous experiences in the relaxation state.

Autogenic Training

Autogenic training differs from progressive relaxation in its emphasis on verbal and visual techniques. Its basis is a psychophysiological principle that says that conditioned patterns of responses become associated with certain thoughts (Girdano & Everly, 1979). Pause for a moment and think about someone you love being in a terrible automobile accident. Imagine the sound of the tires squealing and the sound at impact. What are the resultant physiological sensations? Most likely, this awful thought generated a set of physiological responses in direct contradiction to the relaxation response. Now imagine yourself lying in a hammock. The sun feels warm, a breeze gently passes by, birds chirp, and all is at peace. What that thought most likely triggered was a state similar to a relaxation response with all its accompanying physiological manifestations. In both cases your thoughts altered your physiological state. This connection between the brain and physiological changes is the basis of autogenic (self-generated) training.

Based on correlations between physiological parameters associated with relaxation, Schultz and Luthe (1969), developed an autogenic training program. It was based on a hierarchy of six psychophysiological dimensions: "heaviness in the extremities, warmth in the extremities, regulation of cardiac activity, regulation of breathing, abdominal warmth, and cooling of the forehead." (Hickman, 1979, p. 125). Phrases such as "My right arm is heavy," "My right arm is warm and relaxed," and "I am calm" are examples of commonly used verbal stimuli within an autogenic training program. Each of the six psychophysiological dimensions are practiced in sequential order. Once the goal of complete relaxation is achieved at one level, then the person moves on to the next goal. The relaxation response is achieved when the person is able to move through all six levels.

Hypnosis

Hypnosis is defined as an induced state characterized by *increased acceptance of suggestion* (Benson & others, 1974; Gorton, 1949). Although the use of hypnotic suggestion with athletes has recently been gaining interest, many people are afraid of hypnosis because of misconceptions resulting from the use of hypnosis in theatrical settings. One misconception is that a hypnotist can make other persons perform foolish and embarassing acts against their will. Another misconception is that only a weak person can be hypnotized. In fact, it is those who are strong and willing to give up control who are the more susceptible. Today fears about hypnosis are being alleviated through a more ethical approach to hypnotic suggestion and by a better understanding of the hypnotic state.

The induction of a hypnotic state involves several steps: (1) pre-induction, (2) induction, (3) attainment of the hypnotic state, (4) awakening, and (5) posthypnotic suggestion period.

Pre-induction procedures. The pre-induction period is vital to the success of the subsequent hypnotic induction. Many persons are afraid of being hypnotized; they fear losing self-control, never waking up from the trance, or doing something foolish during the hypnotic state. It is absolutely crucial that the hypnotist gain the trust of the athlete during the pre-induction period and assure the athlete the he or she will remain in control during the hypnotic session and can awake from it at will. At this point the purpose of the hypnotic induction needs to be identified. What is the problem to be remedied through hypnotic techniques? Is it lack of confidence? Feelings of inadequacy? Anxiety concerning leadership ability?

Induction procedure. During the induction period, hypnosis is achieved and increased suggestibility occurs. Many different techniques can be used to induce the hypnotic state. The most common techniques involve the use of visual fixation (staring at one spot), imagery, and relaxation. Usually two or more of these strategies are used in combination. The physiological state reached during hypnosis is identical to that reached in the relaxation response; thus suggestions relating to feelings of relaxation and peacefulness are usually included in the induction procedure.

Attainment of the hypnotic state. When the hypnotic state has been attained, the hypnotist makes positive suggestions for solving the problems identified in the pre-induction period. These positive suggestions are called posthypnotic suggestions because they indicate what behavior should be like after the athlete awakens from the hypnotic state. For example, the suggestion might be made to a bowler that when next in the "address" position, concentration will be focused on the correct mark on the alley, all thoughts will be on a smooth release, and the muscles will feel relaxed. A golfer might receive the suggestion that when next on the green the cup will appear large, that the putting stroke will feel like the motion of a well-synchronized pendulum, and that the follow-through will send the ball directly into the cup.

Awakening. The athlete is usually awakened from the hypnotic state by hearing an appropriate suggestion or signal from the hypnotist. Cooke and Van Vogt (1965) have suggested that at this point the hypnotist should be forceful, enthusiastic, and dramatic. The goal is to leave the awakened subject with a pleasant and healthy attitude toward the experience with hypnosis. Honey (1978) suggests the following steps be included in the awakening method:

1. You are awakening very, very slowly.
2. Your entire body is completely relaxed from head to toe.
3. You feel light, elevated, and exceptionally clear-headed.
4. You are happy with everyone and everything.
5. You are WIDE AWAKE!!'' (p. 61)

Posthypnotic suggestion period. The posthypnotic suggestion period is extremely important in the hypnosis procedure. It is at this point that the positive suggestions provided during the induction phase are enacted in the awakened state. It appears that the effectiveness of the posthypnotic suggestions can be increased if they are coupled with a signal, such as a certain sound or word (LeCron & Bordeaux, 1947).

In athletics these signals, or cues, can be coupled with aspects of the sport situation. For example, a basketball player may hear the positive suggestion "When you are at the free throw line, you will feel confident and poised." A tennis player could use a pre-determined verbal signal, such as saying "calm" just before the serve.

Not everyone can achieve a hypnotic state. Hatfield and Daniels (1981) point out that only 20% to 30% of the population can achieve relatively deep levels of hypnosis. In addition, because of variations in individual experiences and personalities, the number of sessions required to achieve the hypnotic state can also vary. As Dishman (1980) has cautioned, *hypnotic procedures should only be done by qualified practitioners.* Most accomplished hypnotists are certified by the Society for Clinical and Experimental Hypnosis or the Society for Clinical Hypnosis.

Although a teacher or coach should not use hypnotic procedures without the help of a fully trained hypnotist, there is no apparent reason why athletes should not be made aware of the procedures involved in *self-hypnosis* (autohypnosis). Self-hypnosis can be equally effective as an intervention strategy in sport settings. Orlick (1980) describes self-hypnosis succinctly:

> The secret of self-hypnosis is two-fold: (1) you must fixate your conscious attention, and (2) you must relax your body. The moment you do these two things you are actually in self-hypnosis. Pick a spot on the wall in front of you right now and stare at it while you let your body become limp and relaxed. Keep on staring and relaxing for a few moments and you will feel yourself sinking deeper and deeper into self-hypnosis.
>
> That is all there is to it, and even in this very light state, you can begin to program yourself with positive beneficial suggestions. Anyone can put themselves into self-hypnosis simply by fixating their conscious attention and relaxing. With practice you can go deeper and deeper and the programming will become more and more effective. (p. 137)

Regardless of whether the hypnotic state is induced by a qualified hypnotist or by the athlete, the procedure can be used to help the performer gain control over attention and achieve a more relaxed precompetitive state. However, hypnosis is most useful in its ability to provide the athlete with a positive "mind-set" before competition. In a sense it creates a **self-fulfilling prophecy;** someone who thinks that he or she is going to do well can actually fulfill that expectation by succeeding.

Transcendental Meditation (TM)

Meditation procedures such as hatha-yoga, Zen, and transcendental meditation (TM) originated over 4000 years ago in India and other parts of Asia. Each of these systems varies somewhat in how it expands conscious awareness and produces a state of restful alertness (Girdano & Everly, 1979). The devices used include visualization (imaginal rehearsal), concentration on breathing, and recitation of a Sanskrit syllable called a *mantra* (Layman, 1978).

TM was popularized by Maharishi Mahesh Yogi; however, it should be noted that TM is not a religion or an organized system of philosophy. It is a system based on the use of a *mantra* to achieve self-transcendence (Girdano & Everly, 1979). The mantra is selected by the TM teacher; it is secret and unique to each person. The mantra is usually a simple sound such as "mu" or "ahhom."

In practice, the performer sits comfortably in a chair and recites the mantra while breathing regularly for 10 to 20 minutes each day. Interestingly, the principles underlying the practice of TM are similar to the methods used to achieve the relaxation response. Noting this similarily, Benson (1975) devised a simple program that combines the features of several meditation and relaxation programs:

1. Select a quiet place.
2. Sit in a comfortable position with your eyes closed.
3. Relax the muscles from the bottom up (feet first, face last).
4. Breath through the nose and say "one" each time you exhale.

In discussing Benson's meditational relaxation program, Nideffer (1981) makes several important points:

> Although individuals are attending to breathing and counting, it is important that these attentional process be as 'passive' as possible. This means that individuals do not fight to force attention. If they lose count, find themselves distracted, their mind wanders, that is all right. They simply react to each distraction by gently and unemotionally bringing their attention back to counting one on each exhale. It is very important that the individual learn to react in this rather passive unemotional way to distractions. In fact, that is one of the major benefits of meditation for athletes, because the negative spiral is broken by a passive attentional focus. (p. 171)

Summary of Relaxation Procedures

From our overview of the four relaxation procedures of progressive relaxation, autogenic training, hyponosis, and transcendental meditation, two points should be clear. First, all four methods have common procedures designed to achieve the relaxation response. Second, by relaxing, appropriately focusing attention, and reducing anxiety, systematic changes are made in physiological parameters such as oxygen consumption, respiration rate, and degree of muscle tension. The available evidence strongly supports the notion that relaxation procedures can systematically influence the negative effects of the fight or flight response and instigate the relaxation response. What is unclear, however, is how the relaxation response relates to the improvement of sport or athletic performance.

Layman (1978) clearly points out some problems and possibilities specific to meditation and sport performance; however, her insights appear equally applicable to the other three approaches to relaxation.

1. Most of the available information is anecdotal in nature; that is, most of the evidence is based on personal experiences of coaches or athletes. Few well-designed studies are available.
2. On an intuitive level, it would appear that relaxation procedures can positively influence sport behavior because they can improve or facilitate concentration. Improved concentration may then have a positive effect on body control and thus sport performance.

The relaxation procedures described above can interrupt the anxiety spiral. They can make the athlete aware of the relationship between physiological activation, attentional control, and sport performance. Practice at relaxation procedures can allow the performer to gain greater control over physiological activation. Because either excessive or minimal amounts of arousal can be detrimental to sport performance (the inverted-U hypothesis), relaxation procedures can help the athlete to determine his or her current level of activation and modify that level according to the demands of the situation. These procedures also provide the athlete with a means of blocking out environmental or internal cues that can be detrimental to sport performance. In addition, the positive nature of the thoughts or suggestions contained within the procedures focuses attention on desirable possibilities rather than on negative aspects. Finally, these procedures tend to focus attention on the present situation rather than on past failures or mistakes.

Biofeedback

Generally, people are not aware of autonomic changes in parameters such as heart rate or muscle tension until the levels become excessively high. At that point, it may be difficult to consciously reduce those levels. One technique designed to teach persons to control physiological or autonomic responses is biofeedback.

Biofeedback ordinarily involves the use of electronic monitoring devices that can detect and amplify internal responses. Thus they can provide the performer with important information that is not ordinarily available (Ash & Zellner, 1978). These electronic monitoring instruments provide the person with visual or auditory feedback concerning some aspect of physiological responses such as muscle activity or heart rate. For instance, by attaching electrodes to specific muscle groups, information about muscle tension can be fed back to the performer as a changing auditory pitch. As Daniels and Hatfield (1981) write:

> Once the athlete has learned to recognize the signal, changes in pitch frequency become associated with changes in cognitive or physical processes. Soon, the athlete is able to decrease the pitch frequency successfully with certain relaxing, or positive thoughts. The development of cognitive strategies to reduce or increase the signal is the key to biofeedback. (p. 69)

This connection between a state of relaxation and cognitive strategies as they affect physiological responses is very important.

Biofeedback allows the performer to perceive how cognitions and situational factors influence physiological responses. By monitoring physiological activation, the person begins to make connections between thoughts and attentional direction and the resultant physiological effects (Nideffer, 1981). Once these connections are made, physiological control can be increased. By switching attentional focus from negative, anxiety-producing cues to positive, performance-enhancing cues or changing the cognitions or negative thoughts, physiological activation should decrease.

But how do you transfer the awareness of physiological responses or changes into the sport situation? Daniels and Hatfield (1981) suggest that transfer can be facilitated by interspersing sessions of nonfeedback within the training regimen. By increasing the length of these nonfeedback sessions, the performer should become less dependent on the biofeedback signal while still maintaining an awareness of physiological changes. With sufficient practice and experience, athletes can learn to identify the onset of a stress reaction and successfully control it so that sport performance is improved.

The transfer of strategies acquired during biofeedback training to the gymnasium and playing fields is an important concept from another standpoint: cost. When biofeedback techniques are used to enhance athletic performance, the method most often used is electromyography (EMG). The cost of EMG equipment is steep, ranging from $700 to $2000 (Nideffer, 1981). Therefore it is not prudent to continually bring the equipment to the sport setting. Instead, the equipment can be kept inside and nonfeedback sessions can be incorporated into the biofeedback training program.

Because biofeedback training is a recent occurrence in sport, there have been few studies of its effectiveness. Although some limited evidence is available (DeWitt, 1980;

French, 1978), the most comprehensive approach thus far has been that of Landers and his associates (Daniels, 1981; Daniels & Landers, 1981; Wilkinson, Landers, & Daniels, 1981). Landers and his colleagues have been particularly interested in studying the effects of biofeedback on rifle shooting. For example, Daniels and Landers (1981) investigated the effects of either verbal instructions or auditory biofeedback training on shooting performance and physiological responses (for example, respiration rate and heart rate) of eight men who were high-level junior shooters.

The findings indicated that shooters who were trained in auditory biofeedback demonstrated improved performance and consistency of the desired pattern. They also showed a significant increase in awareness and control of the autonomic pattern as compared with the verbal instruction group. Of major importance in the Daniels and Landers study was the finding that auditory biofeedback positively affected shooting performance beyond simply increasing awareness of autonomic response. On this basis, Daniels and Landers suggest that similar approaches could very easily be used in other sports; in particular, closed-skill sports that by their very nature make it easier to assess aspects of psychophysiological responses during participation.

It appears that biofeedback can help athletes develop skills needed to recognize even subtle changes in physiological responses. With proper use, biofeedback techniques appear capable of assisting high-anxious performers to regulate autonomic responses and thus increase the possibility of performing successfully. However, its application is certainly not limited to persons characterized by high levels of anxiety. In the case of the shooters, it allowed those performers to gain a clearer understanding of the relationship between occurrences in the autonomic domain and effects on sport performance.

Cognitive Procedures

Imagery

Imaginal rehearsal (that is, mental practice) for athletes usually takes one of two forms. **Mastery imagery** uses mental rehearsal to increase athletic success by mentally rehearsing a sport skill. Such mental rehearsal involves a process of systematically removing performance errors imaginally and continuing that process until a ''perfect'' mental rehearsal is achieved. The effectiveness of mastery imaginal rehearsal depends somewhat on the skill level of the performer because a perfect mental rehearsal probably cannot be achieved by a person who has not been able to overtly perform the response correctly. However, once any performer has developed a fairly high degree of skill and has a clear idea of the ideal skill execution, then the process of mastery imaginal rehearsal can allow the person to mentally compare responses and thereby eliminate potential errors or incorrect responses.

Coping imagery refers to the process of using imagery to manage stress. The imaginal rehearsal is ordinarily structured on the basis of a *systematic desensitization procedure,* which in turn is based on the *principle of reciprocal inhibition* and the development of a *hierarchy.*

The principle of reciprocal inhibition proposes that it is not possible to experience two conflicting emotions at the same instant; that is, it is not possible to be totally relaxed and highly anxious at the same moment.

Developing a hierarchy is the process of rank-ordering from least stressful to most stressful the steps leading to a high anxiety or stress response. For example, suppose an athlete is bothered by high degrees of precompetitive stress. The highest degree of stress would most likely be experienced immediately before the actual competition, and this situation would represent the highest point in the hierarchy. For most persons, however, the stress reaction builds in a systematic fashion. To construct the hierarchy, the athlete would be asked to indicate the first instance that any precompetitive anxiety is experienced, for example, the moment the athlete awakes on the day of the game. This would represent the first, or lowest, step in the hierarchy. Slightly higher degrees of anxiety might then be experienced on reaching school that day, followed by increasing amounts when entering the locker room. Once all these anxiety-inducing instances are identified and rank-ordered, the hierarchy has been established.

Subsequently, a coping imaginal rehearsal program can be instituted. First, the athlete is taught and becomes proficient in using relaxation procedures. After achieving a state of relaxation, the athlete imagines coping with the situation presented at the lowest step in the hierarchy. The goal is to be able to imaginally cope with the previously anxiety-inducing situation in a state of relaxation. This procedure is repeated systematically until the athlete is able to successfully cope with all of the steps in the hierarchy. Once such coping behavior is accomplished imaginally, the procedure is ordinarily repeated behaviorally; that is, the same systematic movement is made through the steps of the hierarchy but the sequence is based on actual behavior rather than imaginal rehearsal.

Imagery, whether mastery or coping, is an integral part of virtually all stress management programs. Although many highly-skilled athletes, such as Billy Jean King, Jack Nicklaus, and Fran Tarkenton, have reported using imaginal strategies as part of their efforts to enhance athletic performance, most athletes need some degree of practice to master imaginal techniques. Hickman (1979) has developed a training method that any athlete should be able to master with little difficulty. The sequence is as follows:

1. Choose a time and place in which you will be undisturbed for 15 minutes and assume a comfortable posture;
2. Close your eyes, breathe deeply into the chest and abdomen, and relax completely for two or three minutes;
3. Create a blank white screen in your mind, focusing on it very clearly;
4. Imagine a circle which fills the screen and slowly make the circle blue;
5. Develop as rich and deep a blue as possible, then slowly change to another color, repeating this process through four or five colors;
6. Allow the images to disappear, relax, and observe the spontaneous imagery which arises;
7. On your blank screen, create the image of a glass (a simple object), develop it clearly in three dimensions, fill it with a colorful liquid (like coffee or Kool-aid), add some ice cubes, insert a straw, and write a descriptive caption underneath;
8. Allow the image to fade and repeat the process with other objects (choose items associated with your sport);
9. Relax and observe the spontaneous imagery which arises;
10. Select a variety of scenes and develop richly detailed images of them (practice with sport related environments such as a swimming pool, a track, etc.);
11. Relax and observe;
12. Practice visualizing people, including strangers, close friends, and yourself;
13. To end each session, breathe deeply three times, slowly open your eyes, and adjust to the external environment (pp. 120-121).

Once the athlete can visualize a stressful situation, it is time to use imaginal techniques to cope with a competitive stress reaction. In Case Study 1 (p. 134) we provide a step-by-step approach for the use of coping imagery with football players.

Visuomotor Behavior Rehearsal (VMBR)

Although it still has not received sufficient research attention, one of the first methods to include aspects of both relaxation and imaginal rehearsal in a systematic attempt to help athletes achieve increased athletic success was visuomotor behavior rehearsal (VMBR) (Suinn, 1976). VMBR includes three basic steps: relaxation, imaginal practice, and the use of imagery to strengthen motor or psychological skills.

The relaxation procedure used in VMBR is presented in the box on p. 140. In the second step, imaginal practice, emphasis is placed on learning to consciously control the content of imagery until a carbon copy of a real-life occurrence can be generated. As Suinn writes:

> In my work with relaxation and stress management, I have been extremely impressed by the quality of imagery that is possible after deep muscle relaxation. This imagery is more than visual. It is also tactile, auditory, emotional and muscular. One swimmer reported that the scene in her mind changed from black and white to color as soon as she dove mentally into a pool, and she could feel the coldness of the water. A skier who qualified for the former U.S. Alpine ski team experienced the same 'irritability' that she felt during actual races, when she mentally practiced being in the starting gate. Without fail, athletes feel their muscles in action as they rehearse their sport. One professional racer who took the training actually moved his boots when skiing a slalom course in his mind.'' (pp. 40-41)

After developing proficiency at imagining, the third step in the VMBR procedure involves the imaginal rehearsal of a specific sport skill. It is here that Suinn introduces the notion of *transfer,* which is derived directly from the motor learning literature. The principle of transfer says that a skill that is initially practiced in one condition will transfer proportionally to a new situation to the degree that the new situation is similar to the previous situation (Suinn, 1976). In terms of an athletic situation, this means that practice conditions should resemble game conditions to the greatest degree possible. Therefore, baseball practice in full uniform and with game cleats, officials, and spectators should produce more transfer to actual game performance as compared with an informal practice. Obviously, gamelike practices are not always feasible. What is always possible, on the other hand, is imaginal rehearsal, which directly mimics the gamelike atmosphere and experiences. According to Suinn, this is the strength of imaginally rehearsing specific sport skills and contests. By so doing, athletes can practice specific techniques and systematically eliminate performance errors until they are able to imaginally repeat the correct skill execution. If imagined under gamelike conditions, this procedure should facilitate transfer to the actual competition.

Lane (1980) points out four potential benefits of the VMBR procedure for athletes: (1) relaxation and anxiety reduction, (2) error correction, (3) increased ability to concentrate, and (4) increased skill development. In fact, the increased ability to relax and concentrate effectively are necessary to clearly analyze the sport skill and then correct errors. Furthermore, recall from the principle of reciprocal inhibition that a person cannot feel relaxed and anxious at the same time. By instigating a state of relaxation, anxiety should be reduced. And because a person cannot hold two different thoughts at the same time, concentrating on performance analysis and error corrections blocks out harmful or irrelevant thoughts. Thus all the steps of the VMBR procedure can improve sport performance by inducing relaxation, reducing anxiety, increasing effective concentration (or attentional focus), and eliminating performance errors.

Stress Inoculation

One way to change a person's perception of threatening situations is to provide a repertoire of coping skills designed to teach the athlete how to deal with stress. One such procedure, stress inoculation, was developed by Meichenbaum and his colleagues (Meichenbaum, 1977; Meichenbaum & Cameron, 1973; Meichenbaum & Turk, 1976). The procedure is termed **stress inoculation** because the performer is exposed to and learns to cope with stress in increasing amounts. It is proposed that through this process the performer can become immune to stress. The procedure involves several steps: (1) appraisal of the problem, (2) stress education, (3) relaxation training, (4) instructed practice, and (5) actual practice.

Appraisal of the problem. As we indicated earlier, for extremely well-skilled athletes the most obvious indication of stress-related problems is a decrement in performance that is not readily attributable to factors such as fatigue, injury, or poor conditioning. Frequently, the athlete simply indicates that he or she is experiencing a "slump." As Harrison and Feltz (1981) point out:

> It is also important to recognize that physical and mental factors are not necessarily mutually exclusive. Many athletes' "slumps" have started from actual physical problems only to be maintained by anxiety and defeatist cognitions after the actual physical problem was resolved. (p. 55)

For less-skilled performers, it is often easy to observe stress reactions. For example, movements frequently appear to be tense and jerky. Regardless of the athlete's level of skill, whenever a stress-related problem is suspected it is important to seek the advice and assistance of a trained counselor, school psychologist, or sport psychologist who is experienced in the use of stress inoculation procedures.

Stress education. An important element within the stress inoculation program is the phase used to educate the athlete relative to the nature of stress. Here the sport psychologist or stress inoculation trainer encourages the person to explore his or her own ideas about the causes and nature of stress. This process serves as a cognitive preparation strategy that facilitates the person's ability to cope with stress. Basically, the trainer helps the performer formulate a conceptualization of stress in layman's terms (Long, 1980). The performer is asked to verbalize how the stress reaction or process operates for him or her. What triggers it? What happens next? What feelings or thoughts occur? How is sport performance affected?

> For instance, if the individual's response to stress involves an increased heart rate and sweaty palms plus a sense of helplessness, these reactions should be incorporated in the explanation of how stress occurs. This will form the basis for the next step, the 'therapeutic contract': that is, the explicit agreement with the individual as to what problems need to be treated. (Harrison & Feltz, 1981, p. 56)

Once the athlete is able to adequately identify how stress is manifested, the removal of these manifestations are the goals of the stress inoculation procedure. These goals ordinarily fall into two categories: the management of excessive physiological arousal and the substitution of positive self-statements for negative ones.

Relaxation training. Various approaches to relaxation training, such as progressive relaxation or autogenic training, are used to help people learn to control physiological arousal. Although these skills are important to the stress inoculation procedure, greater emphasis is placed on cognitive-skills training.

Instructed practice (cognitive-skills training). The goal of cognitive-skills training is to teach a person to replace negative self-statements with positive self-statements throughout the stress reaction. Positive self-statements can be identified for each phase of the stress reaction. Usually four phases are employed in the cognitive-skills training program.

Preparation for the stress situation. In the first phase the goal is to assist the performer in preparing to face a potentially stressful situation by eliminating negative self-statements and shifting attentional focus to the specific task. Typical positive self-statements include "This may be a difficult situation, but I can handle it" and "I know that I can cope with this task."

Stress confrontation. In the confrontation phase, the objective is not the total elimination of arousal or anxiety but instead its use to maximize sport performance (Harrison & Feltz, 1981). Positive self-statements include "Relax and take a deep breath" and "My arousal means that I am ready to perform well."

Coping with a sense of being overwhelmed. Because a feeling of being overwhelmed by a stressful situation is often experienced, performers should be taught to use positive self-statements to deal with this feeling. Examples of such statements include "I have nothing to prove to anyone by myself" and "Think positively, just concentrate on the task at hand."

Once these positive self-statements are identified, usually the sport psychologist or stress inoculation trainer models the self-statements and then the performer rehearses them under the guidance of the trainer. To complete the training in coping with a sense of being overwhelmed, positive self-statements are identified that can be used by the performer as sources of positive self-reinforcement after successfully coping with a stressor.

Application. The final phase of the stress inoculation procedure is the application of the above techniques. The stress inoculation approach uses steps that are graduated according to the amount of stress. Other intervention strategies such as coping-imagery rehearsal, modeling films, behavioral rehearsal, role reversal, and exposure to real stressors may also be introduced (Long, 1981). As a check that the performer is actually attempting to substitute the positive self-statements for the negative ones, it is wise to have the performer recite those statements during the initial attempts at application (Harrison & Feltz, 1981).

Although the stress inoculation procedure relies on several techniques, its primary strategy is to modify or change the internal statements the performer makes when confronted with a stressful situation. According to Meichenbaum (1977), there are several reasons why a change in internal statements or images may have systematic effects on behavior. Positive self-statements can serve as a source of instructions for behavior. They also can direct attention to task-relevant cues. Finally, such self-statements can modify the way in which the performer experiences and explains the manifestations of increased physiological arousal. Recall that the way a person labels or interprets a situation affects whether or not that situation is perceived as threatening. A cognitive appraisal that results in a perception of threat triggers an anxiety response.

Cognitive-Affective Stress Management Training (SMT)

Cognitive-affective stress management training (SMT) was devised by Smith (1980) and is one of the most comprehensive approaches currently available. Its strength lies in the theoretical model of stress underlying its orientation to stress management and in its inclusion of both cognitively based and physiologically based intervention strategies.

Smith's theoretical model of stress is presented in Figure 5-1. Notice how the model focuses on the assumed relationship among cognitions, physiological responses, and behavior. More specifically, the model takes into account aspects of the situation, the person's mental appraisal of that situation, the physiological response, and the actual behavior.

External Situation

The external situation (Figure 5-1) refers to the observable environmental stimuli; it is the actual sport situation the athlete faces.

Mental Appraisal

According to Smith, the mental appraisal process refers ''to subjective judgments about the nature and meaning of the situation and to judgments about one's own ability to cope successfully with it'' (p. 56). This position is reflected in the model shown in Figure 5-1 by the identification of *(A)* the situation and *(B)* the coping ability located

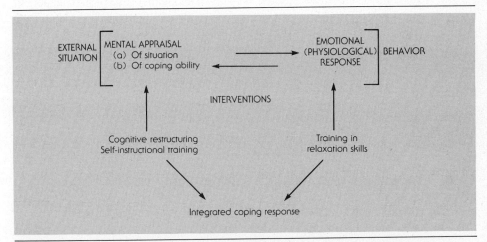

FIGURE 5-1 Mediational model of stress underlying the cognitive-affective stress management program together with major intervention techniques used in development of integrated coping response.

From Smith, R.E. (1980). A cognitive-affective approach to stress management training for athletes. In C.H. Nadeau, W.R. Halliwell, K.M. Newell, & G.C. Roberts (Eds.), *Psychology of motor behavior and sport.* Champaign, IL: Human Kinetics.

under the heading "Mental Appraisal." The athlete's mental appraisal of a situation determines the nature, degree, and content of the emotional responses that follow.

Cognitively based strategies. Most sport situations do not contain objective causes for a stress reaction; it is the athlete's mental appraisals of both the situation and his or her ability to cope with that situation that directly affect the stress response. For this reason, Smith places a great deal of his emphasis on techniques designed to change the self-statements that people make when faced with an ego-threatening situation. Two of these cognitively based techniques are cognitive restructuring and self-instructional training. Both are similar to the stress inoculation procedure designed originally by Meichenbaum (1977). **Cognitive restructuring** attempts to identify and modify irrational self-statements (for example, "I need to succeed at everything" or "I need to be loved by everyone"). Such irrational statements tend to produce high stress reactions because they generate unrealistic and unachievable expectations. **Self-instructional training** differs from other similar techniques in its emphasis on teaching athletes to provide themselves with specific instructions geared to improve attentional focus and problem-solving ability.

Emotional and Physiological Responses

The emotional and physiological responses to a situation are closely linked; the physiological responses to the mental appraisal of a situation greatly affect the content and intensity of the athlete's emotional response. High levels of physiological or autonomic responses tend to cause negative self-statements such as "'Oh, Oh, I'm really getting uptight now' or 'This is horrible, What if I screw up?'" (Smith, 1980, p. 57). Such statements then trigger an anxiety spiral in which negative thoughts increase physiological activation, which in turn causes more negative thoughts.

As we have discussed at some length throughout this chapter, physiologically based intervention strategies, such as relaxation procedures, effectively reduce the stress response. Recall that a state of relaxation is not compatible with a state of high anxiety or stress. Learning to use relaxation strategies can help the athlete combat the debilitating effects of stress. Thus Smith includes training in physiologically based relaxation skills as an intervention technique within the component of emotional (physiological) response.

The combination of cognitively based and physiologically based intervention strategies should result in an "integrated coping response," which should in turn have a positive effect on the athlete's behavior.

Behavior

The athlete's behavior as a result of the interaction of the cognitive appraisal of a situation and the resultant physiological and emotional responses represents the fourth element in Smith's model. Whether social, coping, or motoric, this behavior is affected by the cognitive and physiological responses that precede it.

Besides representing a consensus of the current thinking and research in the field of stress, Smith's model also provides clear implications for the selection and application of appropriate intervention strategies at any of the four component levels. For example, if evaluation apprehension appears to be the primary instigator of a stress reaction, the potential threat can be reduced by decreasing or eliminating the number of observers in the immediate environment. Examples of such a strategy are some youth sports programs that exclude parents from the games to reduce the amount of stress experienced by the young participants.

Administration of the SMT Program

Smith's cognitive-affective SMT program is divided into five phases: (1) pretreatment assessment, (2) treatment rationale, (3) skill acquisition, (4) skill rehearsal, and (5) posttreatment evaluation. The program can be administered on an individual or group basis.

Pretreatment assessment. During this phase, information is gathered through personal interviews and questionnaires. Athletes are also requested to begin self-monitoring procedures such as keeping a notebook to record the frequency and causes of their own stress reactions.

Treatment rationale. The treatment rationale, or educational phase, underlying the SMT program is almost identical to that in stress inoculation; the emphasis is on helping the athlete understand the nature of the stress response. Smith uses the model presented in Figure 5-1 to aid this process. Again, the focus is on having the participants conceptualize the stress response based on an analysis of their own stress reactions and experiences. For example, they might be asked what appears to trigger their stress reaction and what thoughts they experience during anxiety. Participants are then familiarized with the schedule of training sessions.

It is important to emphasize two points during the treatment rationale. First, it is stressed that the program is educational, not psychotherapeutic, in design. Emphasis is placed on the reasons why athletes differ from one another in their ability to cope with stress. Persons who handle stress most effectively are those who have had a combination of previous experiences that have facilitated their ability to cope. The program is designed to provide similar coping skills to others who have not been as fortunate in terms of previous life experiences.

The second point to emphasize is that the program is designed to give athletes *self-control* and that the level of coping ability achieved depends on the amount of effort the athlete gives to the program. This emphasis on attaining self-control is of paramount importance. Ultimately the athlete must come to rely on his or her own coping abilities rather than the trainer or sport psychologist.

Skill acquisition. As shown in Figure 5-1, the major objective of the SMT program is the development of an *integrated coping response* by acquiring both relaxation and cognitive intervention skills. The skill acquisition phase is devoted to teaching the skills associated with muscular relaxation, cognitive restructuring, and self-instructional training described previously.

Skill rehearsal. Stress coping skills are skills like any others: they must be practiced and rehearsed. Smith agrees with Suinn's argument in regard to VMBR that such coping skills should be practiced in real-life settings to be used most effectively. To facilitate this process, various stress-inducing procedures can be used to induce different levels of stress. These include stress-inducing films, imaginal rehearsal of stress-inducing events, and other physical or psychological stressors. In the SMT program a technique called *induced affect* is employed to cause high levels of emotional arousal. Once induced, those arousal responses are reduced through the use of the coping skills previously acquired. Smith (1980) describes the use of induced affect within the SMT protocol as follows:

> In SMT skills rehearsal, the subject is asked to imagine as vividly as possible a stressful situation (for example, getting ready to shoot a free throw in a critical situation). He is then asked to focus on the feeling that the situation has elicited and it is suggested that as he focuses on it, it will begin to grow and to become stronger and stronger. The suggestions

continue as the subject begins to respond to them with increasing emotional arousal, and physical indications of arousal are verbally reinforced and encouraged ('That's good, that's fine. . . . Now just let that feeling grow. . . . It's getting bigger and bigger. . . . Just let it come. . . . It will grow by itself. . . . It's O.K. to let it come, because in a minute you'll see how easily you can turn it off. . . .'). At intervals during the arousal phase, the trainer asks the subject what kinds of thoughts are occurring, and this information is used to elaborate upon the arousal. It also provides information on the nature of the cognitions that accompany (and, it is hypothesized mediate) the arousal. (p. 66)

After achieving a state of induced arousal, the athletes practice their skills for reducing the arousal response. First, only relaxation procedures are employed; then only cognitive coping strategies are used. Finally, the two types of coping techniques are used together to achieve an integrated coping response. These techniques are then tied into the breathing cycle by using both a relaxation response and a positive self-statement:

As the subject inhales, he emits a stress-reducing self-statement. At the peak of inhalation, he says the word 'so' and as he slowly exhales, he instructs himself to 'Relax' and induces muscular relaxation. (p. 66)

At the end of the skill rehearsal phase of the program, the athletes are trained in a meditation procedure similar to that described on p. 119 (Benson, 1975).

At this point, two important issues need to be addressed. First, the orientation of the SMT procedure differs sharply from that of Meichenbaum's stress inoculation in a very specific manner. In Meichenbaum's approach, stress inoculation is achieved by exposing the athlete to gradually increasing amounts of stress and teaching him or her to systematically cope with those increments. In Smith's protocol, the induced affect procedure results in degrees of arousal that are in excess to that experienced in actual encounters with the stressor. Thus the athlete learns to cope with amounts of stress that are greater than that experienced in the real-life threatening situation. As Smith (1980) and others (for example, Ziegler, Klinzing, & Williamson, 1982) have pointed out, at the present time it is not clear which of the two procedures is the most effective.

A second issue is the appropriateness of actually inducing high arousal responses. There are certain ethical questions that can be raised concerning the use of this procedure with athletes. Because of the potential psychological dangers of such a process, it is imperative that only trained clinicians employ such a procedure; the use of such a strategy by an untrained teacher or coach is *highly unacceptable*.

Evaluation. A fundamental part of any stress management training program is evaluation. Ideally, the evaluation process should include pre- and post-treatment comparisons of both cognitive and physiological dependent variables. In addition, performance improvements that occur as a result of participation in the stress management program should be assessed. In terms of the latter, Smith and Smoll (1978) were able to demonstrate performance improvements for high-anxious college football players and an adolescent figure skater who all participated in the SMT program. The figure skater also showed an appreciable decrease on her score on the Sport Competition Anxiety Test (Martens, 1977).

Although the SMT program is new, its comprehensive approach in terms of theoretical rationale, selection of appropriate intervention techniques, and practicality argue for its potential as a successful vehicle for teaching athletes skills to enable them to cope with sport-related stress. It is also important to note that those same coping skills are generalizable to other nonsport situations.

STRESS AND THE UNIFYING MODEL

By this point you should have a fairly clear conception of the multifaceted nature of a stress reaction as it occurs in sport situations. However, the unifying model depicted in Figure 5-2 can help you more fully understand how that process operates. An understanding of how the stress process operates provides the coach, athlete, or sport psychologist with a sound foundation for selecting and using appropriate intervention strategies.

Input

It is important to remember that it is the athlete's thoughts and feelings about the situation, not the external situation itself, that causes a stress reaction. Thus input stimuli can come not only from the external situation but also from the athlete's own cognitions. Because people tend to worry and anticipate threat or failure before it actually occurs, the stress reaction can begin before the performer is physically present in the sport situation.

Intervening at the input level involves either modifying the sport situation or changing the athlete's precompetitive thoughts, images, or self-statements. Two ways of modifying the sport situation are to (1) reduce the evaluation potential present in the setting and (2)

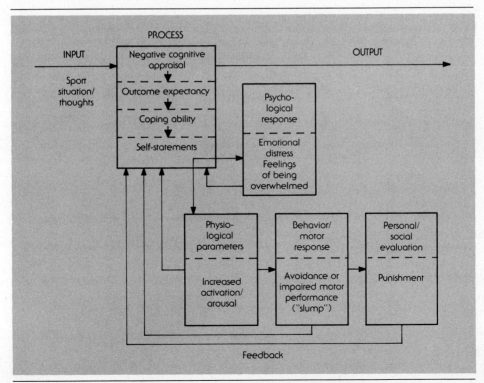

FIGURE 5-2 Stress and the unifying model.

enhance the athlete's sport skills. Several intervention techniques can be used to change the person's precompetitive tendencies to generate a stress response. Imaginal rehearsal, as described in our discussion of visuomotor behavior rehearsal (see p. 124), can be effective, as can a regimen that focuses on coping with stress in a graduated manner, such as the stress inoculation procedure. A systematic attempt to substitute positive, task-related thoughts for negative thoughts can also be effective in combating precompetitive stress responses.

Process

The cognitive appraisal process consists of two dimensions: (1) evaluation of the sport situation, which results in (2) judgement as to the response needed to produce a successful outcome. Based on that information, the athlete also assesses his or her ability to cope with that situation in terms of a subjective estimate of the probability of success or failure. If a negative estimation of coping ability results from this evaluation, a stress reaction is almost sure to follow. This will often result in negative self-statements that will foster allied emotional or physiological effects. Intervention at the cognitive level most often involves a program designed to change those negative self-statements. Examples of such strategies are cognitive restructuring, self-instructional training, and cognitive-skills training.

It is important to emphasize that the stress process must be examined in terms of the interrelationship of all the elements presented in the unifying model. There are definite interactions between input, cognitive appraisal, output, and feedback. For this reason, most stress management programs incorporate strategies designed to intervene at more than one point in the model. This multifaceted conceptualization of the stress process is best exemplified by Smith's cognitive-affective stress management program, the objective of which is the development of an integrated coping response. Within the framework of the unifying model (Figure 5-2), this same orientation is reflected by the arrows that connect all of the various elements. Therefore, although we discuss output variables separately, keep in mind the interrelationships that exist among the elements. Remember also that the most effective approach to intervening within the stress cycle is to incorporate techniques designed to intercede at several levels.

Output

At the psychological or emotional level, a negative cognitive appraisal generally results in feelings of emotional distress. These feelings are a direct result of the athlete's perception of a situation and his or her response to the evaluation of that situation. One technique to modify those feelings is to change the nature of the self-statements. For example, instead of saying "I'm all upset, my heart is racing, I'm going to fail," the athlete can substitute a more positive statement such as "My heart rate tells me that I am ready, I'm really psyched-up."

Harrison and Feltz (1981) also point out that often athletes respond to stress with feelings of being overwhelmed (see p. 137). One way to change this perception is to break the response sequence into separate phases such as the recognition of the manifestations of increased physiological activation, the monitoring of negative or ineffective cognitions, and the thought of being overwhelmed by the situation. Positive self-statements can then be instituted to cope with the responses at each of the three levels identified.

Unsuccessful sport behaviors or ineffective motor responses resulting from stress reactions are most easily understood in terms of cognitive or attentional disruptions and increased physiological activation. Monitoring stimuli such as negative self-statements and increased physiological activation impairs concentration on task-relevant variables. Physiological changes such as increased muscular tension can also impair the ability to effectively execute sport skills. Because it is not always possible to determine accurately exactly what is causing the performance disruption, athletes should be taught coping skills designed to intervene at both the cognitive and physiological levels.

When a stress reaction causes a poor or unsuccessful motor response, the evaluations of that response by the athlete, spectators, and coach are often negative. Such negative evaluations increase the threat potential on future occasions. Thus as the stress spiral increases the likelihood of future failure also increases. The only way to break that spiral is to intervene at one or more levels of the process.

Feedback

All intervention strategies are based on the idea that if the content of the information fed back to the brain can be changed, then the cognitive evaluation of the stimulus conditions can be modified. For example, athletes tend to perceive increases in physiological activation as a signal that they are under stress. This perception then triggers allied cognitive and emotional reactions. By intervening at the physiological level through techniques such as relaxation or biofeedback, physiological activation can be decreased. Such decreases feed back the information that the person is calm rather than stressed. Similarly, the information contained in the statement "I'm scared" feeds back an entirely different message than the statement "I'm psyched-up." Therefore many intervention techniques focus on changing the way athletes talk to themselves or label their thoughts.

IMPLICATIONS FOR SPORT

- A coach must be able to identify accurately athletes who need help to control competitive stress. This can be accomplished through behavior observation, counseling sessions, and standardized tests.
- If athletes have a better understanding of the stress spiral as it operates within themselves, at least two benefits may be realized. The athletes may be better able to "tune in" to themselves and recognize anxiety symptoms. They should also become more receptive to entering an intervention program. This may be even more important for male athletes, who are generally more resistant to trying intervention techniques.
- One way to increase athletes' awareness of the stress spiral is through team discussions in which the athletes explore the causes and effects of elevated anxiety. Such discussions may be as important as physical practice.
- A coach can help players cope more effectively with competitive stress by making practices as gamelike as possible, by explaining that new and difficult skills may be stress-inducing, and by behaving as a nonstressful model.

- When teaching intervention strategies to a team, provide them with practice at a number of different techniques. Each athlete is unique; some strategies may work for one person, whereas different techniques are more effective for others.
- Once athletes have learned to use intervention techniques under the guidance of a coach or sport psychologist, let them use them on their own. The athletes need to learn how to gain their own self-control.
- After practicing intervention techniques, evaluate the practice session. As the athletes become more proficient at using those strategies, discuss how and if they are affecting sport performance.
- Know when to refer athletes to trained professionals. Frequently, highly stressed athletes have other nonsport related problems that require the help of a psychologist or guidance counselor. If you have any doubt, refer the student. Do not attempt to play amateur psychologist; you could do more harm than good.

CASE STUDY 1

A Stress Management Training Program for a College Football Team

Smith (1980) has developed a six-session stress management training program that has been used with college football players (see box on the facing page). It is based on the rationale and procedures associated with his cognitive-affective stress management training program. Although originally designed as an intervention procedure for football players, it can be used with other sport groups. Several different techniques have been incorporated into the sessions. The following is a brief commentary on each of these techniques.

Program Implementation

We suggest that the induced affect procedures described in Sessions 3 and 4 be used only moderately or be eliminated completely if the program is not conducted by a psychologist or a *trained* sport psychologist.

Relaxation Training

Suinn's (1980) relaxation procedure is presented on p. 140. It would be helpful to either read the steps aloud or record them so that the athletes can more easily concentrate their attention on the steps of the procedure. It is important that the athlete remain relaxed throughout the imagery session.

Coping Imagery

The skills needed for imaginal rehearsal can be introduced through the 13 steps described on p. 123 (Hickman, 1979). Once the athletes are able to use imaginal rehearsal effectively, then the following steps can be used to help them develop the ability to use a coping imagery strategy.

1. Construct a step-by-step hierarchy that traces the development of your competitive anxiety reaction. Follow its development from its beginnings until you were actually faced with the same situation.
2. Assume a first-person, or internal, focus.

Schedule of Sessions for the Group Version of the Cognitive-Affective Stress Management Training Program

---

SESSION 1

Orientation and relaxation training. The nature of emotion and stress is discussed as is the nature of coping with stress. Training is begun in deep muscular relaxation, which serves as a physical coping response.

SESSION 2

Continuation of relaxation training and discussion of the role of mental processes in coping with stress.

SESSION 3

Practice in the use of relaxation to control emotional responses induced during the session through imagining of stressful athletic situations. Development of cognitive coping responses.

SESSION 4

Practice in using relaxation and stress-reducing mental statements to control emotional reactions induced through imagination.

SESSION 5

Continued practice in use of coping mechanisms with emphasis on development of the end product of the program; the "integrated coping response."

SESSION 6

Training in the use of a meditation technique having stress-reducing properties.

From Smith, R.E. (1980). A cognitive-affective approach to stress management training for athletes. In C.H. Nadeau, W.R. Halliwell, K.M. Newell, & G.C. Roberts (Eds.), *Psychology of motor behavior and sport.* Champaign, IL: Human Kinetics.

3. Imagine exactly how you felt at each step when you experienced competitive anxiety.
   a. Notice the sensations coming from various parts of your body. Feel them.
   b. Tune into important cues in the environment. See and hear them.
   c. Get close to your feelings. Be aware of how you felt emotionally when you experienced competitive anxiety.
4. Practice making your images vivid.
5. Practice controlling your images so that you can imagine yourself coping with stress at each point in your hierarchy.
6. At the end of the imagery session evaluate your success and plan what you should do for the next session.

Meditation

For the meditation technique contained in Session 6, Benson's (1975) meditational relaxation program (p. 119) can be used.

Positive Self-Statements

Examples of positive self-statements that can be used for developing cognitive coping responses can be found within our discussion of stress inoculation (p. 125) and cognitive-affective stress management training (p. 127).

CASE STUDY 2
Stress Inoculation for a High School Basketball Player*

Player X was the star center for the basketball team of a varsity squad for 2 years and was regularly expected to be the high point scorer for his team.

Midway through his second season, he contracted a viral infection which eliminated him from one game. He returned for the next game, perhaps prematurely, and performed far below his usual level of competence during most of the game. With less than 20 seconds left to play and the score tied, he attempted a difficult shot, even though several fellow players were in a better position. He missed and the ball was recovered by a member of the rival team who then scored the winning shot.

After the game, Player X was harshly criticized by the team coach for his error. He also felt the annoyance of other team members who resented his behavior. Even the school newspaper ran an article the next day which noted that his behavior had probably lost the game.

Player X was still not completely recovered from his illness and now his confidence had been badly shaken by this experience. His performance continued to suffer over the next several games. He began to hand off relatively easy shots to other players and he had a tendency to 'choke' when shooting foul shots.

His coach, realizing that he had returned his player to competition too soon, withdrew him from the next two games. Player X only attributed this to the coach's increased lack of confidence in him and saw it as another instance of rejection and failure. His performance had not improved when he returned to the team and the coach was ready to attribute the sudden decrement in his player's performance to one of those inexplicable 'slumps' which players encounter.

Application of Stress-Inoculation Training to Player X

The coach asked a counselor qualified to handle stress-related problems in athletes, to work with Player X. The counselor determined that the player was experiencing strong anxiety during each game. He was expecting that he would perform poorly and this became a self-fulfilling prophecy. The counselor explained this to the player and gave him concrete examples of how he was inhibiting his own performance. They then agreed to work on the player's anxiety through the technique of stress inoculation.

The educational phase was completed by the counselor explaining to the player how the stress response occurred. In this instance, the act of competing brought about increased physiological arousal. Whereas Player X had previously interpreted his rapid heartbeat and sweating palms as signals that he was 'up' for the game, now he interpreted them as signals of fear that he was going to perform poorly. Careful inquiry by the counselor found that he was making self-statements like, 'I'm going to fail again.' 'If I keep passing the ball, they can't accuse me of not being a team player,' or 'If I stay away from the basket, I won't have to decide about making any difficult shots.'

---

*From Harrison, R.P., & Feltz, D.L. (1981). Stress inoculation for athletes: Description and case example. *Motor Skills: Theory into Practice, 5*,53-61.

The rehearsal phase consisted of teaching the player new physical methods for coping such as deep muscle relaxation procedure. He also learned to replace his defeatist cognitions with new, more adaptive ones. These were learned as part of a 4-point process:

1. Preparing for stress—'Just keep your mind on the game'; 'All I can do is the best I know how. If that's not enough, then tough.'

2. Coping with stress—'Just take each shot one at a time; don't worry about past shots or plays.'; 'O.K. I'm nervous, but that's all right. I can use the nervous energy to perform better.'

3. Coping with being overwhelmed—'The counselor told me this might happen. She said to just do the best I can.'; 'What's the worst thing that can happen? After all, it's only a game.'

4. Reinforcement—'Well, I did it. I'm at least getting better control of my thinking and that's the first step toward improving my game.'; 'Every time I use these procedures I'll get a little better.'

In the application phase the counselor gradually exposed the player to increasingly stressful situations and made sure that he was using the procedures adequately. First, she had the player imagine various scenes of failure and asked the player to use the coping procedures he had learned. After some initial success at this, she took the player to a nearby basketball court to scrimmage with some of his teammates. While they played, the counselor and several confederates played the role of disgruntled fans. At every opportunity they booed the player loudly and verbally attempted to disrupt his performance. Afterwards, the counselor checked with the player to make sure he was able to use the coping procedures. She also asked him to make a mental list of self-statements which he found most effective.

When they both thought that he was ready to return to active competition, the counselor consulted the coach and he agreed to let Player X start in the next game. The player's performance was again below previous levels, but he reported after the game that he felt the anxiety had been more manageable. In particular he reported that relabeling the anxiety as energy was an effective way of keeping it under control.

During the next several games, Player X began to improve slightly. By the end of the season he had returned to his previous level of performance. A 6-month follow-up by the counselor revealed that the player had also been using coping procedures in other ways as well. He reported that he found it useful to prepare for important exams this way and that he thought his work in several subjects had improved as a result. Whereas before he had dreaded studying for tests, he used the positive self-statements he had learned and he found himself getting an early start on studying. Also, during the test, he was much less likely to panic if he did not know the immediate solution to a problem.

SUMMARY

- The major purpose of stress management programs is to provide athletes with coping skills that can be used in the alleviation and control of stress-related problems. However, after athletes have acquired those skills they can be used in other nonsport, stress-related situations such as preparation for examinations and public speaking.
- Control of the physiological manifestations of a stress response is ordinarily gained by using various relaxation procedures such as progressive relaxation, autogenic training, hypnosis, or transcendental meditation, all of which help induce a relaxation response.

- The relaxation response produces physiological changes that are in opposition to those which accompany the fight or flight reaction. The elements needed to produce the relaxation response are a mental device, a passive attitude, a decrease in muscle tension, and a quiet environment.
- Biofeedback is an effective procedure for the allievation of increased physiological activation. Biofeedback provides the athlete with visual or auditory feedback concerning his or her physiological responses to stress.
- Imaginal rehearsal can take the form of either mastery imagery or coping imagery. Mastery imagery provides a means by which the athlete can increase sport success by mentally rehearsing a sport skill in a real-life context; coping imagery involves mentally practicing stress-related behaviors or responses. Regardless of the form of the imaginal rehearsal, to become proficient in using such a covert process, those mental skills must be practiced.
- The visuomotor behavior rehearsal program includes three fundamental steps: relaxation, imaginal practice, and imagery to strengthen motor or psychological skills. After achieving the ability to relax, emphasis is placed on teaching athletes how to control the content of imagery until a carbon copy of a real-life occurrence can be consciously generated.
- In stress inoculation, athletes are taught to cope with stress in ever-increasing amounts to immunize them to stress. It also includes the use of positive self-statements as substitutes for stress-producing negative self-statements. The stress inoculation program generally involves five steps: appraisal of the problem, stress education, relaxation training, instructed practice or cognitive-skills training, and actual practice.
- A comprehensive and theoretically based intervention program is cognitive-affective stress management training, or SMT. The model considers aspects of the situation and the person's cognitive appraisal of that situation in terms of both the situation itself and the athlete's perceived ability to cope with the situation. The cognitive-affective SMT program includes five phases: pretreatment assessment, treatment rationale or education, skill acquisition, skill rehearsal, and post-treatment evaluation. The major objective of the program is to teach the athlete how to achieve an integrated coping response. Specific intervention techniques included within the cognitive-affective SMT protocol include muscular relaxation training, cognitive restructuring, self-instructional training, induced affect, and meditation.
- The unifying model emphasizes the idea that the stress process must be viewed in terms of the interrelationships and interactions that take place among the elements of input, process (cognitive appraisal), output, and feedback.
- Because of the multifaceted nature of the stress process, stress management programs such as cognitive-affective SMT, visuomotor behavior rehearsal, and stress inoculation all provide coping skills that can be used to intervene within the stress cycle at more than one level.
- Because athletes differ in both the manner in which they manifest stress reactions (i.e., cognitive versus physiological) and their ability to cope with stress responses, it is important they be taught several techniques for reducing stress. Once they have acquired multiple coping skills, they can select the ones that work most effectively for them.

DISCUSSION QUESTIONS

1 Identify the differences in the activation of several physiological parameters during the fight or flight response as compared with the relaxation response.
2 Identify the elements needed to induce the relaxation response.
3 Distinguish between *mastery* imaginal rehearsal and *coping* imaginal practice.
4 What is the major difference between the stress inoculation procedure and the cognitive-affective stress management training program in terms of teaching athletes how to cope with stress?
5 Discuss the rationale underlying the integrated coping response.
6 From what you know about the attentional process, discuss how it relates to applying both physiologically based and cognitively based intervention techniques.

GLOSSARY

autogenic training   Techniques involving the use of verbal cues and visual images to achieve a relaxed state
cognitive restructuring   Process of identifying and changing irrational self-statements
coping imagery   Use of systematic desensitization procedures during imaginal rehearsal for the purpose of managing stress
lifetime stress   Stress that is experienced as a result of hassles and problems encountered in daily life
mastery imagery   Use of imaginal rehearsal specifically for improving skill execution
modified progressive relaxation training   Abbreviated version of Jacobson's original progressive relaxation program
self-fulfilling prophecy   Process whereby a person acts out in reality the expectancies held in cognition
self-instructional training   Teaching athletes the use of specific covert instructions designed to enhance attentional control and problem-solving ability
stress inoculation   Process of gradually exposing persons to increasing amounts of stress to build an immunity to stress
tonus   Degree of muscle tension or tone

SUGGESTED READINGS

Borkovec, T.D. (1981). Stress management in athletics: An overview of cognitive and physiological techniques. *Motor Skills: Theory into Practice, 5,* 45-52.
    This article presents an overview of several cognitive and physiological strategies designed to help athletes cope with competitive stress. It proposes a rationale that suggests that persons respond to stress in an idiosyncratic fashion; therefore intervention techniques should be selected from the three categories of cognitive, behavioral, and physiological strategies.

DeWitt, D.J. (1980). Cognitive and biofeedback training for stress reduction with athletes. *Journal of Sport Psychology, 2,* 288-294.
    Two investigations were conducted to study whether a training program that combined cognitive training and biofeedback could assist athletes in reducing stress reactions on competitive settings and could improve competitive performance.

Hall, E.G., & Erffmeyer, E.S. (1983). The effect of visuo-motor behavior rehearsal with videotaped modeling on free throw accuracy of intercollegiate female basketball players. *Journal of Sport Psychology, 5*, 343-346.

The authors studied the effectiveness of VMBR on highly skilled basketball players. Subjects trained in the techniques of VMBR improved in the free throw accuracy and reported feeling kinesthetic sensations in association with visual imagery.

Kirschenbaum, D.S., & Wittrock, D.A. (1984). Cognitive-behavioral interventions in sport: A self-regulatory perspective. In J.M. Silva & R.S. Weinberg (Eds.), *Psychological foundations of sport*. Champaign, IL: Human Kinetics.

In this section, focus is placed on the aspects of thinking and feeling that can be changed to improve sport performance. A model of self-regulation is presented, and a review of major approaches to cognitive-behavioral intervention techniques follows.

Smith, R.E. (1984). Theoretical and treatment approaches to anxiety reduction. In J.M. Silva & R.S. Weinberg (Eds.), *Psychological foundations of sport*. Champaign, IL: Human Kinetics.

Four models for anxiety reduction are discussed. Within the presentation of each model the treatment techniques that they have inspired are identified. Particular emphasis is placed on the potential effectiveness of the coping skills model.

Muscle Relaxation Exercise

Muscle relaxation is sought by coaches and athletes since coordination and sustained performance are hindered by muscle tenseness. Relaxation is desirable in non-physical activities, e.g., mental concentration, since it aids in avoiding distractions to such effort, thus the technique has been used by executives as well.

The directions in the next section are used in a relaxation exercise. As with all physical exercises, the end product is the control by the athlete of muscle groups. In this case the end product is the ability to relax completely within a short time span. With three or four practice sessions, many persons are able to achieve muscle relaxation within 5 minutes. At this point the muscle tension component of the directions can be omitted.

RELAXATION DIRECTIONS

The primary purpose of the procedure is to aid in focusing attention on how it feels to have muscles truly tense and, in contrast, how it feels to be relaxed (or not tense). In each step you will be asked first to tense a muscle group, then to relax. Always pay close attention to the feeling within the muscles. Tense each muscle group only as long as is required for you to attend to the tension generated. For most, this takes about 5 seconds or a count of 5. Relaxation of the muscle groups take about the same amount of time. These times are approximate—do not distract yourself by paying too much attention to counting or timing. Tense the muscles until you can really feel the tension, and then relax.

This set of directions was developed by Richard M. Suinn, Ph.D., Sports Medicine Team, for use by Nordic coaching staff and athletes. Duplication or other use is possible only through direct release from Dr. Suinn, Professor and Head, Dept. of Psychology, Colorado State University, Fort Collins, Colorado 80523.
From Suinn, R.M. (1980). *Psychology in sports: Methods and applications.* Minneapolis, MN; Burgess.

Weinberg, R.S., Seabourne, T.G., & Jackson, A. (1981). Effects of visuo-motor behavior rehearsal, relaxation, and imagery on karate performance. *Journal of Sport Psychology, 3,* 228-238.

   The study attempted to ascertain if imagery combined with relaxation (VMBR) was more effective in improving karate performance as compared with either imagery or relaxation alone. After breaking performance into three subcomponents: skill, combinations, and sparring, a significant difference was shown for sparring.

Wenz, B.J., & Strong, D.J. (1980). An application of biofeedback and self-regulation procedures with superior athletes: The fine tuning effect. In R.M. Suinn (Ed.), *Psychology in sports.* Minneapolis, MN: Burgess.

   This study reviews a multifaceted stress management program. Techniques discussed are those of relaxation training, autogenic phrases, visualization, and biofeedback.

Ziegler, S.G., Klinzing, J., & Williamson, K. (1982). The effects of two stress management training programs on cardiorespiratory efficiency. *Journal of Sport Psychology, 4,* 280-289.

   The relative effects of stress inoculation training and stress management training on cardiorespiratory efficiency were assessed. The major finding was differential effects for oxygen consumption.

The exercise follows a systematic pattern: right hand (or dominant hand), left hand, right bicep, left bicep, forehead, eyes, facial area, chest, abdomen, and both legs and feet. At the start, repeat the exercise for each group twice before going to the next group. Later, omit the tension and the repetition. After completing each muscle group, permit the area to remain relaxed by not moving that area. As a start, someone should read the directions to you.

Hands. First get into a comfortable position, preferably lying down on your back. You may use a small pillow for your head. Choose a time of day when you will not be disturbed for an hour. Many practice in the evening just before falling asleep. The relaxation achieved is an especially good way of going to sleep at night.

Close your eyes so as not to be distracted by your surroundings. Now, tense your right hand into a fist . . . *as tight as you can get it* . . . so that you can feel the tension . . . really tight, the tighter the better, so that you can really feel the tension. . . . Now relax the hand, let the tension remove itself . . . feel the muscles become loose . . . and notice the contrast between the tension a moment ago and the relaxation, the absence of tension. . . . Allowing the fingers to relax . . . and then the entire right hand.

Repeat the exercise for the right hand once.

Continued.

Muscle Relaxation Exercise—cont'd

Now we'll leave the right hand relaxed and focus on the left hand. Tense the left hand by making it into a fist . . . very tight . . . and again notice how that tension feels. . . focus your attention on the muscles as they are tense. . . . All right, now relax the hand, and notice the contrast between the tension of a moment ago and the relaxation. . . . Continue to be aware of the relaxation of the muscles . . . in the fingers . . . and throughout the entire hand.

Repeat the exercise for the left hand once.

Arms (Biceps). We'll leave the hands and the fingers relaxed and move to the biceps. In order to tense the biceps, you will be bending the arm at the elbow and tightening the biceps by moving your hand towards your shoulder. Let's start with the right arm.

Bend your right arm at the elbow so that your hand moves toward your shoulder . . . tight. . . . Keep tightening the biceps as hard as you can . . . focusing your attention on the muscle tension. . . . Really notice how that feels. . . . Now relax . . . letting the arm and hand drop back down . . . and noticing the relaxation, the absence of tension. . . . Feel the relaxation as it takes over the upper arm. . . . Notice the feeling of relaxation in the lower arm, the hand, and the fingers.

Repeat the exercise for the right arm once.

Now leave the right arm relaxed and move to the left arm. Tense up the left arm by bending it at the elbow . . . really tense, as tense as you can get it . . . and focus your attention on the feelings of tension. . . . Now relax, letting your arm drop back down. . . . Notice the difference in feeling between the tension and the relaxation. . . . Permit the relaxation to take over the entire left arm . . . the upper arm . . . the forearm . . . the hands . . . and fingers.

Repeat the exercise for the left arm once.

Forehead. We'll leave the hand and the arms comfortably relaxed and move to the forehead. In order to tense up the forehead, you will frown.

All right, I want you to tense the forehead by frowning. . . . Wrinkle up the forehead area . . . very tight . . . and notice how the tension feels. . . . Now relax. . . . Let the wrinkles smooth themselves out. . . . Allow the relaxation to proceed on its own . . . making the forehead smooth and tension-free as though you were passing your hand over a sheet to smooth it out.

Repeat the exercise for the forehead once.

Eyes. We'll leave the forehead relaxed and move to the eyes. What I want you to do is close your eyes tighter than they are . . . tighter . . . feeling the tension. . . . (Use less time for tension here so as to avoid after-images.) . . . Now relax . . . keeping the eyes comfortably closed . . . noticing the contrast between the tension and the relaxation now.

Repeat the exercise for the eyes once.

Facial Area. We'll leave the eyes relaxed and go on to the facial area. To tense up the facial area, I want you to clench your jaws. . . . Bite down on your teeth hard now. . . . Really pay attention to the tension in the facial area and jaws. . . . (Use less time for tension here.) . . . Now relax. . . . Let the muscles of the jaws become relaxed. . . . Notice the feeling of relaxation across the lips, the jaws, the entire facial area. . . . Just allow the relaxation to take over.

Repeat the exercise for the facial area once.

All right, notice the relaxation in the right hand and the fingers . . . and the feeling of relaxation in the forearm and the upper arms. . . . Notice the relaxation that is present in the left hand and the fingers . . . in the forearm and the upper arm. . . . Let the relaxation take over and include the forehead . . . smooth and without tension . . . the eyes . . . the facial area . . . and the lips and the jaws.

Chest. All right, we'll now proceed to help the relaxation across the chest. I want you to tense up the chest muscles by taking a deep breath and holding it for a moment. . . . Notice the tension. . . . Now slowly exhale, breathing normally again . . . and notice the chest muscles as they become more and more relaxed.

Repeat the exercise for the chest once.

Abdomen. Now we'll move to the stomach. I want you to tense your stomach right now . . . very tight. . . . Pay attention to the tension. . . . Now relax . . . letting the feeling of relaxation take over. . . . Notice the difference in the feeling of tension a moment before and the relaxation.

Repeat the exercise for the abdomen once.

Legs and Feet. Now we'll proceed with the relaxation. To tense your legs and feet, I want you to point your toes downward until you can feel the muscles of your leg tense. . . . Notice the tension. . . . (Use tension for about 3 seconds; avoid cramping of the toes or feet.) . . . Now relax. . . . Let the relaxation take over. . . . Feel the comfort.

Repeat the exercise for the legs and the feet once.

All right, simply enjoy the sense of relaxation and comfort across your body . . . feeling loose and relaxed in the hands and fingers . . . comfortable in the forearms and upper arms . . . noticing the relaxed feeling as it includes the forehead . . . the eyes . . . the facial area . . . the lips and the jaws . . . letting the relaxation include the chest . . . the abdomen . . . and both legs and both feet.

Now, to further increase the relaxation, I want you to take a deep breath and slowly exhale . . . using your rhythmical deep breathing to deepen the relaxation and to permit you to become as relaxed as you want . . . breathing slowly in and out . . . using your rhythm to achieve whatever level of relaxation you want . . . and in the future you can use this deep breathing technique to initiate or to deepen the relaxation whenever you want.

All right, that's fine. . . . Now let your breathing continue normally.

Termination of Exercise. In a moment, I'll count backward from 3 to 1. When I get to 1, you'll feel alert and refreshed . . . no aches or pains. . . . You can retain the relaxed feeling as long as you wish. . . . All right, 3 . . . more and more alert . . . 2 . . . no aches or pains . . . and 1 . . . you can open your eyes.

Continued.

Muscle Relaxation Exercise—cont'd

GENERAL INSTRUCTIONS

1. If the relaxation exercise is being used for the first time, I recommend that someone reads the instructions aloud for another to follow.
2. Whoever reads the instructions should do so in a normal voice, pacing the speed by doing the tension exercises. The aim is to tense the muscle group long enough to be noticeable but not long enough to be painful, to lead to cramps, or to lead to fatigue.
3. Some muscle groups, e.g., the eyes, the jaws, and the feet, should be tensed for a shorter span, about 3 seconds, to avoid painful or cramping results.
4. Once an athlete has used the exercise once upon the direction of someone else (as indicated above), he or she can practice the exercise alone by simply tensing and relaxing each muscle group in sequence.
5. After three or four practice sessions, one can omit the tension part and concentrate on simply having each muscle group become relaxed or limp, again in sequence. With training, a person can develop the relaxation within 5 minutes; with more practice, individuals have been able to initiate relaxation control within 1 minute. Such individuals are able to use the relaxation sitting in chairs or riding in vehicles and can practice it prior to contests. Control in relaxing specific muscle groups is possible with repetition.
6. Repetition of the deep breath technique can be a useful signal for initiation of relaxation on a quick reflex basis.
7. Although the relaxation exercise can be used for other forms of training, the directions here are aimed at teaching an individual how to control muscle groups to achieve *relaxation*. As with any other physical exercise, the success of the exercise requires practice and adherence to the exercise steps. Once a day, five out of every seven days, is a normal routine. More frequent use, such as once daily, speeds up training.
8. For those who wish to speed up the training and who are at training camps with USSA Nordic coaching staff, tape recordings can be made available upon prior arrangement. Contact your coach.

III

COGNITIVE PROCESSES AND SPORT BEHAVIOR

6

ATTENTION, ATTENTIONAL STYLE, AND SPORT BEHAVIOR

Through their training and experience, most coaches and physical education teachers are very effective in analyzing skills in terms of performance errors. Until recently, however, little was known about mental errors. This chapter focuses on attention and how that process relates to the causes and prevention of mental errors.

When we are awake we are bombarded with potential sensory inputs. However, we are certainly not aware of all of them and therefore do not attend to most of them. For instance, you are not generally aware of the pressure that wearing shoes generates. Of course, if your tennis shoes do not fit correctly or your golf shoes rub your heel, then you will concentrate on those sensations. Try this exercise. Pause for a moment and concentrate all your attention on the sensations generated by your shoes. At the same time try to add the numbers 8, 6, 3, and 11. Can you do it? Probably not. One task probably interfered with the other. One characteristic of the attentional process is that often when attention is divided between two tasks, interference in the performance of one of those tasks occurs. Furthermore, attention is somewhat limited. You cannot simultaneously attend to a large number of stimuli; instead you attend selectively to particular sensory inputs. If you selectively attend to a task-relevant cue, then your performance should be enhanced. If you selectively attend to a task-irrelevant cue, then performance should be hindered.

Other factors that can influence the effectiveness of attentional focus are skill level, level of anxiety or alertness, and characteristic manner of attending to the environment. The latter is called **attentional style.** Attentional style is viewed as an individual difference variable. For instance, some persons generally attend to stimuli in a very broad and external manner, whereas others tend to be narrow in attentional scope and introspective. Thus persons with different attentional styles process different cues.

A BRIEF OVERVIEW OF ATTENTIONAL CONSTRAINTS

Ordinarily a book on sport psychology does not discuss attention as a process, or mechanism. Instead, it addresses only the role that the personality variable of attentional style plays in sport performance. We will also explore that question later in the chapter. First, however, it is important for you to have some understanding of the concept of attention.

Limitedness and Interference

Attention should be viewed as a limited resource. Anderson (1980) provides us with an interesting analogy for the **attentional mechanism.** Think of attention as analogous to a fixed electrical current; as with electrical current, only so much attention can be allocated to a number of different tasks. If you attempt to overallocate, what happens? A fuse is blown, or in sport terms, performance deteriorates.

Attention is limited in the sense that a person can attend to a limited number of stimuli simultaneously. If a person tries to attend to too many stimuli at the same time, then interference occurs and performance on at least one of the two tasks decreases. The more difficult a task is, the more attention it requires; therefore if you are asked to perform two tasks at the same time, then the more difficult the one task, the greater should be the deterioration of your performance on the other task. Such performance decrements are generally caused by what is termed **capacity interference.**

Capacity Interference

Capacity interference occurs when two tasks simultaneously compete for use of the attentional mechanism. If the competitive demand exceeds the limited capacity of the attentional mechanism, then performance will decrease on one of the two tasks. In laboratory experiments this performance decrement can be measured, and its amount indicates the attentional demand of the first task.

Structural Interference

Sometimes interference occurs because a person tries to perform two tasks at the same time and both tasks require the use of a common receptor system (such as the ears) or effector system (such as the hands). In this case, interference is caused by the competition for the use of the identical input and output systems (Schmidt, 1982), and is not solely caused by the attentional demands of the task. A common example of **structural interference** is the childrens' trick of rubbing their tummies while simultaneously tapping their heads. Both require the simultaneous use of the hands at two different tasks, and that is what causes the task interference, not the attentional demands of the two tasks. When first attempting such a dual task performance, most children switch their attention to one of the two tasks; whichever task they focus on they do well but performance on the second task falters. Such attentional switching can also be called **selective attention.**

Selective Attention

Selective attention is the process of switching attentional focus to one set of cues while ignoring others. Think about a football quarterback in a third down and long yardage situation. As soon as he has dropped back, set up, and is ready to pass, would it be wise for him to focus attention on all the possible cues available on the field? He better not, if he wants to complete the pass successfully. He must selectively attend to the location and running patterns of his recievers and block out all other environmental cues.

Selective attention is important for success in sport situations. Often, players under pressure selectively attend to the wrong cues; the result is almost always failure. One way a coach can help such a player is to identify the exact cues to which the athlete should attend. This is called cue-reduction feedback (see pp. 72-73). Also, when teaching sport skills, it may be wise to tell the learner exactly what cue attention should be focused on during practice. For most skills visual cues are more important early in learning, whereas kinesthetic cues are more important as skill develops (Fleishman & Rich, 1963). Skill level also relates to attention in other ways.

ATTENTION AND SKILL LEVEL

Recall that attentional capacity is said to be limited. Therefore if two tasks simultaneously compete against one another, then some division of total capacity takes place. One factor that can modify the total capacity demand of a particular task is how much that task has been practiced or how skilled the performer is.

As we explained earlier in the text, Fitts and Posner (1967) classified the stages of skill learning into three phases: *cognitive, associative,* and *autonomous* (see p. 66). During the *cognitive* stage much internal verbalization occurs. For instance, in executing a tennis forehand stroke, the performer might be reminding herself to get an early preparation, to step into the ball, and to follow through. These verbal self-instructions require large amounts of attention. With sufficient practice, the learner moves into the *associative* stage. Errors are reduced and the skill execution takes on a smoother appearance. With continued and frequent practice the *autonomous* stage is reached, in which there is little or no need for internal verbalizations or self-instructions concerning the skill execution. Such highly practiced skills require little attention; thus they do not interfere very much with other skills.

Because continued practice of a skill can lead to its automatization and because attentional demand is then negligible, attentional focus can now be placed on factors other than skill development. Concentration can now be allocated to aspects of game strategy. The most helpful coaching cues at very high levels of player skill are those geared toward playing strategy rather than the motor response.

One way to disrupt the playing performance of highly skilled performers is to direct their attention to aspects of the motor response. This strategy is sometimes called *psyching-out.* By saying to a highly skilled tennis opponent something such as "Whatever you are doing differently on your volley today is sure making a big difference" or indicating to a 220-handicap bowler that "I never noticed you did that movement with your nonball arm before" you can disrupt their skill execution because they then switch attention back to subcomponents of the skill execution. Instead of strategizing about where to hit or locate the ball, attention has been shifted off the strategy and onto some aspect of the motor performance. What was automatic is now being thought about and performance decrements take place.

ATTENTIONAL STYLE AS AN INDIVIDUAL DIFFERENCE VARIABLE

Attentional style differs from one person to another. To date the most useful research on the role of attentional style in sport has been based on the theoretical framework and measurement instrument devised by Robert M. Nideffer (1976, 1981).

Theoretical Model

Although attention can be conceptualized in more than one way, Nideffer's approach is to view attention along two dimensions. He proposes that attentional focus can vary in

TABLE 6-1   Attentional Focus and Sport-Related Situations

Internal	External
Broad	
1. Mentally practicing fastbreak in basketball	1. Linebacker in football
2. Coach thinking about the game plan for a soccer match	2. Halfback in field hockey
Narrow	
1. Mentally practicing a front dive	1. Golf putt
2. Mentally practicing a routine for the balance beam	2. Free throw in basketball

both width (broad versus narrow) and direction (external versus internal). For instance, as you are reading these sentences you probably have a narrow external focus. However, if you stop for a moment and try to imagine a fast-moving basketball game, then you have probably switched to a broad internal focus.

It is important to be able to switch your attentional focus according to the task you are trying to accomplish. Table 6-1 depicts sport-related situations and the corresponding appropriate attentional focus. Notice that an internal focus is effective only for mentally practicing a skill or anticipating a future event. The assumption of an internal focus, whether broad or narrow, at the time of the actual skill execution only hinders performance. Therefore, the "rule of thumb" is that a switch to an external focus should occur the moment the athlete is ready to perform. Review the examples of the broad-narrow dimension in Table 6-1. Notice how the nature of the sport situation coincides with the width of the attentional focus. If the player must process multiple cues in the sport environment, then a broad attentional focus is needed. On the other hand, an athlete who must respond to a single cue, such as a gymnast on the balance beam or a basketball player at the free throw line, must focus attention in a narrow external fashion; to focus attention on a broad-external basis would most likely be disastrous.

Under nonstressful conditions most sport participants are fairly effective at switching their attention as the task or skill demand varies. However, as we will discuss a little later, when arousal or anxiety becomes too high, then mental errors associated with ineffective attentional focusing occur.

Another important point regarding attentional style is that people vary in their usual way of attending to stimuli; thus attentional sytle is an individual difference, or personality variable. Given these variations in attentional style, some athletes should perform certain sport behaviors more effectively than others. Would you want a softball pitcher to have a generalized tendency to focus in a broad-external or narrow-external fashion? Who should make a better point guard in basketball, an athlete with a broad-internal focus or a broad-external focus?

Aspects of Measurement

One way to assess the attentional style of an athlete is to observe under what environmental conditions the person appears to be making mental errors. Based on such observations, the coach or teacher can infer the athlete's preferred attentional style. However, this is probably not the best nor most efficient method. Another way in which attentional style

TABLE 6-2 The Six Attentional Scales of the TAIS

Scale	Abbreviation	Description
Broad-External	BET	High scores indicate an ability to effectively integrate many external stimuli simultaneously
External-Overload	OET	High scores indicate a tendency to become confused and overloaded with external stimuli
Broad-Internal	BIT	High scores indicate an ability to effectively integrate several ideas at one time
Internal-Overload	OIT	High scores indicate a tendency to become overloaded by internal stimuli
Narrow Focus	NAR	High scores indicate an ability to effectively narrow attention when it is appropriate
Reduced Focus	RED	High scores indicate chronically narrowed attention

Adapted from Nideffer, R.M. (1976). Test of attentional and interpersonal style. *Journal of Personality and Social Psychology, 34,* 394-404. Copyright (1976) by the American Psychological Association. Adapted by permission of the author.

can be assessed is through a paper and pencil test. In 1976 Nideffer developed the Test of Attentional and Interpersonal Style (TAIS). It is composed of 17 scales: six measure attentional style, two measure behavioral and cognitive control, and the remaining eight measure interpersonal style. For our purposes we will address aspects of the scales designed to measure attentional style. Table 6-2 contains the names and descriptions of the six attentional scales. Notice how the scales can be used to indicate several different combinations of attentional width and direction. Notice also that three of the scales indicate aspects of effective focusing (broad-external, BET; broad-internal, BIT; narrow focus, NAR), whereas three others assess aspects of ineffective focusing (external-overload, OET; internal-overload, OIT; reduced focus, RED).

Reread the six scale descriptions presented in Table 6-2. Now observe the opposing patterns shown in Figure 6-1 for the ineffective versus the effective attentional profile. Effective attenders indicate that they can deal well with multiple stimuli from both external and internal sources (high scores on BET and BIT) and can effectively switch their attention from broad to narrow focus when necessary (high score on NAR). Ineffective attenders indicate that they tend to become confused and overloaded by the presence of multiple stimuli both internally and externally (high scores on OIT and OET). When such athletes assume either a broad-internal or broad-external focus, they have trouble narrowing their attentional width (high score on RED). Furthermore, the high score on the RED scale indicates that when the ineffective attender does assume a narrow focus, it is so narrow that it hinders performance. For such persons to perform better in most sport situations they have to be taught to switch the direction of attention at will and to narrow or broaden attention as the situation demands.

Any technique involving attentional switching, whether internal-external or broad-narrow, should be helpful. In Chapter 5 we discussed some of these techniques, such as progressive relaxation and transcendental meditation. Chapter 8 includes a lengthy discussion on imagery, which has long been used to help performers gain control of their attentional focus. In addition to these techniques, sometimes performers can gain attentional control through very simple methods. Case Study 1 at the end of this chapter concerns Nideffer's (Nideffer, 1981; Nideffer & Sharpe, 1978) centering procedure.

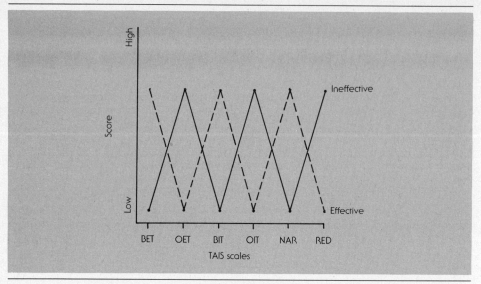

FIGURE 6-1   Effective and ineffective attentional profiles.

Centering is a procedure that uses relaxation techniques and deep breathing to allow a person to gain control of attention. Such attentional control can then lead to better sport performance.

From the discussion above it appears that the profiles generated on the basis of Nideffer's (1976) TAIS can provide insight into the attentional styles of various persons. However, there are currently some questions concerning the theoretical basis underlying that test and other methodological issues.

METHODOLOGICAL ISSUES

Trait Measure

The Test of Attentional and Interpersonal Style (TAIS) is a trait measure of a person's generalized way of attending. The trait nature of the test presents two potential problems. First, it ignores situational factors. Recall that most of the current thinking in sport psychology favors the use of the interactionist paradigm (person × situation). This approach has been more powerful in describing human behavior as compared with the more traditional trait strategy. For example, if a coach used the TAIS to assess the attentional style of all of her field hockey players without taking player position (situation) into account, then little pertinent information would be gained in terms of enhancing sport performance. Second, Zuckerman (1979) has provided evidence to suggest that narrow-state measures are superior to broad-trait measures. Therefore more effective measures should be both state and sport specific.

In support of the superiority of the sport-specific approach to the measurement of attentional style in sport situations, Van Schoyck and Grasha (1981) used both the TAIS and a tennis-specific adaptation of the TAIS (T-TAIS) to study beginning, intermediate, and advanced players. Their results showed that the T-TAIS was more precise and more valid as compared with the more general TAIS. Therefore their data argue for the use of sport-specific measures of psychological characteristics.

Predictive Validity of the TAIS

Another important question to be answered when attempting to assess psychological characteristics such as attentional style is whether or not the test scores do indeed predict performance. In view of the data provided in Table 6-1, it was proposed that particular attentional styles should be systematically related to specific sport settings. For instance, a narrow-external focus is desirable for activities such as a free throw in basketball, whereas a broad-external style is needed for effective performance by a linebacker in football or a halfback in field hockey. Although those relationships are intuitively appealing, for a test to be found acceptable in a scientific sense, evidence must be provided to support those assertions. The question is one of **predictive validity.** Predictive validity refers to the degree to which the test is capable of accurately forecasting the behavior it was designed to assess.

The few studies that have preselected specific scales from the TAIS for behavioral prediction have supported aspects of the TAIS. Reis and Bird (1982) designed a two-part investigation to test the predictive validity of the BET (broad, external focus) and RED (chronically narrowed focus) scales. Subjects scoring high on the BET scale and low on the RED scale were classified as broad attenders. Other subjects who scored high on RED and low on BET were classified as narrow attenders. Initially, subjects were required to perform 16 trials on a pursuit rotor task, a visual tracking task that was considered the primary task in the sense that the subjects were told that performance on the pursuit rotor was most important in the experiment. During the latter part of the experiment, at the same time that the tracking performance was taking place, visual probes (lights) were operating in each subject's visual periphery. The visual probes were considered to be the secondary task. When the subjects saw a light, they were to respond by releasing a reaction time key as quickly as possible. If the BET really can classify persons as being broad attenders, then such persons should have faster reaction times as compared with narrow attenders (high on RED). During the trials in which the subjects had been told that the visual probes would appear, the results provided strong support for the predictive validity of the two scales. Broad attenders had significantly faster reaction times to the visual probes as compared with narrow attenders, although performance by the two groups on the primary task was equal. This was important because if performance by the two groups had not been equal, then it might be argued that the differences were the result of the broad attenders shifting their attention away from the primary task and onto the secondary task.

In the second part of the Reis and Bird experiment, when negative feedback was manipulated experimentally to elevate anxiety it was found that broad attenders had much slower reaction times. The results, particularly in terms of the broad attenders under conditions of high anxiety, indicated that anxiety can reduce the range of cue utilization in the visual periphery (see Easterbrook, 1959). Together the results support the predictive validity of Nideffer's (1976) notion of a broad-narrow dimension to attentional style.

In another investigation, Martin (1983) used the NAR (narrow, effective focus) and the OET (external overload) scales to test predictive validity of those two scales for the basketball free throw percentages of high-school players. He found that the high NAR players had far superior free throw percentages as compared with the high OET performers. In addition to providing evidence supporting the predictive validity of the two scales, these data indicate that such differences in attentional style can be used by coaches as indicators of potentially good or poor free throw shooters. Armed with such information, coaches could then institute attention control programs for players who score high on the OET scale. After completion of training in attentional control programs such as the centering procedure described in Case Study 1 (pp.163-164), coaches could then reassess scores on OET and check for positive changes in free throw percentage.

ATTENTIONAL STYLE AND ANXIETY

Anxiety, Attention, and Cue Processing

In Chapter 4 we discussed two cognitively based explanations for the relationship between level of anxiety and attention. The first was based on Easterbrook's (1959) *cue utilization hypothesis,* which proposed that as anxiety increases there is a reduction in the number of peripheral cues a person can process. The second explanation proposed that as anxiety increases, *attentional shifts,* or *scanning,* take place. Based on the work of Van Schoyck and Grasha (1981), it appears that both explanations should be used jointly. From their perspective, high anxiety has a negative effect on the ability to integrate stimuli (similar to Easterbrook's ineffective cue utilization) and increases the amount of scanning (similar to the attentional shift hypothesis). Both these attentional disruptions can cause the athlete to lose concentration and the ability to attend to the cues most important to performance. These attentional disruptions can help to explain the decreases in performance associated with the right side of the inverted-U (high arousal or anxiety) (see Figure 3-5 on p. 61). For instance, if a basketball player is highly anxious and unable to appropriately allocate attention and maintain concentration, then performance decrements will surely follow. If the player shifts attention to the bench or the stands, game-related cues will be missed.

Attentional Style and Trait Anxiety

Although few studies have specifically tested the predicted relationship among attentional style, anxiety, and sport performance, some limited evidence is available. For example, Bird, Ravizza, and Reis (1983) studied the connection between trait anxiety and attentional style of college students enrolled in either tennis or hatha-yoga classes. Their results supported the findings of Van Schoyck and Grasha (1981). After selecting only persons who were either high or low in trait anxiety, they compared the attentional profiles (based on the TAIS) of the two groups. There were significant differences between the high versus low trait groups in all six attentional scales. In fact, the pattern was highly similar to that depicted in Figure 6-1. The low-anxious group followed the pattern associated with effective attention, whereas the high-anxious group paralleled the pattern proposed for ineffective attention. The high-trait anxious pattern was characterized by both internal and external stimuli overload and the inability to effectively control attentional narrowing; the low trait-anxious pattern indicated an ability to effectively integrate multiple stimuli and to narrow attention when the task called for it. Again you can see why high levels of anxiety are so disruptive to effective performance in sport. If an athlete cannot control attentional narrowing and also tends to become overloaded by stimuli, it is not surprising that sport performance will be hindered.

In a study of pistol, skeet, rifle, and trap shooters, Landers, Furst, and Daniels (1981) also found a strong tendency for high trait-anxious shooters to score higher on the two overload scales (OET and OIT) and on the RED scale as compared with the low trait-anxious shooters, Apparently the high trait-anxious performers, who were also generally the less skilled, had difficulty maintaining effective concentration and narrowing attentional focus. Other than the three scales mentioned above, there did not appear to be any systematic differences between the high and low trait-anxious shooters on any of the other scales. This is not consistent with the pattern of differences generated in the Bird, Ravizza, and Reis (1983) study or in the correlational patterns contained in Nideffer's original paper on the TAIS (1976). However, it is clear that trait anxiety is systematically related to a performer's ability to narrow attention on demand and to maintain concentration during performance.

Attentional Style and State Anxiety

Recall that Nideffer (1976) proposed that attentional style can vary across the two dimensions of width (broad-narrow) or direction (internal-external). From this perspective the focus that is usually dominant is considered to be the person's attentional strength, and less dominant tendencies are considered to be attentional weaknesses. For example, to be effective in basketball a performer must assume a broad-external attentional focus. However, if the player does not switch to a narrow-external focus at the free throw line, the result will be poor free throw shooting. Therefore the usual broad-external style would be considered an attentional strength and the less dominant narrow-external focus would be considered an attentional weakness.

Nideffer (1981) proposed a specific relationship between increases in state anxiety and effects on attentional style. More specifically, he said that as pressure (state anxiety) increases there is an increased tendency for athletes to play to their attentional strengths. Thus if an athlete's greatest attentional strength is the ability to assume a broad-external focus, then that person would be predicted to rely on that attentional perspective under conditions of increased anxiety. Such an occurrence can be facilitative or detrimental to performance. If the task demands the processing of multiple external cues, then performance can be quite good. However, if the player is trying to shoot a free throw wherein it is important to narrow attention, then the shot will probably be missed.

By talking about the notion of playing to attentional strengths under elevated state anxiety conditions, Nideffer is actually referring to a loss of attentional flexibility with an accompanying "locking in" and exaggeration of the dominant attentional focus. His prediction is based on clinical evidence rather than empirical or scientific evidence. Although his prediction may be correct, it has not yet received sufficient verification in controlled, experimental settings. However, accepting his assertion for the time being, several variables must be considered when viewing the proposed relationship between attentional flexibility and anxiety. For example, Keele and Hawkins (1982) have demonstrated some evidence to support the assertion that attentional shifting may be a stable individual difference variable; that is, performers should vary in their susceptibility to anxiety effects on attentional flexibility. In addition, as skill and experience increase, performers are better able to control attentional shifting. Finally, the performer's initial level of anxiety should have some bearing on the predicted effects of increases in anxiety. Nideffer's prediction concerning the notion of playing to attentional strengths should be viewed with the understanding that it must be modified in accordance with the variables presented previously.

CURRENT ISSUES AND CONCERNS

There appear to be three issues of major concern relative to the use of the TAIS in sport settings. First, there is some evidence (Gardner, Holtzman, Klein, Linton, & Spence, 1959; Schlesinger, 1952; Silverman, 1964; Wachtel, 1967; Van Schoyck & Grasha, 1981) that Nideffer's bipolar model is too simplistic to fully explain the human attentional system; a more sophisticated, multidimensional model is needed. Second, on the basis of the small amount of available literature (Bird, Ravizza, & Reis, 1983; Landers, 1982; Landers, Furst, & Daniels, 1981; Nideffer, 1976) there is a possibility that the TAIS is not measuring a construct or constructs that are identifiably separate from anxiety. Briefly, if all of the scales of the TAIS correlate in a systematic fashion with anxiety scores, then it suggests that the TAIS may not be measuring a construct that is totally independent of anxiety (Landers, 1982; Turner & Gilliland, 1977). More specifically, if the relationship generated between the TAIS and anxiety is both systematic and consistent, then it follows that if you knew someone's anxiety score, you could predict the associated attentional profile. Therefore it would be redundant to measure attentional style in addition to anxiety.

On a more positive note, Ed Etzel, a 1984 gold medal Olympian, recently began development of a sport-specific instrument for assessing attention in highly skilled rifle shooters. The Riflery Attention Questionnaire (RAQ) (1979) is based on the five dimensions of attentional capacity, alertness, selectivity, duration, and intensity. Although it is too soon to determine the merit of this instrument, it may prove a significant contribution to the attention–sport performance literature.

ATTENTIONAL FACTORS RELATED TO COACHING EFFECTIVENESS

Concentration

Using a variety of approaches, some investigators have been interested in ascertaining the role that various attentional strategies such as concentration might play in sport performance. In a study of elite wrestlers, Highlen and Bennett (1979) found two aspects of concentration to differ between athletes who qualified for a berth on three Canadian National teams as compared with those who did not qualify. Qualifiers showed greater concentration on specific wrestling moves and generally focused less attention on the audience.

Using an assessment instrument adapted from the Highlen and Bennett (1979) inventory, Gould, Weiss, and Weinberg (1981) also looked at various psychological characteristics of wrestlers. They measured attentional focus by asking the performers to rate the following statement on an 11-point scale: "Rate the frequency that you mentally prepare for a match by focusing your attention (e.g., try to focus all your thoughts on the upcoming match and eliminate any thoughts about external factors.)" (p. 72). Based on the responses to this statement, it was shown that the place winners had significantly superior ratings of attentional focus as compared with nonplacers. Their findings agree with those of Highlen and Bennett.

Using a behavioral observation approach as opposed to a questionnaire strategy, Walker, Nideffer, and Boomer (1977) investigated the relationship between concentration time and diving performance. Concentration times for both front and back dives were measured by timing the period between the diver coming to attention on the board and executing the initial movement of the dive. Dive quality was based on judges' ratings. The data analysis indicated that the best dives were associated with middle concentration times, second-best dives were at the faster concentration time, and poorest performance took place after longer periods of concentration. It could be speculated that during those longer periods of concentration the diver is either experiencing increases in tension or attention shifts to irrelevant cues.

Several implications can be drawn from these studies. First, if superior performers do focus more on the task at hand and less on task-irrelevant cues, then the performance of less successful athletes should be enhanced by redirecting attention to more relevant, task-related cues. Previously, we referred to the notion of selective attention. Because humans have a limited capacity to process multiple cues simultaneously, some cues will be ignored while others are selected for processing. To help an athlete select the most important cues, the coach must select a reduced number of task-relevant cues and direct the athlete's attention to those cues. Through practice and experience, the athlete should then be able to focus more effectively on the most important cues. Coaches should avoid broad commands such as "concentrate" and "watch what you're doing", and instead provide very specific cue-reduction information. This not only increases the chances for better skill execution but also carries a positive rather than a negative message.

The Walker, Nideffer, and Boomer (1977) study on length of concentration time and diving effectiveness should also be applicable to other sports that require some form of address, or "ready set," before skill enactment, such as a gymnast's stance before a vault, the preservice period in volleyball, or the address in golf. Walker, Nideffer, and Boomer suggest that a coach collect statistics during practice and game situations that indicate the relationship between concentration time and quality of performance. This could provide a baseline measure of optimal concentration time for a particular performer. Once that is known, it would not be difficult to observe changes in concentration time before performance. In addition, we suggest that time-certain preperformance rituals be practiced so that length of concentration time becomes standardized. This could optimize length of concentration time for individual athletes and focus their attention in a positive direction; that is, attention would be focused on the tension-reducing aspects of the ritual rather than on extraneous and task-irrelevant cues such as the presence of an audience or judges.

Association versus Dissociation

Recent studies of long-distance runners have questioned whether it is better to attend to internal cues, such as monitoring the pain in the legs or the rate of respiration, or external factors or thoughts irrelevant to the run. As distinguished by Morgan and Pollock (1977), an **associative strategy** is one in which the runner tunes into input from the body and emotions during the race; a **dissociative strategy** is used by runners when they use various techniques designed to distract their minds from the pains that accompany long-distance runs.

Morgan and Pollock reported that elite marathoners tended to use associative strategies, whereas nonelite runners generally employed dissociative techniques. Other writers have suggested that both actually use dissociative coping strategies to deal with the pain that occurs during long-distance running. For example, Nideffer (1979) suggests that the difference between experienced, world-class distance runners and nonelite runners is that elite runners are able to deal with pain more objectively; by objectively associating with pain cues, elite runners are able to dissociate themselves from those pains on an emotional basis. From his perspective, these experienced, highly skilled runners ''step out of themselves'' so that they gain an emotional distance from the pain; they are then able to use those cues to learn and test themselves. Nideffer believes that the less experienced runners are unable to achieve that same degree of emotional separation from the physical cues; thus when they attend to those cues they become frightened or upset and performance is hindered or they stop altogether.

From a somewhat different perspective, Sacks, Milvy, Perry, and Sherman (1981) suggest that it may not be a question of one group of runners using an associative strategy solely and other runners employing only a dissociative coping technique. They studied 10 male runners involved in a 100-mile road race. On the basis of their within-race and after-race interviews with these runners, they speculate that perhaps Morgan and Pollock's original associative versus dissociative conceptualization might have to be modified. They propose that a third type of thinking, called meditative thinking, may be occupying the runner's mind during much of the race. They write:

> During this kind of thinking, runners are focusing neither on themselves nor on some distracting thought, but rather they are not particularly focusing at all. As one runner summed it up: 'The more the race is on, the more you try to concentrate on the race. The mind goes in circles. First on one thing, then the pace, then something else, and then the pace.' The 'something else,' however, may have nothing at all to do with the race or the runner's body. (p. 173)

The last sentence is important because from Morgan and Pollock's perspective, associative thinking is directly related to thoughts concerning the race or bodily inputs.

Currently, it is difficult to draw any firm conclusions from the data presented. Most of it is either based on speculation or on interviews that may include some experimenter bias. Furthermore, the samples are not all similar. In one case marathoners are studied: in another, 100-mile road runners. If that is the current status, why should the question of associative versus disassociative attention be important?

On an intuitive level it would appear that learning to monitor the feedback from your own body and aspects of the race can enhance performance. A runner can use these cues to more fully tune into what is happening within the body and during the race itself. However, this could be an emotionally upsetting strategy for a beginner to employ, particularly if attention is strictly focused internally on bodily pain and emotions. From personal experience, we know that if attention during the early stages of running is focused almost solely on pain and discomfort, then dropping out of a running program is almost sure to happen. On the other hand, a strictly dissociative strategy may be detrimental because attention to internal warning signs of potential injury may be ignored. Therefore it seems reasonable that coaches should attempt to develop the runner's ability to employ an associative strategy only as skill develops. Athletes must learn how to monitor, as objectively as possible, the information that the body provides during the run.

At this time the notions of attentional switching and cognitive coping strategies are receiving much more research attention than they did in the past. It is hoped that in the near future researchers will have a much clearer idea as to which strategy is best to use at what time in terms of both skill level and the race itself.

Coaches' Attentional Style

Like athletes, coaches vary in their attentional styles. Each coach has his or her own attentional strengths and weaknesses. These strengths and weaknesses are also associated with or modified by the particular sport or athlete to be coached. Coaches, like athletes, tend to play to their attentional strengths under conditions of increased pressure or anxiety. Similarly, the coach's state anxiety and ability to shift attention can modify what happens under those anxiety conditions.

In most instances, effective coaching requires good attentional flexibility. The ability to shift from one attentional focus to another allows the coach to "match" attentional style with changes in the game environment. For example, a water polo coach must be able to broaden externally so that the multiple cues in the fast-paced play can be analyzed and corrections made. The next minute attention must be narrowed and the performance of one player must be focused on. However, what would happen as time was running out and the score was very close or tied? Let's take a look at what might happen to a water polo coach whose dominant focus is broad-external under those conditions.

This coach is very good at attending to a fast-moving, external environment. Reading the offensive moves and the defensive responses are usually no problem. The coach can anticipate the plays and see the errors of both teams. As pressure increases, state anxiety elevates. The coach begins to play to the extreme in terms of a broad-external attentional style and rapidly switches attention from one point in the pool to another, from one player to another. As soon as a mistake is seen, the coach overreacts and either criticizes loudly or substitutes immediately. The general pattern is one of reacting too quickly and changing strategy too fast without thinking about possible consequences (Nideffer, 1982).

Taking this same coach, what errors do you think will be made in terms of interacting with the team members? One of the errors almost everyone makes is to expect others to perceive the world in much the same way as we do or to be able to perform the same skills that we are able to perform. More than likely, the coach with the broad-external focus has these same perceptions and will expect the athletes to be able to attend to and to process effectively many stimuli or events in a fast-moving sport situation. What do you think will happen when such a coach encounters an athlete whose dominant attentional style is characterized by a tendency to maintain a different focus such as narrow-external? Most probably, in a pressure situation, that athlete will simply not be able to attend to

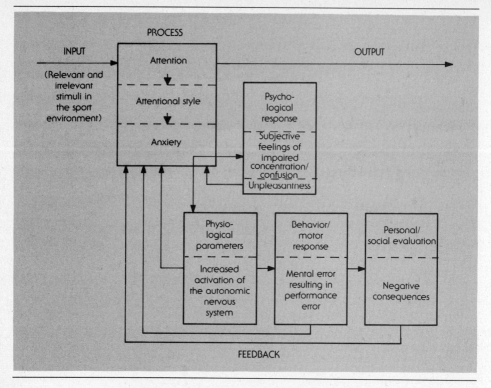

FIGURE 6-2   Attention and the unifying model.

multiple stimuli and will therefore commit ''mental'' errors. The coach may react quickly and call a substitution. The athlete is upset, and the coach thinks that the athlete wasn't really trying at a crucial point in the game. This could be the beginnings of an incompatible coach-athlete relationship. The player will think that the coach doesn't understand and the coach may think that the person is a problem athlete.

Some of these pitfalls can be avoided if a coach knows more about his or her own attentional tendencies and how to control both level of anxiety and attentional focus. Coaching effectiveness both in terms of sport competition and player-coach compatibility can also be enhanced by a more thorough knowledge of players' attentional styles.

Attention and the Unifying Model

The framework of the unifying model provides an ideal way to understand how mental errors relate to attention. As shown in Figure 6-2, when a performer is placed in a sport performance situation, he or she can select from many stimuli, both task relevant and task irrelevant, for processing.

Input

The cues to which the performer chooses to attend determine whether or not a mental error will occur in task performance. Because a performer can attend to a limited number of cues simultaneously, it is most important that the performer select the correct cues.

Landers (1982) notes that performers may have their own cue priority; that is, they tend to process some cues before selecting others. If this is so, then one way to facilitate the input process is to discuss each performer's cue priority to determine if that hierarchy is appropriate for a given task. If not, then the cues should be reprioritized. Another way to help the athlete select the proper cues for processing is to use the cue-reduction approach associated with the notion of selective attention (see p. 148). Here the coach or teacher selects a small number of highly task-relevant cues to which the performer should attend to the exclusion of other competing cues.

Process

The processing of environmental cues can result in a performance error either because the wrong cues were selected in the first place or because the performer is unable to integrate the selected cues into a meaningful whole. For instance, when it is said that a performance error was caused by a reduction or narrowing of the attentional field, it could mean that the performer has either a reduction in the amount of scanning across the visual field or a reduction in focusing so that cues are considered in isolation rather than in an integrated fashion. In each case a performance error should result, but for different reasons.

The cue-selection process is affected by at least two major factors: individual attentional style and level of anxiety. Because people attend differently to their environments, individual athletes will select different cues. Faced with the same situation, a person who tends to view the world from a broad-internal perspective will select cues for processing different from those selected by another person who tends to maintain a narrow-external orientation.

There are several propositions concerning the effects of elevated anxiety on the attentional process and thus on cue selection. Van Schoyck and Grasha (1981) suggest that as anxiety increases there should be an accompanying increase in the range of scanning and a decrease in the capacity to integrate stimuli into meaningful wholes. These effects should then cause a person to feel that he or she is confused and unable to concentrate. If an athlete experiences attentional scanning or an inability to integrate stimuli with accompanying feelings of confusion and lack of concentration, performance is bound to deteriorate. Imagine yourself as a basketball center or an ice hockey goalie experiencing these reactions.

From another point of view, Nideffer (1981) offers a three-stage explanation of the relationship between attentional style and increases in anxiety. First, the performer will tend to play to attentional strengths; if an athlete has a predominately narrow-external focus, then he or she will tend to favor that focus over other possibilities, whether or not it is appropriate for task performance. The second stage involves a performer's tendency to narrow his or her focus involuntarily under increasing anxiety. Nideffer's third stage proposes that with further increases in anxiety, there should be a switch to an internal focus of attention, meaning that the performer will attend to changes in physiological responses or aspects of psychological responses. Take the case of a softball pitcher who has just walked two batters. Anxiety should be high, and attentional focus should narrow. There are two possible responses. If the pitcher throws "strikes" on the next few pitches as a result of the attention narrowing, anxiety should decrease and the pitcher should be back in control. On the other hand, if the severe attentional narrowing causes the pitcher to throw "balls" on the next few pitches, the pitcher's attention should switch to monitoring uncomfortable physiological responses such as rapid heart rate and sweaty palms. This should hinder the performer even more.

It is important to re-emphasize that both anxiety and attentional style can be affected by other factors. For example, with higher levels of experience and skill, an athlete may be able to maintain greater degrees of attentional flexibility and would be less prone to "locking in" to a single attentional style. Also, individual performers appear to differ in their tendency toward attentional flexibility and this could affect their tendency to play to attention strengths. Finally, the state anxiety response is mediated by several factors, such as skill level, trait anxiety, and ability to inhibit the anxiety response.

Output

The output of the attentional process can be viewed at four levels: psychological, physiological, behavioral, and the post-response evaluation. At the psychological level, a performer's inability to effectively integrate the stimuli inputed into the attentional mechanism should result in feelings of confusion and inability to concentrate (Van Schoyck & Grasha, 1981). The performer feels overloaded by too many stimuli or the connections between stimuli are disjointed. As a result the performer's anxiety level increases.

Increased anxiety will usually cause the athlete to notice and probably shift attention to the resulting physiological sensations. Given the limited capacity of the attentional mechanism, it would be difficult, if not impossible, to effectively select task-relevant cues for sport performance while at the same time attending to the pounding of your heart or your rapid respiration.

On the behavioral level, performance is greatly affected by the environmental cues that are selected for processing. A mismatch between cue selection and task demands results in a behavioral (motor) response that is incorrect or impaired. Such a mismatch is called a **mental error.** The probability of a mental error is determined by several factors, such as number and vividness of cues in the environment, skill level, attentional style, and level of state anxiety.

Feedback

When a performance error does occur it is perceived as a negative experience or failure. This perception should increase the probability that when again faced with that same or a similiar situation, the performer will experience increased state anxiety. Again, an anxiety response can affect both attentional style and cue-processing ability.

When the cause of a sport performance error appears to be ineffective cue processing, several approaches can be taken. Intervention strategies such as centering (see Case Study 1) can help the player control attention and reduce anxiety. Selective attention strategies can be used by the coach to help the athlete identify task-relevant cues (see Case Study 1, Chapter 3).

IMPLICATIONS FOR SPORT

- Because the athlete's ability to process cues is limited, techniques such as cue-reduction feedback (that is, selective attention) should be used to promote the processing of relevant cues.

- To avoid interference, do not ask the performer to perform simultaneously two tasks that require identical input or output systems. For example, a basketball coach should not expect a player to look to the bench for a signal while also trying to track the movement of the ball or the opponents.
- During the early stages of skill learning (that is, the cognitive stage) provide the learner with limited but specific cues on which to focus attention.
- After a skill has become automated, provide the athlete with strategy-related cues as opposed to skill-related cues.
- For mentally practicing a sport skill, direct the performer's attentional focus inward.
- Stress that attentional focus should be directed externally at the initiation of the skill execution.
- Because there appears to be a systematic relationship between high anxiety and attentional disruptions, use various intervention strategies to lower anxiety and control attentional focus.
- Instruct performers to focus attention on the task or match rather than on distracting stimuli such as an audience.
- Because there may be an optimal concentration time in events that require a "ready-set," determine that time for each athlete by timing the concentration period and comparing it with the quality of the subsequent performance. Then develop a time-certain preperformance ritual.
- Remember, just as athletes may play to their attentional strengths under conditions of increased anxiety, so too may coaches. As a coach, try to maintain attentional flexibility. One way to increase this awareness for both athletes and coaches is to videotape games and matches, then identify the most stressful moments and observe attention-related behaviors. Ask the athlete to recall differences in attentional focus under conditions of both success and failure. Point out the important, most-relevant cues for specific tasks.

CASE STUDY 1

Attention Control for Athletes

Many motor performance errors can be attributed to either a tendency to shift attentional focus internally to monitor various physiological responses or a lack of attentional flexibility. Although there are numerous intervention strategies that can help allieviate such tendencies, the simple and quick centering procedure described below is usually sufficient for most athletes. This **centering procedure** is based on Nideffer's suggested procedure (Nideffer, 1981; Nideffer & Sharpe, 1978).

1. The athlete should first assume a position with the knees bent and feet spread slightly apart. The weight should be balanced evenly over the feet. Test this position by leaning side-to-side and forward-to-back. The bent-knee position is important because it prohibits the bracing and locking of the knees. In the bent-knee position the athlete should feel muscular tension in the thighs and calves.

2. The next step is the conscious relaxation of the shoulder and neck muscles. The athlete can check the degree of relaxation by moving slightly forward and back, then side to side. Gently shake the arms to make sure they are loose and relaxed.

3. Now the athlete should relax the jaw by opening the mouth slightly to eliminate any tension in the jaw muscles.

4. The athlete should inhale slowly and deeply, breathing from the diaphragm, from deep in the abdomen. The athlete can check his or her breathing by noticing whether the stomach is extended as a breath is taken. While breathing, the athlete should consciously relax the chest and shoulders and when inhaling, should not allow the chest to expand or the shoulders to elevate. This deep-breathing technique should prohibit the tightening of the neck and shoulder muscles and discourage any tendency to hyperventilate.

5. The athlete should slowly exhale while noticing the sensations coming from the stomach area. He or she should feel the stomach muscles relaxing and consciously allow the knees to bend slightly. The athlete should feel the sensation of heaviness as the body presses toward the floor. While exhaling, there should be no lifting feeling during the breathing exercise; instead the body should feel heavier, steadier, and firmer. The athlete's attention to the cues associated with relaxation should prevent any attention being spent on cues that trigger an anxiety response. At this point the athlete should think about some constructive cue relevant to sport performance.

6. To enhance the centering procedure the athlete should be told and reminded about the critical cues that should be attended to during the breathing exercise. In addition, the sport-related cue or cues should be identified before beginning the centering procedure. The exact nature of the sport cues may vary from one person to another. The main purposes of the procedure are the lowering of arousal and the control of attentional focus.

CASE STUDY 2

Attentional Style and Volleyball Performance

In this case study we describe the attentional strengths and weakness of a volleyball player and a head coach, examining how the strengths of each should facilitate performance and identifying some potential sources of performance decrements.

Player A

Player A's greatest attentional strength is a high score on the NAR scale. This player is good at narrowing attention on a particular task. Player A is a good server, blocker, and hitter during practice and most matches. However, during close matches, when tension increases, this player tends to make defensive mistakes in both blocking at the net and positioning to dig a spiked ball. The very high NAR score indicates that Player A is able to focus narrowly and effectively under low or moderate anxiety conditions but with increased stress the athlete tends to lose attentional flexibility. The tendency to narrow dominates and the ability to effectively scan the activity on the court diminishes. Under conditions of anxiety, Player A needs to learn to broaden attention when the situation calls for it.

Coach B

Coach B's strongest attentional ability is reflected by an extremely high score on the BIT scale. This coach is a good planner and analyzer. Practices are well–thought out, organized, and efficient. Game plans are perceptive and use the talents of each team member very well. The only time that coach B tends to make major errors is during crucial, stressful game situations. Under pressure, when play is rapid and the game is close, this coach fails to react quickly enough. Instead of calling a time out and changing the strategy, Coach *B* becomes introspective and tense. Usually, before Coach *B* reacts, the point spread is too wide or the game is already over. Coach *B* should practice shifting attention externally and avoid becoming too analytical under pressure conditions.

CASE STUDY 3
Narrow-External Focus: Tennis Drills

Anyone who has ever taken tennis lessons has probably been told time and time again to "Keep your eye on the ball!" Although most beginners believe they are doing just that, in reality they are not. Most are focusing on their own thoughts, their opponent's movements, or other aspects of the environmental conditions. What the coach or teacher is trying to accomplish by telling the player to watch the ball is a narrow-external attentional focus. However, the instructions are too vague; it is not clear *when* the player should focus on the ball: When the ball is hit? When it clears the net? While the ball is in flight? Below are a few suggestions for enhancing players' ability to track the ball and assume a narrow-external focus. Although we have used tennis as an example, in any sport, drills should be designed to teach athletes task-relevant attentional skills. Success comes not from physical practice alone; cognitive skills and strategies must also be practiced.

Drill 1: Hit and Bounce

The player is told to say "bounce" each time the ball is bounced and "hit" each time the ball is hit. Early in practice it would be wise to have the student say each word out loud so that the coach knows that the verbal labels are coinciding with the action of the ball. (The "hit" part of this drill could also be used effectively in volleyball.)

Drill 2: Rotation and Distance

Once the player is able to track the ball and correctly label either a hit or bounce, then emphasis can be placed on the rotation and distance of the ball. Ball rotation can be called out in terms of *topspin, backspin, sidespin,* or *no spin.* During ground-stroke practice, ball spin should be called out so that the playing partner (or coach) can hear the call. A variation would be to switch attentional focus to the distance the ball travels (within the service court, "short"; between service court and baseline, "good"; within five feet of baseline, "deep"; over the baseline, "long". Once the player gains adequate skill in calling the ball rotation and distance, they can be combined so that both rotation and distance are called. The latter, however, would most likely require that the performer has reached at least the associative if not the automated stage of learning.

CASE STUDY 4
Anxiety, Attentional Focus, and the Tennis Serve

A frequent problem for many skilled tennis players is a sudden and often prolonged slump in service effectiveness. This happens most usually in competition. If the skill is there, what could be the cause?

We had a relatively high-skilled tennis player approach us with just this situation. The problem had been getting progressively worse. First, it was simply a few double faults; later it became a series of games in which his serve was consistently broken. When he approached us he was experiencing high anxiety each time it was his turn at service.

Through our discussions, we determined that there seemed to be a progressively worsening pattern of attentional focus. The early problems appeared to be caused by switching attentional focus to the movement of the arm during service rather than focusing attention on the ball. Recall that after a skill has become automatic, it requires little or no attention. In fact, too much attention to a movement can be detrimental. Motor skill execution is impaired, failure is inevitable, and an anxiety reaction is sure to follow. One of the usual consequences of increased anxiety is a shift of attentional focus to internal responses rather than to environmental factors. In our tennis player's case, by the time he spoke with us he was monitoring physiological responses at the service line rather than attending to the ball toss.

The solution was a simple one. First, we asked if he really did have skill at service. After some attempts at modesty, he agreed that he did. Then we explained some of the principles associated with attentional focus, anxiety, and tennis performance. Our prescription entailed simply telling him to focus totally on the ball toss, to block everything else out. Because the skill was already there, an effective attentional focus should increase probability of success. Success should then lower anxiety and facilitate more effective attentional focus. When we saw him next, his grin alone told us that our strategy had been successful.

SUMMARY

- The attentional mechanism is characterized by several constraints, including limitedness and interference. Because it is not possible to process large numbers of cues at the same time, it is important that selective attention be used for the identification of the most important, task-relevant cues.
- As skill level increases there is less of an attentional demand. By the time a skill becomes automated, it may require little or no attention during performance.
- Attentional style refers to any person's characteristic manner of focusing. According to Nideffer, attentional style can be conceptualized along the two dimensions of width (broad-narrow) and direction (internal-external).
- Individual profiles of attentional style can be generated on the basis of scores derived from the Test of Attentional and Interpersonal Style (TAIS).
- Usually a person can be classified as being broad-external, broad-internal, narrow-external, or narrow-internal in attentional style. However, from Nideffer's (1981) perspective, although most athletes are fairly good at switching attention along both dimensions, under conditions of stress or high state anxiety they tend to play to their own attentional strength; that is, they tend to exaggerate their attentional strength and lose attentional flexibility.
- In addition to a tendency for performers to play to their attentional strength, other possible effects of increased state anxiety have been proposed. It has been hypothesized that with increased anxiety there is a tendency to turn attentional focus inward, narrow

the visual field, increase scanning, and become overloaded with stimuli to the extent that the athlete feels confused.

- In terms of the relationship between anxiety and attentional style, some theorists have speculated that as currently measured by the TAIS, attentional style may not be a totally separate construct from anxiety.
- Several implications have been drawn concerning how attention or concentration may relate to effective coaching. There is some evidence that superior performers are better able to focus their attention on the task to be performed. There may also be an optimal preperformance period of concentration time. Finally, the coach's own attentional style can affect both coaching effectiveness and coach-player compatibility.

DISCUSSION QUESTIONS

1 How do the notions of interference and selective attention relate to the limited nature of the attentional mechanism?
2 What should be the most effective attentional style for the following sport-related situations?
   a Mental practice of a golf swing
   b Execution of an inbounds pass in basketball
   c Design of an offensive game plan in football
   d Execution of a relay handoff in track
3 Identify some current problems and issues associated with the measurement of attentional style.
4 Identify several predicted relationships between increases in level of anxiety and effects on attention.
5 Differentiate between the cognitive coping strategy of association versus disassociation.
6 Discuss how a coach's attentional style may relate to actual coaching effectiveness.

GLOSSARY

associative strategy   Strategy that focuses attention on input signals from the body or emotions during performance

attentional mechanism   Process whereby cues are perceived and processed in the brain

attentional style   A person's characteristic manner of attending to the environment

capacity interference   Cause of performance decreases as a result of attempting to perform two tasks simultaneously when both tasks have high attentional demand

centering procedure   Intervention strategy that incorporates both relaxation and breathing techniques to gain attentional control and lower arousal

dissociative strategy   Strategy that focuses attention on nonperformance factors to distract the performer from pain that can occur during a performance

mental error   Performance error that occurs as a result of attending to an inappropriate internal or external cue

predictive validity   Degree to which a particular test is able to forecast actual performance on an appropriate task

selective attention   Process of attending to one set of cues to the exclusion of other cues

structural interference   Cause of performance decreases as a result of attempting to perform two tasks simultaneously when both tasks require the use of common receptor or effector systems

SUGGESTED READINGS

Landers, D.M. (1982). Arousal, attention, and skilled performance: Further considerations. *Quest,* *33,* 271-283.

This article reviews literature on topics such as peripheral narrowing under stress, the measurement of attention-anxiety, psychophysiological correlates of attention-anxiety, and considerations in applications for control of attention and anxiety.

Nideffer, R.M. (1980). Attentional focus—self assessment. In R.M. Suinn (Ed.), *Psychology in* *sports,* Minneapolis, MN.: Burgess.

Nideffer briefly discusses each of the six attentional scales contained within the TAIS. He provides a quick assessement which can be used by students to determine their own attentional style. The article also presents a representative sample of attentional profiles ranging from a ''choking'' profile to an effective profile for sport performance.

Okwumabua, T.M., Meyers, A.W., Schleser, R., & Cooke, C.J. (1983). Cognitive strategies and running performance: An exploratory study. *Cognitive Therapy and Research, 7,* 363-370.

The authors looked at the issue of whether novice runners can be taught how to use cognitive strategies to improve performance. Regardless of instruction, it appears that inexperienced runners adopted either an associative or dissociative strategy.

Reis, J.A., & Bird, A.M. (1982). Cue processing as a function of breadth of attention. *Journal of Sport Psychology, 4*, 64-72.

Reis and Bird used an experimental design to test the predictive validity of the BET and RED scales from Nideffer's TAIS. They also manipulated state anxiety to observe effects on cue processing ability of broad and narrow attenders.

Van Schoyck, S.R., & Grasha, A.F. (1981). Attentional style variations and athletic ability: The advantages of a sports-specific test. *Journal of Sport Psychology, 3*, 149-165.

The authors devised and tested a tennis-specific version of the TAIS. This article presents several provocative criticisms concerning the usual approaches to attentional measurement.

Vallerand, R.J. (1983). Attention and decision making: A test of the predictive validity of the test of attention and interpersonal style (TAIS) in a sport setting. *Journal of Sport Psychology, 5*, 449-459.

Vallerand attempted to see if the TAIS would be sensitive enough to be able to discriminate between good, average, and poor decision makers. The results did not show support for the predicitive validity of the TAIS.

OBSERVATIONAL LEARNING AND MOTOR PERFORMANCE

Observational learning is the process of observing the behaviors of others and then attempting to imitate those behaviors. This is a powerful and important means of acquiring new, complex skills and refining the execution of already-existing skills. Sport psychologists are interested in observational learning because an athlete's choice of a model can profoundly affect future behaviors. The observational learning process can also influence motivation and level of anxiety.

THE NATURE OF OBSERVATIONAL LEARNING

Several variables affect the observational learning process. For example, is the most effective model one who most closely resembles the observer, or the most highly skilled model? Certain practice regimens or stategies are also important. For example, is it necessary to instruct the observer to try and mentally code information during model observation? At what point during practice is it best to observe a model: before initial physical practice or midway through practice? How much modeling should there be in relation to physical practice?

In teaching complex sport skills, knowledge of how observational learning can affect skill acquisition and refinement is critical. Observational learning is the most important of all methods of teaching sport skills. Sadly, little research attention has been given to this topic.

When physical educators and coaches teach novel or complex motor skills, the most common approach is a demonstration because skill acquisition is enhanced by the use of visual cues as opposed to verbal directions. For example, most of you know how to maintain your balance as you ride a bicycle. Could you verbally explain how you do that to someone else? For a baseball swing, a tennis serve, or a volleyball dive, could you explain the sequencing of the various muscle groups so that someone could actually execute a fairly accurate replica of the skill? In all these cases, verbal cues would be highly inadequate and a demonstration much more effective.

Although coaches and physical educators generally use the term *demonstration* to refer to the use of visual cues in the learning process, sport psychologists often use several other terms. *Observational learning, vicarious learning, imitative behavior,* and *modeling* can all be used interchangeably with the term *demonstration*. Whichever term is employed, it refers to the process by which an observer watches a model and then attempts to match his or her own response to that of the model.

EARLY THEORETICAL INTERPRETATIONS

The Behavioristic Perspective

Although there have been other behavioristically based interpretations of the observational learning process (such as Miller & Dollard, 1941), the most well-known is Gewirtz and Stingle's (1968) **generalized imitation theory.** This behavioristic theory proposes that observational learning is similar to any other type of learning; therefore it can be explained within the confines of the contingencies of reinforcement and the other principles associated with operant conditioning. In other words, reinforcement is the crucial element necessary for the observer to attempt to match the model's response.

Using the S–R–Re (stimulus-response-reinforcement) model, you can see how the modeling process operates from the perspective of generalized imitation theory. The S–R–Re elements refer to the operations of the observer. In this situation, stimulus *(S)* pertains to the model's observed action; response *(R)* is the observer's attempt to match the model's response through imitation. The subsequent application of reinforcement *(Re)* is predicted to strengthen the imitative tendency of the observer. Through this procedure the observer learns how to imitate a model's response. Again, the application of reinforcement is the critical factor for strengthening the imitiative response.

Once the person has learned to imitate, then, based on the **principle of stimulus generalization,** the observer would then tend to generalize the imitative behavior to new situations and new models. The imitative response was initially acquired through observation of a model, it was maintained through the application of reinforcement, and it then tends to generalize to other new observed responses, novel situations, and similar models. For example, suppose that a junior high school volleyball player was reinforced for modeling her behavior after that of her coach. The principle of stimulus generalization predicts that she would be highly likely to transfer the imitative behavior to her new coach when she reached high school.

There is currently some criticism of Gewirtz and Stingle's interpretation of the observational learning process. To propose that human learning is controlled by external determinants alone is simply not an adequate explanation. This does not mean that reinforcement cannot strengthen the imitative response; it means that reinforcement is not always absolutely necessary for the imitative response to occur. If the latter statement is true, then it argues against an interpretation that suggests that reinforcement is mandatory for observational learning to take place.

Symbolic Representational Theory

From quite a different perspective, Sheffield (1961) embarked on a research program designed to illuminate aspects of both filmed demonstrations and programmed instruction. As a result of that work he developed **symbolic representational theory.**

Symbolic representational theory's major tenet was that the function of model observation was to provide the learner with a cognitive, or symbolic, representation of a particular skill. This cognitive representation was then said to function as a guide for subsequent reproduction of the observed skill. It was proposed that by recalling from memory that which was observed, the learner would be able to refer to the cognitive representation to reproduce the act. Thus the primary determining factor in observational learning was proposed to be internal in the form of a cognitive representation.

Gould and Roberts (1982) have summarized several findings of Sheffield and his colleagues:

1. Modeling alone is not sufficient for adequate skill development; some overt practice must occur during the practice regime.
2. For skills that can be broken down into natural units, both model demonstrations and practice should parallel those units. For example, the swimming stroke of the front crawl can be broken down into the natural units of the kick, the arm motion, and the breathing technique. In this case, each unit should be demonstrated separately and then be followed by overt practice.
3. When using a filmed model or demonstration, the model should be filmed from the identical visual angle the observer will experience during overt practice. (This point also applies to live demonstrations.) Otherwise the observer would have to make perceptual adjustments to realign the correct visual perspective. Such adjustments can be distracting and detrimental to the learning process.

SOCIAL LEARNING THEORY

The symbolic representation perspective of Sheffield is a good introduction to the more sophisticated interpretation of Bandura. As opposed to the external determinism of human behavior reflected in the behavioristic interpretation of observational learning, Bandura's (1977) **social learning theory** proposes a framework that views humans as capable of self-direction and self-regulation. Whenever a psychological theory places a strong emphasis on notions such as personal control or self-determinism, then it must also rely on a cognitively based explanation of human behavior. If humans could not think clearly and logically, then it would not be possible to exercise effective and meaningful personal control over our own behavior; thus Bandura's social learning theory is indeed a cognitively based interpretation.

Social learning theory addresses the role of both reinforcement and observational learning. However, the most critical component of social learning theory is the explanation of how observational learning facilitates the learning of new or complex responses. Much emphasis is placed on the use of symbols to represent the meaning of information in memory or cognition and the role of self-regulatory or self-determining processes. Self-regulatory capacities allow persons to interpret, analyze, and transform the stimuli that act on them. Interpretation, analysis, and transformation of stimuli into symbols are cognitive activities. If humans are capable of accomplishing such activities, then we are not passive organisms who simply respond automatically to events occurring in the environment, as behavioristic theories of learning suggest.

Although cognitive in perspective, social learning theory does not totally ignore the effect of reinforcement on behavior. Instead, it takes a more expansive position on the role of reinforcement by identifying three different types.

The Role of Reinforcement in Observational Learning

A major distinction between Bandura's (1977) social learning theory and its behavioristic predecessors (namely, Gewirtz & Stingle, 1968; Miller & Dollard, 1941) concerns the role that reinforcement is said to play in the observational learning process. Recall that the behavioristic position proposed that reinforcement was mandatory for observational learning to be effective, whereas social learning theory says that it is a facilitative rather than a required element.

Bandura (1977) based his position on the role of reinforcement on three weaknesses inherent in the behavioristic interpretation. From his point of view, the behavioristic position cannot explain:

> observational learning where observers do not perform the model's responses in the setting in which they are exemplified, where neither the model nor the observers are reinforced, and whatever responses have been acquired observationally are first performed days, weeks, or months later. (p. 36)

Consider a youngster who sees his or her favorite athlete on television one Saturday morning and does not receive any kind of reinforcement for watching the performance. It is not until the following Thursday on the school's playground that an opportunity arises to try to imitate the behavior the youngster observed. In this situation an imitative response is emitted in a different setting, after a lapse of time, and in the absence of reinforcement. If the behavioristic position cannot adequately explain this situation, how does social learning theory explain it?

Social learning theory proposes that novel responses are coded symbolically (that is, represented mentally) during model observation. It is that ability to code symbolically, not reinforcement, that is the major explanatory concept. However, the role of reinforcement is not ignored within the theoretical framework of social learning theory. Reinforcement is viewed more as an antecedent (before) condition than a consequence (after) of behavior. Anticipation of reinforcement can have a positive influence on both attention to the model's behavior and retention of the observationally acquired information.

From the framework of social learning theory, the consequences of behavior (namely, reinforcement or punishment) regulate behavior through their informational or motivational value. As Bandura (1977) writes:

> For the most part, response consequences influence behavior antecedently by creating expectations of similar outcomes on future occasions. The likelihood of particular actions is increased by anticipated reward and reduced by anticipated punishment. (p. 96)

Response consequences are said to regulate behavior in three ways. The first is the usual application of **external reinforcement.** Second, response consequences can affect behavior by what the observer sees happen to the model after performance. This is called **vicarious reinforcement.** In vicarious reinforcement the observer can imagine experiencing the same consequences as did the model. Third, performers can generate their own self-imposed or self-regulated reinforcement. This is called **self-reinforcement.** These three types of reinforcement can act interdependently to determine behavior. The following section describes how each of these types of reinforcement relate to the observational learning process.

External Reinforcement

The fundamental framework of external reinforcement comprises the contingencies of reinforcement (stimulus–response–reinforcement) (p. 21). For example, suppose that a beginning or intermediate tennis player decides that watching the Wimbledon tournament on television might provide some useful strategies for play at the net. The player watches John McEnroe execute several outstanding cross-court volleys and is "psyched-up" to try that same strategy on the next appropriate occasion. During the next practice a perfect opportunity arises and the athlete makes an excellent point-winning cross-court volley. Both the coach and the player's opponent praise the shot. The player has received external reinforcement (verbal praise) and probably will try the same stroke again in the future.

Vicarious Reinforcement

Bandura (1977) has highlighted several implications concerning the role of vicarious reinforcement in learning in general and in observational learning in particular.

People do not learn everything about the world based on their own experiences, they also learn by observing the actions and consequences that others experience. These observations can influence behavior in much the same way as a person's own direct experiences.

For instance, the type of reinforcement you see others receive can serve as a standard for your own decision as to whether a reinforcement you receive is adequate or inadequate. This situation arises often in team sports. If a coach provides players with inequitable rewards for similar performances, then resentment and conflict arise among players. However, if the coach uses an equitable system of rewards, then usually all team members are satisfied.

In terms of observational learning of motor skills, the observation that the model received a positive reinforcement generally increases the probability that the observer will attempt to reproduce the modeled behavior. However, the positiveness or meaningfulness of the reinforcement is in "the eye of the beholder"; what is rewarding to an athlete may not be meaningful to a chemist.

The absence of negative consequences for socially undesirable behavior and the observation of negative consequences also affect behavior. If a new member on a basketball team observes that the returning players did not receive any reprimand for "horsing around" during practice, then it is likely that the new player will join in on the fun. Thus the absence of punishing consequences functions in a manner similar to positive reinforcement. However, if the new player observes that the players experience punishing consequences for their behavior, that observation will inhibit similar undesirable responses by that player.

Self-Reinforcement

People can also regulate their behavior through self-reinforcement. The process of self-reinforcement involves the athlete setting a goal for achievement and then rewarding himself or herself for attaining that goal. Most highly skilled athletes maintain their workouts and training regimens on the basis of self-reinforcement. They do not need an external source of rewards, such as a coach, to strive to achieve a higher degree of skill or fitness; they set their own performance goals, judge their achievement of those goals, and then either reward themselves or judge themselves negatively.

These personal standards can be influenced by both personal experience and the observation of models. The behavioral standards of children and adults are affected by the standards adopted by the models they observe. When models, such as coaches, adopt a high standard for reward, athletes (observers) tend to do likewise. When models adopt a low standard, athletes tend to follow suit (Bandura & Krupers, 1964; Marston, 1965).

The adoption of a self-reinforcement orientation gives the performer control over the direction and outcome of his or her own behavior. It is this tendency for self-reinforcement that underlies prolonged effort and sustained responses that occur in the absence of any apparent external reinforcement. Self-reinforcement motivates the athlete, the writer, and the researcher to continue to strive for excellence during long periods of working alone.

The Observational Learning Process

Representational Systems

Two cognitive, or symbolic, representational systems associated with the observational learning process are **imaginal** and **verbal.** Verbal representation of observationally derived information can be enhanced by instructing the observer to give verbal labels or codes to each part of a movement. For example, in observing a right-hander's four-step approach in bowling the observer might say "right," "left," "right," "left." For most motor skills however, the imaginal system is the dominant representational system. Usually, the visual sensory information gained through observation of a model is transformed (symbolically coded) into mental images. With sufficient repetition of the modeling experience and mental rehearsal of the codes, these images become more vivid and stable, and the performer can recall these imaginal codes from memory and use them as a guide for response production.

Conceptual (Cognitive) Representation

Social learning theory proposes that the acquisition and reproduction of observationally learned responses are mediated by the construction of a **cognitive representation** of the skill. This cognitive representation performs two functions: (1) it serves as the internal **template,** or model, for the production of a response and (2) it functions as a standard for correcting a response based on the feedback received after that response (Carroll & Bandura, 1982). Although Carroll and Bandura do not specify that the cognitive representation must have two identifiably separate parts, one to generate the movement and the other to represent the template (standard) for the response, current theory in motor learning mandates such a separation (Adams, 1971; Schmidt, 1975). This is because if only one representation of a response were constructed, then there would be no way to compare response feedback and make necessary corrections to the template; thus the same response would recur (Ross, 1983).

In Figure 7-1 two separate components depict the idea of a conceptual, or cognitive, representation of a motor skill (our interpretation may or may not totally agree with that of Carroll and Bandura.) The box on the left shows a template, or comparison center,

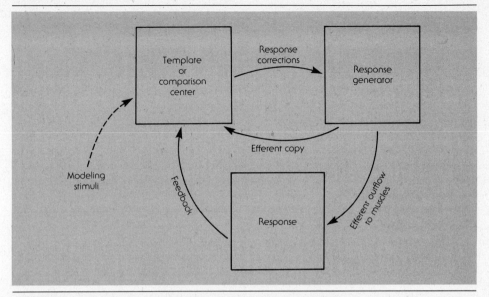

FIGURE 7-1   Schematic model of a cognitive representation.
Adapted from Keele, S.W. (1977). Current status of the motor program concept. In D.M. Landers and R.W. Christina (Eds.), *Psychology of motor behavior and sport*. Champaign, IL: Human Kinetics.

for a particular skill. This is developed by transforming observationally acquired information into symbolic codes. It is strengthened through repeated exposure to modeling stimuli, physical practice, and mental rehearsal of the codes. Such rehearsal may also cause the codes to be modified or reformulated into more concise codes, which reduces the demand on memory. Rehearsal may also enhance the retrievability of the symbolic representations from memory (Carroll & Bandura, 1982).

The box on the right of Figure 7-1 depicts a response, or movement, generator. A response is performed when a pattern of nerve impulses is sent from the brain to the appropriate muscles. This pattern causes the muscles to respond in a particular sequence and timing pattern (Keele, 1977). At the same time, identical information, called efferent copy, is sent to the comparison center of the brain. The efferent copy lets the comparison center know what the muscles were supposed to do. By comparing a response, on the basis of feedback, to the ideal represented by the cognitive template, a performer knows whether the response was correct or incorrect. Based on that comparison, corrections can be sent to the response generator and the performance should move toward a closer approximation of the ideal performance depicted by the template for the response.

In summary, the social learning perspective of observational learning encompasses the symbolic, or representational, systems of imaginal and verbal codes and employs a conceptual-matching procedure. The information gained through observing a model is transformed into symbolic codes, which are then used to develop a cognitive, or conceptual, template (model) of the motor skill. Through further observation, rehearsal of the codes, and matching performance feedback to the template, successive responses should more closely approximate the desired response.

TABLE 7-1   Factors Affecting the Observational Learning Process

Learning Factors	Performance Factors
Attention Processes	Motoric reproduction processes
Retention Processes	Motivation processes

Factors Influencing the Observational Learning Process

As shown in Table 7-1, Bandura has identified two factors or processes that may affect the learning of a skill and two factors or variables that may influence the performance of a response. Because social learning theory takes the position that observational learning functions primarily through information the observer gains from the model, any factor or process that influences the potency of that information affects the observational learning process.

Attention

In observational learning, if the observer does not attend to the model's behavior, then little or nothing will be learned. Bandura (1977) has identified several factors that can influence the attention of the observer to the model's behavior.

Associational patterns have a strong influence on what is learned observationally. People tend to emulate the behaviors of those with whom they most often associate socially; athletes tend to imitate other athletes, artists tend to imitate other artists. These associational patterns generate a stereotypical manner of behaving. Thus if you want someone to be aggressive, have him or her associate with people who exhibit aggressive behaviors. If you want someone to have strong achieving tendencies, have him or her interact with people who are high achievers.

Model characteristics influence the attentional direction of observers. For example, models who have *social power* tend to be imitated more than those who do not. Social power refers to the number of potential reinforcers over which a person has control. High social control may be why athletes tend to imitate a coach or team captain more than the student manager. People who are the recipients of many rewards also tend to be selected as models, as do people with high degrees of personal attraction. Sport examples of such persons are Mary Lou Retton (1984 Olympic gymnast), and Valarie Brisko-Hooks and Carl Lewis (both 1984 track and field stars).

Other factors affecting attention during exposure to a model include *the nature of the response or skill to be demonstrated*. As mentioned earlier (see p. 65), a novel task frequently increases arousal or alertness. This increase can help direct attention to the modeled behavior. The *age of the observer* can also influence what is learned observationally. If a child has not reached a stage of cognitive development sufficient to process the cues necessary to code the modeled behavior, then little will be gained through the demonstration.

Retention

Exposure to a model is of no benefit if the observer does not remember the modeled behavior. To retain the observational information, the observed behavior must be converted into symbolic form (that is, imaginal or verbal codes) and stored in memory. This ability to store modeling information in symbolic form allows the performer to reproduce the observational response after a delay of time. Two major aids to the retention of modeled behavior, in addition to symbolic coding, are mental rehearsal of the symbolic codes and actual performance or practice of the modeled response (Bandura, 1977; Jeffrey, 1974).

Motoric Reproduction Processes

Motoric reproduction processes refer to the ability to enact a physical response on the basis of a symbolic representation of the response. The symbolic codes or cognitive representation serves as a guide to the overt action.

If the performer has the appropriate skills in his or her repertoire of available responses, then reproduction of the modeled behavior should not be a problem. But if some of the necessary elements or skills are lacking, then further practice, modeling, and information feedback will be required.

Motivational Processes

Acquiring information observationally does not mean that the observer will overtly perform the modeled behavior. Bandura (1977) has identified some factors that influence whether or not the observer will perform the response.

The consequences of the model's response play an important role in motivating the observer. If the model is positively reinforced after the response (that is, vicarious reinforcement), then the probability increases that the observer will mimic that same response.

Positive emotional or affective reactions by the model can also facilitate imitative behavior by the observer.

Observational Learning and the Unifying Model

The unifying model can help pull together the various components of the observational learning process (Figure 7-2).

Input

For an observer to learn observationally, the first prerequisite is the presence of a model. The model's behavior is the observer's source of information.

Process

No modeling will take place unless the observer attends to the appropriate model-related cues. Information acquired observationally must be coded in symbolic form, if it is to be retained. Preobservation instructions telling the observer to code the modeled behavior increase the amount of information the observer remembers.

Output

An observer will not perform a response learned through modeling if he or she is not motivated to execute the response. Psychological factors that affect motivation level are the positive nature of the response outcome for the model and the value the observer

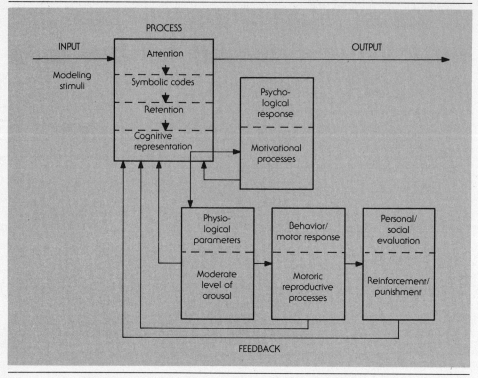

FIGURE 7-2   Observational learning and the unifying model.

attaches to the response. Physiologically, sufficient arousal must be present to perform the modeled behavior. Behaviorally, performance of the observationally learned response requires that the observer have the necessary physical capabilities. Beginning tennis players might be able to acquire large amounts of skill information by observing professionals such as Chris Evert Lloyd or Jimmy Conners; however, they cannot reproduce those skills until they have more experience and greater skill development.

The positive or negative content of the evaluation of performance outcomes affects the observational learning process in at least two ways. Responses that are followed by positive consequences tend to be repeated, whereas responses that generate unpleasant evaluations tend to be extinguished or avoided. Therefore, if the matching behavior of the observer is reinforced, then such matching responses should recur.

Feedback

The role of feedback in the observational learning process cannot be overemphasized, particularly when the skill in question involves complex interactions among parameters such as force, time, and spatial relationships. Feedback can be kinesthetic, visual, or auditory. The error information (knowledge of results) a coach or teacher provides an athlete after a response also functions as feedback. Feedback is used to check the correctness of a movement response by comparing it to the template, or cognitive representation, of the skill.

THE OBSERVATIONAL LEARNING OF MOTOR SKILLS

Model Characteristics

Status and Similarity to Observer

Landers and Landers (1973) tested two different aspects of Bandura's social learning theory. First, they tested whether or not the learning of a novel motor skill through observational strategies would occur in the absence of any reinforcement to either the model or the observer. Second, they tested the notion that models with higher social status (that is, teachers with high skill) would result in superior performance on the part of observers as compared with models with lower social status (that is, peers with low skill).

The results confirmed Bandura's assertion that reinforcement was not a necessary component within the observational learning process. The results showed that subjects who saw a skilled teacher model performed better than subjects who observed an unskilled-teacher or skilled-peer model. However, children who observed an unskilled-peer model performed better than those exposed to an unskilled-teacher model.

There are several plausible explanations for the latter effect. One is that the observers simply matched their behavior to that of the unskilled teacher. Another explanation might be that the observers were embarassed for the unskilled teacher and shifted their attention away from the modeling demonstration. The superior performance by the observers of the unskilled peer can be explained in terms of both Bandura's social learning theory and the social comparison theory of Festinger (1954). Both theories propose that persons tend to identify with others who are most similar to themselves in attributes such as age and ability. The subjects in the Landers and Landers (1973) study were young women enrolled in physical education classes. It seems reasonable that more of these students would consider themselves unskilled rather than skilled; therefore, they would tend to identify more with a model most like themselves, the unskilled peer as opposed to the skilled-peer.

Overall, the findings of this investigation supported Bandura's interpretation of observational learning. Reinforcement was shown not to be a critical variable in that process. The model with the highest degree of social status (skilled teacher) generated the greatest learning effects in observers. Finally, observers tended to benefit more by observing a more similar model (unskilled peer) as opposed to a less similar model (skilled peer).

Although the findings do support Bandura's theoretical interpretation, they also call into question the basis on which models are selected for demonstrations of sport and motor skills. If a skilled teacher is not available to demonstrate, who is ordinarily selected? A skilled peer. That may be fine if all the observers are similarly skilled, such as on a varsity team; however, in beginning skills classes it may not be the best selection.

Gould and Weiss (1981) also addressed the question of model similarity and modeling effects. They were also interested in ascertaining the effect of various statements made by models on observer's performance. Three different types of model self-statements were used: positive, negative, and irrelevant. An example of a positive self-statement was "Doing pretty well so far." A negative self-statement was "I'm not very good at tests like this." Irrelevant self-statements were "This is probably good for the stomach muscles'' and ''We used to do an exercise like this in physical education class'' (p. 21). A fourth group made no statements.

Generally, the findings supported the superiority of similar over dissimilar models for the enhancement of observer performance. Furthermore, the similar–no-statement and similar–positive-statement models were superior to the dissimilar–positive-statement, dissimilar–no-statement, dissimilar–negative-statement, and control (no model) groups.

Together, these two studies argue for the importance of addressing aspects of the social and personal characteristics of models when designing observationally based learning strategies. Also, the Gould and Weiss (1981) investigation suggests that observers attend not only to the model's performance but also to other model actions such as positive or negative remarks.

Model Strategy

Do observers learn strategy as well as skill components from a model? Martens, Burwitz, and Zuckerman (1976) conducted a series of related experiments designed to examine aspects of this question. The first three experiments used four treatment groups, including three different modeling groups—a correct model, an incorrect model, and a learning sequence model—and a no-model control group. The learning sequence model showed a gradual movement from incorrect to correct performance, culminating in a perfect execution of the modeled skill by the last observation (the task was a simple ball roll-up skill).

The results of both the first and second experiments indicated that observers performed better after viewing either a correct or learning sequence model as compared with the no-model control group. However, this superiority in performance was only evident during the early stages of learning. Using a more difficult task, the third experiment indicated that observers do learn to model strategy as well as skill components.

Observer Characteristics

Age

Because social learning theory is a cognitively based interpretation of the observational learning process, it seems reasonable that observers must have a certain degree of cognitive development to receive optimal learning benefits. It is interesting to note that few published investigations address the question of how age relates to aspects of the observational learning of motor skills (Feltz, 1982; Thomas, Pierce, & Ridsdale, 1977; Weiss, 1983).

Thomas, Pierce, and Ridsdale (1977) studied the effect of observing a model either before practice or midway within the practice session on children's performance of a balancing task. Both age groups (second-graders and fourth-graders) benefited from observing a model before their own performance. However, the midway observation of a model had different effects on the two age groups. Midway observation was beneficial to the older children and detrimental to the younger children.

Feltz (1982) examined a similar question. She found that college-age performers had better performance and truer form on a balance task as compared with fourth- and fifth-graders as a function of observing a model. In neither the Feltz nor the Thomas, Pierce, and Ridsdale investigations were performers provided with verbal instructions to help them attend selectively to the most important cues. Given that younger performers probably do not have the same cognitive processing capacities as older performers, such verbal instructions could be used to help younger performers select and attend to task-relevant cues. Support for this assertion comes also from the work of Yando, Seitz, and Zigler (1978), who provided some evidence that when children are not told what cue to pay attention to, they may attend equally to both task-relevant and task-irrelevant cues.

A recent study by Weiss (1983) looked more specifically at how verbal cues accompanying a model presentation affected the motor performance of children in the age ranges of 4 to 5 and 7 to 8. Three experimental groups were formed: a no–verbal cue (silent) model, a model who verbalized task-relevant cues, and a no-model control group.

The most important finding of the Weiss investigation was that age interacted with model type. More specifically, the older children (ages 7-8) performed equally well after observing either a silent or a verbal model. However, the younger children (ages 4-5) performed best only after exposure to the verbal model. Also, although not surprising, the older children had superior performance as compared with the younger children.

The Weiss study highlights some implications for instructional strategies appropriate for the teaching of motor skills to children. The apparent differences in the cognitive capacities between the younger and older children suggest that younger children's motor performance can be enhanced by using both verbal cues and visual cues during a model demonstration. These cues can help youngsters to direct attention to the task-relevant cues most important to performance.

Level of Anxiety

Should high anxiety have a positive or negative effect on observational learning? Currently, the relationship between level of anxiety and effects on observational learning is unclear. Sarason and his colleagues (Sarason, 1968; Sarason, Pederson, & Nyman, 1968) have studied the effects of high test anxiety on the observational learning of verbal tasks. Their evidence suggests that highly test-anxious persons learn more observationally then do less test-anxious persons. These scientists have suggested that highly test-anxious persons may benefit more from exposure to models because, such persons also tend to be more insecure and therefore, tend to look outside of themselves for task-related information. Their analysis is somewhat in agreement with Bandura (1977), who suggests that persons lacking confidence and self-esteem and who are dependent tend to imitate more. However, much controversy still exists. First, Bandura and Sarason, Pederson, and Nyman were not referring specifically to the observational learning of motor skills; their analyses were based on social and verbal skills. Second, as discussed in Chapter 6, there is a wealth of evidence to suggest that increases in level of anxiety should result in attentional disruptions that hinder the identification and processing of task-relevant cues.

Presently, there appears to be only one study that has specifically examined the relationship between level of anxiety and the observational learning of motor skills. Zoeller (1983) investigated timing performance under conditions of either modeling or physical practice. These findings indicated specific differences between the high-anxious groups who had practiced physically as opposed to observationally. The high-anxious–physical practice group demonstrated significantly less errors on the timing task as compared with the high-anxious–modeling group. High levels of anxiety were extremely disruptive to learning observationally, but not to learning through physical practice. It can be presumed that high levels of anxiety disrupted the subject's ability to select and process the appropriate, task-related cues provided by the model.

During observational learning the cues for skill acquisition are external. Therefore, perhaps high levels of anxiety disrupt the attentional processing capabilities of the observers. This explanation seems reasonable, given the relationships discussed previously concerning the connection between ineffective cue processing and conditions of high anxiety (p. 154). One additional point warrants mention. In the Zoeller (1983) study, subjects were not provided with selective attention instructions. Because previous research has shown that such instructions facilitate observational learning (McGuire, 1961; Sheffield & Maccoby, 1961), perhaps the disruptive effects of high anxiety would not have been evidenced so vividly if the subjects had been instructed to attend to only the most critical aspects of the modeled behavior.

Task Characteristics

Novelty and Complexity

Recall from our discussion of the stages of skill learning (p. 66) that in the beginning of skill acquisition, responses are organized through the use of cognitive functions. If a skill is simple and if the performer is physically capable of emitting the desired response, then the presentation of even a single demonstration can enable the performer to establish a cognitive representation. However, if skills are novel and complex, then their development requires more repetitions of the modeled behavior, physical practice, and performance feedback. Together these activities enhance the development of an accurate cognitive representation and provide the corrections necessary for increasingly better skill executions (Carroll & Bandura, 1982).

The position of Bandura and his colleagues concerning the effectiveness of modeling for the acquisition of complex skills is also consistent with that of Gould (1978). Gould's research has indicated that observational learning enhances the acquisition of motor skills that have higher degrees of *information load*. Information load refers to either the number of steps required to reproduce the movement or the degree of strategy inherent in the movement.

The above evidence indicates that the learning of novel and complex motor skills is facilitated significantly by the observation of a model. However, the reproduction of simple skills probably is not affected as dramatically by similar exposure to a model.

Visual Field

In addition to identifying the role that observational learning plays in the acquisition of complex, novel skills, Bandura and his colleagues (Bandura, 1977; Carroll & Bandura, 1982) have also proposed that modeling can facilitate the performance of skills in which certain components must be enacted outside of the visual field.

Particularly in the early stages of skill acquisition, performers are highly dependent on visual information or visual feedback (Fleishman & Rich, 1963). Therefore skill acquisition can be hindered when performers cannot visually monitor aspects of the motor response that occur outside their visual field. For example, bowlers cannot see the height of their backswing and golfers cannot see whether or not they keep their club parallel to the ground at the height of the backswing. In both cases, two problems tend to arise.

First, the performer cannot detect mismatches between the cognitive representation of the skill and actual performance. Second, the athlete may assume that the movement is being performed correctly when it is not (Carroll & Bandura, 1982). Both factors tend to diminish the effectiveness of the performance feedback. Model observations can provide the performer with more accurate skill-related information then they receive from their own overt performance.

Practice-Related Variables

Symbolic Coding

There is a wealth of evidence that when performers are told to transform modeled information into imaginal or verbal codes during observation, motor performance improves (Bandura & Jeffery, 1973; Bandura, Jeffery, & Bachicha, 1974; Carroll & Bandura, 1982; Gerst, 1971; Jeffery, 1976). For instance, instructing an observer to code an observed tennis serve by using the numbers 1 through 6 could enhance the amount learned. When the observer sees the ball toss, the number 1 would be said. The number 3 would be coded with the racket drop in the back. Number 6 would coincide with the completion of the follow-through. If the timing of saying the numbers remains consistent, those verbal labels can help to achieve the correct movement sequence and timing.

When the codes are both meaningful and retrievable to the performer, the symbolic coding function is even more beneficial. To help the athlete make the codes more meaningful, either letter associates or mnemonic devices can be used (Bandura, Jeffery, & Bachicha, 1974). Letter associates are simply the first letter of each word that describes a particular movement. Mnemonic devices are phrases that help retention by making the code more meaningful to the performer. For example, if you observed a model perform a polka step, you would see that the components of that dance step could be broken down into the fundamental movements of hop, step, step. The appropriate letter associates would then be HSS. To construct a mnemonic sentence or phrase, you would simply invent a phrase using each of those letters for the beginning of each word; for example, "Her sad self."

Temporal Spacing and Number of Repetitions

Other factors that appear to affect the observational learning process are whether or not the modeled demonstration is repeated or distributed throughout the practice regime and the total number of times the model is presented to the observer.

To date, only two studies have specifically addressed the issue of the temporal spacing of the model demonstrations throughout the motor skill practice session. Landers' (1975) results indicated some limited support for the facilitating effect of having an observer see a model both before and midway through practice.

Contrary to Landers' (1975) findings, Thomas, Pierce, and Ridsdale (1977) showed that age of the performer affected whether or not seeing a model both before and midway through practice was beneficial. In looking at younger children (age 7), they found that the presentation of a model midway through practice had a detrimental effect on performance. On the other hand, that same midway presentation of a model improved the performance of the older children (age 9). Both groups benefited from exposure to a model before their own performance.

Based on the limited amount of evidence, it appears that the effectiveness of repeated model demonstrations throughout the practice regime is somewhat dependent on the cognitive development of the observers. It may be that the introduction of a model midway within the practice session of younger children disrupts cognitive processing. However, the situation remains unclear. For example, based on the Weiss (1983) investigation discussed on p. 183, if the modeled behavior was accompanied by verbal labels or cues, then such midperformance presentations could enhance rather than hinder the observational learning of younger children. Again, this is an area that needs more systematic research before any firm conclusions can be drawn.

Is it possible to identify the exact number of demonstrations that will most positively affect motor skill acquisition? Based on current evidence, the answer to that question is no. There have not been enough investigations designed to answer this question; however, some suggestive evidence exists. Based on Feltz's (1982) analysis, it appears that the optimal number of model demonstrations depends on two associated factors: the nature of the skill to be demonstrated and the number or length of the practice sessions. Apparently, the more difficult the skill, the more likely repeated exposure to a model (with accompanying physical practice) will benefit response acquisition and reproduction. Furthermore, there may be an inverse relationship between the number of model demonstrations and the length of practice; that is, with more or longer practice, fewer model demonstrations are required to enhance learning as compared with fewer or shorter practices. This relationship also needs further study.

Practice Variability

Practice variability refers to a strategy whereby the performer practices several different but related tasks. This is in opposition to constant practice, wherein the performer repeatedly practices the identical task or goal. For example, in variable practice a basketball player would practice jump shots from several locations on the court. In constant practice the jump shot would consistently be practiced from the same location.

Bird and Rikli (1983) were interested in investigating the effects of variable versus constant practice during both observational learning and physical practice. Their results supported the superiority of variable practice during both observational and physical practice. In addition, subjects in the observational learning–variable practice group were able to perform in a manner highly similar to subjects in the physical practice–constant practice group. This was a particularly important result because the subjects in the observational learning–variable practice group had never performed an overt response during practice. It appears that the observation of a model engaged in a variable practice routine provided a rich enough source of information so that these observers were able to construct a cognitive representation comparable to that of subjects who had actually practiced (physical practice–constant-practice).

Observational versus Physical Practice

How much should an athlete practice physically versus observationally? Several researchers (for example, Bandura & Carroll, 1982; Keele, 1977) have suggested that some amount of physical practice, in addition to observational practice, is necessary for the learning of complex motor skills. However, little research attention has been directed toward determining the ideal ratio of physical versus observational practice.

In an initial study of this issue, Bird, Ross, and Laguna (1982) investigated the effects of seven different practice combinations on the retention of a timing response. The conditions were varied in terms of the amount of physical practice versus observational practice, ranging from 100% physical practice to 100% observational practice. Five combination groups (observational and physical practice) were also included. Analysis of the retention data indicated that four out of five groups that included some combination of observational learning and physical practice performed better than the 100% physical practice group. Only the minimal observational learning group (16% observation, 84% physical practice) was no different than the 100% physical practice group. Within the combined groups (some percentage of time observing a model and some percentage of time practicing physically), subjects who spent at least one-third or more of their practice time observing a model had superior performances.

Bird, Ross, and Laguna's data also indicated that the major activity during the early stages of skill acquisition is indeed cognitive. Apparently, model observation is a better way to develop a cognitive representation early in learning. However, it again needs to be stressed that some physical practice with accompaning information feedback is also required. In fact, in the Bird, Ross, and Laguna investigation, the group that spent 100% of their time observing a model had many more errors than the other groups.

What about the relative effectiveness of observational learning versus videotape feedback (VTFB)? Ross, Bird, Doody, and Zoeller (in press) looked at three different treatments using physical practice and modeling, VTFB, or a combination of modeling and VTFB, respectively. They also included an all–physical practice control group. After a retention period, the modeling group was clearly superior to all the other groups. These data again argue for the potency of a combined modeling and physical practice regime for the acquisition of motor skills. It remains to be seen, however, if that same effect would be evidenced in later learning.

Visual Versus Auditory Modes

Although people usually think of modeling in terms of a source of visual information, other informational modes can function as models. In some tasks, such as timing tasks, it is possible that auditory models may be superior to visual models. To test this assumption, Doody, Bird, and Ross (in press) divided subjects into four groups: an audio group (heard a recording of correctly executed trials), a visual group (saw a model perform the task correctly), a combined audio and visual group, and a control group (all physical practice). The dependent variable was the same timing task employed in the two previous studies. The results indicated that the audio, visual, and combined audio-visual groups were superior to the physical practice group. In addition, both the audio and the combined audio-visual conditions were superior to the visual group. These findings indicate that the use of an auditory or combined audio-visual model may be better than a presentation of only a visual model for tasks characterized by a distinct timing paramenter. These findings are similar to the tennis practice technique suggested by Gallway (1974). He suggests that during a rally, players should use the auditory cues of saying "bounce" and "hit" while visually tracking the ball. Many tennis players have found this combination of visual and auditory cues extremely helpful.

The research program of Bird, Ross, and Doody is important for several reasons. It is the first systematic test of hypotheses derived from contemporary motor learning research to assess their capacity for explaining the processes underlying observational learning of motor skills. In most previous research, immediate or performance effects were assessed and effects on learning were then inferred. However, in most of the current investigations, long-term, or retention, effects were measured directly.

Also, in the vast majority of observationally based studies of motor skills the data were collected in field settings and limited in terms of the skill modeled. Such an approach leads to two problems. First, it is difficult to gain full experimental control under field conditions. Second, by using highly specific skills, researchers may learn something about how observational learning affects the acquisition of that particular skill; however, they may not be able to generalize that information to other skills because those findings may not indicate much about the skill components being acquired observationally. Bird, Ross, and Doody used a timing task in their research. Previous research has shown that relative timing is an integral and invariant process within a motor program (for our purposes a motor program can be considered to be the same as a cognitive representation). Therefore, the results of studies using a timing task can be more easily generalized to other tasks that have a major timing component. The use of a task that reflects a major component of a motor program, combined with the highly controlled conditions of a laboratory setting, allows researchers to more fully demonstrate the mechanisms and processes underlying the observational learning of motor skills. Future research is needed on other parameters associated with motor programs, such as force and speed, in both laboratory and field settings.

IMPLICATIONS FOR SPORT

- Some overt practice must accompany the observational learning of sport skills. Apparently, a minimum of one third of practice time needs to be devoted to physical practice.
- When sport skills have natural subcomponents or segments, the modeling demonstrations should mirror those units. A good example is the side stroke in swimming, which involves different motor patterns for the arms and legs.
- Perform the demonstration so that the athlete views it from the same visual angle he or she will experience during actual performance.
- Because coaches have high degrees of social power, they frequently serve as role models. Thus coaches should exhibit the same behavior they would like to see in their athletes.
- Provide athletes with preobservation instructions concerning what cues to observe during a demonstration. Instruct them to symbolically code those cues during the modeling session and to imaginally rehearse them afterward.
- Models who are reinforced and who exhibit positive emotional (affective) reactions can increase the observer's motivation to attend to the demonstration.
- Promote self-regulation on the part of athletes by encouraging them to set goals and to reward themselves for achieving those goals.
- When choosing a model, a skilled teacher or coach is best. If this is not possible, select a model who is most similar to the particular class or team.
- When using demonstrations, particularly with younger children, use both verbal and visual cues.

- Because high degrees of anxiety appear to disrupt the observational learning process, establish a calm and supportive atmosphere before a demonstration.
- Use modeling strategies to introduce new skills that are complicated and require high degrees of procedural or cognitive demand.
- Demonstrations may be particularly effective for skill components that must be executed outside the performer's visual field.
- Space the demonstrations throughout the practice session and provide several opportunities to observe the model.
- Have the students or athletes observe a model under as many different circumstances as possible.
- For skills that require a timing component, use both visual and auditory cues. The tennis serve is a good example of such a skill.

CASE STUDY 1

Observational Learning and Motor Skill Acquisition

As discussed throughout this chapter, there are several factors that can influence the effectiveness of a model in teaching sport skills. This case study uses the breaststroke in swimming to demonstrate how the acquisition of this skill can be enhanced through observational strategies. The observational training program is divided into three parts: pre-observation, observation, and post-observation.

Pre-observation

Try to increase observer alertness and attention by indicating that the skill to be demonstrated (breaststroke) will be practiced in the pool immediately after the observational period. The anticipation of future evaluation usually increases attention to the modeled behavior.

Provide instructions that direct the observer's attention to the most relevant parts of the skill. The component parts of the breaststroke can be broken down into three movements: (1) the arm pull, (2) the whip kick, and (3) the glide. To facilitate the synchronization process, put verbal labels on the three skill components: "pull," "kick," "glide". After the observer is familiar with the verbal labels, instruct him or her to say those labels as the appropriate movement occurs during the observational period.

Remind the observer to attend only to the order in which each skill segment occurs during the modeled demonstration.

Observation

Select either a skilled-teacher model or plan to obtain a film strip of a correct model. Repeat the modeled demonstration at least two times.

Post-observation

Have the observer mentally rehearse the verbal labels and concentrate on the timing of the skill while saying each label.

Have the observer physically practice the breaststroke and provide information feedback after the overt response.

Have the observer imaginally rehearse the skill. Then have the observer physically practice the stroke again and provide positive reinforcement if the skill execution approximates the desired standard. Provide further information feedback to decrease any mismatch between overt performance and the performance standard.

Suggest that the observer take time to verbally and imaginally rehearse the movement pattern before the next attempt at overt performance.

Instruct the observer to mentally compare actual skill execution with the mental picture of the skill and make the necessary adjustments in the next performance attempt.

CASE STUDY 2

Observational Learning and Motor Skill Refinement

Case study 1 addressed specifically the question of how observational learning might be used to enhance the initial acquistion of a new motor skill. This case study focuses on how observationally based strategies might be used to refine or further develop an already existing motor skill.

As many teachers and coaches know, one of the most difficult problems encountered when working with athletes of intermediate or high levels of ability is trying to convince performers that they are not accurately performing a portion of a sport skill that is outside their field of vision. Below we have listed some steps that can be used to help solve this type of problem by fostering a better match between actual performance and the performer's cognitive template.

1. Point out the performance error and provide corrective feedback relative to the standard of performance.
2. Have the performer execute the skill again. If the response more closely approximates the standard, provide postive reinforcement and more corrective feedback. If there is little or no change in the quality of the response, follow steps 3 through 10.
3. Provide a correct model demonstration, pointing out the most relevant cues.
4. Repeat the model demonstration and remind the observer about the cues most relevant to performance.
5. Have the performer execute the overt response. Provide corrective feedback or positive reinforcement. If there is still little change in the match between the standard and the overt response, then introduce videotape feedback.
6. Videotape the performer's response.
7. Repeat the modeled demonstration, including instructions to attend to the movement pattern that takes place outside the model's field of vision.
8. Have the performer view the videotape of his or her own response, comparing the movement pattern of the model with his or her own movement pattern.
9. Have the performer mentally rehearse the correct movement pattern.
10. Have the performer attempt the correct physical response. Provide corrective and positive feedback. If a severe mismatch between the overt response and the standard still exists, repeat the modeling, videotape, and physical practice procedures.

SUMMARY

- Earlier theoretical interpretations of the observational learning process included the behavioristic approach of Gewirtz and Stingle (1968) and the symbolic representational position of Sheffield (1961). The behavioristic interpretation assumed that reinforcement was crucial to learning through observation, which is a mechanistic position that interprets behavior from the point of view of external determinism. The symbolic representation position held that information acquired observationally was reformulated into symbolic codes and is a cognitive perspective of skill acquisition.
- Currently, the most accepted theoretical perspective concerning the process of observational learning is Bandura's social learning theory, which is also a cognitively based interpretation. However, it is a more sophisticated and more fully-developed framework that argues that aspects of the person, behavior, and environment must be considered to act interdependently as influences on performance.
- A major difference between Bandura's social learning theory and the earlier behavioristic positions is the role in which reinforcement is said to play in the observational learning process. The behavioristic position proposes that reinforcement is mandatory, whereas the social learning perspective posits that it is facilitating rather than necessary.
- The three types of reinforcement that can influence the modeling process are external reinforcement, vicarious reinforcement, and self-reinforcement.
- In terms of observational learning, social learning theory proposes that two representational systems, imaginal and verbal, are used to code information acquired observationally. The imaginal system is the most potent in terms of coding information associated with complex motor skills.
- Social learning theory also says that observational learning involves a conceptual, or cognitive, representation of motor skills. The cognitive representation serves as both a standard of comparison, or template, and as a movement generator. After performing a motor response, the feedback generated as a consequence of that response is compared with the template in the cognitive representation and corrections are made on the basis of this comparison. Through this matching process, overt performance should then move increasingly closer to the desired or ideal response.
- Bandura (1977) indicated that the learning of a skill through observational strategies is affected both by the amount of attention that the observer gives to the modeled behavior and the amount of observationally derived information the observer remembers. The overt performance of skills acquired observationally depends on both the motoric reproduction capacity of the observer and the incentives or motivation attached to the modeled behavior.
- The framework of the unifying model can further a better conceptual understanding of the multifaceted nature of the observational learning process by identifying influencing variables at the stages of input, process, output, and feedback.
- Research evidence on the observational learning of motor skills has revealed that several variables can affect this process, including characteristics of the model and the observer, and the nature of the task to be learned.

- Practice-related factors can also hinder or encourage learning through model observation.
- Learning can be affected positively by providing instructions that indicate that the observer should symbolically code the information gained observationally.
- Other factors that appear to influence the quality of the practice regime are the temporal spacing of the model within the practice session, the number of model repetitions, whether the practice is variable or constant, and the relative amount of vicarious versus physical practice.

DISCUSSION QUESTIONS

1 Of the theoretical interpretations of observational learning that have been presented, which is the most comprehensive orientation (that is, generalized imitation theory, symbolic representational theory, and social learning theory)?
2 Identify and define three types of reinforcers.
3 What is the rationale underlying the argument that the cognitive representation of a motor skill must have two separate components: a template, or comparison center, and a movement generator?
4 Identify as many factors as possible that could affect whether or not a motor skill is learned observationally.
5 Identify as many factors as possible that could determine whether or not an observer will actually perform a skill learned through observation of a model.
6 Throughout this chapter, several areas in need of further research were identified. Take one of those and design an investigation that could provide some much-needed information concerning the observational learning of motor skills. Based on what you now know about modeling, be sure to advance a hypothesis for your proposed study.

GLOSSARY

cognitive representation Mental representation or internal template for the production of a response and a standard for making response corrections based on feedback
external reinforcement Reinforcement that originates from outside the person
generalized imitation theory Behavioristic theory that proposes that modeling can best be explained through the contingencies of reinforcement
imaginal representation system Symbolic coding of information in pictorial, or visual, forms
kinethesis Sensory information regarding position and movement that arises from body parts such as the limbs, neck, and trunk
long-term memory Permanent information storage component of the brain
mnemonic device An aid or linguistic formula designed to improve retention of information
operant conditioning Conditioning in which a response is followed by a reinforcing event, increasing the strength and likelihood of recurrence of that response
principle of stimulus generalization Principle that states that once a response has become associated with one stimulus there is a tendency for the response to transfer to new, similar stimuli
reciprocal relationship A mutual, equivalent, or interchangeable relationship
replica Facsimile of an original; for example, an observer's matching response based on the model's original response

self-reinforcement   Self-generated reinforcement

social learning theory   Cognitively based theory of observational learning that emphasizes the role of symbolic coding and self-determining processes

symbol   A representation of the meaning of information in memory or cognition

symbolic representational theory   First cognitively based theory of observational learning

template   A cognitive plan or mental model that is a mirror image of a motor skill or movement pattern

verbal representational system   Symbolic coding of information in linguistic forms

vicarious reinforcement   Reinforcement that the model receives after performance

SUGGESTED READINGS

Bandura, A. (1977). *Social learning theory*. Englewood Cliffs, N.J.: Prentice Hall.

   This is an easy-to-read book that presents the basic tenets of social learning theory. It emphasizes the role of observational learning and reinforcement in the acquisition and maintenance of behavior.

Flanders, J.P. (1968). Review of research on imitative behavior. *Psychological Bulletin, 69*, 316-337.

   Flanders' classic review paper on the observational learning process covers several variables thought to affect the modeling process and various theoretical perspectives.

Gould, D.R., & Roberts, G.C. (1982). Modeling and motor skill acquisition. *Quest, 33*, 214-230.

   The authors review the literature concerning the modeling process as it operates in motor skill acquisition. Topics include modeling theory, task specificity, symbolic coding, temporal spacing of demonstrations, social factors, and the role of modeling in anxiety reduction.

Ladd, G.W., & Mize, J. (1983). A cognitive-social learning model of social-skill training. *Psychological Review, 90*, 127-157.

   This article explores the purposes, methods, findings, and future directions of social-skill training research. It identifies important or promising variables for behavior change.

Landers, D.M. (1978). How, when, and where to use demonstrations: Suggestions for the practitioner. *Journal of Physical Education and Recreation, 49*, 65-67.

   In this article, Landers draws on the available research evidence to provide some useful guidelines that teachers and coaches can use to most effectively present modeling demonstrations.

Weiss, M.R. (1982). Developmental modeling: Enhancing the children's motor skill acquisition. *Journal of Physical Education, Recreation and Dance, 53*, 49-50.

   Weiss presents important developmental factors that teachers should be aware of when using observational learning strategies with young children. Emphasis is given to the variables of cognitive-developmental level and motivation orientations.

Weiss, M.R. (1983). Modeling and motor performance: A developmental perspective. *Research Quarterly for Exercise and Sport, 54*, 190-197.

   In this article, Weiss assessed the variables of age, type of model, and verbal self-instructions during children's observational learning. Results supported the premise that age-related or developmental factors play an important role in the modeling process.

IMAGERY, SPORT, AND MOTOR BEHAVIOR

The study of imagery is concerned primarily with how people represent and process information mentally or symbolically. Within the field of sport and physical education, what is now referred to as imagery was originally called mental practice. Early mental practice studies focused on determining whether mentally practicing a motor skill before physical practice would be of benefit. Generally, the results indicated that some mental practice is better than no practice. As the research process and strategies became more sophisticated, researchers began to question the variables that might intervene within the imagery process. For example, how does the nature of the skill in terms of its motor, strength, or cognitive demands affect imagery? Other research has focused on how individual differences in imaginal ability and content of the imaginally related instructions affects the imaginal rehearsal. As the research questions became more penetrating, scholars attempted to develop theories that could explain more fully the actual operation of the imagery process.

THE NATURE OF IMAGERY

For as long as scholars have studied the psychological factors underlying the learning and refinement of motor and sport skills, they have tried to understand how imagery (mental practice) might relate to the production of an overt response. To answer such imagery-related questions it is important to know something about the nature of images. At an intuitive level, the most easily understood description of mental images is based on the description proposed by dual code theory.

Dual Code Theory

Dual code theory proposes that information is represented in memory in the form of either verbal codes or visual images. The verbal memory system is said to be designed to store symbolic information of an auditory or articulatory origin, such as linguistic units. Common auditory images might be the "cracking" sound heard as the golf club makes contact with the ball or the sound of an arrow hitting a target. Visual memory can be thought of as storing information associated with spatial organization or relationships. Close your eyes for a moment and mentally picture a fast-moving basketball game. Imagine a fast break, with the players moving swiftly down the court. To imagine such a scene, you must have previously stored visual information about basketball in memory. The visual and verbal symbolic codes are considered to be the most dominant or relevant; however, the proponents of dual code theory do not ignore the possibility of the existence of other memory systems such as those associated with smell, touch, or taste.

Fundamental to the dual code framework is the idea that memory systems are connected directly to specific sensory modalities such as vision and audition. These two systems are said to be independent from one another; as such, either system can operate singly or jointly during the imaginal rehearsal. The dominance of one of the two systems would depend on the nature of the task to be rehearsed and other factors such as the previous experience of the person. For example it would seem reasonable to assume that the mental rehearsal of a visually-dominant task such as a hit in volleyball would be conducted primarily by means of retrieving visually-coded symbols from the appropriate memory system. However, the mental rehearsal of a piano sonata would seem to be more logically based on auditory codes.

Although dual code theory still has strong proponents (Paivio, 1971; 1973), it also has several critics (Kieras, 1978; Lang, 1979; Pylyshyn, 1973). Many people tend to accept the dual coding position because it appeals to a person's intuition or experience. For example if you ask most people how they experience images, they will generally respond by saying that they see mental pictures or mental displays. This is a **phenomenological** description in that it is based on personal experience. According to dual code theory, images are said to be represented in memory either imaginally or verbally because that is how they are experienced. Is this reasoning valid?

Propositional Theory

Several lines of research argue against the dual coding interpretation. The first criticism is that such dual coding of separate images for individual responses is an inefficient explanation of the capacity of human memory. In terms of visual memory, it would require that the human brain contain an expansive array of graphical displays, or visual codes; it would be like conceiving the visual memory as a giant slide carousel containing one mental picture for each motor response that was stored.

Also, there is growing evidence that verbal information is not retained in its original form. Instead, it is argued, the associated meaning is remembered. Much the same thing appears to happen with visual memory; it is not the details that are retained in memory but rather the meaning underlying the interpretation of the visual display (Anderson, 1980). In a similar vein, researchers who have been most interested in the retention and representation of motor skills have also proposed that such information is represented in a more generalized or abstract form rather than as mental pictures or verbal representations (Keele, 1977; Schmidt, 1975).

Although there are some underlying differences in how various researchers have described mental representation of information, the major difference among the various theorists appears to be in the label they attach to the mechanism used for representation of information in cognition. Some refer to it as a *motor program* (Keele, 1977); some prefer to call it a *generalized schema* (Schmidt, 1975); and some have called it a *conceptual representation* (Carroll & Bandura, 1982). Imagery theorists, on the other hand, have generally preferred the term *proposition* or a **propositional network** (Kieras, 1978; Lang, 1979; Pylyshyn, 1973). All, however, apparently agree that information, including imaginally based information, is coded in memory in some abstract form rather than as identifiably separate graphical or mental replicas of a skill or response.

In viewing the analysis of mental imagery from the perspective of propositional theory, a few important points need to be emphasized. Propositions are thought to be general, abstract forms of representation that contain logical relationships among concepts (Kieras, 1978; Lang, 1979). In constructing a mental image for a particular skill, the pertinent set of propositions (that is, a propositional network) is said to be retrieved from long-term memory. Propositional networks contain information about relationships and relevant descriptions. A most important characteristic of the description of the propositional network for a mental image is the assertion that the propositional network for an image contains modality-specific information (Lang, 1979). For instance, it can represent information such as muscular activity requirements, sense organ adjustments, and physiological parameters such as degree of muscular tension. Imagine yourself in a weight room doing a bench press. You imagine the feel of force and tension in the arms, shoulders, and back. You imaginally reflect on the sensations associated with an increase in muscular tension. Then, when you imagine the press being over, you feel the sense of relief and sudden muscular relaxation. The images described would be coming from the kinesthetic modality and generated on the basis of kinesthetic information contained in the appropriate propositional network.

A word of caution is necessary. Although propositional theory is currently the most popular in terms of understanding the representation of imaginal information in memory, it too is not without its critics. The major question appears to be whether human memory is exclusively propositional or if it is possible that three separate codes exist (abstract, or propositional, verbal, and visual) (Anderson, 1980). An exploration of this possibility is not feasible here. However, if you are interested in exploring this possibility further, you might find the computer-simulation model of visual imagery presented by Kosslyn and Schwartz (1977) to be informative.

THEORETICAL INTERPRETATIONS OF THE IMAGERY PROCESS

The Inflow Model

The inflow model proposes a neuromuscular explanation of the effects of mental imagery. It originated in the late nineteenth century, when Carpenter (1894) proposed the **ideo-motor principle** of imagery (mental practice). The ideo-motor principle proposes that imagery facilitates the learning of motor skills because of the nature of the neuromuscular activity patterns activated during the imaginal process. These slight (low-gain) neuromuscular patterns are said to be identical, but reduced in magnitude, to those produced during overt performance of the same response. Therefore, although the magnitude of the efferent activity is reduced during imagery, this activity is a *mirror image* of the overt performance patterns. When the neuromuscular activity mirrors actual physical performance, it is said to be localized. This localization of the neuromuscular activity during imagery provides feedback to the movement schema (that is, propositional network) in the brain. The feedback could then be used either to make cognitive comparisons and then corrections in the motor response or to provide a preparatory set for future performance.

Figure 8-1 is a graphical representation of how the inflow model is proposed to function. During imaginal rehearsal of a motor skill (see box at top of figure) the associated propositional network is retrieved from long-term memory. The imaginal activity then

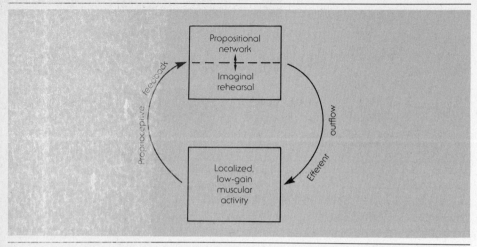

FIGURE 8-1   Schematic representation of the inflow model.

produces efferent outflow to the same muscles that would be used during overt performance
of that same skill (*arrow* on right). Although the magnitude of the efferent activity is
reduced during imaginal rehearsal as compared with overt performance, it is said to be
localized in the appropriate skill-related muscles (box at bottom of figure). As a consequence of the low-gain muscular innervation, proprioceptive feedback is sent back to the
propositional network (*arrow* on left). Thus the model is called an inflow model. The
feedback information is then used for future response corrections based on modification
and refinement of the propositional network. Thus the crucial variable in the inflow model
is the **proprioceptive feedback** that is a consequence of the imaginal rehearsal.

A fundamental assumption of the neuromuscular (inflow) explanation is that the muscle
innervation that accompanies imagery is *localized* to the muscles involved in the imaginal
rehearsal. Is this assumption supported by the evidence? Although some researchers have
reported supporting evidence (Jacobson, 1931; Schramm, 1967; Suinn, 1976), those
reports appear somewhat biased because of insufficient experimental control. On the other
hand, two more current lines of research demonstrate more experimentally acceptable
evidence to support the neuromuscular explanation (Hale, 1982; Lang, 1979). However,
in neither of the two latter cases were motor performance effects measured. Currently
researchers are undecided on the acceptability of the neuromuscular explanation in terms
of localized muscle innervation and imaginal rehearsal effectiveness.

If, on the contrary, the neuromuscular activity that accompanies imaginal rehearsal is
nonlocalized, what function (if any) could it play in enhancing motor performance? Several
researchers (Feltz & Landers, 1983; Keele, 1977; Schmidt, 1982) have proposed that
submaximal levels of muscle tension can function as a preparatory "set", or "priming
device," for future performance. It is hypothesized that under such conditions the athlete
can activate performance facilitators such as setting the optimal level of arousal or selectively attending to task-relevant cues while ignoring irrelevant cues.

The essence of the controversy surrounding the neuromuscular explanation is the
question of localization. Currently the available evidence does not allow the assumption
of localization to be accepted with any great degree of confidence. However, there is

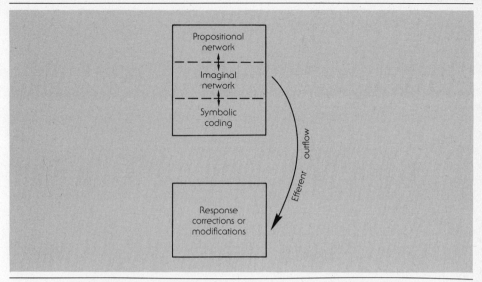

FIGURE 8-2   Schematic representation of the outflow model.

some evidence that supports the position that some efferent activity probably will accompany imaginal rehearsal, particularly when the subject is familiar with the task or is trained in imagery techniques (Hale, 1981; Feltz & Landers, 1983). If this is so, then the inflow aspects of imagery should not be ignored or abandoned totally.

The Outflow Model

The crucial variable associated with the outflow model of imagery effects is the cognitive activity of **symbolic coding.** Thus it is highly similar to Bandura's (1977) social learning interpretation of the observational learning process. As displayed in Figure 8-2, the symbolic coding, or outflow, model suggests that during imaginal rehearsal, the propositional network (box at top of figure) is retrieved from long-term memory and then during imaginal rehearsal information concerning the skill is coded symbolically so that modifications or corrections can be made in the network. Such propositional changes should then be used as a basis for sending efferent outflow to the muscles. This should result in response corrections or modifications in overt performance (box at bottom of figure). Notice then, that the crucial variable in the outflow model is symbolic coding as opposed to the proprioceptive feedback, which is said to be crucial in the inflow model.

Two major lines of research have been used to argue that symbolic coding is the crucial variable underlying the effectiveness of imaginal rehearsal. The first focuses on the stage of learning of the performer; the second emphasizes the degree of cognitive demand inherent in the task.

Stage of Learning

The early stages of motor skill acquisition require large amounts of cognitive activity (Fitts & Posner, 1967). Cognitive activity is considered an outflow variable in that these activities are used to modify the efferent outflow to the muscles. The modified outflow then affects the subsequent overt performance of that skill. Schmidt (1982) defines the possible nature of these cognitive activities in the early stage of skill development nicely. He says that the novice performer

> can think about what kinds of things might be tried, the consequences of each action can be predicted to some extent based on previous experiences with similar skills, and the learner can perhaps rule out inappropriate courses of action. (p. 520)

Status of the research. Some studies have found that imagery enhances learning during the early stages (Minas, 1980; Wrisberg & Ragsdale, 1979); whereas others have argued that imagery is most effective in the later stages of learning (Corbin, 1967; Phipps & Morehouse, 1969). However, on the basis of an analysis of a large number of imagery studies, Feltz & Landers (1983) found no clear-cut support for either argument. This controversy is discussed more fully later in this chapter.

Cognitive Demand

The idea that the degree of cognitive demand inherent in a task directly relates to the effectiveness of mentally practicing the task has received considerable support from several studies (Minas, 1978; Ryan & Simons, 1981; Wrisberg & Ragsdale, 1979). Basically, these investigations have shown that imaginally rehearsing tasks with high cognitive demand produce superior effects as compared with physically practicing those same tasks. On the other hand, when task performance required little cognitive activity, imagery was not very helpful. These differences received further verification when Feltz & Landers (1983) made similar cognitive versus motor task comparisons across 60 studies. They found strong support for the assertion that imagery facilitates the performance of tasks that require significant amounts of cognitive activity.

What does the current evidence tell us about the ability of the outflow model to explain imagery effects? The strongest evidence is that cited above relative to cognitive demand of the task and the associated benefits that can be derived from the symbolic coding activities that occur during imaginal rehearsal. However, common sense dictates that if a task is primarily cognitive, then it will have stronger outflow (symbolic coding) than inflow (proprioceptive feedback) requirements. Furthermore, many tasks cannot be classified as either primarily cognitive or motoric tasks.

In addition, if cognitive demands tend to become reduced as skill development increases (Fitts & Posner, 1967), then it should follow that cognitive processing demands should decrease as skill development increases. If so, then as skill development increases outflow requirements should be reduced and, in many instances, inflow requirements should become more important.

In other words, when a person reaches a high degree of skill at a certain task—that is, skill execution reaches the automated stage—does that person need to cognitively organize and mentally rehearse the skill before execution? No. Therefore the cognitive activity of symbolically rehearsing skill components should not greatly enhance skill execution. How does a highly skilled performer know immediately when a performance error has occurred? It seems most reasonable that the person uses the proprioceptive feedback associated with the motor response to compare the actual response with the cognitive representation of that response. Thus for a skilled performer it is the inflow information that is compared with the cognitive representation of the skill that provides the vehicle for error detection.

To summarize, a few points need to be emphasized. Although the outflow model has demonstrated some empirical basis for its ability to explain the effectiveness of imagery, it does not seem capable of excluding the possible role of inflow mechanisms in the enhancement of skill development through imagery. It also seems reasonable that the cognitive rehearsal strategies used by low- versus high-skill performers may differ in content. As mentioned above, more than likely the novice performer uses imaginal activities to aid development of a cognitive representation of the desired response. Then, as in the observational learning process, in combination with overt practice and performance feedback, the cognitive representation is strengthened and modified. Because the highly skilled performer already has a well-developed cognitive representation (propositional network) for a specified skill, it seems that imaginal rehearsal would be most effective for practicing strategy-related variables or even redirecting attention away from environmental factors that might cause elevated levels of anxiety. From our perspective, the important question is not whether imaginal rehearsal is better early or late in learning but instead, how should the imaginal rehearsal be structured given the stage of learning of the performer? It seems that an exclusive adoption of either the inflow or the outflow model is too simplistic to explain imagery effects on performance. The major issue may not be that of which is the crucial or mandatory variable (that is, proprioceptive feedback or symbolic coding) in imaginal rehearsal but rather, how do each of these activities function within the imaginal process?

FACTORS INFLUENCING IMAGINAL REHEARSAL

Performer Characteristics

Sensory Modalities

Although images can be formulated in relationship to any of the seven **sensory modalities,** the two modalities of most importance to imaginal rehearsal of motor skills are vision and kinesthesis. Just as there are individual differences in psychological characteristics such as attentional style and trait anxiety, people also vary in their propensity to construct images in one modality rather than another. This claim has a long history in the imagery literature but its role in sport performance received little attention until Mahoney and Avener (1977) assessed the form of imagery used by elite gymnasts.

Instead of using the terms *visual* or *kinesthetic* images, Mahoney and Avener described the gymnasts as being either external (visual) or internal (kinesthetic) in regard to imaginal focus. Using this classification system, they found that the gymnasts who qualified for the 1976 U.S. Olympic team reported using internal (kinesthetic) imagery more frequently than external (visual) imagery.

> In external imagery, a person views himself from the perspective of an external observer (much like in home movies). Internal imagery, on the other hand, requires an approximation of the real-life phenomenology such that the person actually imagines being inside his/her body and experiencing those sensations which might be expected in the actual situation. (p. 137)

External imagery takes a third-person perspective wherein the person steps outside himself or herself and then visualizes the performance. Internal imagery is predominantly kinesthetic and assumes a first-person perspective.

Such findings are important in terms of their potential for enhancing sport performance. If such findings were evident in elite performers in several different sports, then it could be suggested that it might be wise to design training programs to teach athletes how to image internally.

After publication of Mahoney and Avener's initial data, several sport psychologists studied other sport groups to ascertain whether or not "internality" of imagery was related to success in a variety of sports. Athletes were assessed in wrestling (Highlen & Bennett, 1979), racquetball (Meyers, Cooke, Cullen, & Liles, 1979), and skiing (Rotella, Gansneder, Ojala, & Billing, 1980). The studies of both wrestlers and racquetball players found no relationship between imagery style and athletic success. And, in complete disagreement with the gymnastic's data of Mahoney and Avener, Rotella and colleagues found that "the more successful skiers indicated that they developed visual images of the course, whereas less successful skiers indicated that they developed visual images of their own body skiing" (p. 352). Thus both groups adopted an external perspective; however, the object of their imagery differed.

One explanation for the conflicting results of the above studies may be that the ideal imagery perspective varies according to the nature of the sport. This assertion is supported somewhat by the fact that the only other available study that assessed the relationship between imagery style and success in gymnastics also found that internal (kinesthetic) imagery was more effective than external (visual) imagery (Start & Richardson, 1964).

In the investigations that either did not replicate the gymnastic data (Highlen & Bennett, 1979; Meyers, Cooke, Cullen, & Liles, 1979) or demonstrated opposing findings (Rotella, Gansneder, Ojala, & Billing, 1980), the nature of the sports were quite different from gymnastics. Sports such as skiing, wrestling, and racquetball involve *open* skills because the performer must attend to external, environmental factors to be successful. On the other hand, a sport in which the environment is static, such as gymnastics, involves *closed* skills. Successful performance of closed skills demands consistency in skill execution, whereas in open skills success largely depends on reactivity or response variability. Thus it may be that internal (kinesthetic) imagery might be more useful for imagining a closed skill, whereas external (visual) imagery should best facilitate the imaginal practice of an open skill.

An alternative explanation for these conflicting findings has been advanced by Epstein (1980), who conducted a study of imagery style and dart-throwing ability. She concluded that

> it was virtually impossible to characterize subjects as strictly internal or external imagers because individual's images varied considerably both within and between images. In other words, the notion of stable and extreme imaginal styles was not supported by the data. (p. 218)

Current literature on the relationship between imagery style and sport performance presents both unanswered questions and many possibilities for future study. For example, it may be that imagery perspective does tend to switch back and forth in a manner similar to attentional style. If the sport in question requires processing of multiple and changeable environmental cues and much planning of strategy, then such imaginal switching could be highly beneficial. On the other hand, if preperformance imaginal rehearsal was conducted for a closed skill such as gymnastics, diving, or free-throw shooting, then an internal, or kinesthetic, perspective could aid performance. If such relationships are shown to be true, then even if a person does not naturally possess the appropriate imaginal perspective, it is possible that he or she can be trained to adopt the most ideal perspective (see pp. 205-206).

Vividness and Controllability

Several researchers have explored how individual differences in imagery vividness and controllability might affect the quality of the imagery rehearsal. *Vividness* refers to the clarity and detail of an image. A vivid imaginer would be able to describe even the smallest detail, such as the bumps on a basketball or the bend of the grass on the putting surface in golf. *Controllability* pertains to how well a person can manipulate the content and action of an image. A gymnast or diver with high controllability would be able to mentally regulate the most minute movements of all of the body segments during a skill execution.

Vividness and controllability are important; many athletes attribute much of their success to their ability to visualize vividly and with control (track and field, Fosbury, 1974; tennis, Gallwey, 1974; skiing, Gallwey & Kriegel, 1977). In referring to his success in golf, Jack Nicklaus indicated that he "goes to the movies in his head." First, he attempts to clearly visualize exactly where he wants to place the ball on the fairway. Next, he pictures the ball landing at the target. Then he imagines the ball on its way to that precise location. Finally, he imagines himself making the exact swing needed so that the first two images will become a reality (Nicklaus, 1974, 1976). Nicklaus' imagery strategy reflects both vividness and controllability. His experiences with imagery are probably very close to those of Magic Johnson, a basketball player with the Los Angeles Lakers. A friend reported overhearing Johnson say that when he plays basketball he can visualize where everyone is on the court, even if the other player is outside of his visual field. This ability to vividly imagine the location and movement of both teammates and opponents may account somewhat for his superb ability at passing the ball so quickly and accurately. Perhaps he has anticipated the location of the receiver imaginally.

If so many highly skilled athletes have reported that they have high degrees of vividness and control in their own imagery, then certainly there must be a lot of scientific evidence to support this same notion. That is not the case. In studying the effects of vivid and controlled imagery on performance of a gymnastics skill, Start and Richardson (1964) found no strong evidence to support the facilitory effect of these two individual difference variables. On the other hand, Sheehan (1966, 1967) found that vivid imagers performed better than nonvivid imagers when they had more experience with the stimulus in question or when the stimulus was complex. Rawlings and Rawlings (1974) also found that persons with high levels of imaginal control performed better than their counterparts.

Again, these seem to be intuitive answers rather than scientifically based statements of fact or relationships. However, Lang's (1979) work with emotional imagery may provide some insight into the question of imagery vividness. His work has indicated that when nonvivid imagers were given instructions to image vividly (and were trained in imaginal rehearsal), they tended to demonstrate effects similar to characteristically vivid imagers.

The variables of imagery instructions and imagery training programs may provide the basis for understanding why the evidence cited above seems so contradictory. It appears that frequently, although subjects may have been selected on the basis of either high or low scores on vividness or controllability, they were not provided with precise instructions for what they were supposed to do during the imaginal rehearsal. Because the imaginal activity is obviously not open to direct observation, it is difficult to know what the subjects were actually doing during the imagery session, yet the inclusion of instructions and training programs can positively affect the role of mental imagery in motor performance.

Instructional Strategies

Labeling of Imaginal Codes

Evidence from several studies supports the premise that the effects of imagery may be more potent if specific instructional strategies are used. Such strategies include the labeling of movement components and instructions to code movement information symbolically (Hall, 1980; Hall & Buckolz, 1982-83; Ho & Shea, 1978; Housner & Hoffman, 1981; Shea, 1977). Movement labels could include Gallwey's (1974) "bounce, hit" tennis strategy or verbalizing "slow, slow, quick, quick, slow" for the Texas two-step. In support of the use of movement labels, Shea (1977) found that subjects who were given relevant movement labels were better able to remember that movement than subjects who either received no labels or who were given irrelevant labels. Also, Ho and Shea (1978) found similar positive effects when the relevant labels were provided either by the subject or by the experimenter. These findings are consistent with the symbolic coding evidence that was discussed in Chapter 7 (see p. 176).

Two additional factors appear to increase the value of labeling for motor skill learning: the ease with which a label evokes an image (that is, its availability) and its concreteness. Both can positively affect subsequent recall of movement patterns (Hall, 1980). Also, a combination of labeling and imaginal rehearsal appears to be superior to labeling alone (Chevalier-Girard & Wilberg, 1978). Again, these statements are consistent with the observational learning literature, which indicates that when symbolic codes are both meaningful and retrievable to the performer, the symbolic coding function is more beneficial to later performance (Bandura, Jeffery, & Bachicha, 1974).

In summary, relevant movement codes should be identified and rehearsed mentally. Make sure they are clear, precise, and meaningful to the performer. One strategy is to have the athlete watch a film or videotape of the skill while the coach and athlete use their movement "vocabularies" to identify appropriate cues. The labels or codes must have meaning to that performer or they will not evoke the desired image. Labels that have one meaning to a coach may have a different meaning, or no meaning, for an athlete. For example, a coach who says "keep your eye on the ball" may have a specific tennis goal in mind; however, the athlete may have a clearer idea of the goal by just being instructed to say "hit" as the ball contacts the racket.

Even though cue-related instructions are provided to subjects and even though such instructions do tend to enhance later performance, direct observation of what is actually taking place during imagery is not an easy process to assess directly. A recent study by Kohl, Roenker, Turner, and White (1983) attempted to determine if it is possible to enhance imagery rehearsal through external means.

The task they used was the pursuit rotor, a tracking task in which the speed with which the target moves in a circular pattern can be preset by the experimenter. Before imaginal rehearsal, all subjects viewed a demonstration of the pursuit rotor task, which included an auditory signal (a beep) that could be heard at the end of each revolution of the target. Thereafter, subjects were divided into three treatment groups: no instructions (control group), standard imagery instructions (uncued imagery), and standard imagery instructions in addition to an auditory cue (cued imagery). The subjects in the cued auditory group were instructed to imaginally time their pursuit rotor performance on the basis of the auditory cue; that is, they were told to imaginally time their practice so that their completion of a revolution would coincide with the onset of the auditory cues. The results showed that the externally cued imagery group performed better than the other two groups. However, the performance of the uncued imagery group was also superior to the control group.

Although the investigation by Kohl and colleagues was somewhat exploratory, when viewed in conjunction with the other available evidence it provides further insights into how a teacher or coach might better facilitate the organization and content of a performer's imaginal rehearsal. Their findings suggest that certain tasks may lend themselves to external cuing that can be used in addition to labeling and instructions to facilitate the imaginal rehearsal of the pertinent movement information. It appears that timing tasks would be most appropriate for such external cuing. One such task might be the relative timing between the release of a pitch in baseball or softball and the start of the batter's swing. Timing the height of the tennis serve to coincide with the height of the ball toss could also be cued externally during imaginal rehearsal. One possibility would be to videotape the athlete's serve during practice repeatedly until an ideal (or close to it) relationship occurred between the height of the racket and the height of the ball toss. An auditory "beep" could then be used to coincide with the height of the "perfect" toss. The athlete could view the film several times, noting the time elapsed before hearing the beep, and then imaginally rehearse the serve, using the same beep to facilitate the desired timing. Before using such imaginal rehearsal, however, the athlete must have first mastered the techniques associated with the imaginal rehearsal process.

Preparing the Athlete

To have an effective imaginal rehearsal session the coach or teacher must prepare the performer by following several important steps:

1. Make sure the athlete is in a relaxed state.
2. Identify the specific skill or strategy to be rehearsed.
3. Direct attention either internally or externally.
4. Determine skill-related movement labels or cues.
5. Tell the athlete to devise a mnemonic device based on those cues. A mnemonic device is a phrase or sentence devised to facilitate retention.
6. If appropriate, provide external auditory cues.
7. Tell the athlete to get in "the here and now"; to stay in the present rather than the past or future.
8. Instruct the athlete to focus on feelings and sensations present during a successful performance of that same skill.
9. Instruct the athlete to image vividly, to see as much detail as possible, and to focus on different parts of the image.

10. Instruct the athlete to control the image. Try to manipulate changes or actions occurring within the image.
11. Instruct the athlete to give a verbal report of what took place during the imagery session. Press for increasingly precise descriptions of the imagery content.
12. Selectively reinforce desired verbal responses.
13. Conduct multiple practice sessions and instruct the athlete to practice on his or her own.

Once athletes have mastered these steps they will be able to image vividly and effectively on their own. Coaches should encourage them to do so.

How might you use mental imagery to enhance performance of the back dive? First, you would practice relaxation procedures (see pp. 140-144) until the performer is highly proficient at achieving the relaxation response. Then you might direct attention internally to the feel of the movement. The skill-related cues could be "balance," "head back," "bend," and "fall." A mnemonic devise could be "bringing home buns and franks." The performer is now ready to rehearse mentally. First, have the performer achieve a state of relaxation. Once relaxed, instruct the performer to concentrate on emotions and sensations happening in the present. Now tell the performer to think about how he or she felt when the back dive was done correctly, to remember what thoughts were taking place. What sensations came from the muscles? Tell the performer to make the image vivid. Ask what was going on just before, during, and after the successful performance. Instruct the performer to concentrate on the actions, feelings, and sequence of the muscles. Repeat the imagery session several times. After the imagery session is over, ask the performer to accurately describe the content. Push for clarity and detail. Try to shape the desired imagery content through positive reinforcement.

Practice Characteristics

Length of Imagery Practice Session

Feltz and Landers (1983) analyzed the effectiveness of imaginal or mental practice for both the number of minutes spent and the number of trials devoted to such activities. On the basis of their review, one finding is clear; the nature of the task must be considered when determining the optimal amount of time to be spent in imaginal practice. They classified tasks as cognitive, motor, or strength. Their analysis indicated that cognitive tasks required only a few minutes or trials for the positive effects of imaginal practice to be realized. In contrast, tasks characterized by predominant motor and strength demands usually required much more time or a greater number of trials. Also, the nature of the task appeared to determine how effective the imaginal practice session was. More specifically, cognitive tasks showed much larger performance effects as compared with either motor or strength tasks. Thus imaginal rehearsal of tasks with high degrees of symbolic processing requirements appeared to benefit most from imaginal practice. As a result, they suggest that "if larger effects are to be achieved in motor and strength tasks, more time needs to be spent in mental practice (both in minutes and number of trials) than for tasks that are high in cognitive elements" (p. 46).

Feltz and Landers (1983) propose further that activities that are rehearsed mentally should vary as a function of the nature of the task. For cognitive tasks, it appears that imaginal rehearsal of the symbolic components of the task can rapidly aid the learner in making relationships that are relevant to performance. Thus, through cuing and instructions, emphasis should be placed on the symbolic coding of task components. In the case of primarily motor or strength tasks, which have low degrees of symbolic content, they indicate that imaginal rehearsal should be devoted to setting appropriate levels of arousal or to directing attention to task-relevant cues.

In a sense, their argument suggests that when a task is high in cognitive demand, the primary function of the activities that take place in mental rehearsal is *informational* in nature; that is, the rehearsal provides a vehicle that allows the performer to learn more about the important relationships between task components and to then symbolically code that information for future task performance. If, conversely, the task is low in cognitive elements (that is, a motor or strength task), then it appears that the primary function of the mental rehearsal is *motivational* in that the performer is actively involved in attempting to establish an ideal preperformance level of arousal. By focusing on task-relevant cues rather than irrelevant or distracting cues, the performer has redirected attention away from cues that might raise arousal or anxiety to a degree that would be detrimental to performance. Feltz and Landers (1983) also propose that just before performance, highly skilled athletes set appropriate tension levels and direct attention to the beginning of the skill execution (where attentional demands are the greatest, see Posner & Keele, 1969).

It is clear that the effectiveness of imaginal rehearsal depends on several factors, including both the nature of the task and the content of the imaginal rehearsal. In addition, the skill level of the performer should probably be addressed when structuring the content of the imaginal rehearsal. The beginner needs some overt practice, accompanied by proprioceptive feedback, to develop an adequate conceptual representation. It appears that when a skill has become automated, effective imaginal rehearsal should focus on aspects of strategy development, setting of optimal arousal level, or attentional direction.

Imaginal Practice versus Physical Practice

Imaginal practice is a skill like any other skill; proficiency requires practice. Imaginal practice accompanied by appropriate cuing and instructions can allow performers to gain greater vividness and control over the content of the image. After taking into account the skill level of the performer and the nature of the task, decisions can be made concerning the amount of practice time that should be devoted to this activity. When making those decisions, keep in mind that it appears that some imaginal practice is better than no practice (Feltz & Landers, 1983); however, unstructured imaginal practice might be worse than no imaginal practice at all (Dunlap, 1983). Therefore always provide specific information about what is to be rehearsed mentally. Be sure to provide appropriate labels and cues.

Also, imaginal practice can have some advantages over physical practice. Two of those advantages, according to MacKay (1981), are the elimination of problems associated with fatigue and the fact that imaginal practice can progress more rapidly than physical practice. This is similar to what we saw in observational learning. Beginners sometimes experience confusion and performance decrements during physical practice because they must continually switch their attention to aspects of response selection, response execution, and the consequences of the response (Bandura, 1977). With precise directions, imaginal rehearsal allows the performer to focus attention on highly selected features of the task. With such increased efficiency in attentional focus, learning can be positively affected.

IMAGERY AND THE UNIFYING MODEL

The status of the research evidence concerning imaginal rehearsal appears to leave still many unanswered questions. Based on what is known presently, however, the unifying model can put that knowledge into a more understandable framework. Figure 8-3 depicts the imaginal process within the confines of the unifying model.

Input

Before beginning the imaginal rehearsal, the coach or teacher should provide cues and instructions that bring the performer's attentional focus to the nature and purpose of the imaginal practice session (extreme left of Figure 8-3). The cues should be as concrete and meaningful as possible. The learner can also be advised to use these cues as mnemonic devices for purposes of retention. Instructions for beginners should direct their focus to either the internal (first-person perspective) or external (third-person perspective) qualities of the image. Although there is not much empirical evidence to support one of these two perspectives over the other, there is some logical basis for selecting one over the other. During the early stages of skill learning, performers seem to depend more on visual cues and less on kinesthetic cues (Fleishman & Rich, 1963). Therefore in most cases it seems prudent to structure the imagery session toward rehearsing external cues. An exception to this rule would be the rehearsal of a closed skill, in which case the processing of

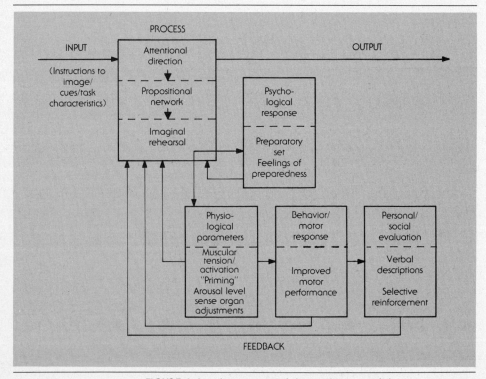

FIGURE 8-3   Imagery and the unifying model.

changing cues in the external environment would have little bearing on skill improvement. Examples of closed skills are archery (given that wind is not a factor), riflery, and a kip in gymnastics.

You can also prepare the learner for imaginal rehearsal by using models or film strips before the imagery session. Finally, the performer should be in a relaxed state before the imagery rehearsal. High levels of anxiety can have a detrimental effect on the quality of the rehearsal.

Process

The attentional direction the performer assumes before the imaginal rehearsal determines the content of the session. Based on the propositional network of that skill, imaginal rehearsal can focus on either the visual (external) elements or the kinesthetic (internal) characteristics. Visual characteristics could include the flight of the ball as it moves through space, the formation assumed by opponents before the snap or toss of the ball, and the positions of teammates on the field or court. Kinesthetic characteristics could include the sequence of muscle activity, the amount of tension in the muscles, or appropriate eye movements.

Output

As you can see in Figure 8-3, the output of the imaginal rehearsal session can be viewed on four levels. Depending on the exact content of the imaginal rehearsal, the accompanying psychological response can range from minimal to extremely powerful. For example if someone asked you to imagine yourself trapped in a cave with hundreds of snakes and spiders and no escape route, you would most likely have a strong negative psychological reaction to the content of your imagery. If someone asked you to imagine yourself at the free throw line in basketball or as the field-goal kicker in football with the game tied and one second to go, you might also experience a potent psychological response.

This same psychological reaction would not ordinarily be predicted to occur when you are simply imagining yourself practicing a sport skill. An exception might be a case in which you are using imaginal techniques to provide yourself with a mental ''set'' for future performance. Used effectively, imaginal strategies should be able to focus your attention positively so that you feel ready, relaxed, and prepared for action.

At the level of physiological responses that accompany imaginal rehearsal, several implications are important. Imaginal rehearsal can be used to adjust identifiable parameters such as respiration or heart rate. The neuromuscular activation that generally accompanies imagery is thought to either ''prime'' the muscles for future activity or to provide proprioceptive feedback to the propositional network, or motor program. Imaginal strategies can also provide a way for the performer to raise or lower arousal levels so that the performer can move closer to an optimal level of arousal before making a motor response.

In sport psychology, imaginal techniques are often used to enhance an athlete's probability of performing successfully. In some cases this is achieved by using imaginal strategies early in skill acquisition to assist in the construction of a strong and accurate propositional network. In other cases such techniques can be used to help control dysfunctional tendencies such as ineffective attentional focus or excessive arousal. In all cases the goal of the imaginal rehearsal is to facilitate an improved or superior motor response. Therefore the purpose of the covert activity of imaginal rehearsal is to facilitate the quality of the overt response.

A positive self-evaluation of the effects of imaginal practice can increase a performer's motivation to undertake those same activities in the future. Therefore it is important that the coach or teacher structure the imagery session so that the probability of a successful effect on overt performance is increased. In addition to the input considerations discussed above, the probability of success of the imagery experience can be increased through the use of the two postimagery procedures: verbal report and selective reinforcement. After completion of the imaginal rehearsal, the athlete should be asked for a verbal report of the content of the imagery session. The goal is to make the verbal report resemble as closely as possible the intended objectives of the imaginal rehearsal. If the goal was to emphasize visual characteristics (external factors), then those characteristics should be reported verbally; if the objective of the session was imaginal rehearsal and control of kinesthetic responses (internal factors), then the verbal report should primarily reflect internal muscular and sensory responses. As Lang (1979) has suggested, it is possible to shape the content of the verbal report by shaping the behavior; when the performer verbalizes a desired description, he or she should be given positive reinforcement. A simple nod of the head or saying "that's right" can effectively modify the content of the verbal report.

Feedback

The activities that occur at each of the four levels of output can affect the development of the appropriate propositional network. At the psychological level, if the result of the imaginal rehearsal induces a feeling of preparedness for overt performance, then that positive motivational set can increase both the probability of a successful response and a desire to once again imaginally rehearse the skill.

The exact role that physiological feedback plays in the imagery process is not yet clear. If the innervation of the muscles is indeed localized, then the accompanying proprioceptive feedback can be used to modify and update the propositional network. If it is nonlocalized, then it is either irrelevant to subsequent performance or it "primes" or "sets" the muscles for future response. This is a crucial question that needs answering.

The motor response provides feedback that can be used to make corrections and changes in the propositional network. This feedback is of particular importance to the beginner, as the propositional network is not well-developed.

The external feedback provided by verbal reports of the imagery content and the shaping procedures used by the coach or teacher can also induce changes in the content of the propositional network. These procedures are necessary to mold the verbal report in a way that matches the desired content of the image.

The process of imagery training is not a "one-shot deal." It takes planning, patience, and repetition. Although researchers are just beginning to gather well-founded, scientific evidence concerning how imagery works and how it can best be structured for the imaginal rehearsal of motor skills, current evidence suggests quite strongly that this procedure has much to offer in terms of facilitating the learning and performance of sport and motor skills. We hope the information contained in this chapter will give you the incentive and the means to begin using imaginal techniques to enhance both your own and others' sport performance.

IMPLICATIONS FOR SPORT

- Build in relaxation procedures before the imagery sessions.
- Always have athletes mentally rehearse sport skills that have high cognitive demand. Have them focus on task-relevant cues.
- For tasks that have primarily motor or strength components, a large number of imaginal rehearsal sessions are necessary to achieve beneficial effects. Performance of such tasks may be enhanced if the focus of the imaginal practice is on setting appropriate arousal levels as opposed to attending to task-relevant cues. Use the imagery session for motivational purposes.
- With highly skilled athletes the content of the imaginal rehearsal should usually be strategy preparation rather than skill development.
- For closed skills it appears that an internal (kinesthetic) focus may be most facilitative during imaginal practice, whereas an external (visual) focus may be best for open skills.
- For beginners, it may be wise to have them adopt an external (visual) focus.
- Always instruct athletes to image vividly and to be in control of their images.
- Identify pre-imagery movement labels and cues that are concrete and meaningful. Instruct athletes to construct their own mnemonic devices using those movement labels and cues.
- For selected tasks that have a strong timing component, such as a tennis serve, try to provide external auditory cues.
- Because imaginal rehearsal avoids problems associated with fatigue and proceeds more rapidly than physical practice, it can be efficient. Have athletes practice it often.
- Use appropriate models and films to enhance the effectiveness of the imaginal rehearsal session.
- Particularly when athletes are initially developing their imaginal rehearsal skills, provide a postsession evaluation period in which the coach selectively reinforces responses that reflect the desired content of the image.
- Remember, good imaginal rehearsal is a developed skill. Athletes need frequent and meaningful practice to achieve success.

CASE STUDY 1

Imaginal Rehearsal of a Golf Putt

Both skilled and unskilled athletes can benefit from the imaginal rehearsal of sport skills. For example, Carol Johnson, a world-class collegiate gymnast in the 1970s was born with the use of only one arm. Carol was subject to several injuries to the knees. After one of those accidents, she was forced to abstain from any physical practice for quite a long period before a major competitive event. Being the ''scrappy'' competitor that she was, she decided to practice her routines mentally. She also visualized herself performing a new and difficult trick on the uneven parallel bars. Her imaginal rehearsal of the new trick was so effective that her first physical try at it was flawless. Her coach, Lynn Rogers, was amazed because he knew that she had never tried it before.

All of us cannot do (nor should we probably try to do) what Carol Johnson was able to accomplish through imaginal rehearsal. However, there are good reasons to believe that all sport performers can benefit from well-structured imaginal rehearsal. We refer again to the techniques used by Jack Nicklaus to demonstrate how imaginal strategies might be used to enhance golf putting performance.

Many golfers can drive a ball with good distance and accuracy, but they lose strokes because of poor putting. Remember, no matter how difficult or easy a particular hole is, two strokes are always alloted for putts. A missed putt is a lost stroke that cannot be regained, even if you "scramble." Many putts are missed not because of lack of skill but because of psychological factors such as lack of confidence, stress, and inappropriate attentional control.

By providing yourself with a mental checklist and an imaginal practice regime, you can avoid many of those barriers to putting success. Remember that when Nicklaus mentally "goes to the movies," he imagines the sequence in reverse order. The first thing he visualizes is the ball going into the cup. His last mental image is the execution of the ideal swing. This strategy makes sense; the visualization of a successful conclusion is a confidence builder. By imagining the appropriate swing just before the actual swing, the immediate, correct imaginal rehearsal takes place just before the overt response. This mental review of a successful outcome achieved on the basis of a correct stroke focuses attention on positive, skill-related cues as opposed to potentially negative or disruptive cues.

To structure your mental rehearsal of a successful golf putt, at least two activities should take place before each and every putt. First, you need to establish a *putting checklist*. This should include: (1) condition of the green (such as direction in which the grass is growing, slope, and moisture); (2) distance the ball is from the cup; and (3) point of aim (taking into account the potential for slight or sharp breaks).

Based on the outcome of your putting checklist, you are now ready to mentally rehearse your correct putting stroke. Stand over the ball with knees in a relaxed position. Take a moderately deep breath. Now, focus your attention on only the cup. "See" the ball drop into the cup. "See" the ball following the correct putting line. "See" yourself correctly positioned with your eyes directly over the ball. "See" your putter lined up square to the target. "See" the clubface strike the ball firmly, yet gently. "See" your follow-through moving squarely through the putting line. You are now ready to make what you just visualized become a reality.

CASE STUDY 2

Imaginal Rehearsal Designed for Gaining Control

One of the most common problems that athletes encounter is "choking" or "falling apart" psychologically under competitive conditions, although they may be able to achieve an almost errorless performance during practice. To use imagery-based techniques effectively to help athletes learn to cope with negative environmental and personal influences, you must first determine the exact nature of the factor(s) triggering the athlete's response.

One way to approach the problem is to discuss the differences between what is happening during a successful performance versus an unsuccessful performance. The problem with this approach is that many athletes are not "tuned in" to themselves sufficiently; thus they are not capable of identifying those cues. There are two techniques that can be used to help an athlete learn to recognize cues that are hindering performance.

First, an athlete can be instructed to carry a "cue identification log" to all practices and competitive events. An entry should be made anytime the athlete feels an increase in anxiety or tension. After a sufficient period of time, relationships between internal and external cues and resulting anxiety responses can usually be identified.

Another approach that can be used separately or in addition to the cue-identification log involves making visual and mental comparisons between successful and unsuccessful skill executions. Coaches are certainly familiar with this approach when it is used for biomechanical comparisons; we are suggesting it for psychological comparisons.

A videotape recording should be made of *that* athlete's successful performance. This should usually be done in practice. Then, a second videotape recording should be made of the same athlete's unsuccessful attempt at performing the same skill.

The procedure then involves using imaginal analyses to determine what environmental or pscyhological factors were different in the two unlike performances. First, have the athlete visualize, under the successful condition, what he or she was thinking about, feeling, attending to. The next step is to make a comparison under the unsuccessful condition.

Potential areas of concern or negative cues are: (1) becoming overloaded by irrelevant, environmental cues, (2) becoming distracted by negative thoughts, and (3) feeling extreme muscle tension. The first two problems are caused by ineffective attentional direction (which may or may not be accompanied by a high level of anxiety). The increase in muscle tension is more definitely related to elevated anxiety.

Imaginal rehearsal can alleviate all of those problems. If muscle tension appears to be the primary causative factor, then the centering procedure described in Chapter 6 (Case Study 1) should be practiced. The "successful" videotape should then be viewed several times. Afterward the athlete should repeat the centering procedure and then attempt to imaginally rehearse the correct skill execution.

Fundamentally, the same imaginal procedures can be used for redirecting an ineffective attentional focus. However, in those cases emphasis should be placed on visualizing placing attentional focus on correct, performance-relevant cues during the imaginal rehearsal. In either case, a few points should be remembered:

1. Athletes must receive some training and practice at both imagery and centering skills. They should also have previously mastered a relaxation technique.
2. Videotape playback is a good tool to use in stimulating the imaginal comparisons.
3. In some cases the imaginal rehearsal will have to proceed on a part-by-part basis. In such cases, the skill will have to be divided into its logical subcomponents. Then each part must be visualized as being successful either by adding more disruptive cues and learning to effectively ignore them or by controlling excess tension during that part of the skill. Once this is accomplished, additional subcomponents can be added until the entire motor sequence is rehearsed successfully.
4. The ultimate goal is to make the imaginal rehearsal a mental replica of a successful performance as it would occur under actual competitive conditions.

SUMMARY

- The nature or form of images has generally been described from two different perspectives: dual code theory and propositional theory. Dual code theory proposes that imaginal information is represented as either verbal or visual codes. Propositional theory suggests instead that such information takes a more generalized or abstract form. Currently, propositional theory appears to have more support than dual code theory.

- Two primary models have been used to describe the process of imagery. The inflow, or neuromuscular, model rests on the assumption that during imagery there is an accompanying innervation of muscles that is localized but reduced in magnitude. The outflow model predicts that the primary causative factor of the positive effects of mental imagery is the symbolic coding activity that takes place during that activity.

- Several different factors can affect the quality or effectiveness of imaginal rehearsal. The ideal imagery perspective in terms of internality or externality appears to differ among various sports. However, it appears that an internal focus may be better for closed skills, whereas an external orientation may be more suitable for open skills. It also appears that persons who have vivid images and who can control those images benefit more from imaginal rehearsal as compared with persons who do not possess those characteristics.

- Imagery vividness and effectiveness can be enhanced through mnemonic devices such as the use of concrete, meaningful labels and the rehearsal of those codes. There also appears to be some evidence that aspects of imaginal rehearsal can be controlled through the use of external cues, such as auditory signals, that coincide with a selected aspect of imagery content.

- When attempting to determine the ideal length of the imaginal practice session a primary factor to be considered is the nature of the task to be rehearsed. Cognitive tasks require much shorter periods of imaginal practice as compared with strength or motor tasks. However, it has also been suggested that the content of the image should perhaps also vary as a function of the nature of the task.

- For cognitive tasks, it appears that imaginal rehearsal should be focused on the symbolic components of the skill, whereas for strength and motor tasks, imaginal instructions should emphasize activities designed to set appropriate levels of arousal or to focus attention on task-relevant cues. One point seems clear. Regardless of the orientation of the imaginal instructions, some instructions should be provided to structure the imaginal rehearsal.

- In many instances, imaginal rehearsal may be superior to physical practice. Imaginal practice may allow the beginner to focus undivided attention on important cognitive aspects of a skill, whereas physical practice might require continual attentional shifting. Imaginal rehearsal can provide the more proficient performer with an anxiety control mechanism and a vehicle for planning future strategies. In some instances imaginal practice can proceed at a faster rate than physical practice, while at the same time avoiding problems caused by fatigue.

DISCUSSION QUESTIONS

1 Discuss the current controversy surrounding the inflow model, or neuromuscular explanation, of the imagery process.
2 How does imagery perspective, in terms of internality versus externality, appear to be related to the nature of the sport skill?
3 How does imaginal rehearsal appear to be related to the stage of skill development of the performer?
4 Select a sport skill that you are familiar with and do the following:
   a. Identify several movement labels that are both concrete and meaningful.
   b. Construct some potential mnemomic devices based on the labels you identified above.
   c. Based on the above, identify possible components of the postimagery verbal report that you would reinforce positively (shaping of behavior).
5 Identify as many factors as possible that should be considered when designing an imaginal rehearsal session. Take into consideration variables such as individual differences in imaginal ability, stage of learning or skill development, and nature of the task.
6 Contrast the position of dual code theory with propositional theory in regard to how images might be represented in memory.

GLOSSARY

ideo-motor principle   Proposal that low-gain neuromuscular patterns (efferent activity) are produced during imaginal rehearsal; these low-gain patterns are said to mirror those generated during overt performance
phenomenological description   Description of an event or process that is based on personal experience
propositional network   Manner in which images are stored in memory; abstract forms that contain information about relationships, relevant descriptions, and modality-specific information
proprioceptive feedback   Sensory information that arises from the muscles and joints (kinesthetic feedback) or the inner ear (vestibular feedback) and provides information relative to position or movement
sensory modalities   Any of the seven faculties connected with the ability of the brain and nerves to receive and react to stimuli such as sounds, sights, and smells
symbolic coding   Process of coding information so that the meaning is represented in memory; visual and verbal codes are common symbolic representations

SUGGESTED READINGS

Feltz, D.L., & Landers, D.M. (1983). The effects of mental practice on motor skill learning and performance: A meta-analysis. *Journal of Sport Psychology, 5*, 25-57.
   Using a meta-analytic strategy, this investigation analyzed the results of 60 different studies designed to answer the question of whether or not mental practice before motor performance has a facilitative effect on subsequent performance. In addition, several alternative explanations and theoretical interpretations of the mental practice process are discussed.

Hale, B.D. (1982). The effects of internal and external imagery on muscular and ocular concomitants. *Journal of Sport Psychology, 4,* 379-387.

This experiment tested the localization of activity in the ocular and muscular systems as a consequence of imagining either externally or internally. Rationale for the study was based on Jacobson's early work and Lang's more recent bio-informational theory of emotional imagery.

Heil, J. (1984). Imagery for sport: Theory, research and practice. In W.F. Straub & J.M. Williams (Eds.), *Cognitive sport psychology,* Lansing, NY: Sport Science Associates.

Heil covers research and theory on imagery across the three areas of cognitive psychology, clinical psychology, and the world meditative traditions. Heil also draws some practical implications and stresses the necessity of extended practice for imaginal rehearsal to be effective.

Housner, L.D. (1984). The role of visual imagery in recall of modeled motoric stimuli. *Journal of Sport Psychology, 6,* 148-158.

In this experiment, high and low visual imagers watched a model and then attempted to reproduce a variety of leg, trunk, arm, and head movements. The results provided support for the assertion that visual imagery may play a role in the recall of modeled motoric stimuli.

Lang, P.J. (1979). A bio-informational theory of emotional imagery. *Psychophysiology, 16,* 495-512.

Lang presents a comprehensive review of the literature on imagery, incorporating evidence from fields such as cognitive psychology, behaviorism, and psychophysiology to develop an integrated theory of imagery. Finally, Lang proposes a training program for enhancing imaginal rehearsal.

Ryan, E.D., & Simons, J. (1983). What is learned in mental practice of motor skills: A test of the cognitive-motor hypothesis. *Journal of Sport Psychology, 5,* 419-426.

The effects of mental rehearsal were examined in two tasks that differed in degree of motor involvement. The results suggest that mental rehearsal is more effective for tasks that have a strong cognitive demand.

Suinn, R.M. (1984). Imagery and sports. In W.F. Straub & J.M. Williams (Eds.), *Cognitive sport psychology,* Lansing, NY: Sport Science Associates.

In this article, Suinn first makes a distinction between mental rehearsal and imagery rehearsal and then traces the status of relevant research in each of the two areas. Suinn uses several case and experimental studies to discuss the intervention program called visuo-motor behavior rehearsal (VMBR).

9

COGNITIVE BASIS OF MOTIVATION IN SPORT

Motivation is anything that impels an organism to action. Action is reflected in the *selection, intensity,* and *persistence* of behavior. Drive theory (Chapter 3) was the earliest and most traditional approach to describing the factors underlying motivated behavior. However, when the premises of drive theory were found to be somewhat lacking, scholars turned to more cognitive, or organismic, explanations. They began to explore questions such as "How do an athlete's thoughts affect performance?" "How do emotions relate to motivation?" In addition, two important themes evolved in the sport motivation literature. The performer's perception of self-competency and personal control over outcomes appear to be directly related to motivation. In this chapter we discuss a representative sample of current theories and explore their application in sport and motor skills settings.

COMPETENCE AND INTRINSIC MOTIVATION

Several different theories have been proposed to explain our apparent motivation to feel competent and in personal control of the events that affect us. Although the names of the theories have varied, from *intrinsic motivation* (Deci, 1972) to *personal causation* (deCharms, 1968) to *effectance motivation* (White, 1959) and *competence motivation* (Harter, 1981), all these perspectives view humans as being positively motivated to strive for accomplishment and achievement. A prime example of such striving is the desire to achieve excellence in sport. Although any of the current theories is slightly different from the others, each alludes somewhat to three fundamental elements within the motivation process. First, people have a *need* to feel competent, self-determined, and in control. Second, the basic goal is to have an effect on the environment or to master the environment. Third, the *reward* for competency based or mastery responses is intrinsic. It is reflected in positive affect and self-reinforcement as opposed to the receipt of an extrinsic reward. Of the theoretical formulations that have been developed to describe and explain mastery behavior, one that appears well suited for application to the realm of sport is Harter's (1981) **competence motivation.**

Development of Competence Motivation and Intrinsic Motivation

The essence of the competence motivation position is that humans are born with the capacity and motivation to experience joy or happiness generated by their own actions or responses. With increasing age, however, there are wide variations, or individual differences, in the degree to which people seek out **mastery experiences** such as sport or enjoy the positive affect that accompanies those experiences. Infants and very young children participate in mastery activities simply for intrinsic reasons, for the challenge and the resulting joy and fun. They do not need external (extrinsic) rewards to motivate their behavior; it is enough to fulfill the needs of curiosity, control, and challenge. It's fun! However, with increasing age, mastery seeking declines for many persons. What causes this decline?

Harter (1981) has identified the nature of the *evaluative response of significant others* to the mastery-seeking behavior of a person as a crucial variable in that process. Throughout this text we have stressed the potency of evaluative responses in affecting behavior and the power of the observational learning process in regard to acquiring skills and knowledge. Both factors affect the development of mastery behavior.

When a child enacts a mastery-related response, parents and significant others, such as coaches, evaluate it. The usual basis for this evaluation is the degree of success the child's response produced. Thus, based on their *own* standards of correctness or excellence, significant others convey powerful evaluative information to the youngster. The child uses that information to begin the internalization of his or her own *system of mastery goals, criteria for judging future success or failure, and establishment of perceptions concerning control* (Harter, 1981).

It is also important to note that by evaluating the child's action on the basis of response outcome alone, the positive emotions the child experienced during the mastery response are often ignored. This sends a clear message to the child that it is outcome, rather than positive affect, that is important, even though that is not the sole message that most adults would want to convey to children.

Besides providing competency information on the basis of evaluating performance, significant others such as teachers and coaches influence the development of competence motivation by functioning as models. The child observes the standards used for evaluation by significant models and then internalizes this information in developing a sense of competence. Sense of competence relates directly to a person's perception of his or her ability. The child also notices and can internalize aspects of the affective reaction of the model.

Based on her work with Connell (1980), Harter further proposes that as the internalization of mastery goals, criteria for success and failure, and perceptions regarding sources of control becomes more crystallized, the child develops a *cognitive representation of perceived competency*. Once the cognitive representation is adequately developed it is capable of generating its own affective reactions to mastery-seeking responses.

More specifically, up until about the age of 5 or 6 years, children's affective reactions appear to be undifferentiated. Events are either good or bad, happy or sad. By school age, and with the development of the internalized, cognitive representation of sense of competence, affective reactions to events or responses can be differentiated. Reactions can be more specifically described, such as feelings of pride, happiness, or anger. When affective reactions are positive, they tend to enhance the probability that mastery striving will occur. Negative affective reactions tend to undermine mastery behavior by reducing feelings of competency. Shame or anxiety about potential failure in sports should reduce the probability that a mastery-oriented response will recur.

At about the same time that affective reactions become differentiated, competence is also differentiated into the cognitive, social, and physical (sport ability) domains. When this occurs, there are observable differences in the degree to which a person is motivated to perform in each of those domains. As we all know, not all highly skilled athletes are equally motivated on the playing field and in the classroom. Similarly, not all "eggheads" are also "jocks."

Extrinsic Rewards, Competency, Motivation, and Sport

Doubts (negative affect) about self-competence can make a person more externally oriented. Therefore by school age and continuing through later life there appears to be a strong connection between a person's cognitions relative to goal setting, criteria for success and failure, and perception of control and his or her sense of competence. This is true at all levels of sport, whether youth sports, interscholastic, intercollegiate, or professional sports. According to **cognitive evaluation theory** (Deci & Ryan, 1980), the performer's perception of personal competence and self-control over behavioral outcomes are extremely powerful variables underlying intrinsic motivation. When people take part in activities just for the sake of doing so rather than for extrinsic rewards, they are said to be intrinsically motivated (Deci, 1971). Therefore, when a person feels that he or she is competent and is personally responsible for sport outcomes, that person is generally intrinsically motivated to participate. A major factor influencing the perception of personal responsibility for success and failure is the application of *extrinsic rewards*. When intrinsically motivated activities are rewarded extrinsically, several possible consequences exist. From Deci's (1978) point of view, future intrinsic motivation can remain the same, be enhanced, or be depressed. His analysis is founded on the notion that rewards can serve two different functions: *controlling* and *informational*.

Controlling rewards. If the controlling aspect is emphasized, persons begin to perceive a correlation between the enactment of the behavior and the receipt of a reward. They begin to perceive that the reward is controlling their behavior. Under such conditions intrinsic (competency-based) motivation should decrease. This is because a contingency has now been perceived between making a response and receiving a reward. Persons may then reason some way such as "no reward, no response." For example, an athlete who is rewarded for participating in an intrinsically interesting activity, such as playing softball or baseball, might decide not to play that game in the future if there is no extrinsic reward for doing so. How many professional athletes would continue to participate in their sport with no monetary rewards? Probably not very many. Yet for the majority it certainly was not money that motivated them to participate initially. How many athletes on scholarship would be motivated to continue their athletic participation if the scholarship were no longer available? According to Ryan (1979), not very many would. He found that 75% of the athletes he assessed were primarily motivated by their scholarship rather than intrinsic factors.

Informational rewards. Informational rewards tell the performer something about his or her competence at a task. When rewards are given contingent on quality of performance outcome, they are powerful sources of information about competency. When the informational aspect of a reward is both salient and positive, then intrinsic motivation should be enhanced. However, under those same conditions, if the nature of the extrinsic information is negative, then it can have a detrimental effect on intrinsic motivation.

Keep in mind that the most frequent extrinsic reward that a coach gives is positive verbal feedback. How does positive feedback affect intrinsic motivation? Vallerand (1983) and Vallerand and Reid (1984) found that positive feedback enhanced both intrinsic motivation and perceived competence, whereas negative feedback decreased intrinsic motivation and perceived competence. Their results argue strongly that coaches should use positive rather than negative feedback whenever possible. Be positive!

The analysis presented above argues that extrinsic rewards should only be given when the quality of the performance meets some pre-established standard of excellence and when the rewards provide information relevant to competence and self-determination. The performer should be made aware of the basis on which the reward was provided. For example, before performance the coach and athlete might determine a specific performance goal that is related to one of the three dimensions of motivation (that is, persistence, selection, and intensity). In volleyball an intensity-related goal could be to increase the number of blocks attempted by three. If that goal is accomplished during the match, then the coach should verbally praise the player. Therefore it is not only the objective result (success) of the blocks attempted that is important; so are the number of blocks attempted. In addition, the controlling aspect of rewards should be minimized or eliminated. This is done to avoid having the performer adopt a perspective that the activity is done to receive a reward because such a perspective directs the performer's focus toward external rather than internal motivation.

There are many occasions within sport settings when participant's perceptions and motivational orientations can be changed by introducing extrinsic rewards. The giving of medals, trophies, and certificates is common in organized athletics. Is it possible that these awards can undermine athlete's sport motivation?

Yes. However, several other factors should be taken into consideration. There is some research evidence that the nature of the reward (or in sport, the award) affects whether it will or will not decrease intrinsic motivation. Deci (1972, 1978) and others (Vallerand, 1983; Vallerand & Reid, 1984) have shown that *verbal rewards* or feedback do not usually have an adverse effect on intrinsic motivation. However, more *tangible rewards,* such as medals or money, can have a negative effect. Recall, however, that Deci (1978) also proposed that the nature of rewards must also be looked at in terms of their controllability and informational components.

If by giving an athlete an extrinsic reward a perception develops that behavior is being controlled externally, then this perceived change in the source of the reward will indeed reduce intrinsic motivation. Under those same conditions, the performer's perception of competence and self-determination should also be affected adversely. For example, suppose a young boy has tried out for a soccer team simply because he enjoyed that activity. Each night after practice he goes home and expresses all the fun and enjoyment he experienced that afternoon. His parents then decide that they will begin attending the practices and games; they get extremely involved and decide that their son could do even better and would have more enjoyment if he received a reward for his participation in soccer. The parents tell him that they will take him out for ice cream every night after practice. They follow this procedure for a few weeks; however, with the passage of time their interest diminishes and other events conflict with soccer. The parents attend fewer and fewer practices and games. As a result there are fewer and fewer trips to the ice cream parlor. What would be predicted to happen to their son's intrinsic interest in playing soccer? If a strong connection had been made between playing soccer and getting a reward of ice cream, the removal of the extrinsic reward should diminish interest in soccer.

If, on the other hand, extrinsic rewards are provided on the basis of the quality of performance, then they can be sources of information and can enhance intrinsic motivation.

Such rewards can also increase perception of self-competency and self-determination. Suppose that at the end of the soccer season a player received an award for being the most improved player on the team. How should this reward affect her sense of competence and intrinsic motivation? It should indicate that the efforts put forth throughout the season have paid off. Her perception of self-competence should be enhanced and her intrinsic motivation should be increased.

The misuse of extrinsic rewards in sport settings can have drastic and negative effects on motivation. Most participants perceive sport activities as fun and enjoyable in and of themselves; the introduction of sophisticated systems designed to reward participation in such activities can be quite detrimental. Several scholars (for example, Harter, 1981; Halliwell, 1978) have suggested that, particularly in youth sports, parents and coaches should redirect attention away from the idea of providing extrinsic awards based on the outcome (success or failure) and on to the affective aspects of the game. Other theorists have suggested that rewards should be based on the particular performer's achievements as compared with past experience rather than on comparisons made between or among the players (Roberts, 1984).

Achievement Goals

Roberts (1984) has identified a constellation of three different types of achievement goals that might determine why people participate in sport activities: (1) to seek social approval, (2) to demonstrate ability (competitive ability), and (3) to be task-involved (sport mastery).

According to Roberts, some performers participate in sport activities primarily to gain the approval of others such as teammates, spectators, and coaches. Game outcome is of less importance than is the **social approval** from significant others. Such approval is usually contingent on demonstrating effort; therefore persons who have social approval as the predominant motivational force do exhibit effort but do so for external reasons.

From Roberts' perspective, persons who have a goal of **competitive ability** participate in sport to see how their ability matches up to that of other performers. These persons consistently employ social comparison processes whereby they evaluate their own ability against that of their opponents. Such ability comparisons are most often made on the basis of competitive outcome (success and failure) because persons whose motivation is generated on the basis of competitive ability can best demonstrate that ability through objective criteria such as winning the game or match. As a result, outcome (winning) becomes the most important criterion for sport participation.

This focus on outcome as the primary criterion for evaluation can be detrimental to achievement strivings. Suppose, for example, that the athlete really does try hard but consistently loses. What should be the resulting effect on perceived competence? It should decline. After all, the performer did exert effort, but lost anyway; therefore the explanation must be that ability is lacking.

The **sport mastery** orientation is closely related to competence motivation and intrinsic motivation. An athlete who has the predominant sport participation goal of performing well, regardless of outcome, is considered to be sport-mastery oriented. This type of performer cares about improving skill rather than beating others. Level of ability or achievement is judged in comparison to that performer's past achievements rather than by making comparisons against others.

In terms of competence, self-determination, and positive affect, it seems more desirable that people participate in sport activities for reasons of sport mastery as opposed to competitive ability or social approval. One way to enhance adoption of a sport-mastery orientation is to use a reinforcement system that provides rewards contingent only on improvement in an athlete's performance compared with that person's previous performance. On the contrary, adoption of an outcome-oriented reinforcement contingency can undermine perceived competence. Furthermore, because only one person or one team can be the winner, all the others must be losers. If outcome is the only criterion used to evaluate sport behavior, then all those losers will experience negative affect as a result of sport participation. It seems much more desirable to use a strategy in which individual efforts and improvement are rewarded regardless of outcome.

Another important aspect of Roberts' work involves the question of how sport achievement orientation may relate to *dropping out* of sport. Of the three orientations identified, social approval, competitive ability, and sport mastery, which do you think would most relate to children dropping out of sport? If you thought the answer would be the social approval orientation, think again. Such people can very easily gain social approval in sport contexts because if they exhibit effort in the sport situation, then significant others will probably reward them.

Now think about the difference between being focused on competitive ability and being sport mastery–oriented. In the case of competitive ability, evaluation of ability is generally made on the basis of the game outcome. Failure indicates lack of ability regardless of individual effort. One way to avoid such failure evaluations is to simply drop out of sports. However, Roberts points out that this does not usually occur until around age 12. It seems that before that age, children do not have sufficient cognitive development to distinguish between effort and ability. At about age 12, children realize that ability, to a large extent, determines sport outcome. They begin to understand that for some children even large amounts of effort are not going to ensure success. In addition, most significant others emphasize success as being based on outcome. Thus it seems reasonable that if an adolescent perceives his or her ability to be low, then dropping out of sports is one way to avoid the negative consequences associated with failure. This explanation may also account somewhat for the significant numbers of women who drop out of sports during their teenage years and avoid public display of their sport ability throughout later life. The recent interest and participation of some women in noncompetitive activities such as jogging and aerobics also lends credence to that explanation. It was interesting to observe the marketing strategies used in many ''women's'' magazines during the beginning of the jogging craze. One such magazine promoted the sale of jump ropes to women by saying they could work out in the privacy of their own homes, where no one could see them! This phenomenon is also evident in many health clubs that have ''women only'' exercise rooms.

Roberts has also suggested than an alternative to dropping out would be to redirect achievement orientation to the task itself. The goal should be sport mastery, and emphasis should be placed on performance of the activity rather than outcome. Social comparisons should be avoided, and the use of self-evaluations should be encouraged. If you want to enhance individual sport motivation, then the selection, intensity, and persistence dimensions of motivation, not outcome, should be used as criteria for self evaluation. Such a strategy should enhance perception of competency, self-determination, and positive affect. The goal should be to make sport participation fun, not anxiety inducing.

The previous discussion should have provided some insight into how sense of competence, extrinsic rewards, and achievement goals interrelate to affect motivation in sport. We hope you also noted the powerful role that a person's thoughts and cognitions play in the motivational process.

ATTRIBUTION THEORY

The focus of attribution theory is the relationship between the explanations a person gives for performance outcomes and effects on subsequent actions (Kukla, 1972). Those explanations rest on a person's **perception of causality.** Thus attribution theory is a cognitive approach to motivation because it assumes that people attempt to understand and explain events to provide themselves with a rational basis for their own behavior. Instead of using complicated formulas and constructs to predict behavior, attribution theory uses the vocabulary of the layman; hence, it is referred to as naïve psychology.

The attributions a performer uses to explain either success or failure in sport settings can influence both expectancy of future performance outcomes and the emotions (affect) the performer experiences regarding the outcome in question. For example, suppose that a high jumper has a particularly excellent jump that exceeds his personal best. When asked to explain why he thinks he did so well, he replies that he really tried hard. He is then attributing the successful outcome to effort. This attribution should have two associated effects. First, the high jumper should perceive that he can repeat the successful performance in the future and will most likely be motivated to do so. Second, by attributing the successful outcome to an internal factor, effort, the accompanying affect should be feelings of pride.

But suppose the jumper attributed the same outcome to luck. Will the effects on motivation and affect be identical? No. Luck is an external factor not under the performer's control. It may or may not be present on a future occasion. In addition, there would be little reason to experience high degrees of positive affect (pride) concerning a performance accomplishment that occurred because an element such as luck was on your side. Clearly, causal attributions used by a performer can influence both expectancy of future performance outcomes and affect.

Weiner's Model of the Attributional Process

Although several attribution theorists have proposed models of the attributional process (Heider, 1944, 1958; Jones & Davis, 1965; Kelley, 1973), Weiner and colleagues (Weiner, 1972, 1979; Weiner, Frieze, Kukla, Reed, Rest, & Rosenbaum, 1971) have provided the most popular model. This model has two very important aspects: **causal elements** and **causal dimensions.**

Causal Elements

Causal elements refer to the reasons people give for experiencing either success or failure. Although there are many causal explanations performers could evoke, such as officiating bias or fatigue, the attributions usually studied are those made to *ability, effort, task difficulty,* and *luck.* The two most important causal elements are the internal factors of ability and effort.

Causal Dimensions

The four causal elements identified above can be classified along three dimensions: locus of causality, stability, and controllability (Weiner, 1979). *Locus of causality* refers to the location of the cause in terms of being either internal (inside the person) or external (outside the person). For example, ability is classified as being internal, whereas task difficulty is classified as being external. *Stability* pertains to whether or not the element is changeable. Effort is variable or changeable, whereas ability is ordinarily perceived to be stable. *Controllability* refers to whether or not the element is perceived to be under the control of the performer. For example, luck is an uncontrollable element, whereas effort is under the performer's control.

Controllability greatly affects motivation. If, after failure, a performer attributes the outcome to a causal element not under that person's control (such as bad luck or lack of ability), then the performer does not perceive himself or herself to be the controlling factor in the outcome. If a performer attributes failure to lack of effort, he or she perceives a covariation between effort and outcome; if one element (effort) is changed or varied, then the other element (failure outcome) should also be changed or varied. Thus the performer perceives himself or herself to be in control of the outcome of a response. This is a positive sign that achievement responses will recur.

Expectancy and Affect

The stability dimension is most closely associated with future expectancy of success or failure. By attributing a positive outcome to a stable factor such as ability, there is every reason to believe that the same outcome will recur. Conversely, attributing a failure outcome to lack of ability should foster the perception that future failure is inevitable. If that stable attribution was used in a consistent fashion, then it could lead to impaired motivation based on feelings of incompetency and perhaps *learned helplessness*. Learned helplessness is a perception of "uncontrollability," an independence between a person's responses and their consequences (Dweck, 1975; Seligman & Maier, 1967).

According to Weiner's original model, locus of causality is predicted to be most closely associated with affective responses. As shown in Table 9-1, specific feelings apparently are generated as a result of attributing outcomes either internally or externally (Weiner, 1981). Notice that internal attributions for success tend to enhance feelings of self-competency and self-worth, whereas internal attributions for failure tend to generate feelings of guilt. Although performers may feel grateful or thankful to others who help them to succeed, there also appears to be a danger that such attributions will cause persons to become more externally oriented. These external attributions could undermine performers' sense of personal control over performance outcomes. What would then be predicted to happen to motivation? It should decrease.

Attributions and Sport Behavior

Achievement Motivation

Based on the theoretical framework of McClelland, Atkinson, and Lowell (1953), a major area of research concerning individual differences has been **achievement motivation.** From this perspective, persons are perceived to have one of two primary motives, either to approach success (M_{as}) or to avoid failure (M_{af}). "Approach-success" persons

TABLE 9-1   Relations Between Locus of Causality and Emotions.

Locus	Outcome	
	Success	Failure
Internal	Pride Confidence Competence Satisfaction	Guilt
External	Gratefulness Thankfulness	Anger Surprise

From Weiner, B. (1981). The role of affect in sports psychology. In G.C. Roberts & D.M. Landers (Eds.), *Psychology of motor behavior and sport.* Champaign, IL: Human Kinetics.

are sometimes referred to as high achievers, whereas "avoid-failure" persons are often called low achievers. Several researchers have demonstrated a consistent pattern concerning achievement motivation and causal attributions (Gilmore & Minton, 1974; Lefebvre, 1979; Weiner & Kukla, 1970). High achievers tend to take personal responsibility for success by attributing it to their own ability. Low achievers deny personal responsibility for success by attributing causality to an external source. Thus high achievers reap affective benefits associated with success in achievement situations; low achievers do not. High achievers also see themselves as personally responsible for failure by attributing it to lack of effort. Therefore they perceive that they can change their own destinies simply by varying the amount of effort exerted. Behaviorally, you should be able to identify high achievers by their motivation to enter into achievement settings such as sport. In addition, these are the performers who tend to persist at a task even after failure because they believe that if they just try harder, they will be successful. On the contrary, given the chance, low achievers will avoid such achievement situations. Also, because they perceive that failure is caused by a lack of ability, low achievers do not tend to try again or persist after failure. They simply stop trying. They become passive.

Of greatest interest in the coaching or teaching of sport skills is whether the maladaptive pattern of attributions exhibited by low achievers can be changed so that it mirrors that of high achievers. Furthermore, if such change is possible, will it be reflected in behaviors such as approaching achievement settings and persisting after failure? If our thoughts and perceptions really do determine our behavior, then a change in attributions should result in an observable change in behavior.

The procedure used to alter attributions for failure is called either an **attribution retraining treatment** (Dweck, 1975) or an **achievement change program** (Weiner, 1981). The goal of such programs is to alter the attributions for failure and therefore increase achievement strivings or persistence (that is, motivation). A good example of such a program is that used by Dweck (1975).

Dweck and her colleagues (Dweck, 1975; Dweck & Reppucci, 1973) hypothesized that a long-term training program that taught learned helpless children (extremely low achievers) to take personal responsibility for failure by attributing it to lack of effort would subsequently increase task persistence. They used two experimental groups. One was a "success-only treatment" wherein the subjects were able to complete all experimental trials successfully. The success-only treatment was included because some theorists and many teachers believe that children can avoid the unpleasantness of failure if they do not have to experience it. The other experimental approach was an "attribution retraining treatment." This differed from the success-only treatment in that failure occurred in about 20% of the experimental trials. When failure was evidenced, it was clearly attributed by the experimenter to lack of effort.

The results of the study showed strong support for the assertion that if persons are taught to attribute failure to lack of effort (reattribution training), then they will begin to show increased persistence behavior after failure. According to Dweck, failure can become a cue that effort must be increased. The use of the effort attribution indicates to the person that failure results from a lack of motivation rather than a lack of ability. Motivation is changeable and under the control of the performer. Also of interest was the finding that the subjects who experienced only success did not show any consistent improvement in their response after failure. On the contrary, performance was markedly impaired after failure.

The notions of learned helplessness, low achievement motivation, and reattribution training have distinct possibilities for applications within sport situations. Clearly, reattribution techniques could be used to increase the persistence behavior of persons in sport settings. However, caution should be exercised. We suggest you follow the steps below when using reattribution procedures in sport and motor skills settings:

1. Select a goal that can definitely be attained if the performer exerts sufficient effort. This selection process is of critical importance.
2. Provide preperformance instructions that tell the person that successful performance depends on exerting effort.
3. After the performance attempt, ask why either the successful or unsuccessful outcome occurred. Positively reinforce effort attributions.
4. When the performer is *consistently* achieving about an 80% to 90% success rate, establish a new goal and repeat the sequence of steps.

These steps can help facilitate the perception that effort determines outcome. And because the performer really is achieving success, perception of his or her ability should be enhanced. Once both of these perceptions are held, the previously low achiever is beginning to think like a high achiever, and motivation to perform and persist at similar tasks in the future should increase. You should be able to observe these motivational changes in the form of increased approach and persistence responses.

Dweck (1980) has also speculated on how aspects of learned helplessness might be manifested even in elite athletes. In such cases, the helplessness would most likely not be observed over the long run. However, during a game or a match, if a failure begins to trigger thoughts of imcompetence or pending doom, then feelings of helplessness will probably follow. Dweck uses the example of tennis star Evonne Goolagong-Cawley, who was fine when things were going her way; but when events didn't go in her favor, she tended to fall apart.

> She has, in fact, made statements to the effect that when this occurs she truly feels she has no control over the situation. This pattern may characterize teams, as well as individuals. There are those teams that display remarkable ability when things are going smoothly and they are winning, but cannot seem to do anything right when the tide turns. There are teams that seem to fall apart when their lead shrinks, even though they may still be well ahead of their opponents at that time. (p. 9)

The statements made by athletes relative to control and the attributions given for mistakes can provide valuable insights into distructive perceptions the performers may hold. That information can then be used to structure "mini" reattribution procedures. This should be particularly effective with high-level athletes whose ability level is not at issue.

Egocentrism, or a Self-Serving Bias

Although individual differences in achievement motivation do influence the attributional process, there also appear to be some general patterns among people. The most common of these is the tendency to employ a **self-serving, or egocentric, bias.** People tend to ascribe success to internal elements and failure to external elements; by so doing, they are able to enhance their egos after success and protect it after failure.

How does the self-serving hypothesis hold up in sport settings? Almost all the investigations have demonstrated a tendency for sport participants to attribute success internally (for example, Bird & Brame, 1979; Scanlan & Passer, 1980). However, no clear or consistent pattern appears to exist when attributing failure. Several variables appear to mediate between losing and making attributions. For instance, the decisiveness of the outcome (Iso-Ahola, 1977; Spink, 1978), whether a player's subjective evaluation of the outcome is consistent with the objective outcome (Spink, 1980), the degree of cohesion within the sport group (Bird, Foster, & Maruyama, 1980), and whether the attribution is made in private or public (Rejeski & Brawley, 1983) can all influence the attributions made for failure outcomes. This is an area that still needs attention. It is particularly important to conduct further research aimed at understanding the factors influencing explanations of negative sport outcomes because those are the attributions that can have a detrimental effect on future motivation to participate in sport.

Gender Differences and Sex-Role Stereotypes

Research studies concerning differences in attribution patterns as a function of gender have indicated that men and women generally follow the same patterns (Iso-Ahola, 1979; Roberts, Kleiber, & Duda, 1981). However, there is evidence to suggest that sex-role stereotypes may exist.

In the only investigation that has taken a developmental approach to the study of attributions within sport settings, Bird and Williams (1980) assessed observers ranging in age from 7 to 18 years. Their results indicated that as the youngsters got older, sex-role stereotypes for sport performance become more apparent. The younger children attributed outcomes for both boys and girls similarly. However, by age 13, sport outcomes for girls were attributed to the external factor of luck, whereas those same outcomes for boys were ascribed to the internal factor of effort. Thus their findings indicated that by adolescence, boys are perceived as being in control of their own achievement outcomes; girls are viewed as being at the mercy of the environment. It is also important to point out that these sex-role stereotypes were held equally by both boys and girls.

However, other evidence suggests that when children are making judgments about their own performance, rather than the performance of others, this pattern does not always arise. For example, Iso-Ahola (1979) examined the sex-role stereotypes of fourth-grade boys and girls. He found no indication of differences in the attributions for own success or opponent's success as a function of gender. The differences between the Bird and

Williams findings and those of Iso-Ahola indicate that attributions made by sport participants may not be identical to those made by observers.

Interestingly, the same study (Iso-Ahola, 1979), uncovered a provocative stereotype
on the part of boys. When a boy lost to another boy, he would accept lack of personal
ability as the cause. However, when a boy lost to a girl, he would not accept his lack of
ability as the cause. It appears that boys may become self-protective after losing to a
girl. Such a loss goes against the sex-role stereotype that boys are more competent than
girls at sport skills.

Taken as a whole, the research evidence provides a strong basis on which to argue
that the cognitions that a person holds and the attributions a person uses to explain the
causes underlying performance outcomes have definite effects on motivation. In addition,
attributional patterns may vary as a function of achievement motivation, self-serving
biases, and gender of the performer.

SELF-EFFICACY THEORY

Another major contribution to sport motivation research is Bandura's (1977) **self-efficacy
theory.** According to Bandura, self-efficacy refers to the strength of a person's
conviction that he or she can successfully make a response that is required to produce a
certain outcome. Thus self-efficacy theory draws strongly on a cognitive interpretation
of motivation. Bandura proposes that cognitive processes play a dominant role in both
the acquisition and retention of new behavior patterns. Information is acquired either
directly or vicariously (model observation) and is then coded symbolically into a cognitive
representation that can guide future behavior. In terms of motivation, the cognitive representation is thought to be capable of predicting future outcomes: "The capacity to
represent future consequences in thought provides one cognitively based source of motivation. Through cognitive representation of future outcomes individuals can generate
current motivators of behavior" (Bandura, 1977, p. 193).

The cognitive representation can also influence motivation by functioning in the goal
setting and self-evaluation processes. For example, an athlete might cognitively set a goal
of running a race at a specific pace. The goal setting serves as a motivator of behavior.
After the run, an evaluation is made against the standard represented in cognition. If
success was the outcome, self-reward or self-reinforcement should follow. This is a
pleasant experience and can motivate future behavior. Failure should cause dissatisfaction
and can influence the athlete to make behavioral changes that will lead to more successful
performance. Thus the cognitive processes associated with both the expectancy of future
behavior and the evaluation of the outcome of that behavior can affect motivation.

Efficacy Expectations versus Outcome Expectations

Bandura (1977) emphasized that a distinction must be made between **efficacy expectations**
and **outcome expectations.**

Figure 9-1 represents the difference between efficacy expectations and outcome expectations. An efficacy expectation represents the strength of the conviction that the
person is capable of producing a certain outcome. This is why the box labeled *efficacy
expectations* is located between the person and the behavior. From Bandura's perspective

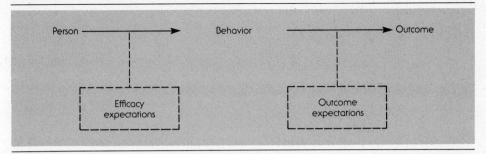

FIGURE 9-1   Diagrammatic representation of the difference between efficacy expectations and outcome expectations.
From Bandura, A. (1977). Self-efficacy: Toward a unifying theory of behavioral change. *Psychological Review, 84,* 191-215.

the motivational force underlying behavior is directly related to the nature of the efficacy expectation held by the performer. Thus his perspective on motivation is called self-efficacy theory. Now notice that the box labeled *outcome expectations* is situated between the behavior and the outcome. This is because an outcome expectancy pertains to a person's estimation that a particular behavior will produce a certain outcome. Another way of looking at these two expectations is in terms of their informational versus motivational roles. The knowledge that a certain response is required to produce an outcome (outcome expectation) does not guarantee that the performer will attempt the response. Usually, a behavioral response will occur only if the performer holds the conviction (high efficacy expectation) that he or she can successfully enact the required response. For example, a beginning tennis player may know that the correct response for a lob is a smash (outcome expectancy). However, the performer may not attempt that response because of the perception that he or she cannot successfully execute the required stroke (low efficacy expectation).

Efficacy expectations are viewed as being specific to given activities rather than being global, or generalized. A person's perception of self-efficacy can influence both choice of activities and persistence of coping efforts in the face of anxiety-producing situations. Perceived self-efficacy can also determine the amount of effort a person expends and how long he or she persists when faced with obstacles (Bandura, 1977).

Sources of Efficacy Expectations

Bandura (1977) has identified four sources of information that influence efficacy expectations: (1) performance accomplishments, (2) vicarious experience, (3) verbal persuasion, and (4) emotional arousal.

Performance accomplishments are seen as the most powerful source of efficacy information because this information is based on a person's own personal mastery experiences. Multiple successes lead to strong positive efficacy expectations, whereas repeated failures generate strong negative efficacy expectations. Because performance-based information is so potent in terms of affecting perceived efficacy, performance-based behavior change programs are the most powerful.

Vicarious experiences provide people with a great deal of information and can influence the perception of their own efficacy at a task through the observation of models. For example, when a person observes someone else perform a threatening task without adverse consequences, this experience can trigger an expectation by the observer that if he or she intensifies effort and persistence, improvement or success can follow (Bandura, 1977). When vicarious modeling is used to reduce observer threat, several modeling variables need to be considered, including the amount of effort displayed, the similarity of model to observer, and the clarity of the outcome conveyed.

Verbal persuasion is a common technique used to influence or change behavior. Coaches frequently use verbal suggestions to convince athletes that they are indeed capable of mastering or coping successfully with a task. Neither verbal persuasion nor vicarious modeling is as powerful in affecting self-efficacy as are performance-based approaches.

Emotional arousal is frequently used to provide information concerning a person's competency. According to Bandura (1977), "People rely partly on their state of physiological arousal in judging their anxiety and vulnerability to stress" (p. 198). Very high states of arousal or anxiety can have negative effects on performance; therefore a person who experiences high levels of arousal or anxiety usually expects to perform poorly. From Bandura's perspective the relationship between arousal and self-efficacy is inverse; as arousal increases, self-efficacy decreases. Although there have been some critics of Bandura's interpretation of the role of arousal and anxiety, it would only complicate matters unnecessarily to present the conflicting arguments here (see Borkovec, 1978; Feltz, 1982; Lang, 1978).

As mentioned previously, performance-based procedures are the most powerful vehicles for behavior change. These procedures are designed to provide a person with direct mastery experiences. Thus, from the perspective of self-efficacy theory, successful performance is the primary vehicle for changes in perceived efficacy.

Self-Efficacy and Sport Behavior

Participant Modeling

Participant modeling consists of three fundamental elements: *modeling, guided participation,* and *the attainment of performance success.* Fundamentally, it consists of structuring the environment with response-induction aids through the following procedures:

1. The "therapist" or another model performs the activity in easily mastered steps. The model should demonstrate effort, should be as similar as possible to the observer, and should demonstrate achievement through effort.
2. The performer attempts the task with the guided, physical assistance of the teacher or therapist. The goal is to achieve success.
3. Once the learner is able to successfully execute the task requirements with the assistance of the model or other physical aids, then such support should be gradually withdrawn.
4. The participant modeling procedure is complete when the performer is able to master the task in the absence of any external assistance.

The achievement of such success should then positively affect the efficacy expectation. Because the performer has achieved actual performance success, this should feed back to formulate the cognitive appraisal that the same successful outcome can be achieved on future occasions.

Participant modeling is ordinarily used when performers perceive a task to be threatening and therefore exhibit avoidance behavior. A sport skill that is quite threatening to most performers is the back dive. Feltz, Landers, and Raeder (1979) selected that skill to test the relative effectiveness of participant modeling as compared with presentation of a live or videotaped model. Given the fear-provoking nature of the back dive, they hypothesized that subjects involved in a participant modeling condition would perform better than other subjects who were involved in either the live model or videotaped model group.

All subjects completed a Diving Efficacy Scale to determine their perceived efficacy at the back dive task (see box below). All subjects rated their perceived efficacy for each item on a 100-point scale. Only subjects who were less than 100% confident on item 8 of the scale were selected for inclusion in the experiment.

In the participant modeling condition, the model provided a verbal description of the task followed by two live demonstrations. The model then accompanied the subject onto the diving board and helped guide the dive in two ways. A rubber strap was wrapped around the lower thighs to help keep the legs together (physical guidance). The model held onto the subject's waist until the correct arch was achieved (model guidance). These subjects received participant modeling only on the first four trials in a sequence of eight trials. The diving self-efficacy scale was re-administered after trials 4 and 8. The procedure used in the live and videotaped conditions was identical to that used in the participant modeling condition, with the exception that no rubber strap or model guidance was used.

The findings indicated that the participant modeling group generated more successful dives and stronger perceptions of self-efficacy as compared with subjects in the live model and videotape model groups. Thus the results of the study provided support for Bandura's (1977) assertion that participant modeling should be an effective means of improving performance and efficacy expectations in situations in which a task has threatening qualities. Because all three conditions were performance-based, the results also argue for the relative effectiveness of participant modeling over live and videotaped models in situations in which performance anxiety is present. However, there is other evidence that participant modeling and live modeling may be equally effective.

McAuley (1983) studied the relative effectiveness of live and participant modeling on three factors: self-efficacy, anxiety, and sport performance. A no-model control group was also included. The task was a complex gymnastic skill that involved a dive forward

---

Diving Efficacy Scale Items

1. Jump off side of pool, feet first.
2. Jump off 1-m board, feet first.
3. Jump backward, off side of pool, feet first.
4. Jump backward, from 1-m board, feet first.
5. Dive off side of pool.
6. Modified forward dive (without spring takeoff) from 1-m board.
7. Running forward dive (with spring takeoff) from 1-m board.
8. Modified back dive (without spring takeoff) from 1-m board (leaning back and falling in).

From Feltz, D.L., Landers, D.M., & Raeder, U. (1979). Enhancing self-efficacy in high-avoidance motor tasks: A comparison of modeling techniques. *Journal of Sport Psychology, 1,* 112-122.

roll mount onto the beam from a springboard. All subjects had no previous gymnastics experience, so it can certainly be argued that such a task would probably trigger threat or anxiety responses. McAuley's results indicated that both modeling groups exhibited lower anxiety and higher efficacy expectation as compared with the control group. McAuley also found no difference in perceived efficacy or anxiety between the two modeling groups. Based on Bandura's framework, it would have been expected that the participant modeling group would have higher efficacy expectations and lower anxiety as compared with the live modeling group. Of further interest is the finding that the performance of the participant modeling group was superior to that of the live modeling group, and both modeling groups performed better than the control group.

The results of the Feltz, Landers, and Raeder (1979) investigation and those of McAuley do not agree on the relative effectiveness of participant versus live modeling in the learning of a threatening sport skill. Because these are the only two studies that have addressed this question in the sport literature, it is not yet possible to resolve the issue. However, it is clear that modeling in one form or another can help students to learn skills that are anxiety provoking.

Manipulated Self-Efficacy

Weinberg and colleagues (Weinberg, Gould, & Jackson, 1979; Weinberg, Yukelson, & Jackson, 1980) have conducted two investigations designed to assess the effect of manipulated self-efficacy on a muscular endurance task performed under competitive conditions. Weinberg, Gould, and Jackson (1979), had subjects compete face-to-face in a muscular endurance task that required subjects to extend their leg horizontally for as long as possible. Self-efficacy was manipulated by telling the subject that the other competitor (actually a confederate) was either a varsity track athlete (manipulated low self-efficacy) or a person who had a knee injury (manipulated high self-efficacy). Results supported self-efficacy theory in that the high self-efficacy group maintained the leg extension longer than the low self-efficacy group.

Because a face-to-face competitive situation can provide performance cues to subjects, Weinberg, Yukelson, and Jackson (1980) designed the second study to look at those same effects in back-to-back competition. They also addressed the question of whether or not performance would be influenced by the request for either private or public expectancy expectations. The efficacy results were the same as in the previous study, thus extending the face-to-face findings to a back-to-back competitive setting. There was no significant effect provided by soliciting efficacy statements in either a public or private situation.

Although research in aspects of self-efficacy in sport settings is rather new, it appears that its premises can help us to better understand aspects of motivation. It is particularly applicable to sports that include threatening activities, such as diving and gymnastics, and also seems to provide a functional framework for highly anxious or low-achieving students.

Some support for the relationship between anxiety and self-efficacy comes from a recent study by Yan Lan and Gill (1984). They had subjects perform an easy (high-efficacy) task and a difficult (low-efficacy) task. They used the Competitive State Anxiety Inventory-2 (CSAI-2) to assess cognitive worry, somatic anxiety, and self-confidence. They also measured heart rate. The easy task generated higher self-efficacy; subjects reported lower cognitive worry and somatic anxiety, higher-self confidence, and had lower heart rate. The fact that the easy task enhanced self-efficacy suggests that intervention strategies might be effectively aimed at increasing self-efficacy in addition to reducing anxiety.

MOTIVATION AND THE UNIFYING MODEL

In presenting the orientations of competence motivation, attribution theory, and self-efficacy theory some common themes and notions appear to run throughout each perspective. The framework of the unifying model should be helpful in pulling those commonalities together and providing a clearer conceptual basis for understanding aspects of sport motivation.

Input

As shown on the left side of Figure 9-2, each of the perspectives on motivation looks at a situation in which a person is faced with a choice of either approaching or avoiding a sport achievement or mastery task. Those tasks are most usually characterized by having challenging components and clear outcomes in terms of success or failure. In sport situations, the decision to attempt a task also means that the performance outcome will be public and therefore subject to the evaluations of others. The motivation underlying whether or not the person will approach or avoid such tasks is a result of several factors.

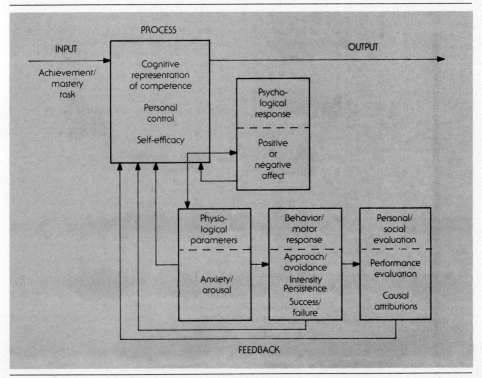

FIGURE 9-2   Motivation and the unifying model.

Process

Very young children appear to have an inborn motive to explore and master their environment. Their mastery behavior is intrinsic and requires no external rewards. However, through the process of socialization, orientation underlying motivation can be changed. When the performer exhibits mastery responses, significant others, such as parents or teachers, evaluate those responses. As development proceeds in conjunction with observational learning, instructions, and evaluative feedback, the person begins to internalize a cognitive representation of both a standard of performance evaluation and a sense of perceived competence and personal control. Through this process the person establishes a perception of his or her ability to make the responses necessary to achieve success. This perceived sense of personal control appears to underlie a person's motivation in sport settings.

Output

The result of the performer's cognitive appraisal of his or her perceived ability is reflected at several levels. At the psychological level, a positive self-evaluation of ability to produce successful mastery responses is accompanied by positive affect and feelings of self-worth. On the contrary, a negative self-evaluation should generate negative emotions such as feelings of helplessness, guilt, or shame.

A negative self-evaluation of perceived ability to successfully perform a mastery task can also increase physiological arousal and feelings of apprehension and anxiety. In addition, the perception of high degrees of physiological arousal can have associated effects that are detrimental to performance. For instance, people may monitor physiological arousal as an indication of how anxious they feel. If the information they receive tells them that they are highly anxious, then their expectation of success can decrease. In addition, as discussed earlier in the text, there is an inverse relationship between high degrees of anxiety and successful performance on complex motor tasks.

At the behavioral level, the outcome of a person's cognitive appraisal of whether or not he or she can produce a successful response determines much about whether the situation will be approached or avoided. A positive evaluation increases the probability of an approach response that will be characterized by an intense effort to master the task. In addition, because mastery is the goal, this person will tend to persist at the task after failure. If the result of the cognitive appraisal reflects lack of control over performance outcome or low perceived ability, then one way to avoid the negative affect that accompanies such an evaluation is to avoid the situation altogether. If the situation cannot be avoided, then the expectation will be failure rather than success. And in all likelihood that is just what will occur—failure.

If that failure outcome is attributed to a stable factor such as lack of ability, then there is no reason to suspect that a different outcome will occur in the future. Repeated attributions to lack of ability can lead to feelings of even lower competence and eventually learned helplessness. Teaching persons to attribute performance outcomes to elements that are variable and under their personal control, such as effort, can help alleviate negative self-evaluations and feelings of uncontrollability. However, as proposed in self-efficacy

theory, the most powerful vehicles for behavior change involve actual performance successes. That is why achievement change or reattribution programs include multiple opportunities for performance success.

The results of these success experiences, coupled with attributions to effort, send
information back to cognition, which can modify the outcome of the cognitive appraisal
on future occasions. This same rationale underlies the participant modeling approach to
facilitating approach behavior to threatening tasks. The actual experience of successful
performance in the absence of adverse consequences should lead to positive feelings of
self-efficacy.

Apparently, one way in which such negative self-evaluations can be avoided in the
first place is by having the coach or teacher shift the criterion of evaluation away from
person-to-person comparisons. This can be done by positively emphasizing the performance accomplishments of the performer based on his or her past outcomes. Such accomplishments should be recognized by positive verbal praise. Also, mastery strivings
and intrinsic motivation should be enhanced when attention is focused on the positive
affective benefits inherent in the activity as opposed to the outcome of the behavior in
terms of success or failure.

Feedback

The output information feeds back to the cognitive representation. Positive information,
whether in terms of the content of the affect or the outcome of the performance, will
enhance a person's sense of competence and efficacy. Negative feedback will do the
opposite. Thus thoughts and emotions do indeed precede and determine behavior. The
determination of a large percentage of those thoughts and emotions is based on the content
of the information fed back to cognition.

IMPLICATIONS FOR SPORT

- Coaches and teachers should emphasize the informational rather than the controlling
  nature of extrinsic rewards. Reward performers on aspects of sport mastery and improvement rather than outcome in terms of objective success.
- Try to reward athletes in a manner in which they will gain information about personal
  competency. This will make the reward more meaningful to the performer.
- Before rewarding a performer, mutually establish a performance standard or goal based
  on that person's previous performance.
- Try to avoid making social comparisons between athletes. Each is unique.
- Discuss the positive affective reactions that players may have experienced during the
  game or match. This will highlight their importance.
- Whenever possible, use verbal praise or positive feedback instead of tangible rewards
  such as trophies and medals.
- Emphasize the ''effort-outcome'' connection during individual conferences and team
  meetings.

- Athlete motivation will be enhanced when performance goals require some amount of effort. Select goals that are specific to a particular practice session or game. Always evaluate how well the athlete did in achieving the goals. Verbally praise success; set new and more achievable goals after failure.
- When athletes show increased persistence or intensity, praise them.
- Small amounts of failure may actually motivate the athlete to persist by indicating to the athlete that more effort is needed. Increased effort should result in better performance and increased skill.
- Coaches should stress that players are in control of their own performance but not necessarily the team outcome.
- When athletes attribute success to ability, this should increase expectancy of future success and thus motivate subsequent sport performance. This same ability attribution can be disastrous in the case of failure. In the latter case, try to substitute the "effort-outcome" connection.
- A lack of task persistence after failure may be a sign that either low achievement motivation or learned helplessness is a problem. If you see this happen on several occasions, first elicit the athlete's reasons for failure. If the answer is lack of ability, then design and implement a reattribution procedure.
- Encourage internal (ability or effort) attributions for success. Those success attributions enhance feelings of self-competency and self-worth.
- When performers express feelings of physical inadequacy when faced with an anxiety-producing skill, use the processes associated with participant modeling.
- Remember, sufficient performance success should result in the perception of personal control and the expectancy of future success. Those perceptions then positively influence the motivation to participate in sport and to persist after failure.

CASE STUDY 1

Teaching and Coaching for Sport Mastery

This case study focuses on the objectives, strategies, and implementation of a program designed to enhance an orientation toward sport mastery.

One of the most common problems, even for highly skilled bowlers, is a tendency to fall apart during competition. The element that is different in competition is the presence of social evaluation. In other words, during practice bowlers tend to be more concerned with their own performance and score and less interested in the outcome of others. During competition, performers consistently monitor the scores of opponents to see how their performance compares. This shift of focus from a self-based orientation to a social-comparison orientation can be detrimental to bowling performance. One strategy to alleviate this problem is to design a program that redirects focus to evaluation of self rather than opponents.

The first step would be to set up a conference wherein discussion will initially focus on the reasons why the athlete thinks his or her performance deteriorates under competitive conditions. Emphasize the idea that level of skill development itself does not vary much from practice to competitive situations; therefore the underlying cause of performance decrements must be psychological. What is the bowler thinking about during competition that is different from thoughts during practice? Most likely, it will be revealed that competition evokes some anxiety based on concerns about social comparisons of overall score. After all, that is what determines who wins and who loses.

If the teacher or coach can switch the standard of evaluation from being socially-based to being self-based, this strategy can actually enhance competitive performance. First, the athlete's current average during practice should be identified. This serves as a realistic representation of actual skill development and should be used as the criterion for subsequent evaluation of competitive performance. It presents an individualized standard of excellence rather than a socially based criterion. The next step is a process whereby the coach and athlete attempt to identify some limited, achievable goals. These are within-performance goals that eventually may lead to better overall performance. These goals must be achievable through increased effort by the performer. A good example in bowling would be to attempt to increase the number of spares picked up in each game by one. It is the effort put into the achievement of the limited, achievable goal(s) that should then function as the criterion (criteria) for both external and self-evaluation. The teacher or coach should verbally praise the intensity and persistence the athlete displays in attempting to reach the limited goal. It is also important to have the athlete evaluate his or her own status relative to the achievement of the limited goal. Such self-based evaluations indicate that the athlete has internalized the goal and also foster the development of a self-reinforcement orientation. Although outcome evaluations probably cannot be ignored entirely, it should be emphasized that the achievement of successful outcomes are dependent on the accomplishment of each of the limited goals. Emphasis should also be placed on the idea that the most important outcome evaluations are those that compare an athlete's current performance against his or her previous performance.

For the bowler it is obvious that achieving the goal of increasing the number of spares picked up in each game by 1 is also going to positively affect the performer's game score. It is this cause and effect relationship that should be stressed. Once the athlete can reach the limited goal(s) fairly consistently, then it is time to begin the sport mastery program again. New, limited goals should be identified, reinforced in terms of motivational dimensions such as effort and persistence, and self-evaluated. This should lead to better overall performance, reduced competitive anxiety, and increased positive affect. Most important, this program should generate a sport mastery orientation that is based on a desire for increased self-competency rather than an orientation that is directed to social comparisons of competitive outcomes.

SUMMARY

- A major factor influencing the degree to which positive self-competency and mastery strivings are exhibited by a person is the evaluative reactions of significant others such as parents, coaches, and teachers. These reactions become internalized and represented cognitively. The cognitive representation reflects the mastery goals, criteria for success and failure, and perceptions of personal control over performance outcome.
- A person's perception of personal control can be affected negatively by the receipt of extrinsic rewards that are perceived to be controlling rather than informational. When the controlling aspect of a reward is emphasized, the person may perceive a correlation between the enactment of the behavior and the receipt of a reward. This perception then undermines intrinsic, or competency-based, motivation.

- One way to use rewards to enhance sport mastery or competency-based motivation is to provide them on the basis of a person's current performance relative to his or her past performance rather than on the basis of interpersonal comparisons. Such a procedure can increase the sense of self-competency, self-determination, and positive affect associated with sport participation.
- As opposed to looking specifically at how rewards may influence motivation, attribution theory focuses on the explanations a performer gives for achievement outcomes. It is proposed that the attributions a person uses to explain either success or failure in achievement settings can influence both expectancy of future performance outcomes and the affect he or she experiences regarding the outcome in question. The most common causal explanations are effort, ability, task difficulty, and luck. Those four causal elements can be classified along the three dimensions of locus of causality, stability, and controllability.
- High achievers generally take personal responsibility for both success and failure in achievement situations. They tend to attribute success to their own ability and failure to a lack of effort. Because effort is an unstable element, high achievers perceive that they can change an unsuccessful performance outcome simply by increasing amount of effort. Low achievers, on the other hand, tend to deny any personal responsibility for a successful outcome by attributing it to some external cause. However, they do tend to accept responsibility for a negative outcome by ascribing causation personally to their own lack of ability. Reattribution or achievement-change programs have been designed to change the attribution patterns demonstrated by low achievers or persons exhibiting learned helplessness so that they begin to reflect the more positive orientation of high achievers.
- Because attributions reflect the perceptions of causality that people hold, attribution theory is a cognitive interpretation of motivation.
- Another cognitively based theory of motivation is self-efficacy theory. Self-efficacy is conceptualized as the strength of a person's conviction that he or she can successfully execute a behavior required to produce an identifiable outcome. Self-efficacy theory proposes that efficacy expectations are influenced by four sources of information: performance accomplishments, vicarious experiences, verbal persuasion, and emotional arousal. Because performance outcomes are viewed as the most powerful source of influence, behavior change programs associated with self-efficacy theory are primarily performance-based in nature. The most prominent of these is participant modeling, which consists of three fundamental elements: modeling, guided participation, and attainment of performance success. Both modeling and participant modeling have been shown to enhance performance in sport activities that have threatening components, such as a back dive or a complicated mount onto the balance beam in gymnastics.

DISCUSSION QUESTIONS

1 Identify the difference between vicarious modeling and participant modeling.
2 What are some common underlying themes in the perspectives of competence motivation theory, attribution theory, and self-efficacy theory?
3 Think of a sport skill with some degree of threat involved with its performance. Design a participant modeling program for that skill that could be successful in reducing threat and in alleviating performance anxiety or avoidance behavior.

4 What are some of the behavioral manifestations of the following individual differences: high sport mastery orientation, high achievement motivation, and high sense of self-efficacy?

5 Explain how a cognitive representation is thought to develop and to influence mastery or competency motivation.

6 Discuss the proposed relationship between external rewards and sport motivation.

7 When using reattribution procedures, what could result if a teacher or coach selected a performance goal that was not achievable for the performer?

GLOSSARY

achievement motivation Dominant motivational orientation in situations characterized by the attainment of clear success or clear failure; the two primary motives are either to achieve success (M_{as}) or to avoid failure (M_{af})

attribution retraining program (achievement change program) Procedure designed to increase persistence after failure by teaching persons to attribute failure to lack of effort

causal dimensions Three dimensions (locus of causality, stability, and controllability) along which the causal elements contained within attribution theory are classified

causal elements Explanations (attributions) that are generally given for a particular outcome; the most common are ability, effort, task difficulty, and luck

cognitive evaluation theory Theory that proposes that two variables—perception of personal competence and perception of self-control—underlie the degree of intrinsic motivation

competitive ability Motivational or achievement goal of judging self-skill or ability by making comparisons with others

competence motivation Desire to engage in mastery activities for intrinsic rewards such as joy or happiness

differentiated motivation Separation of the motivational system into domain-specific dimensions such as cognitive, social, and sport achievement motives

efficacy expectations Strength of a person's conviction that he or she is capable of producing a certain outcome

intrinsic motivation Motivation to perform a skill or activity in the absense of any external reward or incentive

mastery experiences Activities in which the person has an observable effect on the environment, usually evidenced by objective success or failure

outcome expectations Person's knowledge about what behavior is needed to produce a certain outcome

perception of causality Person's beliefs about the causes underlying outcomes, particularly whether or not the performer is the causative agent or if some external factor is the causative agent

self-efficacy theory Cognitive approach to motivation that focuses on the strength of a person's conviction that he or she can successfully make a response that is required to produce a certain outcome

self-serving bias (egocentric bias) Self-protective or ego-protective strategy whereby people tend to take personal responsibility for success but deny responsibility for failure

social approval Motivational or achievement goal of receiving the approval of others

sport mastery Motivational or achievement goal of performing well to improve or perfect skill, regardless of the accomplishments of others

uncontrollability The perception of independence between a person's own response and the consequence of that response; this perception discriminates between the learned helpless person and the mastery oriented person.

SUGGESTED READINGS

Bandura, A. (1977). Self-efficacy: Toward a unifying theory of behavioral change. *Psychological Review, 84*, 191-215.

This is a landmark paper outlining one of the most popular cognitively-based theories of motivation. After developing the rationale underlying the theory of self-efficacy, the participant modeling procedure is described as a means of changing avoidance behavior.

Brawley, L.R. (1984). Attributions as social cognitions: Contemporary perspectives in sport. In W.F. Straub & J.M. Williams (Eds.), *Cognitive sport psychology,* Lansing, NY: Sport Science Associates.

Brawley initially orients the reader to the study of attribution through the presentation of an organizational model, then presents an overview of recent investigations of attributions in sport settings. Brawley concludes with a discussion of suggestions for future research.

Barling, J., & Abel, M. (1983). Self-efficacy beliefs and tennis performance. *Cognitive Therapy and Research, 7*, 265-272.

The authors tested the relationship of self-efficacy expectations to tennis performance. They found self-efficacy expectations to be related to both self and coach's ratings of tennis performance.

Feltz, D.L., & Brown, E.W. (1984). Perceived competence in soccer skills among young soccer players. *Journal of Sport Psychology, 6*, 385-394.

Feltz and Brown modified Harter's perceived competence scale to make it specific to soccer. They attempted to determine whether perceived physical competence, general self-esteem, or perceived soccer competence would be the best predictor of soccer-playing ability. Results provide some support for the use of sport-specific measures of psychological constructs.

Harter, S. (1981). The development of competence motivation in the mastery of cognitive and physical skills: Is there still a place for joy? In G.C. Roberts & D.M. Landers (Eds.), *Psychology of Motor Behavior and Sport,* Champaign IL: Human Kinetics.

This is an examination of how a sense of competence develops in young children. Harter explores variables that influence competence motivation and discusses the measurement of competence motivation.

McAuley, E., Russell, D., & Gross, J.B. (1983). Affective consequences of winning and losing: An attributional analysis. *Journal of Sport Psychology, 5,* 278-287.

The authors examined the relationships between causal dimensions and affective reactions to outcomes in table tennis. For winners, in particular, attribution processes were found to be important factors affecting affective reactions.

Rejeski, W.J. (1983). A model of attributional conflict in sport. *Journal of Sport Behavior, 2,* 156-166.

Rejeski presents an attributionally based model for understanding potential conflicts between coaches and athletes. The central theme is the usual diversity between the perceptions of actors and observers. Both theoretical and practical implications are advanced.

Vallerand, R.J., & Reid, G. (1984). On the causal effects of perceived competence on intrinsic motivation: A test of cognitive evaluation theory. *Journal of Sport Psychology, 6,* 94-102.

This investigation was designed to determine whether the effects of verbal feedback on intrinsic motivation are mediated by perceived competence. Results indicated that positive feedback increased and negative feedback decreased both intrinsic motivation and perceived competence.

Weinberg, R.S. (1984). The relationship between extrinsic rewards and intrinsic motivation in sport. In J.M. Silva & R.S. Weinberg (Eds.), *Psychological foundation of sport.* Champaign, IL: Human Kinetics.

Weinberg discusses the effects that external rewards are predicted to have on intrinsic motivation. The article provides an overview of important theories and research and concludes with implications for coaches and physical educators.

IV

AGGRESSION, GROUP PERFORMANCE, AND COACHING BEHAVIOR

10

AGGRESSION AND SPORT

The study of aggression in sport is important for several reasons. Social scientists have frequently argued that sport is a reflection of society as a whole. Thus sport is often said to be a *microcosm* of the larger society. If so, then the aggressive behavior seen so frequently in sports events merits attention. Does the violence that is part of professional ice hockey and football really mirror the values of Western culture? Or is aggressive behavior limited to a few sports? In analyzing aggressive behavior in sport settings, two apparently contradictory questions arise. Does aggressive behavior in sport serve to reduce future aggression by providing a positive means for expression of aggression? Or does sport participation promote and encourage aggression by teaching and actually welcoming aggressive behavior? Any attempt to resolve this contradiction must begin with a better understanding of the nature of aggression.

THE NATURE OF AGGRESSION

During the last 10 to 15 years there has been much controversy in the sports psychology literature concerning an acceptable definition of aggression. Silva (1980a) has done much to clarify that situation by using the terms **hostile aggression** and **instrumental aggression** to differentiate between two types of aggressive behavior.

Hostile Aggression

Aggressive behavior, whether it is labeled hostile or instrumental, refers to an observable act that is intended to inflict physical or psychological harm on another person or oneself. In hostile aggression the primary reinforcement is the satisfaction of seeing the pain or injury that is inflicted. Thus the purpose of such aggression is the achievement of the *end product,* namely, physical or psychological injury. A playground basketball player who intentionally pushes an opponent into the basket upright just to see the other player get hurt is using hostile aggression.

Instrumental Aggression

Instrumental aggression can be differentiated from hostile aggression on the basis of the reason why the performer inflicts or attempts to inflict injury. Although in instrumental aggression the player also intends to cause pain or injury, the act is done to receive an external positive reinforcer. The receipt of a positive reinforcer should then increase the probability that the athlete would repeat the aggressive behavior. In the basketball example above, if the player pushed the opponent into the upright to receive a positive reinforcer such as the coach's praise, the roar of the crowd, or an athletic scholarship, then that act would be classified as instrumental aggression. Thus in the case of instrumental aggression the aggressive response serves as a *means to an end* rather than the end itself. However, in both cases, because injury was the intent neither is acceptable in sport! Why then do we so often hear both coaches and players yelling ''Be aggressive?'' Is that what they really mean? Do they mean that players should go out onto the field, the court, or the ice and intentionally inflict injury? Sadly, in some cases they probably do. But it is hoped that in the vast majority of instances what they actually mean is that players should be *assertive* rather than aggressive in their behavior.

Assertive versus Aggressive Behavior

Assertive behavior involves the use of high degrees of physical or verbal force or the demonstration of unusual physical energy and effort (Silva, 1980a). Assertive behaviors differ from aggressive responses in two ways. First, the intent of the assertive behavior is to achieve a goal and *not* to inflict injury. Second, assertive behavior falls within the rules of the game.

Suppose an act causes injury to a player but does not violate any written game regulations or rules. How is it determined whether that act is assertive or aggressive behavior? That becomes the duty of the officials. It is probably also the reason why many athletes become proficient at looking so innocent after a forceful or injurious play.

Thus the only way that a response can be labeled ''aggression'' is through observation of the behavior and subjective evaluation of the player's intention. When making those judgments, coaches and officials generally use clues from the previous actions of the athlete in question. They may take into account such factors as recent unfriendly interactions between the players, negative verbal interchanges, and prior fouls. The player behaviors that are most easily classified as being aggressive rather than assertive are those that result in injury and that clearly violate the rules of the game. Slashing in ice hockey, sticks in field hockey, and clipping in football are illegal because they often result in injury. As a consequence, these behaviors are penalized as soon as they are observed by the officials.

THEORETICAL EXPLANATIONS OF AGGRESSION

Is it necessary that athletes aggress in the first place? If the rules of sports are designed to punish such behaviors, and if such acts can hinder a team's progress, why does aggressive behavior occur with such frequency? One explanation is that humans are born with an innate drive, or instinct, that compels them to agress. However, other theories take issue with that explanation.

Instinct Theory

Instinct theory had its beginnings in the writings of Sigmund Freud. Briefly, he proposed that humans are born with a conflict between a life instinct and a death instinct. The life instinct was said to be manifested in the sexual drive, whereas the death instinct was thought to be represented by a need to aggress. The death instinct was said to work toward the person's own destruction; therefore to avoid this drive to harm oneself it could be satisfied by aggressing against others. This proposed externalized death instinct was then used to explain why humans appeared to be inevitably involved in violent conflicts such as wars. It was an instinctual human drive! From this perspective, because aggression is based on an innate, or biological, drive it must be fulfilled. Thus aggressive behavior was viewed as being inevitable. However, on the brighter side, it was proposed that its enactment could be regulated or controlled through activities such as games or sports.

More recently than Freud, other theorists have also argued that instinct theory provides the most acceptable explanation for human aggressive behavior. Ethnologists* such as Lorenz (1966) and Ardrey (1966) argue that man is an animal like any other animal and has the same biological instincts, including the need to aggress. This position says that over time energy is built up and must be discharged through activities such as aggression for fulfillment to be achieved. Once the energy is dissipated, there is less liklihood of extreme violence (Berkowitz, 1970).

How does this interpretation relate to sport participation? Ethnologists argue that we should provide people with frequent opportunities for participation in vigorous physical activities such as sport so that they can discharge their aggressive behaviors in controlled situations. Such sport participation should then lead to a reduction in the need to aggress. The latter argument is founded on the **catharsis hypothesis.**

Catharsis Hypothesis

Catharsis comes from the Greek word *kathairein,* which means "to cleanse." As used here, *catharsis* refers to the release of aggressive tendencies. The catharsis hypothesis predicts that bottled-up emotions can be discharged or purged by expressing them through aggression (Berkowitz, 1970). Early proponents of physical education classes in the public schools based their arguments on thinking similar to the catharsis hypothesis. They felt that physical activities would allow students to release their pent-up emotions and therefore make them more docile in the classroom. Many athletes and weekend sports enthusiasts also argue that participation in vigorous physical activity allows them to "blow off steam" and that they feel much more relaxed after such activities.

Indeed, most of the research that has addressed the question of aggression in sport has also tried to test the validity of the catharsis hypothesis. Generally, this research approach has looked at how either direct participation or observation of physical activity affects subsequent level of aggression. (Catharsis as it relates to fan behavior is discussed later in the chapter.) Based on an analysis of the experimental literature, most scholars have concluded that participation in vigorous physical activity does *not* produce a cathartic effect. Instead it appears that such activities result in higher degrees of aggression. Although little evidence has been gathered in field settings, one study by Zillmann, Katcher, and Milarsky (1972) found that after subjects finished a bout of exercise they were more willing than a control group to express aggression through the administration of an electric shock to another person. Taken as a whole, the available evidence does not support the idea that vigorous physical activity will result in a decreased desire to exhibit aggressive behaviors. If this is so, then some doubt must be cast on the validity of the

---

*Ethnologists are scholars who study animal behavior.

instinctual interpretation (catharsis hypothesis) of human aggression. Currently, there are two primary counter-explanations: the frustration-aggression-displacement hypothesis and social learning theory.

Frustration-Aggression-Displacement Hypothesis

Probably the most famous theory of aggression is the learning-based explanation originally formulated by Dollard and Miller and others (Dollard, Miller, Doob, Mourer, & Sears, 1939) and called the **frustration-aggression-displacement (F-A-D) hypothesis.** The major premise of their position was that aggression always occurs as a consequence of *frustration,* which was defined as the blocking of instrumental goal attainment by someone or something. Once the goal is blocked, frustration occurs; there is an increase in arousal, and an aggressive response is predicted to follow. If the frustrated person cannot, for any number of reasons, act out the aggressive response on the person who blocked the goal attainment, then the aggressive response is predicted to be *displaced* onto another person. As shown in Figure 10-1, the gradient of stimulus generalization is used to determine onto whom the aggressive response will be displaced.

Suppose, for example, that a young athlete tries out for her school's volleyball team. She is highly motivated to make the team (her instrumental goal). She has purchased her own volleyball and has been practicing for months. She tries out, and the coach cuts her on the first day of practice. The coach has blocked her attainment of her goal. The athlete is frustrated and feels motivated to aggress against the coach. Will she do it? Probably not because the coach is 6'2" tall and an authority figure.

However, the F-A-D hypothesis predicts that under conditions of high frustration, aggression will occur. On the horizontal axis of Figure 10-1 it is predicted that she will seek out a new stimulus (in this case another person) onto whom to displace the aggressive

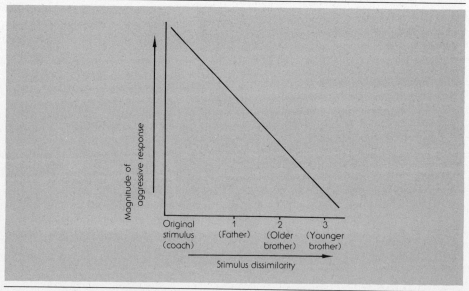

FIGURE 10-1   Aggression and the gradient of stimulus generalization.

response. On the basis of physical similarity, she perceives her father to be similar to her coach. He is an adult male of about the same height and is definitely an authority figure. Will she aggress against him? Probably not, but by looking at the vertical axis in Figure 10-1 we can see that if she had, the magnitude of her response would still have been quite strong. Who's next? Her older brother? He is also 6'2" and very strong; again, not a suitable choice. But there is her little brother; if she can catch him, he'll be the target. However, by the time she has displaced her aggression onto the stimulus (her younger brother) who is three times removed from the original stimulus (the coach), the magnitude of her aggressive response would be predicted to be rather low. The younger brother might just get a pinch or poke as opposed to a punch.

What is the current status of the F-A-D hypothesis? One major problem lies with the idea that frustration is the single cause of aggressive behavior. Although frustration can certainly instigate an aggressive response, it seems reasonable to argue that aggression can have other causes. A second problem rests with the notion of the physical similarity between possible targets for displacement. Physical similarity is really in the "eye of the beholder"; it cannot be measured in a scientific sense. A third problem with this explanation is its inclusion of the catharsis hypothesis within its framework. Given the lack of evidence supporting that hypothesis, it calls into question the tenets of the F-A-D hypothesis also. Recall also that the catharsis hypothesis was based on the idea of an instinctual foundation of aggressive behavior. Although most current theorists have rejected the instinctual explanation of human behavior, others have taken a more moderate approach (Berkowitz, 1965). We will return to that issue after briefly discussing the social learning interpretation of aggression.

Social Learning Theory

Social learning theory argues that it is not necessarily frustration that triggers an aggressive response, that instead aggressive behavior is learned behavior. The primary advocate of social learning theory is Bandura (1973, 1977). Bandura proposes that behaviors are acquired through the two primary mechanisms of *reinforcement* and *modeling*. If a person is positively reinforced for being aggressive, then that person is likely to exhibit those same behaviors again in the future. For example, a failure by either parents or coaches to punish aggressive behaviors should result in increased aggression by the child.

The most significant models in early childhood are parents. There is a significant body of literature to support the assertion that aggressive parents generally have aggressive children (Martens, 1974). However, those same children may not exhibit that aggressiveness in the company of their parents. Fearing punishment and further parental aggression, they wait for a more suitable "victim" among their peers. If peer-inflicted aggression is not curbed or punished, it should lead to incidences of aggression against opponents on the playing fields and courts.

In short, social learning theory predicts that aggression will tend to generate more aggression. With more observational learning and additional reinforcement a person can acquire a stable disposition to aggress against others. This should result in a predisposition to behave aggressively in sport settings. It would then appear that the "enforcer" in ice hockey wasn't born that way; he learned those aggressive behaviors.

A classic investigation of how modeling and reinforcement can be used to instigate aggressive behavior in children was that of Bandura, Ross, and Ross (1961). The children were divided into two groups: an experimental group who viewed an adult model aggressively strike a bobo doll and a control group who observed a passive adult model. A bobo doll is a large plastic doll weighted on the bottom so that it will not fall over when punched. When used in investigations such as this one, positive reinforcement for punching behavior can be received either by having the eyes light up or from dispensing marbles from the doll's stomach. They found that when the children observed a model receiving reinforcement for punching the doll aggressively, the children tended to follow suit by acting aggressively themselves.

Based on their results, Bandura & others rejected the catharsis hypothesis and argued instead that aggression is a learned behavior. They proposed that aggression is a *circular* phenomenon in that an initial aggressive act triggers future aggressive responses.

Smith (1978) provides some interesting and perhaps shocking insights into how both reinforcement from coaches of youth players and modeling of professional players generates violent aggression in North American ice hockey. He says that the primary source of amateur hockey violence lies in the ranks of the professional game. Children watch such violence either on television or at the rink and see that it often provides a vehicle for player success and recognition. These children want to advance through the system and eventually become professional players, and such advancement is highly competitive; therefore they reason that one way to be selected and to move up is to be tough, to be a "hit man," or a designated fighter. This reasoning is further supported through the attitudes and behaviors of youth coaches. As Smith writes:

> We found ten-year-old Atoms who could handle heavy bumping, picked for teams over other more skilled, but less tough (and usually smaller) aspirants. Fourteen-year-olds with marginal playing ability are upwardly mobile in the Metropolitan Toronto Hockey League's elite AA division primarily because they can fight. One such was the "Animal," as he was known to other players around the circuit. When opposing coaches prepared for games against the "Animal's" team, they always made special plans to "handle" him. The Flyers' (a fictitious name) plan on one occasion was explained by their coach in a pregame talk, which we tape recorded: "Look, if this character starts anything, take him out early. We can't have him charging around hammering people. Somebody's going to have to straighten him out. Just remember, get the gloves off and do it in a fair fight. If you shake him up early he can't keep it up. Besides, it's best to take the penalties early in the game before we get too tired to kill them effectively." The adolescent bully is hardly a recent social phenomenon, but his sponsorship by adults on the scale evident in minor hockey may be somewhat unique. (p. 143)

Smith's analysis and example provide pertinent insights into how coaches and the media can instill aggressive tendencies into the behavioral system of young (or older) athletes. His position is also consistent with the social learning interpretation of aggression. However, others have taken issue with the idea that a learning-based explanation of aggression is the only acceptable one.

Berkowitz's Reformulation

Berkowitz (1965) has taken the position that aspects of both the F-A-D hypothesis and social learning theory can be combined to best explain human aggression. He proposes that both innate determination and learning experiences can coexist in humans. It is important to note that Berkowitz is not saying that an aggressive tendency is biologically determined, or instinctual, in origin. When he uses the term *innate,* he means that humans may have a predisposition to respond to frustration with aggression; however, that predisposition can be modified through the learning process. His major point is that even though frustration may not always result in aggression, the presence of frustration increases a person's *readiness* to aggress.

Berkowitz (1981) has identified some important variables that can influence whether or not aggression will occur as a result of frustration:

1. If through reinforcement and modeling a person has learned to exhibit a nonaggressive response to a certain situation, then there should be little liklihood that an aggressive response will occur. This might be exemplified in a sport situation wherein a coach exhibits nonaggressive behavior and also fails to positively reinforce or punishes athletes who demonstrate aggressive responses. On the other hand, an aggressive coach is also a potent source of modeling information. Just as aggressive parents tend to have aggressive children, aggressive coaches are more likely to have aggressive players.
2. If stimuli are present that have been previously associated with an aggressive response, then the probability is high that aggression will recur. If a person has previously associated aggressive behavior with the presence of stimuli such as guns or being cursed at, then an aggressive response is more likely under either one of those two conditions at some future time.
3. If the person perceives that the frustration is legitimate and therefore does not blame the instigator, then the probability is low that aggression will recur. Certainly on a cold, snowy day with the field wet and slippery it would be an illegimate response for the offensive coach to blame the tailback if he fell and missed gaining some important yardage.

To summarize, current thinking and experimentation on aggression leads to the conclusion that although aggressive behavior may have some roots in innate determinants, its expression can be modified through learning. The two most powerful learning factors are reinforcement and observational learning (see Chapter 7 for a more detailed discussion of these variables).

Some mention of the possibility of a physiological basis underlying aggressive tendencies also appears warranted. The fundamental idea of physiological theory is that there are inborn neural systems in the brain that, when activated by certain stimuli, cause aggressive responses. Some experiments have induced human aggression by stimulating parts of the brain electrically. For a more lengthy discussion, refer to Moyer (1976).

PLAYER-RELATED VARIABLES

Competition

One probable source of aggression in sport competitive situations is the inevitable presence of frustration. Frustration was defined as the blocking of an instrumental goal; in competitive sport the whole idea is to block the goal achievement of the opponents while at the same time moving yourself or the team toward the achievement of those same goals. Therefore, from what we know about the frustration-aggression connection, it seems highly reasonable that competition may generate aggressive behaviors.

A classic study of the relationship between competition and aggression was that discussed by Sherif and Sherif (1953). It was a three-stage investigation that took place in a summer camp for boys. In the first stage the campers were allowed to participate fully in all the camp's activities. The setting was highly informal. In the second stage the boys were separated into two distinct groups within which they participated in the camp activities. In the third stage the two groups met in competition and were also presented with multiple frustrations.

The results indicated that only minimal amounts of aggressive responses occurred during the first and second stages. In the third stage, high degrees of aggression were evident, to the point that the groups had to be broken up and other competitive events scheduled against members of another camp. Another finding of interest was that more aggression was shown both after frustration and after failure.

These results were consistent with our earlier discussion regarding the triggering effect of frustration. In terms of the failure data, the above findings are similar to those of Ryan (1970), who also found that subjects who were successful in a competitive setting showed less tendency to aggress as compared with their less-successful counterparts.

Two additional factors affecting the relationship between competition and aggression were identified by Martens (1974). He proposed that when opponents are nearly equally matched, a loss will produce greater degrees of frustration because victory could have gone to either player. Secondly, when the rewards associated with winning are high, losing will cause greater frustration than when they are not so meaningful. We can assume then that high degrees of frustration and thus a greater probability of aggression will occur in competitive situations characterized by a close contest with the possibility of potent rewards. Although these predictions have not yet been tested adequately, on an intuitive basis they seem reasonable.

Excitement and Arousal

An important issue relative to whether or not excitement or arousal will instigate an aggressive response concerns the type of aggression that is experienced. In instrumental aggression there should be little or no effect in terms of increased physiological activation because there is no negative cognitive set such as anger; the aggressive response is executed to achieve a goal. On the other hand, in hostile aggression there should always be increased arousal. Does this mean that increased arousal will always cause increased aggressive behavior?

Based on our earlier discussion of the role that aggressive stimuli can play in instigating a violent response, it seems reasonable to argue in the following way. If a player is in a state of high excitation or arousal and there are aggression-related stimuli in the sport environment, then it is highly likely that an aggressive response will follow. If no such stimuli are present, then high degrees of excitement should not necessarily generate an aggressive response.

In support of this argument, Geen and O'Neal (1969) found that persons who were first aroused and then watched a boxing film exhibited more aggressive behavior as compared with persons who only saw the film. Therefore it appears that the aggressive stimuli accompanied by increased arousal triggered greater tendencies to aggress. This finding was also supported by an investigation by Berkowitz and LePage (1967), who used the presence of a pistol or a rifle to generate increased aggressive behavior in already aroused subjects. Zillmann & others (1972) also supported this effect by showing that aroused subjects who were exposed to aggressive environmental stimuli demonstrated significant aggressive responses. Taken together the evidence shows fairly strong support for the idea that persons in states of high arousal or excitement tend to exhibit aggressive behavior if aggressive environmental stimuli are present. For example, if a player in a state of high excitement sees other players or the coach acting aggressively, it is highly likely that the performer will follow suit. Under those same conditions, abusive or disruptive fan behavior could also trigger aggressive behavior by the player.

Cognitive and Affective Factors

Suppose an athlete experiences frustration, and arousal becomes high; is it definite that the athlete will aggress? Certain thoughts might run through the performer's mind to inhibit the aggressive response. One cognitive activity might be to estimate the probability of retaliation by the target of the aggressive act. If this probability is high, then other factors, such as relative physical size of the opponent, come into play. The athlete may also consider the possible negative effects if he or she decides to aggress. Would it be worth being suspended, heavily penalized, or even dropped from the team? The intent of the opponent must also be evaluated.

Intent of the Opponent

Why did the opponent aggress? Did he or she intentionally aim to inflict injury? If the answer is yes, then the player's decision is more than likely retaliation through counteraggression. This effect was shown in an investigation by Harrell (1980). In studying high school basketball players, a major finding was that aggression could best be predicted by the degree of previous aggression exhibited against the player. There seemed to be a desire to "balance out" the amount of aggression demonstrated by two teams. Thus again it appears that there may be an aggression cycle wherein initial aggression causes further aggression. You can witness this phenomenon during the National Basketball Association playoffs, in which so often one player aggresses against an opponent, the opponent aggresses back, and pretty soon there are groups of players fighting on the court. This aggression cycle is being seen more frequently in supposedly noncontact sports such as professional baseball. From what you know about the observational learning process, what should be seen more frequently in youth basketball and baseball?

Guilt

After committing a blantantly aggressive or violent act, athletes often experience some degree of guilt. However, because of the acceptance of violence in sport, many athletes feel that such behaviors are legitimate, in which case they should not feel any guilt or remorse (Feigley, 1983). They feel that by acting aggressively they will be viewed more positively by their coach, teammates, and fans.

To test this idea of the legitimacy of hostile aggression in sport, Silva (1979) studied 122 male volunteers in either a sport (basketball) situation or a nonsport (peg-board) situation. Trained confederates were used throughout the study to instigate the hostile or assertive behaviors. The results indicated that after hostile aggression in the nonsport setting, high levels of guilt were experienced; however, hostile aggression in the basketball setting did not create high levels of guilt.

What do these findings mean? More than likely athletes learn that aggressive behavior is considered a legitimate part of sport and that it is OK to behave that way. They may come to perceive that hostile aggression leads to success and thus to positive reinforcement. Given this perception, why would they feel any guilt? Silva (1979) has suggested that the most powerful way that such perceptions can be changed and aggressive behavior reduced is through a modification of the reinforcement structure of sport teams. He writes:

> A 5-min. penalty, an official's warning, or a personal foul do little to curb the occurrence of hostile and violent acts. Such negative reinforcers hold little real-life consequences for the player. By making direct acts of physical violence result in suspension and personal fines for the initiator, and the possibility of extended suspension for the continual exhibition of violence by a player, the meaningfulness of the personal costs incurred will have a deterring effect upon violent behavior. This approach is similar to what has been successfully employed in American collegiate hockey. (pp. 106-107)

Physical Fitness

Although few scholars have explored the relationship between physical fitness and tendency to aggress, some insight into this issue can be gained from the work of Zillmann. Zillmann's (1979) position is that highly trained or physically fit persons react with low degrees of physiological activation when faced with either physical exertion or emotion-inducing stimuli in the environment. If his position is correct, then highly fit athletes should be less likely to exhibit high degrees of arousal when faced with aggressive cues in the environment. Without the increased arousal to "ready" the organism for an aggressive response, hostile behavior is less likely.

In support of this assertion, Zillmann, Johnson, and Day (1974) have shown that the recovery time of the fit person is faster than that of the unfit person. However, we cannot accept the idea that fitness alone will alter a person's tendency to behave aggressively. Other mediating factors, such as the behaviors learned in a particular sport position (a lineman in football or a "hit man" in ice hockey), could have a definite effect on an athlete's propensity for aggression. In addition, the expectations about desired behavior which the athlete perceives on the part of the coach, other teammates, and the fans may also influence whether or not aggressive responses will be made.

Performance Level

Should an athlete's level of performance improve or worsen after an aggressive response? In analyzing this issue, Silva (1980b) has proposed that athletic performance should decline. He based his argument on two potential effects. First, by shifting attention to the goal of aggressing against an opponent and away from the task itself, performance decrements should occur. Second, the heightened arousal that accompanies an aggressive response might push a person's level of arousal beyond the optimal level. Thus, according to the inverted-U hypothesis, the performer would be operating on the right side of the inverted-U.

Although Silva's position seems intuitively appealing, it must be mediated by the characteristics of the particular athlete. For instance, in some cases the increase in arousal may move the player from a state of lethargy or insufficient arousal to a more optimal level. Overall, however, from what we know about attentional shifts and optimal level of arousal, usually aggression should have a negative effect on sport performance.

GAME-RELATED VARIABLES

The classic investigation of possible relationships between game occurrences and aggression (as defined by number of fouls) was done by Volkamer (1971), who collected his data on more than 1800 soccer matches. We will use his findings to highlight instances that seem to provoke athlete aggression. Listed below are some of the more pertinent results.

Objective Outcome

Losers committed more fouls than winners. This would seem reasonable, considering the frustration that usually accompanies a loss.

Home versus Away

Visitors tended to commit more fouls than the home team. This could be a result of several factors, including the "goading" that the home team often displays toward the visiting team. Some caution needs to be exercised concerning this finding, however, because when studying ice hockey teams, Wankel (1972) did not reveal the same result. Furthermore, in studying basketball performance before an abusive audience, Thirer and Rampey (1979) found that the home team committed more fouls. Therefore we do not currently know if the difference is between soccer versus ice hockey and basketball or if there really is a difference between home and away aggression.

Point Spread

When the score is close or tied, there tends to be less aggression. Why? When the score is extremely close, one foul can determine the outcome of the game. Therefore under such conditions both players and coaches tend to be more cautious and thus less aggressive. Also, when there is a large discrepancy between the scores of two teams, fewer fouls occur as compared with a match in which moderate amounts of points separate the opponents.

Total Number of Points Scored

When more points or goals are scored, fewer acts of aggression occur. Conversely, when fewer points or goals are scored, more aggression takes place. From Volkamer's point of view, this may be because goal scoring tends to reduce arousal, whereas a failure to score may generate increases in player activation.

Team Standing

It appears that teams in the lower standings aggress more than higher ranked teams. However, when the lower ranked teams played the upper ranked teams, they both committed more fouls as compared with teams in the middle ranks. This may be because the middle ranked teams have less to lose; the championship is not at stake and they will not come in at the bottom of the standings.

Although Volkamer's findings do provide some basis for predicting aggressive behavior in sport, some caution should also be exercised in totally accepting the findings. First, soccer was the only sport analyzed. Second, the dependent variable used to represent aggression was the number of fouls. Recall that for a behavior to be correctly classified as aggression the intent of the perpetrator must be the infliction of injury. Surely, not all fouls are committed for the purpose of inflicting injury to another player. In many instances the foul could be the result of assertive rather than aggressive behavior. Silva (1980a) offers a more thorough discussion of the issues and problems surrounding the accurate measurement of aggression in sport settings.

COLLECTIVE AGGRESSION

Reports of fan violence at sporting events are increasing. For example, in the Soviet Union the newspaper *Komsomolskaya Pravda* chastized sport fans for their disruptive behavior: "Drunken louts, foul-mouthed boors, oleaginous scalpers and female groupies are penetrating Moscow spectator sports in disturbing numbers" (Arms, Russell, & Sandilands, 1980). In another example from the United States, a basketball game between high school students in New Jersey caused a riot among fans one week, followed by an altercation between two opposing groups of cheerleaders the next week (Turner, 1970). When groups of persons simultaneously exhibit violent or hostile behavior, it is called **collective aggression.** These two brief examples alone demonstrate why an understanding of collective aggression in sport settings is so important.

Observation of Aggressive Sport Behavior

The majority of collective aggression studies have tested the cathartic versus the enhancement interpretations. The cathartic position says that fan arousal and aggression should decrease as a function of observing aggression in sport settings. The enhancement position proposes that such observation of aggressive displays should increase fan arousal and aggression.

In one of the earliest studies, Goldstein and Arms (1971) used the annual Army-Navy football game to test these opposing interpretations. Men departing the stadium after the game scored higher on a paper and pencil test of hostility as compared with a sample of men who were just arriving at the game. It was also of interest to note that the postcompetitive hostility ratings were equally high for the fans of the winning team and the losing team. They also included a control group that consisted of men coming to and leaving a highly competitive gymnastics meet. Those same comparisons revealed no difference in hostility scores.

In a later investigation, Arms, Russell, and Sandilands (1980) studied ice hockey rather than football, and swimming competition was substituted for gymnastics. They also included professional wrestling as an example of *stylized* aggression. Stylized aggression can be seen in sports such as professional wrestling and roller derby wherein aggressive acts are perceived to be fictional or theatrical rather than real. Therefore in this investigation professional wrestling was used to represent stylized aggression whereas ice hockey was classified as realistic aggression.

Their results were consistent with the Goldstein and Arms (1971) data wherein it was shown that fans who watched either professional wrestling (stylized aggression) or ice hockey (realistic aggression) demonstrated increased levels of aggression or hostility. Fans who attended the competitive swimming meet showed no such elevations in aggression or hostility.

Before going any further it is important to discuss a study completed by Russell (1981). Two ice hockey games were used in the investigation. One was very violent and the other was a relatively nonviolent match. At various times during each of the games, randomly selected subjects were measured for their level of arousal and aggression. The data analysis left little doubt that the degree of violence observed in the game was directly associated with degree of fan arousal and aggression.

These three studies tell us some interesting things about fan observation of sport aggression. First, it appears that observation of violent competitive sport increases fan arousal and thus could "ready" the fan for subsequent aggressive behavior. This conclusion argues strongly against the cathartic explanation and in favor of the enhancement explanation. Also, it appears that such fan observation of player violence may cause a **disinhibition** of aggressive tendencies (Bandura, 1973). Fans observe players acting in violent ways with no apparent reprisals. That observation, accompanied by the spectators' feelings of **anonymity** (Berkowitz, 1978) can lead to an increased tendency to behave in hostile or violent ways.

Let's review this process once more. The fan observes aggressive behavior by players. Such observations increase excitement and arousal, which "readies" the spectator for aggression. The fan also observes that the players do not receive severe punishment for violent actions. The fan feels a sense of anonymity, which lowers any feelings that punishment will be the result of aggressing. All these factors lead toward a disinhibition of the hostility reaction. Now switch your thoughts to the team members who observe fan violence or abusive fan behavior. How should this observation affect performance? As we mentioned earlier, if the players are in a state of high arousal or excitement, violent or abusive fan behavior can be a triggering stimulus for player aggression. Aggression should hinder team performance. For both players and fans, it appears to be a circular phenomenon; aggression leads to more aggression.

The evidence on collective violence also appears to show that it may be both the nature of the competitive activity in terms of its potential for the exhibition of violence and the actual amount of violence that occurs during a particular match that must be taken into account. For example, although the realistic aggression seen in ice hockey did raise spectator arousal and hostility, when the actual amount of game violence varied, so did fan reactions. It should then follow that if player aggression or violence could be curbed, so would fan violence. This is an issue of critical importance.

Causes of Fan Misbehavior

Although violent fan reaction to player aggression is a serious problem it has received scant research attention. To gain further insights into the process and causes of fan misbehavior, Cavanaugh and Silva (1980) assessed spectator perceptions regarding the causes underlying those behaviors.

They assessed a total of 1747 spectators attending one of three hockey games. The questionnaires were distributed before the game to avoid any reactivity to the game itself. Below are some of their more important rankings within the categories of characteristics of the game, the spectator, or the environment.

Game Characteristics

Five of the eight top-ranked factors were related to characteristics of the game. We present them below, with their actual rank in the parentheses following each factor. A rank of 1 was the highest or most important:

Referees (2)
Rivalry (3)
Nature of the game (5)
Time remaining/losing (7)
Score (8)

Notice that each of the above characteristics relates directly to the game. Furthermore, each provides a stimulus setting that should be capable of either frustrating or arousing the fans.

Spectator Characteristics

Generally, the respondents ranked both being young (1) and being under the influence of alcohol (4) as important factors capable of precipitating fan misbehavior. However, as Cavanaugh and Silva point out, it is interesting to note that college-age subjects did not rank age as being that important. They gave it a rank of 11.

Environmental Characteristics

It only seems reasonable that the respondents would rank crowd density (6) as being a facilitator of fan misbehavior. The highly uncomfortable feeling of being closed in at a sporting event is surely likely to cause increased arousal and frustration. As the authors point out, "Sporting facilities that jam spectators into a small area or provide little space around spectators were perceived as environments conducive to fan misbehavior" (p. 197).

The results of this study can provide new directions and insights into the causes of collective violence as it occurs in sport settings. Because the issue of cartharsis appears to be pretty well resolved, it seems appropriate to move in new directions. It is particularly important that we look for ways to curb the violence that has become so integral to both player and fan behavior. The suggestions below are designed to achieve that goal.

IMPLICATIONS FOR SPORT

- Because increased excitement or arousal tends to make an athlete more ready to aggress, instruct performers to use intervention strategies to reduce activation level (see Chapter 5).
- Make a concerted effort to only hire officials who are noted for penalizing aggressive behavior, officials who understand the difference between aggressive responses enacted with the specific purpose of inflicting injury and assertive responses that involve increased energy or force to obtain a legitimate goal.

- Because we know that professional sports models are a potent source for the learning of aggressive behaviors, highlight and emphasize the contributions of nonaggressive professional sport models.
- When athletes do commit aggressive or violent behaviors they must be punished. The punishment should fit the crime; benching an athlete who has purposely attempted to inflict injury on an opponent is not severe enough. That athlete should be suspended for an appropriate length of time.
- In team meetings, discuss why the media, particularly television, "hypes" acts of professional athletic violence. It boosts ratings!
- Because losing tends to be frustrating, do not overly stress outcome in post-game discussions. Instead, focus on the positive events that took place during the competition. Try to reduce player arousal by establishing a calm and supportive atmosphere. Act the same after a win as after a loss.
- Always stress self-control and sportsmanship rather than hostility and violence. This applies to opponents as well as individual behavior. As Corran (1980) has warned, do not try to motivate athletes by referring to dirty tactics and unfair practices of opponents. Such attempts will most likely lead to more aggression.
- Because aggressive behavior is learned through both reinforcement and modeling, it can be controlled or modified through these same processes. Particularly with young athletes, these strategies should be used to focus on skill improvement and self-control rather than potentially harmful and violent thoughts and behaviors.
- Because aggressive stimuli present in the sport environment can instigate a hostile response when a player is in a state of high arousal, carefully observe each player to see what usually triggers that person's aggressive response. Remember, whether or not a particular stimulus is perceived to be aggressive varies with each person. For one athlete an insulting remark may do it, whereas for another it would take a physical blow that was perceived to be done with the intent to inflict harm. It may be necessary to remove the player from the game when that triggering stimulus occurs and calm the athlete by discussing what is legal and using relaxation strategies.
- Positively reinforce athletes when they have exercised self-control by not aggressing when provoked. Many intervention strategies, such as imagery and attentional control (see Chapter 5), can be used to help the athlete in gaining greater self-control.
- Because hostile or violent fan behavior can trigger aggressive responses by athletes, make sure that there is good crowd control. Do not allow excessive misbehavior on the part of spectators—it's contagious!
- Condition athletes so that they achieve high levels of physical fitness. Being fit may allow athletes to recover more quickly from high levels of arousal or excitement and thus it may help them to more easily control aggressive tendencies. This may be even more important in team sports involving high degrees of player contact, such as football, ice hockey, and water polo.
- What about the player who feels guilty or uncomfortable about exhibiting *assertive* behavior even when the situation calls for it? Counsel the player and try to determine the reason for his or her discomfort. Use practice sessions to provide situations in which such behaviors can be tried out. Use coping imagery and modeling techniques to help the athlete and positively reinforce appropriate attempts at such behavior.

- Remember, the coach is often a strong model. Do not let your expectations for player behavior appear to be supportive of aggressive behavior.
- Do not exhibit aggressive or hostile behaviors yourself. To a large degree your players are a reflection of you! The coach's behavior can be either a positive or negative role model for fans; aggressive responses by the coach can lead to similar responses by fans.
- Because alcohol consumption is perceived as a major cause of fan misbehavior, prohibit its sale. Instruct cheerleaders, ticket takers, and others to watch for alcohol in the stands and to report it to the security officers. Alcohol consumption by minors should be considered intolerable and punishable.

CASE STUDY 1

The Overly Aggressive Basketball Player

One type of problem athlete with whom many coaches must deal is the athlete who cannot control aggression when highly aroused. Although the performer may have good or even exceptional physical skills, he or she has not learned enough self-control to behave well in spite of high arousal.

When the game is going well and the score is in the home team's favor, everything is fine and the athlete may even be a team leader in scoring. But wait until the pressure starts! When arousal gets too high, this athlete tends to act aggressively by pushing and shoving under the boards and fighting violently for possession of the ball. If the performer has not already fouled out, the coach can make a quick substitution. That may be all right for the game at hand, but it does not solve the problem. Below are some ideas that might assist a coach in helping this performer learn more self-control and reduce aggressive tendencies.

Origin of the Problem

Both the coach and the athlete need to understand why the problem exists. Frequently, such lack of self-control and the resultant aggressive response are the result of some aspect of early child-rearing patterns. Several methods can be used to gain an insight into the origin of the problem. In a private and nonthreatening location, discuss the problem with the athlete. Discretely probe for reasons why the athlete behaves in this fashion. Ask the athlete to write an autobiography, *which will be kept confidential!* The autobiography should focus on situations and factors that have triggered aggressive behaviors in the past. Look for a pattern that will provide insights into the causes underlying the need to aggress. If parents attend practices or games, observe their behaviors and reactions to the athlete's performance. Do they tend to become boisterous and demanding? Remember, aggressive parents often have aggressive children. Ask for insights into why the performer feels that he or she must aggress under stressful conditions. Finally, see if you can get the athlete to express exactly what it is that "ticks off" the aggressive response. What is the instigating stimulus or stimuli? These explorations should help both the coach and the athlete gain a clearer perspective of the causes underlying the need to aggress in sport situations. Once that is accomplished, it is time for the athlete to try to change the aggressive tendency and gain more self-control.

The Self-Control Contract

The self-control contract is a document that should be mutually designed by the coach and the athlete. It should list various potentially aggressive behaviors and precisely define what the punishment will be for each offense. Make the punishments potent enough so that they will inhibit the athlete's tendency to aggress. These should be punishments that are above and beyond any penalties administered by the official. They should be kept private between the coach and the athlete. The athlete needs to know that if the aggressive behavior is not curbed, then the ultimate punishment will be exclusion from the team. The athlete needs to know that aggressive or hostile behavior simply will not be tolerated and that the coach is willing to make the decision to drop the athlete from the team. Also, stress that the athlete is ultimately in charge of his or her own behavior.

Interventions for Self-Control

As mentioned previously, the athlete must first master relaxation skills. One method is the muscle relaxation technique described in Chapter 5, which can be practiced until proficiency is gained. Once this is accomplished, it seems wise to focus attention on what self-statement patterns are operating within the aggressive player. Remember, an internal focus can disrupt sport performance if the person is either monitoring the effects of increased physiological activation or covertly making negative self-statements. Novaco's (1979) work on the cognitive regulation of anger and stress can provide helpful insights for assisting athletes in managing aggressive behavior. He proposes a four-step self-statement program.

Preparation for the provocation. This occurs before competition. The performer trys to reduce the psychological "set" to aggress in two ways. First, the athlete tries to emphasize the *impersonal* rather than personal nature of the competition. *Positive self-statements* are then substituted for negative thoughts. Instead of saying "If anyone on that team starts something, I'm going to finish it," the athlete might say "I know that I play better when I keep my cool."

The impact. This stage occurs at the time of the competition. The performer again repeats positive self-statements such as "I'm calm and I know that I can do OK, let the other team make the mistakes" or "I know that I can do well if I don't lose control."

Handling arousal. The athlete should anticipate increased activation and try to handle it both cognitively and by translating it into a positive force or skill component. Rather than saying "Oh my God, my heart is racing, I know I'm going to miss this basket," the athlete should interpret the increased arousal as being "psyched-up" and ready to perform. Remember, such increases in arousal can ready the athlete either for aggression or for thinking game-related and positive thoughts.

The period of reflection. To reduce the potential for retaliation after an aggressive response has occurred, positive self-statements can also be used. The athlete should practice positive self-statements such as "OK, it's over and forget about it" or "You did all right, you didn't lose your temper this time." The athlete should focus on reducing annoyance and switching attention away from the incident. Such statements might include: "No sense staying mad, it won't help my game" or "Forget it, the next play is about to begin."

With care and planning by the coach and cooperation by the player, these techniques can help the athlete gain self-control and improve sport performance. Remember, however, that simply changing an athlete's self-statements does not guarantee that behavior will be changed. To do that with any degree of stability, the athlete's thoughts must be changed. Emphasizing the impersonal nature of sport competition and the desirability of self-control should facilitate such positive thought changes.

SUMMARY

- Aggressive behavior always refers to an act that is committed with the intent to inflict injury.
- In hostile aggression, the sole purpose is to gain the satisfaction of seeing the pain or injury that was inflicted.
- The more common type of aggression evidenced in sport situations is called instrumental aggression. Instrumental aggression can be differentiated from hostile aggression on the basis of why the athlete inflicted the injury. Instrumental aggression is used when the injury is inflicted to receive an external reinforcer such as praise from the coach or applause from the spectators.
- As opposed to aggressive behavior, assertive behavior is characterized by high degrees of physical energy and effort toward achieving a goal. Such behavior falls within the rules of the game and is not done with any intent to commit injury.
- Aggression has been interpreted within the framework of three major theories. Instinct theory proposes that man is born with an instinctual, or innate, drive to aggress and that acting out aggressive feelings will serve as a catharsis so that subsequent need to aggress will be lessened.
- The frustration-aggression-displacement (F-A-D) hypothesis proposes that frustration is the cause of aggressive behavior. Furthermore, if a frustrated person cannot act out the aggressive response on the instigator of the frustration, then that person will try to displace the aggression on someone else who is similar to the instigator in physical characteristics.
- An alternative explanation of aggression is the social learning position, which says that aggressive behavior is learned through modeling and reinforcement. Also, rather than serving a cathartic function it is proposed that the enactment of an aggressive response results in a circular phenomenon in which an initial aggressive act triggers future aggressive responses.
- Berkowitz has reformulated the theoretical interpretation of aggression by proposing that human aggression can best be explained by combining aspects of both the (F-A-D) hypothesis and social learning theory. He proposes that humans may be born with a tendency to respond to frustration with aggression; however, that tendency can be modified through reinforcement and modeling.
- Several variables are related to whether or not an athlete will aggress in a sport situation. One is the frustration that almost always operates in athletic competition; each team attempts to block the goal seeking of the opposing team. Extremely high levels of excitement or arousal also appear to ready the performer for aggression. If the athlete is in a state of high arousal, and if there are aggressive stimuli in the environment, then it would be predicted that an aggressive response will follow. However, certain

thoughts or cognitions may influence the decision of whether or not to aggress. The performer will probably consider such things as the liklihood that the other person will retaliate and the opponent's intent to inflict injury.

- Physical fitness may also mediate within the aggression process because more physically fit individuals tend to recover more quickly from high activation and, therefore, their readiness to aggress may be more quickly dissipated.
- Volkamer (1971) has identified several game-related variables that appear to be related intimately to player aggression. He found that losers commit more fouls than do winners and that visitors tend to commit more fouls than the home team. Also, in terms of point spread, when the contest is very close both teams tend to commit fewer fouls. However, when there is a large discrepancy between the scores of two teams, fewer fouls occur. When more points or goals are scored, fewer acts of aggression take place. Finally, teams in the lower standings aggress more than higher ranked teams.
- When groups of people simultaneously exhibit violent or hostile behavior it is called collective aggression. When fans observe highly aggressive sporting events, they tend to have increased feelings of arousal or aggression. When Cavanaugh and Silva (1980) assessed spectator's perceptions of the causes of fan misbehavior, they found that aspects of the game (namely, referees, rivalry, nature of the game, time remaining/losing, and score), characteristics of the spectator (namely, age and alcoholic consumption), and the amount of crowd density all were seen as potential causes of misbehavior.

DISCUSSION QUESTIONS

1 Differentiate among the three following terms: hostile aggression, instrumental aggression, and assertive behavior. Can you provide an example for each within a sport setting?
2 What appears to be the most acceptable explanation of aggressive behavior? Why is that position more tenable than the alternative interpretations?
3 How does physical fitness appear to be related to aggression? Will increased physical fitness necessarily lead to reduced aggression?
4 Does competitive sport actually encourage aggression?
5 Is the number of player fouls an accurate measure of aggression?
6 What is meant by the circular effect of aggressive behavior? How does that explanation differ from the catharsis hypothesis?

GLOSSARY

anonymity As used here, the feeling that one is unknown

catharsis hypothesis Proposal that bottled-up emotions can be purged or reduced through aggressive behavior

collective aggression Simultaneous exhibition of violent or hostile behavior by a group of people, such as sport fans

disinhibition Releasing of restraints or controls of a person's actions; the person is no longer inhibited

frustration-aggression-displacement (F-A-D) hypothesis   Proposal that frustration is the cause of aggression and that if the frustrated person cannot act out the aggressive response on the instigator of the frustration, then it will be displaced onto another person

hostile aggression   Intentional infliction of injury that is done for the satisfaction of seeing someone hurt or in pain

instrumental aggression   Intentional infliction of injury that is done for the purpose of receiving positive reinforcement, such as a coach's verbal praise

SUGGESTED READINGS

Feigley, D.A. (1983). Is aggression justifiable? *Journal of Physical Education, Health, Recreation, and Dance, 54,* 63-64.

In this article, Feigley explores violent behavior and poor sportsmanship in sport from the self-justification notion of cognitive dissonance theory. Stresses the need for increased self-awareness and for understanding the nature of self-justification.

Harrell, W.A. (1980). Aggression by high school basketball players: An observational study of the effects of opponents' aggression and frustration-inducing factors. *International Journal of Sport Psychology, 11,* 290-298.

After observing the aggressive behavior of high school basketball players it was shown that the most significant predictor of both aggression and fouls was the amount of aggression directed toward a player by an opponent. Other factors that were studied included field and free-throw shooting percentages, number of turnovers, and home versus visiting team score differences.

Leith, L. (1982). The role of competition in the elicitation of aggression in sport. *Journal of Sport Behavior, 5,* 168-174.

Leith provides an overview of the relationship between aggression and sport competition. Discusses how factors such as frustration, decisions by referees, amount of player contact, and perceived intent of the aggressor might be related to aggressive behaviors in competitive settings.

Lennon, J.X. (1980). The effects of crowding and observation of athletic events on spectator tendency toward aggressive behavior. *Journal of Sport Behavior, 3,* 61-68.

In this article, Lennon assesses the effects of crowding and type of sport being observed on the tendency of spectators to commit violent acts. Although crowding did not appear to cause aggressive responses, viewing a football game as opposed to a gymnastics meet did increase aggression levels.

Russell, G.W. (1983). Crowd size and density in relation to athletic aggression and performance. *Social Behavior and Personality, 2,* 9-15.

This article examines the effect of crowd size and density at ice hockey games on performance and aggression. Russell suggests that the framework of the inverted-U hypothesis can be used to explain the relationship between crowd size and player aggression.

Silva, J.M. (1983). The perceived legitimacy of rule violating behavior in sport. *Journal of Sport Psychology, 5,* 438-448.

Silva investigated the question of whether sport socialization influences the degree of perceived legitimacy of rule-violating sport behavior. He looked at respondent's gender, amount of physical contact characteristic of the sport, number of years of participation, or the highest level of participation in an organized sport.

Thirer, J. (1978). The effect of observing filmed violence on the aggressive attitudes of female athletes and non-athletes. *Journal of Sport Behavior, 1,* 28-36.

Filmed violence was used to determine whether female athletes and non-athletes would show any increases in aggressive attitudes. Non-athletes exhibited increased aggression after viewing filmed violence, although athletes did not.

11

SPORT GROUP PRODUCTIVITY AND PROCESS

The major emphasis in all the previous chapters has been on psychological variables that can influence the sport performance of individual athletes. Knowledge of such information is crucial to effective coaching and teaching of sport skills. However, a large percentage of sport performance occurs in a group setting. Any time that players must interact to achieve a positive sport outcome, various interpersonal dynamics and processes must be considered in addition to attempting to optimize individual sport performance.

Although few, if any, coaches would disagree with that statement, surprisingly little research attention has been given to the study of the variables and factors underlying effective sport group performance.

Several important questions arise concerning sport group productivity: How does individual motivation operate in group settings? Does rate of player assimilation or turnover affect group productivity? How does degree of cohesion relate to team performance? The answers to these questions form the basis of this chapter.

GROUP PRODUCTIVITY

Player Ability

When recruiting athletes for sport teams, many coaches believe that the major rationale underlying player selection should be the *ability level* of the individual performer. They believe that ''you can't win unless you have the horses!''; therefore they perceive group productivity as a direct result of the sum of athletes' abilities. Is such a position justifiable? It would be easy to argue that a professional ice hockey team would most likely get the best of a collegiate ice hockey team and that an Olympian sprinter should run faster than a novice. However, when considering teams within the same skill level or league, can you argue as convincingly that the team with the more highly skilled athletes should consistently beat teams with less highly skilled participants?

Consider the bowl games in collegiate football or the playoffs for the Super Bowl in professional football. Time and time again there are upsets in these games, and lower ranked teams pull together and outperform the favorites. For a team to win a football game, more is required than simply generating outstanding performances from individual athletes. Instead, effective coordination among players must occur within both the offensive and defensive units. Therefore, when a particular sport structure demands coordinated interactions among team players, the sum of individual player ability is not always the most effective predictor of actual team productivity. This was dramatically demonstrated in the 1980 Winter Olympics, when the United States men's ice hockey team pulled together and won stunning upsets over supposedly more highly skilled opponents.

An innovative study by Jones (1974) sheds further light on this issue. Using individual statistics as the measure of individual ability, Jones was interested in determining how well those measures of individual sport ability could predict actual team performance in several professional sports. Of particular interest are the results he obtained for baseball versus basketball teams. How well do you think that the sum of the individual athlete's ability for each of the two types of teams was able to predict success or failure for the team as a whole? Should we be able to predict differences in team outcome based on the sum of player ability for both types of teams? His results indicated that for baseball, prediction of team outcome based on individual athlete ability could be made with about 90% accuracy. However, the findings for basketball showed only a 35% degree of accuracy in predicting team outcome. Why such a wide discrepancy between the predictive accuracy of those two types of teams? Think for a moment about how each of those two sports vary in their structure. Success in baseball requires a strong battery (that is, pitchers and catchers) and players with good fielding and hitting skills. The majority of the players do not continually interact with one another during the game. In basketball, on the other hand, the team that wins is the one in which the players consistently interact with one another effectively throughout the game. Basketball has been called a ''means-dependent'' or **interacting,** sport, which means that an effective play execution by one player moves the entire team closer to the ultimate goal of winning. Winning requires effective inter-player cooperation and interaction. Even if a basketball team were composed of the most highly skilled players, if those players did not cooperate with one another their team would probably not emerge as the victor. For this reason, sport psychologists became interested in trying to determine exactly what processes or dynamics could be used to enhance interplayer coordination in teams that by their structure demanded that coordination. Their goal was to determine how group processes could be used to facilitate sport group productivity when it appeared that such group interactions were tied intimately to actual team performance. Some impetus to this line of inquiry was provided when Steiner (1972) proposed his model of group productivity.

Steiner's Model

Steiner's model is a general one that takes the following form:

Actual productivity = Potential productivity − Losses due to faulty group processes

Actual productivity is reflected by what the sport group achieves in terms of objective measures, such as win-loss ratio. **Potential productivity** is what it is hypothesized the team could achieve if it used all its resources to the optimal level. A team's resources are obviously affected by the nature of the task; for example, having a high degree of explosive leg strength might be considered a highly desirable resource in pole-vaulting or basketball but of little relevance in table tennis or bowling. Individual player skill or ability, as those qualities relate to a particular sport, also are a primary component of potential productivity. However, as we noted previously, if a sport requires coordinated efforts among team members, then loss of potential productivity can occur as a result of ineffective group interactions or processes.

Two primary explanations have been proposed concerning possible causes underlying ineffective group processes: *coordination problems* among group members and *decreases*

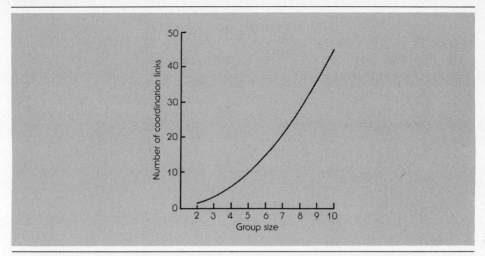

FIGURE 11-1   The number of coordination links as a function of group size.
From Carron, A.V. (1980). *Social psychology of sport*. Ithaca, NY: Mouvement Publications.

in individual motivation in group settings. As a group size increases, the number of individual efforts that must be coordinated increases in a systematic fashion. Figure 11-1 illustrates how the number of coordination links increase as group size increases. The smallest possible group size (two persons) has only one coordination link, whereas (as shown in Figure 11-1) a group as large as 10 persons contains 45 coordination links. Therefore, as Carron (1980) points out: "while a 10-person group has approximately three times the available resources to draw upon when compared to a triad, it has nine times as many coordination links to maintain" (p. 208). The point is that although an increase in group size does indeed result in a larger pool of possible resources, the increase in group resources will not necessarily result in increased productivity. Any decrease in the effectiveness of coordinating those links could be predicted to result in a decrease in actual group productivity.

The Ringlemann Effect

An alternative explanation to the causes underlying faulty group processes is that of potential losses in individual motivation that may occur in group settings. The basis of this explanation is called the **Ringlemann effect.** This effect is based on an early un-published study conducted by a German psychologist named Ringlemann whose results have been widely cited in other group research investigations (Davis, 1969; Ingham, Levinger, Graves, & Peckham, 1974; Steiner, 1972). Ringlemann apparently had workers pull to their maximum on a rope either alone or with one, two, or seven other persons. He then used a strain gauge to determine how hard they pulled as measured in kilograms of pressure (Latane, Williams, & Harkins, 1979).

Not surprisingly, the total pulling power exhibited by any of the groups surpassed that of a single person. However, in no case did the sum total of the group's pulling power equal the absolute total of the individual members of the group. For example, in groups of three, members only pulled at a rate of two and a half times the average individual performance, and when group size reached eight, pulling power was only four times rather than eight times the average individual performance (Latane, Williams, & Harkins, 1979). Thus Ringlemann's findings indicated two important occurrences: (1) individual effort decreases in a group setting and (2) the decrease in individual effort increases as the size of the group increases.

In terms of implications for sport psychology, the Ringlemann effect is provocative. Is it true that members of sport teams don't try as hard or perform at a lower level as compared with participants in individual sports? If so, why would successful basketball coaches such as Dean Smith of the University of North Carolina spend so much time emphasizing the necessity of players and coaches being a "family?" Why would most other coaches of team sports give pep talks regarding similar notions such as group morale, group cohesion, or "togetherness?" Why do we so often hear slogans such as "there is no 'I' in the word team?"

It appears then that coaches' objectives of facilitating group unity argue against the effects shown by Ringlemann's research. On the other hand, if Ringlemann's initial findings were accurate, they could provide one reason why losses as a result of faulty group processes occur (Steiner, 1972). Given this controversy, other researchers have become interested in attempting to first replicate Ringlemann's early findings and then determine whether the underlying cause was a loss in the group's ability to coordinate their efforts or a loss in motivation. A final objective was to ascertain if it were possible to prevent such group losses in productivity.

The first two of these objectives was addressed in a two-part investigation carried out by Ingham, Levinger, Graves, and Peckham (1974). In a controlled, laboratory setting they used a rope-pulling task to see if Ringlemann's early findings would be replicated. Their results indicated that as the size of the group increased, *up to a group size of three,* average pulling performance decreased. However, this was only a partial replication of the earlier findings in that in group sizes of four, five, and six no further decreases were evidenced.

Part two of the Ingham and others study looked at the question of decreased performance as a function of either poor coordination among group members or loss of individual motivation in group settings. They used an innovative experimental protocol that eliminated the possibility of coordination losses by having blindfolded subjects pull the rope alone while thinking that the other five confederates were also pulling. They found the same effect relative to decreases in individual performance in three-person groups. Again, this decrease did not become more pronounced as group size increased. Given that they had experimentally eliminated the possibility of such losses being caused by losses in group coordination, they were able to conclude that the causative factor underlying the Ringlemann effect was loss of motivation by persons in group settings.

Social Loafing

Intrigued by the results of both the early work of Ringlemann and the more recent findings of Ingham and others, other researchers became interested in attempting to understand more about how group processes can affect group productivity. Most prominent among such investigators is the work of Latane, Williams, and Harkins (1979). They reasoned that persons are more likely to work hard in proportion to the amount of pressure they feel to do so. Therefore with increased group size pressure becomes more dispersed, and each person should feel less and less pressure to perform. They called this decrease in individual effort caused by the social presence of others **social loafing.** From their perspective, the most plausible cause of social loafing appeared to be **identifiability.**

According to Williams & others (1981), people appear to be more apt to perform a task better if their efforts or their work is identifiable to other people. This should be especially so when the other people are important to performers in terms of their ability to supply desired reinforcements. On the other hand, when performers' efforts or outputs are unidentifiable, performers are said to feel less motivated to perform with the same degree of intensity. Put another way, the underlying cause of social loafing is the notion of the unidentifiability of the performer's effort. In fact, the data obtained from the second phase of the Williams and others (1981) investigation showed rather convincingly that when performers' efforts were clearly identifiable, social loafing was eliminated.

Why should identifiability be so important to individual performance in group settings? Using the theoretical notion of learned helplessness, Williams and his colleagues suggest that identifiability is crucial because it assures an awareness of the connection between effort and outcome. Recall that from the perspective of learned helplessness theory, when people perceive no relationship between responses and their outcomes (regardless of whether the outcome is positive or negative), they learn to experience feelings of helplessness or uncontrollability, which are predicted to lead to a loss in motivation.

Because research into social loafing and identifiability is relatively new, there is not much available information. One exception is a study conducted by Latane, Harkins, and Williams (1980) who looked at this question within the framework of competitive swimming. A total of 16 collegiate swimmers each swam one lap in two 400-meter freestyle relays and two 100-meter individual freestyle events. The swimmers were not informed of the true nature of the experiment but instead were told that their starting techniques and certain timing methods were of interest. The manipulation of identifiability versus unidentifiability consisted of either announcing or not announcing the results of the individual freestyle events. In addition, winners of the relay events were given T-shirts, whereas the losers did not receive any reinforcement.

Unidentifiability appeared to produce social loafing in the relay events as compared with the individual freestyle events. The average time for the individual freestyle events was 61.34 seconds, and the average relay time was 61.66 seconds. This situation was reversed under the condition of identifiability, wherein relay times averaged 60.81 seconds and the individual freestyle times averaged 60.95 seconds. Although the differences between the average times obtained under any condition were small, such differences are typical of the difference between places in competitive events (Latane & others, 1980). Their results provide "food for thought" in that high degrees of identifiability not only eliminated social loafing in the group situation (relay events) but also appears to have increased individual swimmer motivation. (For a further look at the notion of identifiability, social loafing, and coaching implications, see Case Study 1 on p. 280.)

Player Assimilation and Turnover

Assimilation refers to the length of time it takes a new player to be accepted as a full-fledged, active team member. Player turnover pertains to the rate at which new members are acquired and old members are released. Because sport teams tend to be stable, the question of group formation (that is, initial establishment of a team) is of less importance than player assimilation and turnover. Large degrees of player turnover can negatively affect team productivity and success; however, some player turnover is necessary, otherwise everyone on the team will grow older and lose their skills at the same time. Marin (1969) analyzed the 1955-1959 records of the National Football League and found that although more experienced teams did not always win, they won more frequently than less experienced teams. In another investigation, Donnelly (1975) found an inverted-U relationship between length of player's team membership and team effectiveness; that is, as player experience increased, up to a certain point, team effectiveness also increased. However, beyond that optimal point a performance decline was observed. Interestingly, the same relationship also applied to the coach's tenure with the team! Thus it appears that generally neither very inexperienced nor very experienced players and coaches are as effective as are those with moderate amounts of experience.

What about when new members join a team? How long does their assimilation take? Are there strategies that can accelerate player assimilation? When players join a new team, it usually takes at least a year before they become starters. Therefore it is important that coaches facilitate their assimilation into the sport group. Two aids to the process are a sociogram and a sociomatrix. A *sociogram* is a brief list of questions such as "To whom do you prefer to pass?" "Who do you trust the most on the team?" "What starting lineup would you select?" The answers to such questions can provide insight into player preferences and interplayer relationships. A *sociomatrix* is simply a behavioral observation technique whereby the coach can tally passing preferences among the players. If trends emerge that show that a particular player is being ignored or overly preferred, then perhaps a team discussion is in order. In addition, armed with the information gained from either technique, the coach can vary combinations used in either practices or games. The coach may also gain insights into potential problems among players, such as rivalries or cliques. The development of such negative interactive patterns can be extremely detrimental to team performance and to important group processes such as cohesion.

COHESION AND SPORT GROUP PERFORMANCE

A common belief among coaches of team sports is that team members need to have feelings of group unity, togetherness, or cohesion to be successful. Of the terms mentioned above, the most commonly used one is *cohesion*. Carron (1982) defines cohesion as "a dynamic process which is reflected in the tendency for a group to stick together and remain united in the pursuit of its goals and objectives" (p. 259).

Although the idea that cohesion is directly related to sport team success may be reasonable or even accurate, there currently is little hard evidence to support that notion. On the contrary, most everyone has witnessed exceptions to this rule. We have all seen teams in which the players didn't appear to like one another and yet somehow they won the game or match. Are there explanations for these apparent conflicts in philosophy and reality? Currently there are only a few strong lines of research to provide us with some insight into the relationship between group processes such as cohesion and team outcome. Before discussing that evidence, however, it is important to further define the construct of cohesion and examine how it is commonly measured within sport settings.

The Nature and Measurement of Cohesion

One of the earliest conceptualizations of cohesion was proposed by Festinger, Schachter, and Back (1950). They suggested that cohesion was the sum of all forces that act on members so that they remain in a group. Their position at first appears to be reasonable; however, there seems to be a great deal of difficulty in accepting that definition. What are those forces, and exactly how would they be identified or measured?

Hagstrom and Selvin (1965) tried to shed some light on this question. Using a statistical procedure called factor analysis, they tested about 16 possible ''forces'' for their relevance to cohesion. From their analysis, they identified two important components: social satisfaction and sociometric cohesion. **Social satisfaction** pertains to the group member's satisfaction with the group in terms of its ability to allow a person to obtain desired goals. **Sociometric cohesion** refers to the amount of positive affect, or ''liking,'' among group members. Thus Hagstrom and Selvin proposed what is referred to as a bidimensional model of cohesion, containing a social (or affective) dimension and a task component. Although the bidimensional model has been used traditionally in group dynamics research, its use in sport research has been rare (see Bird, 1977). Instead, the vast majority of sport researchers have tended to adopt a slightly different bidimensional approach to assessing cohesion within sport teams, apparently because of the availability of a single sport-specific inventory, the Sport Cohesiveness Questionnaire (Martens, Landers, & Loy, 1972). Table 11-1 contains the seven components contained in the Sport Cohesiveness Questionnaire. The first two components (interpersonal attraction and personal power or influence) are considered to be sociometric indices, whereas the remaining five (value of membership, sense of belonging, enjoyment, teamwork, and closeness) are considered to be more direct measures of cohesion (Williams & Hacker, 1982). Some advances in the measurement of sport cohesion have been made recently with the development of the Sport Cohesion Instrument (Yukelson, Weinberg, & Jackson, 1984). This is a multidimensional approach that assesses aspects of both group goals and objectives, and positive interpersonal relationships.

TABLE 11-1   Cohesion Items from the Martens, Landers, and Loy (1972) Sports Cohesiveness Questionnaire

Item	Question
Interpersonal attraction	On what type of friendship basis are you with each member of your team?
Personal power or influence	For many reasons some of the members of a team are more influential than others. How much influence to you believe each of the other members of your team have with the coach and other teammates?
Value of membership	Compared to other groups that you belong to, how much do you value your membership on this team?
Sense of belonging	How strong a sense of belonging do you believe you have to this team?
Enjoyment	How much do you like competing with this particular team?
Teamwork	How good do you think the teamwork is on this team?
Closeness	How closely knit do you think your team is?

From Carron, A.V. (1980). *Social psychology of sport.* Ithaca, NY: Mouvement Publications.

Sport psychologists have been interested in measuring the degree of cohesion within various sport teams for two major reasons. The first, and certainly the most popular, has been an attempt to determine if high levels of cohesion will have a positive effect on team outcome in terms of success. The second has been an interest in how degree of cohesion might be related to player satisfaction.

Cohesion, Performance Outcome, and Player Satisfaction

During the 1960s and 1970s it appeared that the status of the literature on the cohesion-performance question was equivocal at best. Sometimes strong relationships seemed to be apparent (for example, Ball & Carron, 1976, Bird, 1977; Bird & Brame, 1978; Martens & Peterson, 1971; Widmeyer & Martens, 1978) but at other times there appeared to be a negative or inverse relationship between degree of cohesion and successful team outcome (Landers & Luschen, 1974; Lenk, 1969).

Some resolution to this problem occurred when Landers and Luschen (1974) proposed that group structure needed to be taken into account when addressing the cohesion-performance question. They restricted their analysis to a simple, two-way classification of sport teams. *Interacting* teams are organized so that success can only result when the team members work together in an effective and coordinated manner. As we mentioned earlier, on such teams the athletes are interdependent or ''means-dependent'' in that as one member moves toward the goal, all team members benefit. Examples of interacting sport teams are basketball, soccer, and volleyball. On the other hand, *coacting* teams have a structure in which team members perform independently of one another during the pursuit of a common goal. In addition, as pointed out by Steiner (1972), coacting sport groups ordinarily require that all team members perform similar skills, and final team performance is generally determined by the sum or average of the individual athlete's performance. Teams such as riflery or bowling teams would be classified as coacting groups.

After classifying teams as being either interacting or coacting in terms of structure, Landers and Luschen (1974) were able to show that coacting sport groups who were successful generally had lower levels of cohesion. On the contrary, interacting teams who demonstrated success generally evidenced higher levels of cohesion as compared with their less successful counterparts. It is on this basis that current research and theorizing relative to the cohesion-performance relationship restricts itself to sport teams that fall within the classification of interacting teams.

The important questions to be addressed are: What, if any, is the causal relationship between degree of cohesion and sport outcome; and what, if any, role does player satisfaction play in the cohesion-performance relationship? On the surface, these questions appear to be simple enough. However, in reality the situation is complex and currently unresolved. Given the tenuous nature of the present situation, we present, with some caution, what appear to be some of the trends in the current evidence.

The results of several studies (Bakeman & Helmreich, 1975; Carron & Ball, 1977; Williams & Hacker, 1982) suggest that there is good reason to believe that there is a much more causative relationship between performance and cohesion than exists between cohesion and performance. In other words, it appears that success generates higher degrees of cohesion but higher degrees of cohesion do not cause performance success. Although this may be discouraging to coaches who are interested in producing successful teams, perhaps there is a more important reason for attempting to foster higher degrees of cohesion within interacting sport teams. Some research evidence (Bird, Foster, & Maruyama, 1980; Williams & Hacker, 1982) suggests that members of sport teams that exhibit high degrees of cohesion also experience higher levels of satisfaction (positive affect). Therefore, regardless of the presence of any causative relationship between cohesion and sport performance outcome, it seems that coaches would be wise to instigate cohesion-enhancing strategies throughout the season. Certainly it can be argued that player satisfaction or pride in performance is of equal or greater importance than success or failure as a team.

Strategies for Enhancing Cohesion

When athletes participate in sport activities, they can simultaneously hold two primary achievement motives. One is their own personal motive to achieve success. Independent of that motive is the group-oriented motive, which can be used to facilitate group cohesion by employing strategies similar to those used to enhance individual motivation.

Enhancing Individual Motivation

Zander (1975) has proposed that there are three frequently used methods for increasing individual achievement motivation in sport settings. The **supportive approach** is premised on the notion that a well-satisfied athlete, as compared with a less-satisfied athlete, will be motivated to try harder and thus perform better. We can see examples of this reasoning throughout the whole realm of the sporting world. For instance, in collegiate athletics some performers receive room and board or even academic tutors on campus. The reasoning underlying such actions is that such benefits will induce the person to perform well in the future. Thus they are not given contingent on performance; instead they are dispensed before any desired response. Recall the principle of contingency discussed in Chapter 2 and Thorndike's law of effect. Together they suggest that rewards should be provided only after a desired response occurs and certainly not before. Preperformance rewards in no way guarantee that the athlete will be motivated to try hard at some future date; thus the supportive approach to motivation building must be regarded as highly ineffective in building individual sport motivation. There is no reason to believe that it would be any more effective in building team-oriented motivation.

A second approach to motivation development suggested by Zander is called the **reinforcement approach.** This strategy calls for the application of positive reinforcements *contingent on* the emission of a desired response. Once a goal or standard is established and the athlete achieves it, a reward is provided. The reinforcement approach is used commonly in athletic settings. Trophies are distributed at the annual sports banquet, stars are provided for football helmets, and a pat on the back is given for a good play.

Are there any potential disadvantages to adhering strictly to the reinforcement approach? In team sports several problems could occur. Players who are unequally reinforced can become rivals rather than cooperative coworkers. Such rivalry can certainly undermine cohesion within the team. From the perspective of the coach other potential problems can arise. The most fundamental problem is associated with the relative potency of the reward. The coach has only so many potential rewards to distribute, with the passage of time the rewards can lose their potency. For example, what important rewards remain after a player has received the most improved player award, has earned the outstanding player of the year award, and has been elected captain of the team?

A third approach identified by Zander is the **pride in performance approach.** This approach is oriented toward enhancing individual pride, or positive affect, through a process in which limited, realistic, but challenging goals are established. The goals are limited in the sense that they should pertain to specific accomplishments, such as increasing free throw percentage or decreasing fouls in basketball, rather than setting an objective such as being named the outstanding player of the conference. It is also important to note that goals should be established that can only be achieved through increased effort by the performer. Achieving such goals should enhance both pride in performance and the expectancy of future success at that or similar goals. The effective use of the pride in performance approach requires that the coach know enough about each individual athlete so that the goals that are set are within the ability level of the particular athlete. Such goal setting must be accomplished on the basis of the *notion of mutuality;* that is, in consultation between the coach *and* the athlete. They should not be established only by the coach. Once realistic and achievable goals are established mutually, then it is imperative that they be evaluated. Through the process of goal evaluation, the coach can determine that the individual player has actually internalized and adopted that goal for himself or herself. Once it has been established that the athlete has both adopted and achieved the goal, then positive reinforcement should follow and new, limited goals should be identified.

Enhancing Group Motivation

In discussing Zander's three approaches to enhancing athlete motivation, we have been exploring avenues for increasing individual achievement motivation. However, it is important to point out that those strategies are equally applicable to facilitating a group-oriented or cohesion-building program. In particular, the reinforcement approach and the pride-in-performance approach are best suited for building group-oriented motivation.

As mentioned earlier, athletes can simultaneously hold both an individually oriented and a team-oriented motive to achieve success. Both Forward (1968) and Zander (1969) have proposed that these motives are *independent.* Therefore the strength or potency of one motive is not necessarily connected or related to the other. On teams classified as being interactive, it is imperative that coaches attempt to strengthen both the individually oriented and the team-oriented motivation of players.

Recall that to achieve success on interacting teams the players must effectively coordinate their mutual efforts. In terms of overall outcome, no one player can achieve success unless the team also achieves success. Therefore on such teams players become intimately involved not only with their own accomplishments but also with the team's achievements. Successful achievement by the team as a unit is mandatory for a strong group-oriented motive to emerge. How can team success be facilitated?

The key to guaranteeing team success and subsequent team-oriented motivation and pride lies with the process of establishing *team, or group-contingent, goals.* The mutually agreed on goals must be developed in consultation with all members of the group and must not be imposed by the coach. They must be realistic, limited, and attainable only through the coordinated efforts of *all* the players. When establishing these goals, the criterion by which such goals will be evaluated must also be identified. As in the process of developing pride in individual performance outcome, team attempts at goal attainment must be evaluated mutually by both the coach and all the athletes on the team. During this evaluation process it can be determined if the goal is indeed realistic or if it is too difficult. In the latter case the goal must be redefined so that it falls within the capability of that particular group. For example, if the team originally set a goal of decreasing turnovers in a basketball game by 30% and subsequently found that they were only able to achieve a 10% decrease, then perhaps setting a new goal of 15% would be both more realistic and more achievable.

Again, the goals selected for the group should be limited rather than generalized. For example, a limited goal in volleyball would be to increase the number of blocks by five. A general goal would be to win the match. The process should be one whereby goals are defined and evaluated throughout the entire season. Why is this so important? Because successful team outcome for an interacting team can only be achieved through the co-ordinated efforts of all of the players, the setting of goals that can only be obtained through such efforts leads to two very positive outcomes. First, the attainment of such goals actually improves the skill level of the team because the only way in which the goal could be achieved was through effective intermember efforts. Second, the successful accomplishment of such goals leads to pride in team performance and enhances cohesion. Together, both should generate increased feelings of satisfaction and team pride for all of the team members and higher expectancies for future team success.

IMPLICATIONS FOR SPORT

- For interacting sport teams, effective interplayer relationships may be more important than individual abilities alone; therefore positively reinforce player responses that reflect those desirable cooperative responses.
- In team sports, individual motivation can be enhanced by making each member's efforts identifiable. Reward and publicize those efforts.
- Use a sociogram or a sociomatrix to gain insights into player perceptions of other team members and possible group problems such as rivalries or cliques.
- Implement a cohesion-enhancing program through positive reinforcement and realistic goal setting.
- *Mutually* establish both individual player goals and team-contingent goals.
- When setting goals:
  Make them operational (that is, measurable)
  Make them short term (that is, next game or practice); the long term goals will then take care of themselves
  Make them limited (that is, specific number by which to reduce turnovers or fouls)
  Mutually identify only a limited number of goals; do not overload players with too many goals
  List the goals in the locker room
  Verbally remind players of the goals
  Always evaluate goal achievement after both practices and games
- Once goals have been achieved, mutually develop a new set of short-term goals.

- Do not maintain unattainable goals; be willing to revise both team and individual goals.
- Devise techniques that help make substitutes feel a part of the team (such as special assignments or practices). This will enhance player assimilation.

CASE STUDY 1
Social Loafing, Player Identifiability, and Football Performance

Social loafing, or decreased player motivation, can occur whenever group members perceive that their roles or contributions to the team are not important. The structure of a football team is a sport setting in which social loafing might frequently occur; the quarterback and the running backs tend to receive the most recognition from both the fans and the media. To prevent decreases in motivation caused by lack of identification of the contributions of the less visible players, coaches should highlight the successful achievements of all the players. Suggestions for increasing player identifiability are presented below:

1. When viewing postgame films, pause and compliment good defensive plays. Do not focus only on player mistakes.
2. When talking with the media, emphasize the unique contributions of some of the lesser known players.
3. In team meetings, stress the importance of each player's contribution to the team.
4. Take the time and make the effort to positively reinforce all players.
5. Post the picture of the offensive and defensive linemen of the week.

CASE STUDY 2
A Cohesion-Building Program for Interacting Sport Teams

Success on interacting teams such as volleyball or hockey results only from highly effective interplayer coordination of efforts. A cohesion-enhancing program can increase the quality of players' mutual efforts and the degree of team pride or satisfaction. Below are some steps to use when initiating a cohesion-enhancing program.

1. Identify major team weaknesses caused by poor coordination of player efforts.
2. Call a team meeting. Ask players to (1) identify team-oriented strengths and weaknesses, (2) discuss probable causes underlying team weaknesses, and (3) mutually establish a small number of limited, achievable goals that can only be achieved through the combined efforts of all of the players. The goals should be for the next game or practice, not for the entire season.
3. Emphasize the goals during practice and any time-outs called during a game or match. Reinforce the team as a unit whenever it appears that they are working together toward achieving the established team goals.
4. Conduct a postgame evaluation session. After a win, positively reinforce the team as a unit and then mutually establish new goals for the next game. After a loss, identify the probable causes and then mutually redefine a new set of team goals.

SUMMARY

- Steiner's model of group productivity states that the actual productivity of the sport group is a function of its potential productivity minus any losses caused by faulty group processes. Potential productivity is the hypothesized productivity of the team if it used all its resources to the optimal level.
- Two possible causes of faulty group processes are poor coordination of effort among team members and decreases in individual motivation that occur in group settings. The latter is referred to as the Ringlemann effect, or social loafing.
- One way to eliminate social loafing in sport teams is to increase the identifiability of each of the participants; that is, each athlete should feel that his or her contribution plays an important role in the team's achievements.
- In regard to sport teams, the group process that has received the greatest amount of research attention is cohesion. The results of several investigations suggest that there may be good reason to believe that there is more of a causative relationship between performance and cohesion than there is between cohesion and performance. More specifically, on interacting teams a successful sport outcome appears to increase degree of cohesion; however, degree of cohesion may or may not affect outcome in terms of success or failure. In addition, there is evidence that high degrees of cohesion are systematically related to positive affective responses by the participants.
- High cohesion appears to increase player satisfaction; because high degrees of cohesion can lead to positive feelings on the part of athletes, it may be prudent for coaches to initiate cohesion-enhancing strategies within their practice regime. Two ways to accomplish such a goal are the reinforcement approach and the pride-in-performance approach. In both approaches, limited but achievable team goals are identified. Reinforcement is then applied on a team rather than an individual basis.

DISCUSSION QUESTIONS

1 What appears to be the major factor underlying social loafing?
2 What are the three primary factors underlying group productivity?
3 How does group structure appear to be related to desirable levels of cohesion?
4 Differentiate between actual productivity and potential productivity.
5 For teams classified as being interactive, what appears to be the relationship among the factors of cohesion, performance outcome, and player satisfaction?
6 Using Case Study 2 as your guide, design a cohesion-enhancing program for an interacting sport with which you are familiar.

GLOSSARY

actual productivity   Measure of a team's achievement in terms of objective measures such as win-loss ratio

bidirectional   As used here, this term refers to a measurement approach that includes two separate components

dynamics   In the study of groups, this refers to interactions that take place among members

identifiability   Process of making a person's efforts or contributions to a group visible or clear

interacting sports teams   Teams that by their structure require that all members continually coordinate their efforts to be successful

potential productivity   Possible achievement of a team if it used all its resources effectively

pride in performance approach   Process of attempting to increase motivation by having athletes and coaches mutually establish limited, achievable goals

reinforcement approach   Process of attempting to increase motivation by positively reinforcing athletes, contingent on emission of a desired response

Ringlemann effect   Effect of losses in individual motivation in group situations

social loafing   Decreases in individual effort or motivation in group settings

social satisfaction   Dimension of cohesion that pertains to the degree to which team membership allows persons to achieve desired goals

sociometric cohesion   Dimension of cohesion that pertains to the degree to which group members like one another

supportive approach   Process of attempting to increase motivation by providing athletes with positive reinforcements prior to actual performance

SUGGESTED READINGS

Carron, A.V. (1982). Processes of group interaction in sport teams. *Quest, 33,* 245-270.

   Carron synthesizes research on sport groups. He presents a model for group interaction, identifies important personal and environmental factors, discusses the notions of group interaction and integration, and highlights the role of both personal-social and achievement factors.

Carron, A.V. (1982). Cohesiveness in sport groups: Interpretations and considerations. *Journal of Sport Psychology, 4,* 123-138.

   This is an overview paper that analyzes several aspects of cohesiveness in sport groups. Topics include the current conceptual perspectives, definitional efforts, implications and limitations of sport-related approaches, and directions for future research.

Carron, A.V. (1984). Cohesion in sport teams. In J.M. Silva & R.S. Weinberg (Eds.), *Psychological foundations of sport,* Champaign, IL: Human Kinetics.

   Carron begins by defining cohesion and tracing how it develops in groups. He then looks at the nature of cohesion as it operates within sport teams and concludes with several practical implications for working with athletic teams.

Gill, D.L. (1984). Individual and group performance in sport. In J.M. Silva & R.S. Weinberg (Eds.), *Psychological foundations of sport,* Champaign, IL: Human Kinetics.

   Emphasizes several factors that can influence group performance and productivity. After presenting pertinent theoretical frameworks, important implications for working with sport groups are presented.

Taylor, D.M., Doria, J., & Tyler, J.K. (1983). Group performance and cohesiveness: An attributional analysis. *Journal of Social Psychology, 119,* 187-198.

   These researchers used an attributional strategy to determine if failing ice hockey teams can also be cohesive. Losing teams were found to exhibit a group-serving rather than a self-serving pattern.

Williams, J.M., & Hacker, C.M. (1982). Causal relations among cohesion, satisfaction, and performance in women's intercollegiate field hockey teams. *Journal of Sport Psychology, 4,* 324-337.

   This investigation looked at the interrelationships between team outcome, player satisfaction, and degree of cohesion. A circular relationship between cohesion and performance was suggested by the results. It was also proposed that player satisfaction may play a mediating role within the circular relationship between cohesion and performance outcome.

LEADERSHIP AND COACHING BEHAVIOR

This chapter focuses on aspects of leadership and coaching behavior. We will try to answer questions such as: "Is one type of leadership style more effective than others?" "How important is it that the coach and the athlete are compatable?" "Is it possible to change coaching behavior so that it "fits" better with a particular sport or athlete?"

PERSPECTIVES ON LEADERSHIP

Perspectives on effective leadership style have varied from trait approaches to behavioral approaches to situational approaches. In this section we will take a look at the most predominant of those frameworks.

Trait Approaches

What makes a great leader? The excitable and pugnacious character of a Bobby Knight? The down-to-earth and calm countenance of a John Wooden? Early theorists hoped it would be possible to identify a consellation of **personality traits** that would be capable of differentiating potentially great leaders from less effective ones. They felt that great leaders might all possess superior personality characteristics; therefore they took the position that enduring personality traits separated the great from the mediocre. Their's was called the **great man theory** of leadership.

Most of the research conducted within this framework was done within the realm of management science. Although researchers may have started with "a burst of glory," their findings revealed little evidence to support their position. Based on the literature from management science, it appears that the "great man" theory of leader effectiveness holds little promise in terms of helping us understand the true nature of the leadership process. However, our primary concern is leadership as it occurs in the realm of sport and athletics. How does this theoretical orientation hold up in those situations?

Recall from Chapter 2 that we had to conclude that the trait approach to understanding aspects of personality and sport behavior had several inherent problems. With the possible exception of elite athletes, the trait approach provided little insight into how personality relates to sport performance. Those same problems appear again when this approach is used to describe the desirable qualities of coaches and other sport leaders. This again seems intuitively reasonable. Trait theories are built on the assumption that highly effective leaders will be characterized by an identifiable set of personality characteristics that will facilitate their success in *all* situations. As such, traits are perceived as being universal (general) in nature, and the uniqueness of the specific situation is virtually ignored. However, what would happen to the predictive ability of a trait interpretation if the nature of the particular situation were also addressed? That is exactly the approach that Fiedler (1967) took in his **contingency theory** of leader effectiveness.

Trait × Situation Approaches

Fiedler's (1967) contingency theory is based on the idea that two major factors influence leadership effectiveness: (1) leadership style (personality traits) and (2) the favorableness of the group situation in terms of allowing the leader to exhibit power and influence. Fiedler conceptualized two dimensions as being of greatest importance to leadership style: the personality dispositions of being either socio-emotional in orientation or being task-oriented. A **socio-emotional orientation** is one in which the leader is supportive of others, is concerned about the interrelationships among group members, and is less concerned about the task per se. A **task-oriented leader** places successful completion of the task as the top priority. This type of leader places much less emphasis on interpersonal relationships among group members.

To determine the predominant leadership or personality styles of persons, Fiedler took an innovative approach. He developed an assessment instrument called the Least Preferred Co-Worker Scale (LPC) to measure the degree of empathy or esteem that the leader holds for the group member whom he or she prefers the least. The scale generates a single score; a high score indicates a therapeutic, socio-emotional leader, and a low score indicates a task-oriented leader.

The second factor in Fiedler's contingency theory refers to the favorableness of the group situation in terms of allowing the leader to demonstrate power or control. This is also called **situational favorableness** and is the result of three subfactors: leader-member relationships, task structure, and position power.

Leader-member relationships pertain to the quality of the relations or interactions between the leader and the group members. A warm and trusting relationship between leader and members should allow the leader to exert more influence and control over the group.

Task structure is associated with the clarity with which the goals of the task are apparent. In a situation in which there is high task structure, those goals will be clear and little or no ambiguity will be present. From Fiedler's perspective, when high task structure is present it is easier for the leader to exert power or control. Conversely, when task structure is low because of unclear paths to goal attainment, it is more difficult for the leader to control the group and thus to achieve the goal. Task structure is almost always high in sport situations, as the goal is clear—winning. However, task structure can be lowered in those same situations when the coach does not clearly outline the specific behaviors needed to achieve success.

Position power is associated with the amount of authority the leader has in terms of controlling positive reinforcements and assigning punishments. Thus it relates to the degree of authority the leader has over group members. The head coach would generally have more position power than the assistant coach. The head coach has the final say over such decisions as amount of playing time versus "bench warming" time.

Of the three subprocesses mediating the favorableness of the situation, the most important is the quality of leader-member relationships, whereas the least important is position power. Without warmth and trust between leader and members, accompanied by clear group goals or objectives, task success is highly improbable. Therefore, even if the leader wields considerable position power, without cooperation from group members and an identifiable goal little will be accomplished.

Based on his conceptualization of leadership style and situation favorableness, Fiedler proposed two major hypotheses:

1. Task-oriented (low LPC) leaders should perform best in situations that are at either extreme of favorableness; that is, in situations that are either highly favorable or highly unfavorable.
2. Socio-emotional (high LPC) leaders should perform best in situations that are moderate in favorableness.

Carron (1980) summarizes Fiedler's theory nicely:

> Thus, the main tenets of the Contingency Theory are that: group-work situations differ in their degree of favorableness; individual leaders vary along a continuum from task to person orientation; and any individual can be an effective leader provided his/her leadership style coincides with a situation of appropriate favorableness. (p. 115)

It is important to note that when applying Fiedler's theory to practical settings, it is highly improbable that a person's personality can be changed to meet the specific situation. Recall that personality traits are considered to be stable; thus from this perspective a more reasonable strategy would most likely be to match a particular person or coach with the situation most suited for his or her preferred leadership style. Before we rush ahead and do that, we better take a look at how well Fiedler's framework has held up in sport and athletic settings.

To date there appears to be only three investigations that have attempted to test Fiedler's contingency theory within sport settings. Using a total of 43 basketball teams, Inciong (1974) assessed the leadership style of 60 coaches through the Least Preferred Co-Worker Scale (LPC). In addition, Fiedler's (1967) Group Atmosphere Scale was used to measure coach-athlete relationships. Position power and task structure were not measured. Group effectiveness was inferred on the basis of the team's won-loss record. Based on Fiedler's theory, Inciong hypothesized that the coaches' scores on the LPC would be correlated positively with performance outcome in situations that were moderately favorable. It was also proposed that the LPC scores would be correlated negatively under either very favorable or very unfavorable situations. The findings indicated that the obtained correlations were in the predicted direction; however, their magnitude was so low that they could not support the use of Fiedler's model in that basketball setting.

In a study of 40 minor league hockey coaches, Danielson (1976) also tested Fiedler's predictions. He used the LPC to measure leadership style, the Group Atmosphere Scale to assess coach-athlete relationships, and the Goal Direction Scale of the Learning Environment Inventory (Anderson, 1973) to measure task structure. He did not attempt to measure position power. His results showed that regardless of the favorableness of the situation, the more socio-emotional, or personally oriented, the coach, the more successful the team.

It would be unwise, however, to conclude on the basis of a single study that a socio-emotional approach to coaching is always the most desirable. Recall that Danielson only tested youth hockey players. A more comprehensive test would be one in which level of skill was varied over at least two levels. That was the approach taken by Bird (1977a) in her study of women collegiate volleyball players.

Bird used the LPC to measure head coaches' leadership style, the Group Atmosphere

Scale to measure leader-member relationships (cohesion), and Fiedler's (1967) Measure of Position Power to determine position power. Position power was moderately high; thus the athletes perceived that the coaches had moderately high control over both reinforcements and punishments. Although she did not directly assess task structure, she argued as follows:

> In reference to volleyball teams, task structure is usually considered to be relatively high. The goal of the team is obvious, winning. Team members ordinarily perform rather specialized roles such as setters and hitters. Members are not, therefore, totally interchangeable. (p. 177)

Based on Fiedler's theory it was hypothesized that winning volleyball teams should have greater cohesion (that is, better coach-athlete relations) and a task-oriented coach. The first prediction was supported; however, as can be observed in Figure 12-1, leadership style of successful teams varied as a function of level of competition. In the more highly skilled division (Division 1), winning coaches were perceived as being more socio-emotional and losing teams viewed their coach's leadership style to be more task-oriented. The converse was shown for the less skilled division (Division 2). On the basis of those findings it could be speculated that players on more highly skilled teams are sufficiently task-oriented themselves and therefore do not need the added direction of the coach. This may be particularly true in this case because the players in the high-skill group (Division 1) were members of what would be considered to be the most highly skilled women's teams in the United States. In regard to the less-skilled players (Division 2), perhaps a more effective coach is one who conscientiously provides instructions and feedback that focuses player attention on the goal of winning.

An alternative to the trait × situation approach is to assess leader *behaviors* rather than personality or leadership traits. The behavioral approach has two schools of thought:

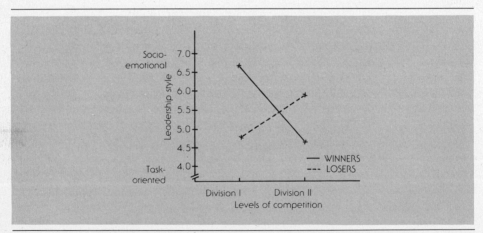

FIGURE 12-1   Leadership in relation to team success and level of competition.
From Bird, A.M. (1977). Leadership and cohesion within successful and unsuccessful teams: Perceptions of coaches and players. In D.M. Landers & R.W. Christina (Eds.), *Psychology of motor behavior and sport.* Champaign, IL: Human Kinetics.

those who believe that *universal* leader behaviors can be identified and those who argue that *situationally specific* leader behaviors should be of primary interest.

Behavioral Approaches

Whether one takes the position that universal behaviors or situation-specific behaviors that characterize successful leaders can be identified, both are optimistic schools of thought. As opposed to the "great man" theory of leadership or Fiedler's personality trait approach, the behavioral approach argues that effective leadership skills can be learned, that it is nurture, not nature, that makes a great leader. If effective leadership skills can be taught, then which is better: to identify a set of universal leadership behaviors that can be effective across multiple situations, or to attempt to identify behaviors that are highly effective in a selected situation?

Universal-Behavioral Approaches

The impetus underlying the popularity of the universal-behavioral approaches came from work that was carried out at about the same time at both Ohio State University and the University of Michigan. Perhaps the most significant product of this work was the development of the Leader Behavior Description Questionnaire (LBDQ). The LBDQ yields two separate leadership scores: initiating structure and consideration.

Initiating structure pertains to the leader's behaviors when attempting to organize and define the relationship between himself or herself and the subordinates. It assesses the leader's behaviors when developing working procedures, opening channels of communication, and determining organizational patterns. The higher the score, the more effective the leader is in performing those tasks. *Consideration* is related to the behaviors that the leader uses when attempting to establish friendships, mutual trust, respect, and warmth between the leader and the subordinates. An example of how these two leadership behaviors have been applied to sport is provided by the Bird (1977b) investigation.

Using the LBDQ, Bird measured how both Division 1 and Division 2 collegiate volleyball players perceived their coaches' leadership style in terms of the two factors of initiating structure and consideration. Using win-loss ratio as the criterion for success, it was shown that the winning players, regardless of division, rated their coaches as being high in initiating structure. Also of interest was the finding that level of competition (skill level) tended to interact with degree of leader behavior–consideration that was perceived. Notice in Figure 12-2 that winners in Division 1 (high skill level) rated their coaches as also being high in consideration, whereas the Division 2 (lower skill level) athletes rated their coaches relatively lower. Now observe that the opposite patterns emerged for the losing volleyball players. It is also interesting to note the similarity between Figures 12-1 and 12-2. Both studies of leadership and success in volleyball (Bird, 1977a; Bird, 1977b) tend to support the notion that effective coaching style or behavior might be situation specific.

Two assessment instruments have been developed specifically to measure coaching behaviors. Danielson, Zelhart, and Drake (1975) developed the Coach Behavior Description Questionnaire (CBDQ) on the basis of the LBDQ. As can be seen in Table 12-1, they were able to identify eight behaviors that were typical of hockey coaches. More recently, also using the LBDQ as a basis, Chelladurai and Saleh (1980) developed the

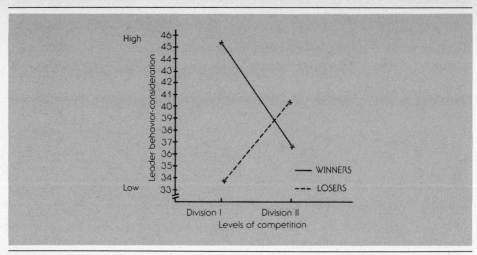

FIGURE 12-2   Team success X level of competition for leader behavior-consideration.
From Bird, A.M. (1977). Development of a model for predicting team performance. *Research Quarterly, 48*, 24-32.

TABLE 12-1   Multidimensional Scaling of Commonly Perceived Coaching Behaviors

Dimension Name	Behavior Descriptions
1 Competitive Training	Behavior concerned with motivation of athletes to train harder and better
	Emphasis on winning via better training and performance
	Little emphasis on behaviors involving coach-athlete relationship and individual and group participation in decision making
2 Initiation	Behaviors involving an open approach to problem solving using new methods
	Little emphasis on organization in the form of equipment provision
	Little emphasis on criticism of performance
3 Interpersonal team operation	Coordination of team members in an attempt to facilitate co-operation at possible expense of protocol
	Behaviors concerned with getting members to interact so that the team functions efficiently
	Little emphasis on criticism of performance
4 Social	Socially oriented behavior outside the athletic situation
	Little emphasis on consistency of performance, organization, or team morale
5 Representation	Behaviors concerned with representing the team favorably in contacts with outsiders
6 Organized communication	Behaviors concerned with either organization or communication with no concern for interpersonal support
	Little emphasis on either criticism or reward
7 Recognition	Behaviors concerned with feedback and reinforcement of both performance and team participation in decision making
	Little emphasis on winning, socialization, or team interaction
8 General excitement	Arousing behaviors involving disorganized approach to team operation
	Little emphasis on recognition or team integration

From Danielson, R.R., Zelhart, P.F., & Drake, C.J. (1975). Multidimensional scaling and factor analysis of coaching behavior as perceived by high school hockey players. *Research Quarterly, 46*, 323-334.

TABLE 12-2　Chelladurai and Saleh's (1978) Leader Behavior Dimensions in Sport

Dimension	Behavior Descriptions
Training behavior	Behavior designed to improve the performance of athletes by technical instruction and in team sports to coordinate the activities of the team members
Democratic behavior	Behavior with participation by the athletes in decision making relative to the establishment of group goals and methods of achieving those goals
Autocratic behavior	Reflects the extent to which the coach separates himself or herself from the athletes and stresses his or her own authority
Social support behavior	Pertains to how much the coach is involved in the satisfaction of the interpersonal needs of the athletes
Positive feedback	Extent to which the coach expresses appreciation to athletes and compliments them on their performance and contribution

Adapted from Chelladurai, P. & Saleh, S.D. (1980). Dimensions of leader behavior in sports: Development of a leadership scale. *Journal of Sport Psychology, 2,* 34-45.

Leadership Scale for Sports (LSS). They identified five typical coaching behaviors. The names of those scales and their associated coaching behaviors are contained in Table 12-2. Notice that at first glance the items identified by Chelladurai and Saleh do not appear to parallel those obtained by Danielson & others. However, on closer inspection Danielson & others' dimensions of competitive training, social behavior, and recognition are quite similar to Chelladurai and Saleh's factors of training behavior, social support, and rewarding behaviors. The two additional factors identified by Chelladurai and Saleh appear to be related more to the coach's decision style in terms of both self and athletes. As discussed in earlier chapters, the development of sport- or coach-specific measures should facilitate greater understanding of effective coaching behaviors.

Situational-Behavioral Approaches

The fundamental tenet of Hersey and Blanchard's (1979, 1982) situational leadership theory is that the leader's (coach's) behavior must change as a function of the *maturity* of the group participants. According to Hersey and Blanchard, maturity is defined as "the capacity to set high but attainable goals (achievement motivation), willingness and ability to take responsibility, and education and/or experience of an individual group" (p. 161). Case (1984) suggests that the leader use a 4-point scale to classify the maturity level of the team as follows: low, low to moderate, moderate to high, and high. Once so-classified, then Hersey and Blanchard suggest that the degree to which either task behavior or relationship behavior is emphasized should vary according to the maturity level of the team members. Their scheme is depicted in Table 12-3, which shows that as maturity of the followers increases, leaders should systematically decrease task-oriented responses and increase relationship-oriented responses. Subsequently, as skill level reaches even higher levels, they suggest that both task-oriented and relationship-oriented behaviors be decreased.

It should seem readily apparent that the notion of maturity should exist in sport and other physical activities. In paraphrasing Hersey and Blanchard, Chelladurai and Carron (1983) write:

TABLE 12-3 Hersey and Blanchard's Classification of Maturity Level and Leadership Behavior

Maturity Level	Leadership Style	Task vs. Relationship Behavior
1 Low	Telling	High Task-Low Relationship
2 Low to Moderate	Selling	High Task-High Relationship
3 Moderate to High	Participating	Low Task-High Relationship
4 High	Delegating	Low Task-Low Relationship

Based on data from Hersey, P., & Blanchard, K. (1982). *Management of organizational behavior: Utilizing human resources*. Englewood Cliffs, NJ: Prentice-Hall.

Athletic maturity can be viewed as the relative mastery of skill and knowledge in sport, the development of attitudes appropriate to sport, and experience and the capacity to set high but attainable goals. Because opportunities for participation in sport reflect a pyramid profile with advancing age and since the exclusive and selective nature of sport insures that only those athletes with the requisite abilities, knowledge, attitudes, and experience advance to each successive level in that pyramid, it can be assumed that athletic maturity increases as the athlete progresses through the competitive levels of elementary, high school, university, and professional sport. (p. 372)

The change in leadership style as a function of athletic maturity is highlighted by Hersey and Blanchard's use of the terms *telling, selling, participating,* and *delegating* (see Table 12-3). When athletic maturity is low, task orientation is facilitated by telling players exactly what is expected or required. As maturity increases, a selling strategy can enhance both task motivation and coach-athlete relationships. When performers have reached rather high skill levels, the coach should adopt a participating role wherein emotional support and encouragement are provided to athletes and they begin contributing more to team goals and organization. In professional sports, or in other instances of extremely high skill levels such as the Olympics, Hersey and Blanchard suggest that the primary coaching strategy should be to wisely delegate authority and responsibility to individual athletes.

If the concept of athletic maturity and variations in effective leadership style does exist in sport settings, then we should see systematic differences exhibited by successful coaches at different levels of skill. More specifically, at the lowest level of skill, primary emphasis would be placed on task-oriented behaviors. There should then be a switch to relationship-oriented behaviors at moderate levels of skill. Finally, with the attainment of high degrees of skill, there should be a withdrawal of both task-oriented and relationship-oriented behaviors because when a team has reached its highest degree of maturity, the team members should be self-directive and should no longer need the emotional support of the coach.

Using two scales from the LSS (Chelladurai & Saleh, 1980), Chelladurai and Carron (1983) attempted to determine the validity of the predictions of situational leadership theory in sport settings. The scales used were training and instruction behavior and social support behavior. Training and instruction behavior was thought to be analogous to the task behavior dimension of Hersey and Blanchard's (1982) theory, whereas social support behavior was presumed to be analogous to relationship behavior. They tested 262 male

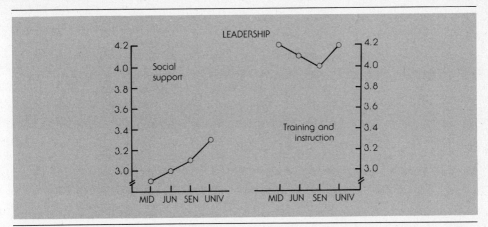

FIGURE 12-3 Social support and training and instruction behavior of high midget (MID), high school junior (JUN), high school senior (SEN), and intercollegiate (UNIV) basketball players.
From Chelladurai, P. & Carron, A.V. (1983). Athletic maturity and preferred leadership. *Journal of Sport Psychology, 5,* 371-380.

basketball players at four ages and skill levels: high-school midget division, high-school junior division, high-school senior division, and university intercollegiate division. The LSS that was completed was a form that assessed *preferred leadership,* not actual leadership, of coaches.

The results are depicted graphically in Figure 12-3. One readily noticable trend indicated that the desire for social support behavior progressively increased with levels of competition. Regarding preferences in training and instruction, the findings showed a distinct decrease in preference for such coaching behaviors from the midget to the high-school senior level, with a sharp increase in preference at the university level. The results of the Chelladurai and Carron investigation did not coincide with the predictions of situational leadership theory.

In discussing the reasons why no support was shown, the authors identified some possible explanations and questions. One area of concern was the limited age range used in their study. Subjects in their study ranged in age from 14 to 20 years of age. Yet as the authors point out, the

> full spectrum for the development of athletic maturity extends from approximately 8 to 10 years to approximately 35 years, a span of 25 to 27 years. Therefore, the Hersey and Blanchard model can only be adequately tested if athletes representing the entire spectrum are included in the sample of subjects. (p. 378)

The second question Chelladurai and Carron raise is the applicability of situational leadership theory to sport situations. They argue that traditional sport practices that publicly claim to enhance self-discipline may hinder the development of athletic maturity through its traditional emphasis on autocratic behaviors. Sage's (1978) quote from All-Pro football player George Sauer illustrates their argument nicely:

It's interesting to go back and listen to the people on the high school level talk about sport programs and how they develop a kid's self-discipline and responsibility. I think the giveaway, that most of this stuff being preached on the lower levels is a lie, is when you get to college and professional levels, the coaches still treat you as an adolescent. They know damn well that you were never given a chance to become responsible or self-disciplined. Even in the pros you are told when to go to bed, when to turn your lights off, when to wake up, when to eat, and what to eat. (p. 158)

At the current time it is not clear whether or not Hersey and Blanchard's theory of situational leadership has any application in sport settings. What first must be determined is whether maturity, as defined by those theorists, actually does change as a function of skill development and experience. Also, as Chelladurai and Carron (1983) point out, future research must include a sample that is representative of the entire age spectrum, teams that are both successful and unsuccessful, coaches who are both successful and unsuccessful, and measures that are sport-specific.

Although the Chelladurai and Carron findings did not support the fundamental predictions associated with situational leadership theory, their findings show once again that situational factors such as age and experience (skill level) do appear to be related to effective coaching behaviors.

Type of sport. Chelladurai (1984) was interested in ascertaining how preferred leadership style might be related to player satisfaction within athletic teams that differ in degree of player dependence and task variability. Wrestling and track and field were classified as being independent tasks, whereas basketball was categorized as a dependent task. Both basketball and wrestling are classified as variable, or open, sports, but track and field is considered to be a nonvariable, or closed, sport. Although Chelladurai assessed all of the five scales of the LSS, we will discuss only his findings relative to the two scales most closely associated with relationship- versus task-oriented behavior: the training and instruction (task oriented) and the social support (relationship) scales.

Chelladurai found that in all three sports athletes expressed the most satisfaction when the coaches' primary emphasis was on training and instruction. On the other hand, although performers in both basketball and wrestling preferred high degrees of social support, this behavior was not seen to be as important in track and field. This discrepancy may be a result of the open nature of basketball and wrestling versus the closed nature of track and field. Particularly in team sports such as basketball, perhaps the social support of the coach increases the *identifiability* of each athlete's contributions (see Chapter 11). Such support is not necessary in sports such as track and field because the outcome of each person's efforts are clearly evident. These findings provide some insights into how effective coaching behavior might vary according to the nature of the sport (that is, open versus closed).

Degree of stress. According to Korten (1962), there appears to be a linear relationship between degree of stress and player receptivity to an autocratic, or task-oriented, leadership style. More specifically, as stress increases, receptivity to a task-oriented leadership style also increases. On the other hand, with low degrees of group stress it is proposed that athletes would be more receptive to a democratic, or socio-emotional, orientation by the coach.

Korten's (1962) analysis of stress and leadership is associated closely with Fiedler's

(1967) contingency theory of leadership. Recall that Fiedler proposed that task-oriented leaders should perform best under conditions of either situation favorableness or unfavorableness. In terms of stress, it can be argued that if the source of stress is external to the group, then the group members will tend to become more cohesive. High degrees of cohesiveness are thought to reflect good leader-member relationships. Thus external stress should result in a favorable situation for the coach. Under favorable conditions a task-oriented coaching style would be predicted to be best.

Now, suppose the source of stress was internal to the group. Perhaps there are conflicts or rivalries among various players. This would result in dissention and an unfavorable situation for the coach. From Fiedler's perspective, under such unfavorable conditions the most effective leader would again be the one who exhibits a task orientation.

It is clear from this discussion that when high degrees of stress are present, regardless of the source, a task-oriented leadership style should be most effective. However, when little or no stress is present, a democratic, or socio-emotional, style should most facilitate player performance.

It is important to emphasize that under conditions of high stress, a task-oriented leadership style should be one that focuses player attention on the goals at hand, *not* one that is punitive. The idea is to help players attend to important sport-related cues and not the factors that are causing the stress.

In summary, what the literature on stress and leadership seems to indicate about leadership behaviors is that coaching behaviors need to change as a function of the degree of stress present; that is, coaches need to learn how to role-play, or switch their orientation according to the degree of stress affecting the group. Amounts of external group stress can be inferred on the basis of factors such as unfavorable media comments or spectator misbehavior at games. Coaches can gain valuable insights into potential internal stress through the use of a sociogram or a sociomatrix (see Chapter 11). Both devices can provide information about possible cliques, team isolates, or inter-player preferences. Another approach would be the measurement of team cohesion (Martens, Landers, & Loy, 1974; Yukelson, Weinberg, & Jackson, 1984).

Group size. It appears that group size should have some relationship to the most effective style of leadership. In large sport groups such as football, players will be more receptive to a more task-oriented, or autocratic, style of coaching. It seems reasonable that a more directive style of coaching is necessary when the group size is large; there are more activities to coordinate, more people with whom a coach must deal, and more areas for potential problems.

Although a task-oriented coaching style would seem to be more effective when dealing with large groups, recall from the discussion of social loafing in Chapter 11 that it is also extremely important that each participant feel that he or she has some visibility or identifiability as an individual. Therefore it is imperative that the coach take some time with each athlete to provide individual attention and socio-emotional support. Under this pattern of coaching flexibility, the coach would assume a task orientation to the group and a consideration orientation with individual players. In addition, in large groups a primary role of assistant coaches should be to provide emotional support to players. A task-oriented head coach who is supported by one or more socio-emotionally oriented assistant coaches may provide the best combination of leadership styles.

INTERPERSONAL COMPATABILITY

When coaches and athletes enter the sport situation they do so with both their personal needs and their unique perceptions of reality. This situation raises several important issues. How do differing coach-athlete needs affect compatability and social interactions? Do coaches perceive themselves in the same way that athletes see them? Is it possible to change or modify coaches' behaviors?

Coach-Athlete Compatability

The most frequently used framework within which coach-athlete interpersonal relationships have been studied is Schutz's (1966) **theory of interpersonal compatability.** From this perspective, it is proposed that people have three basic interpersonal needs to be satisfied in a social relationship: control, inclusion, and affection.

Control refers to the relative need to dominate, or to exert influence over others. *Inclusion* pertains to the need to associate, to interact, and to establish a set of mutual interests with others. *Affection* refers to the need to develop close emotional ties with others and to develop affectionate and loving relationships. It is important to note that these needs represent a "two-way street"; that is, they represent both the behavior that an individual demonstrates to others and the behavior that the person wants to receive from others.

Based on the framework presented above, a compatible relationship would be one in which the needs of two persons are both being met. An incompatable relationship would exist when the needs of two persons are not complementary and are therefore not being met. Founded on that idea, a few researchers have attempted to study coach-athlete compatibility.

In the initial investigation, Carron and Bennett (1977) contrasted compatible versus incompatible coach-athlete dyads. They hypothesized that the dimensions of control and affection would be best able to discriminate between the compatible and incompatible dyads.

The way they selected their subjects is of particular interest. University coaches were asked to identify those athletes who were perceived to be most coachable and least disruptive—most removed from being "problem" athletes. The coaches were then asked to identify athletes who were at the opposite end of that spectrum. They used the Fundamental Interpersonal Relations Orientation-Behavior (FIRO-B) (Schutz, 1966) to assess two aspects of behavior (behavior a person expresses and behavior a person wants others to express) and three interpersonal needs (control, inclusion, and affection).

In support of their hypothesis, Carron and Bennett (1977) found control and affection to be of some importance in differentiating between compatible and incompatible dyads. However, the most crucial interpersonal need in terms of discriminating between compatible and incompatible dyads was found to be inclusion. Their findings on inclusion indicated that "the relationship within the incompatible dyads was characterized by relatively detached, withdrawn, isolated behavior on the part of both the coach and athlete" (p. 677). In other words, when a player has the same inadequacies or problems as the coach (low inclusion behaviors), then it is highly likely that the coach will have some difficulty in relating to that athlete. What will most likely result is a perception on the coach's part that the athlete is a "problem" athlete and a perception on the athlete's part that the coach is cold and distant. Perhaps if both coaches and athletes became more aware of these incompatible need structures, both would be more receptive to behavior changes. Such awareness might then reduce the probability of coach-player incompatibility and conflict.

In a later study, Carron and Chelladurai (1978) wanted to ascertain if any differences existed between the perceptions of athletes versus coaches regarding the enactment of the need-related behaviors associated with inclusion, control, and affection. On the control dimension both coaches and athletes agreed; coaches should exhibit control behavior and athletes should be the recipients of those behaviors. In terms of affection, both coaches and athletes thought that they should be the receivers, not the givers, of affection. A similar pattern emerged for the inclusion dimension. Both coaches and athletes perceived they would be the unlikely instigator of inclusion-related behaviors. These data argue that the perceptions held by both coaches and athletes could form the basis of potentially incompatible interpersonal relationships.

Team Climate and Player Satisfaction

Another variable intimately related to coach-athlete interactions is team climate. Fisher, Mancini, Hirsch, Proulx, and Staurowsky (1982) define team climate on the basis of "the quantity, quality, and sequence of the interactions that occur among all team members (athletes and coaches included)" (p. 388). Feeling that the coach, as the team leader, would exert a definite influence on team climate, those investigators designed a study to look at the relationship between coach-athlete interactions and players' perceived satisfaction.

Subjects were male varsity high school basketball players and their coaches. All subjects completed a social climate scale, and practice sessions were videotaped for later analysis of coach-athlete interactions.

Several important findings emerged from the analysis. Members of satisfied basketball teams tended to initiate more interactions with their coaches, whereas members of less-satisfied teams generally had their responses elicited by the coach. Coaching suggestions were more frequently offered during active play on satisfied teams. On less-satisfied teams the coaching suggestions tended to interrupt the flow of action, and those interruptions were generally followed by structured drills. Therefore members of more-satisfied teams seemed to be more active within the learning process, whereas members of less-satisfied teams assumed a more passive, rote style of learning.

Furthermore, although members of both types of teams received a great deal of information feedback from their coaches, in less-satisfied environments coaches gave 70% more information to the athletes. As we have discussed repeatedly throughout this text, such an excessive amount of feedback may cause information overload that disrupts athlete performance. When too much information is provided, the athlete does not know what is important and what is not and therefore may attend to irrelevant rather than relevant cues. Such information overload can also heighten anxiety by generating feelings of inadequacy. When anxiety increases past an optimal point it is highly probable that an ability to process task-related cues will be hindered. Thus we see a vicious circle of information overload, increased anxiety, and decreased ability to process important cues.

The situation described above could become even worse. Fisher & others, also found that coaches on more-satisfied teams also tended to be more accepting of the athletes and generally praised them more often. In contrast, coaches of less-satisfied teams were more directive and critical, which can increase player anxiety and decrease player satisfaction.

Satisfied players also saw practice time as more interesting and innovative as compared with their less-satisfied counterparts. Satisfied athletes were not bored by practice; instead it appeared that they perceived those times as meaningful and interesting.

It was also found that coaches and players differed in their perception of current and ideal team climates. Coaches perceived both to be the same, whereas athletes saw the need for change. Coaches also tended to see team climate in a favorable light, whereas athletes perceived it to be less favorable. Other studies have also shown similar discrepancies between the perceptions of coaches and athletes.

Coach-Athlete Perceptions of Coaching Behavior

Bird (1977a) found that collegiate volleyball players generally viewed their coaches as more socio-emotional, although the coaches saw themselves as being more task-oriented. This discrepancy between the perceptions of athletes and coaches was also found by Percival (1971). In that investigation, both coaches and athletes were asked to rate coaches on several factors such as personality, methods, knowledge, and mechanics. Using a 1 to 10 scale, the coaches rated themselves higher than did the athletes.

These studies indicate that coaches may be positively biased in favor of themselves and that they may not be perceiving reality correctly. What can be done to alter this situation? The most effective strategy for change appears to be a program designed to objectively feed back to the coach information about the exact patterns of interaction that are occurring between the coach and players.

Changing Coaching Behavior

Currently, the best example of a program designed to improve coachs' perception of coach-player interaction is the Coaching Behavior Assessment System (CBAS) designed by Smith, Smoll, and Hunt (1977). It was designed to allow systematic observation and coding of coaching behaviors in the setting in which they occur, whether in the field or the gymnasium. It deals with two classes of behaviors: reactive behaviors and spontaneous behaviors. *Reactive* behaviors occur as a response to a preceding player or team response. *Spontaneous* behaviors are instigated by the coach but not on the basis of an immediately preceding event. Reactive behaviors can occur in response to a desirable performance, a mistake, or a misbehavior on the part of the athlete. Spontaneous behaviors are subdivided into two categories: game-related and game-irrelevant behaviors emitted by the coach. Thus the CBAS emphasizes the interaction between a player's response and a coach's reaction to that response. To more fully understand the coach's responses, it is necessary to examine how Smith and his colleagues (Smith, Smoll, & Hunt, 1977; Smith, Smoll, & Curtis, 1978) have defined each of the responses. Table 12-4 presents each of the 12 behavioral categories and their descriptions.

TABLE 12-4 Behavioral Categories of the CBAS

Behaviors	Descriptions
Reactive	
1 Positive reinforcement or reward (R)	A positive reaction by the coach to a desirable response by one or more players. R may be verbal or nonverbal.
2 Nonreinforcement (NR)	A failure to reinforce a positive behavior; in essence the coach simply fails to respond.
3 Mistake-contingent encouragement (EM)	Encouragement of a player by a coach following a player's mistake.
4 Mistake-contingent technical instruction (TIM)	Telling or showing a player who has made a mistake how to make the play correctly. TIM requires that the coach instruct the player in some specific way.
5 Punishment (P)	A negative response by the coach following an undesirable behavior. Similar to R, P may be either verbal or nonverbal.
6 Punitive TIM (TIM + P)	Is used when TIM and P occur at the same time.
7 Ignoring mistakes (IM)	A lack of response, either positive or negative, to a mistake on the part of a player or a team.
8 Keeping control (KC)	Responses that are designed to maintain order.
Spontaneous	
9 General technical instruction (TIG)	Communication providing instruction relevant to techniques and strategies of the sport in question.
10 General encouragement (EG)	Encouragement that does not immediately follow a mistake.
11 Organization (O)	Behavior directed at administrative organization, such as reminding the players of the batting order.
12 General communication (GC)	Interactions with players that are unrelated to the game situation or a team activity.

Adapted from Smith, R.E., Smoll, F.L., & Hunt, E., (1977). A system for the behavioral assessment of athletic coaches. *Research Quarterly, 48*, 401-407.

In a later study, Smith, Smoll, and Curtis (1979) designed an investigation to test the effectiveness of a preseason training program for little league coaches. Their major purpose was to see if they could help coaches to relate more effectively with the performers through the use of an intervention program that was conceptualized on the basis of a cognitive-behavioral framework. As Smith & others write:

> The techniques chosen were designed to make coaches more aware of their behaviors, to create expectancies concerning the likely consequences of various coaching behaviors, to increase their desire to generate certain consequences rather than others, and to develop or enhance their ability to perform desirable behaviors effectively. It was expected that cognitive changes of this nature would promote and mediate positive changes in overt coaching behaviors. (pp. 60-61)

For the coaches in the experimental group, the training session lasted approximately 2 hours. A review of past research was presented, and the behavioral guidelines to be used were provided both verbally and in written handouts. The guidelines emphasized "the desirability of reinforcement, encouragement, and technical instruction designed to elicit and strengthen desirable behaviors" (p. 62). More explicit goals were to facilitate positive interactions between athletes and coaches as well as among teammates and to decrease any player fears concerning failure. The box below presents some excerpts from the written handout given to the coaches in the experimental group. During the training session, experimenters modeled both good and bad methods of responding to player behavior. In addition, behavioral feedback and self-monitoring strategies were used in the hopes of increasing self-awareness and fostering compliance with the coaching guidelines.

During the first 2 weeks of the season, coaches were observed and their behaviors were coded on the basis of the CBAS. Based on those observations, profiles were mailed

---

Excerpts from the Behavioral Guidelines of the CBAS

REACTIONS TO PLAYER BEHAVIORS AND GAME SITUATIONS

1 Good plays

Do: REWARD!! Do so immediately. Let the players know that you appreciate and value their efforts. Reward *effort* as much as you do results.

Don't: Take their efforts for granted

2 Mistakes, screw-ups, boneheaded plays, and all the things the Cincinnati Reds seldom do

Do: ENCOURAGE immediately after mistakes. That's when the kid needs the encouragement most. Also, give corrective INSTRUCTIONS on how to do it right, but *always* do so in an encouraging manner.

Don't: PUNISH when things are going wrong. Punishment isn't just yelling at kids; it can be any indication of disapproval, tone of voice, or action.

3 Misbehaviors, lack of attention

Do: Maintain order by establishing clear expectations. Emphasize that during a game all members of the team are part of the game, even those on the bench. Use REWARD to strengthen team participation.

Don't: Get into the position of having to constantly nag or threaten the kids in order to prevent chaos. Don't be a drill sergeant. The idea here is that if you establish clear behavioral guidelines early and work to build team spirit in achieving them, you can avoid having to repeatedly KEEP CONTROL.

GETTING POSITIVE THINGS TO HAPPEN

Do: Give INSTRUCTION. Establish your role as a teacher. Try to structure participation as a learning experience in which you're going to help the kids develop their abilities. Always give INSTRUCTION in a positive fashion.

Do: Give ENCOURAGEMENT. Encourage effort, don't demand results. Use it selectively so that it is meaningful.

Do: Concentrate on the game. Be "in" the game with the players. Set a good example for team unity (remember the powerful effects that modeling can have on behavior).

Don't: Give either INSTRUCTION or ENCOURAGEMENT in a sarcastic or degrading manner. Make a point, then leave it. Don't let "encouragement" become irritating to the players.

Adapted from Smith, R.E., Smoll, F.L., & Curtis, B. (1979). Coach effectiveness training: A cognitive-behavioral approach to enhancing relationship skills in youth sport coaches. *Journal of Sport Psychology, 1,* 59-75.

to each of the participating coaches. In addition, coaches did postgame self-monitoring after each of the first 10 games of the season. This was a quick estimate of the amount of time the coaches perceived that they were engaging in the recommended behaviors during the game.

The findings of the study indicated that a training program can have a positive influence on coaching behaviors. Although there was no significant difference between the number of games won or lost by the trained versus the untrained coaches, the players under a trained coach evaluated both the coach and the team climate more favorably. Of the observed behaviors exhibited by the two groups of coaches, the only significant difference was in the frequency with which positive reinforcement was provided.

Trained coaches were perceived by their players as more reinforcing, more encouraging, more technically instructive, and less punitive. Of perhaps even more significance was the finding that children with low self-esteem showed the largest difference in terms of positive attitudes toward trained versus untrained coaches. They also perceived the largest difference between trained and untrained coaches along the behavioral dimensions of mistake-contingent encouragement, punishment, and general technical instruction. This suggests that children with low self-esteem may be particularly sensitive to variations in such behaviors (Smith & others, 1979). It was also shown that children who played for trained coaches exhibited marked increases in postseason self-esteem.

Regardless of any observable effects on team outcome in terms of winning and losing, the training program designed by Smith and others (1979) provides clear evidence that such behavior change approaches can enhance the quality of the athletic experience of the participants. This is particularly true for children who are low in self-esteem because these are the children most likely to suffer adverse psychological consequences in competitive sport situations such as little league baseball. Therefore one of the greatest contributions the field of sport psychology can make is to train coaches to become more aware of how their behaviors can affect the cognitions and affect of their players. The future is promising. The tools and knowledge are available. Let's go for it!

IMPLICATIONS FOR SPORT

- When athletes are young and poorly skilled, the coach should be directive and task oriented (although never punitive). However, as athletes mature they should be given more autonomy in decision-making. At the same time the coach can become more supportive and relationship oriented.
- It appears that in closed sports (such as track and field, gymnastics, and diving) a coaching style that emphasizes training and instruction is most effective. For open sports (such as basketball and wrestling), coaching behaviors that reflect aspects of both training and instruction with accompanying social support result in improved player satisfaction.
- When either internal or external stress appears to be affecting your team negatively, increase your task orientation. Redirect player attention to the sport goals.
- Do not overload players with too much information. Use the principles of selective attention so that a few task-related goals are emphasized. This strategy can also reduce player anxiety.

- If you are a coach of a large team, particularly an interactive sport team, practice coaching flexibility. Be task-oriented with the team but be sure to provide social support to each player. Make sure that individual efforts and contributions are recognized and reinforced.
- Because inclusion appears to be highly related to the amount of compatibility between coaches and athletes, use inclusion-enhancing strategies. Try to interact with the athletes; discuss mutual interests and goals. These inclusion behaviors may be most important with athletes whom you consider to be real or potential problem athletes. In the case of problem athletes, if you are too uncomfortable to make such gestures, see if you can delegate that responsibility to an assistant.
- Try to make practices interesting and innovative. This will improve player motivation and satisfaction. Avoid consistently repeating the same structured drills.
- Reward *both* effort and outcome. Be positive rather than critical or sarcastic in your interactions with players.
- Coaches may not perceive their own attitudes or behaviors accurately. As a coach, try to find out how others perceive your behavior. Try to be objective and flexible. Use coaching evaluation techniques in which the player's know that their responses will remain anonymous. Observe your own behaviors on film or videotape. Try using the factors contained within the CBAS. You may be surprised at the results.
- Know thyself. If your coaching style is primarily task-oriented and if you find being flexible difficult, select assistants who have complementary rather than identical coaching styles.

CASE STUDY 1

Situational Leadership Theory and Coaching Style

Recall that Hersey and Blanchard's (1979, 1982) situational leadership theory proposed that leadership style should be adjusted according to the maturity level of the athlete(s). Maturity level can be classified as (1) low, (2) low to moderate, (3) moderate to high, and (4) high. Each maturity level is then proposed to work best with a particular coaching orientation: (1) telling, (2) selling, (3) participating, or (4) delegating. *Telling* involves a high task orientation and a low relationship orientation style. *Selling* involves both a high task and a high relationship orientation. *Participating* involves a low task and a high relationship orientation, and *delegating* involves both a low task and a low relationship orientation. Below are descriptions of two different sport teams and suggestions for how each might be coached on the basis of situational leadership theory.

Team 1: Youth Swim Team

You have just agreed to be the head coach of a newly-formed youth swim team. Although all members can swim, none has any competitive experience. You would have to rate their maturity level as low because they will probably not be able to set high but attainable goals. They also may be neither willing nor able to assume much responsibility. Situational leadership theory would say that the most effective coaching style in this instance should be *telling;* thus your coaching responses should be primarily task directed. You need to establish both team and individual goals and use positive reinforcement primarily for successful, goal-related responses. They will also need large amounts of mistake-contingent technical instruction and mistake-contingent encouragement.

Team 2: Collegiate Varsity Volleyball Team

This team consists of a full roster of well-experienced, highly skilled players. In fact, many of the players have attended Olympic training camps in addition to previous collegiate competition. Their maturity level would have to be rated as at least a 3. Therefore situational leadership theory would say that the appropriate coaching style should be *participating*. This style requires that the coach's primary emphasis be placed on relationships, or providing large amounts of socio-emotional support. Because the players have the skills already, task-orientation need not be overly emphasized. Make sure that you give individual encouragement and support. Convey the message clearly that you recognize and appreciate each person's contribution to the team.

CASE STUDY 2
Contingency Theory and Coaching Style

Fiedler's (1967) contingency theory proposes that there are two types of leaders: those who are task oriented and those who are socio-emotional in orientation. The effectiveness of each type of leader is said to be a function of the favorability of the situation. Situational favorabless is proposed to be mediated by three subfactors: leader-member relationships (cohesion), task structure (goal clarity), and position power (control over reinforcements). Task-oriented leaders are then predicted to be more effective under either highly favorable or highly unfavorable conditions, whereas socio-emotional leaders should do best under moderate levels of favorableness. Read each of the coaching situations described below and then see if you agree with our selection of an appropriate coach.

Team 1: Bobby Socks Softball—Bay City

In Bay City the parents really take a strong interest in Bobby Socks softball. Most of them attend all of the games; you can hear them yelling and screaming from the stands. They are not shy about making pointed suggestions to either the coach or to the players who are at bat or on the field. Because of parental pressure, many of the players argue among themselves and have often been known to criticize the coach. The social climate in Bay City has resulted in an unfavorable situation for the coach, who has lost some position power. Leader-member relationships are poor. What this team needs is a task-oriented coach. Otherwise, team success will have to wait for another world!

Team 2: Bobby Socks Softball—Falcon Crest

It's the preseason parents' meeting for the Bobby Socks softball team called the Winettes. Everyone is anxious to have the best season ever. The parents have identified several goals for the season: (1) to improve the season standing over last year, (2) to attempt to enhance team cohesion and player-coach compatibility, and (3) to give the new coach complete authority over the running of the team. At the end of the meeting a new, task-oriented coach is selected. They then raise glasses to toast their wisdom. Do you agree with their selection? We do, as the new coach will have an extremely favorable situation within which to work.

SUMMARY

- Leadership has been studied within several theoretical frameworks. The earliest was a trait approach called the "great man" theory of leadership. This position sought to find a constellation of superior personality traits that would differentiate between highly effective and less effective leaders. One major weakness of that approach was a failure to take the specific situation into account.

- In an attempt to remediate that problem, Fiedler proposed contingency theory, which falls within the trait × situation framework. This theory proposes that effective leadership is a function of both personality characteristics and identifiable characteristics of the situation. The two personality dimensions of most interest are task-oriented and socio-emotional leadership styles. The second factor in Fiedler's theory concerned the favorableness of the situation in regard to allowing the leader to exhibit power or control. Contingency theory predicts that task-oriented leaders will be most effective in either very favorable or very unfavorable situations, whereas socio-emotional leaders should perform best under conditions of moderate favorableness. The research that has been conducted within sport settings is inconclusive relative to this theory.

- Another approach to the study of leadership has been theories that concentrate on behaviors rather than personality characteristics. Such behavioral approaches can be classified as being either universal or situational. Regardless of how a particular behavioral approach is classified, however, all take the position that leadership skills are learned, not innate.

- The most prominent universal-behavioral approach came out of Ohio State University. This approach uses the Leader Behavior Description Questionnaire (LBDQ) to assess both initiating structure and consideration. Although the available evidence is scanty, it would appear that rather than being stable as would be proposed by measures such as the LBDQ, effective coaching behaviors should be more situationally specific.

- One situationally based behavioral approach is Hersey and Blanchard's situational leadership theory. This position argues that the coach's behavior must change as a function of the degree of maturity of the participants. Fundamentally, this theory proposes that as the maturity of the followers increases, leaders should systematically decrease task-oriented responses and increase relationship-oriented responses. As skill level reaches even higher levels, it is suggested that both task-oriented and relationship-oriented coaching behaviors be decreased. In other words, at very high levels of skill the coach can delegate most of the authority to the players. In testing the predictions of situational leadership theory, Chelladurai and Carron (1983) found little encouragement for the support for this theory in a sport setting. However, in looking at the situational specificity of coaching sport groups, some mediating factors may play important roles: type of sport (that is, open versus closed), degree of stress, and group size.

- Two important points appear to stand out regarding coaching behavior and sport groups. First, whatever the label used, the two dimensions of task-orientation and socio-emotional support appear consistently throughout the literature. Second, from the current status of the literature it would appear that a coaching style that is flexible relative to the demands of the situation will be most effective.

- In terms of coach-athlete compatibility, the most frequently used framework is Schutz's (1966) theory of interpersonal compatibility. This theory proposes that people enter into interpersonal relationships with at least three needs: control, inclusion, and affection. These needs are reflective of both the behavior a person demonstrates to others and the behavior the person desires to receive from others. In assessing these needs within athletics, Carron and Bennett (1977) found that inclusion was the most important need in terms of understanding why some coach-athlete dyads were incompatible. In a later investigation, Carron and Chelladurai (1978) found that both athletes and coaches agreed on who should exhibit control behavior: the coach. However, when it came to affection and inclusion, their perceptions varied. Both coaches and athletes perceived that they should be the receivers of affection, and neither perceived that they would be the likely instigator of inclusion-related behaviors.
- There are several differences between the perceptions of more satisfied versus less satisfied basketball players (Fisher, Mancini, Hirsch, Proulx, & Staurowsky, 1982). For example, satisfied players tended to initiate more interactions with their coach and were actively involved within the learning process. They also saw practice time as being more interesting and innovative.
- Several studies have indicated a disparity between how the coach perceives his or her behavior and how the athletes perceive that coach's behavior. One way to achieve more coherence between perception of reality and actuality may be through the use of coaching training programs such as the Coaching Behavior Assessment System (CBAS). Coaches who completed such training were perceived by their players as being more reinforcing, more encouraging, more technically instructive, and less punitive. It is also important to note that children who had low self-esteem showed the largest positive differences in their perceptions of trained versus untrained coaches. Furthermore, children with low self-esteem showed marked increases in postseason self-esteem after playing for coaches who completed the training program.

DISCUSSION QUESTIONS

1 What appears to be the major flaw of the trait approach to leadership?
2 Identify and discuss the major components of Fiedler's contingency theory of leadership.
3 Taking either the task-oriented or the socio-emotional type of coach, identify both pros and cons of that style and apparent situational influences affecting the desirability of that style.
4 What appears to be some major differences between the perceptions of coaches and athletes?
5 How does team climate seem to be related to player's perceptions of the athletic experience?
6 Identify some possible causes of a coach perceiving a person to be a "problem athlete."
7 What appears to be the major advantages to training programs such as the CBAS?

GLOSSARY

contingency theory Approach to leadership that takes into account aspects of both personality traits and the favorableness of the group situation

great man theory Trait approach to leadership that proposes that all great leaders would possess a superior constellation of personality traits

personality traits Enduring predispositions or tendencies to behave in certain ways; also called individual difference variables because these are the unique psychological characteristics that make one person different from another

situational favorableness Factor within contingency theory that addresses the question of the degree to which the group situation will allow the leader to exhibit power, influence, or control; it takes three factors into account—leader-member relationships, task structure, and position power

socio-emotional orientation Orientation reflected by a leader who is supportive of others, concerned about interrelationships among group members, and not overly concerned about the task

task-oriented Characteristic of a leader who places highest priority on the successful completion of the task

theory of interpersonal compatibility Theory that incorporates the three interpersonal needs of control, inclusion, and affection to explain the relative compatibility within interpersonal relationships

SUGGESTED READINGS

Caccese, T.M., & Mayerberg, C.K. (1984). Gender differences in perceived burnout of college coaches. *Journal of Sport Psychology, 6,* 279-288.

Using the Maslach Burnout Inventory, this study assessed the level of perceived burnout in male and female college coaches. Several gender-related differences emerged, including the perception by female coaches that they had higher levels of emotional exhaustion and significantly lower levels of personal accomplishment as compared with their male counterparts.

Chelladurai, P. (1984). Leadership in sports. In J.M. Silva & R.S. Weinberg (Eds.), *Psychological foundations of sport,* Champaign, IL: Human Kinetics.

This chapter discusses several aspects of leadership in sport, including the interface between motivation and leadership and the relationship between individual differences and preferred leadership. It also proposes a multidimensional model of leadership.

Rees, C.R. (1983). Instrumental and expressive leadership in team sports: A test of leadership role differentiation theory. *Journal of Sport Behavior, 6,* 17-27.

This investigation examined intramural basketball players' preferences for leadership style. In addition to several other aspects of leadership preferences, support was found for leadership role integration as opposed to differentiation.

Rees, C.R., & Segal, M.W. (1984). Role differentiation in groups: The relationship between instrumental and expressive leadership. *Small Group Behavior, 15,* 109-123.

The authors assessed the amount of role differentiation between instrumental and expressive leadership styles of collegiate football teams. In addition to finding some support for relatively high degrees of role integration, implications concerning leadership style and status were discussed.

Richardson, B. (1980). How to ruin an athlete. In R.M. Suinn (Ed.), *Psychology in sports,* Minneapolis, MN: Burgess.

This facetious and amusing article looks at how certain coaching behaviors can be used to effectively and swiftly end an athlete's career. Those behaviors are broken down into three aspects: the workouts, the races, and the social life.

Yukelson, D., Weinberg, R., Richardson, P., & Jackson, A. (1983). Interpersonal attraction and leadership within collegiate sport-teams. *Journal of Sport Behavior, 6,* 28-36.

This investigation examined leadership status and friendship status among members of baseball and soccer teams. Players assessed as being high in leadership status were perceived to be better performers, upperclassmen, and internal in locus of control. Players with lower leadership status displayed the opposite characteristics.

GLOSSARY

achievement motivation   Dominant motivational orientation in situations characterized by the attainment of clear success or failure; the two primary motives are either to achieve success (M_{as}) or to avoid failure (M_{af})

activation   A neuropsychological term that can be used interchangeably with arousal and refers to the intensity of behavior; it is generally measured through central assessments (such as brain activity) or peripheral assessments (for example, heart rate, muscle tension, and respiration)

actual productivity   Measure of a team's achievement in terms of objective measures such as their win-loss ratio

aerobic   Submaximal exercise of a cardiovascular nature, such as jogging or bicycling over long distances

affect   Positive or negative emotional state

agonist muscles   Muscles that perform a specific movement; for example, the biceps are the agonist muscles for arm flexion

androgyny   In terms of personality, the simultaneous possession of the healthiest psychological characteristics usually associated with feminine and masculine personality profiles

antagonist muscles   Muscles that oppose a specific movement if they are not relaxed; for example, the triceps of the upper arm are the antagonist muscles for arm flexion

anonymity   As used here, the feeling that one is unknown

antecedent   An event or set of circumstances that occurs before another event

applied research   Research undertaken for purposes of immediate and practical application

approximation   In sport performance, any skill performance that closely resembles a desired act or goal

arousal   The degree of physiological activation present at a particular time

associative strategy   Strategy that focuses attention on input signals from the body or emotions during performance

attentional mechanism   Process whereby cues are perceived and processed in the brain

attentional style   A person's characteristic manner of attending to the environment

attribution retraining program (achievement change program)   Procedure designed to increase persistence after failure by teaching persons to attribute failure to lack of effort

authority   A person with vast knowledge or experience in a particular field

autogenic training   Techniques involving the use of verbal cues and visual images to achieve a relaxed state

basic research   Research conducted for the purpose of gathering information simply to increase knowledge; it usually has no immediate appplication and may have no future application

bidirectional   As used here, this term refers to a measurement approach that includes two separate components

capacity interference   Cause of performance decreases as a result of attempting to perform two tasks simultaneously when both tasks have high attentional demand

catharsis hypothesis   Proposal that bottled-up emotions can be purged or reduced through aggressive behavior

causal dimensions   Three dimensions (locus of causality, stability, and controllability) along which the causal elements contained within attribution theory are classified

causal elements   Explanations (attributions) that are generally given for a particular outcome; the most common are ability, effort, task difficulty, and luck

causal relationship   A relationship in which one variable can be said to have an identifiable effect on a second variable

centering procedure   Intervention strategy that incorporates both relaxation and breathing techniques to gain attentional control and lower arousal

cocontraction   The simultaneous contraction of two opposing muscle groups

cognitive evaluation theory   Theory that proposes that two variables—perception of personal competence and perception of self-control—underlie degree of intrinsic motivation

cognitive representation   Mental representation or internal template for the production of a response and a standard for making response corrections based on feedback

cognitive restructuring   Process of identifying and changing irrational self-statements

collective aggression   Simultaneous exhibition of violent or hostile behavior by a group of people such as sport fans

competence motivation   Desire to engage in mastery activities for intrinsic rewards such as joy or happiness

competitive ability   Motivational or achievement goal of judging self-skill or ability by making comparisons with others

competing response tendencies   The notion that correct responses compete with incorrect responses

competitive state anxiety   The level of anxiety that a particular sport situation generates in a performer

competitive trait anxiety   The anxiety a performer generally experiences in sport situations

coincident   A relationship in which two events occur at the same time or in which two objects occupy the same position in space at the same time

conclusion   A summary statement or judgment based on the outcome of an experiment

control group   The group in an experiment that is not exposed to the independent variable

control variable   A variable that could affect the dependent variable or the independent variable; therefore it must be controlled either experimentally or statistically or it must be eliminated before the study

contiguity   Refers to at least two events that occur closely together in time

contingency theory   Approach to leadership that takes into account aspects of both personality traits and the favorableness of the group situation

coping imagery   Use of systematic desensitization procedures during imaginal rehearsal for the purpose of managing stress

crucial experiment   An experiment in which two conflicting hypotheses are tested simultaneously

cue-reduction feedback   Feedback that presents a limited number of task-related cues

dependent variable   The variable thought to be affected in an experiment and therefore measured during data collection

deprivation   A state in which a person is deprived or denied something

differentiated motivation   Separation of the motivational system into domain-specific dimensions such as cognitive, social, and sport achievement motives

disinhibition   Releasing of restraints or control of a person's actions; the person is no longer inhibited

dissociative strategy   Strategy that focuses attention on nonperformance factors to distract the performer from the pain which can occur during a performance

drive   The motivational component of drive theory

dynamics   In the study of groups, this refers to interactions that take place among members

efficacy expectations   Strength of a person's conviction that he or she is capable of producing a certain outcome

empiricism   A scientific method using observations made concerning a particular event or phenomenon

external causation model   A model in which human behavior is said to be determined by environmental effects

external reinforcement   Reinforcement that originates from outside the person

flooring effect   A situation in which a performance or score cannot become any lower or worse than it already is

frustration-aggression-displacement (F-A-D) hypothesis   Proposal that frustration is the cause of aggression and that if the frustrated person cannot act out the aggressive response on the instigator of the frustration, then it will be displaced onto another person

generalizability   In science, the degree of applicability of the results of a particular investigation to larger samples or populations or different situations

generalized imitation theory   Behavioristic theory that proposes that modeling can best be explained through the contingencies of reinforcement

great man theory   Trait approach to leadership that proposes that all great leaders would possess a superior constellation of personality traits

habit strength   The degree of association between a stimulus and a response

hostile aggression   The intentional infliction of injury that is done for the satisfaction of seeing someone hurt or in pain

hypothesis   A prediction or educated guess that an investigator makes before beginning a study

identifiability   Process of making a person's efforts or contributions to a group visible or clear

ideo-motor principle   Proposal that low-gain neuromuscular patterns (efferent activity) are produced during imaginal rehearsal; these low-gain patterns are said to mirror those generated during overt performance

idiosyncratic   Uniquely characteristic of a particular person

imaginal representational system   Symbolic coding of information in pictorial, or visual, forms

independent variable   The variable that is said to be the cause underlying some observed effect and is often manipulated or varied during an experiment

individual difference framework   The study of either one or two variables on which persons are known to vary

innate   Inborn or instinctual

instrumental aggression   Intentional infliction of injury that is done for the purpose of receiving a positive reinforcement, such as a coach's verbal praise

interacting sport teams   Teams that by their structure require that all members continually coordinate their efforts to be successful

interactionist paradigm   The simultaneous study of some aspect of the person and the social situation

intrinsic motivation   This term pertains to the motivation to perform a skill or activity in the absence of any external reward or incentive

internal mediational model   A model in which human behavior is said to be based on cognitive activities, during which information is processed and rational decisions are made

inverse relationship   A relationship between variables wherein as one increases the other decreases

inverted-U hypothesis   A proposed curvilinear relationship between level of arousal and quality of motor performance

kinethesis   Sensory information regarding position and movement that arises from body parts such as the limbs, neck, and trunk

lactate   A metabolic waste product

law of effect   If the consequences of a response are positive, then the probability increases that the same or a similar response will recur under the same set of stimulus conditions; if the consequences are negative, then the probability of response recurrence decreases

lifetime stress   Stress that is experienced as a result of hassles and problems encountered in daily life

linear   A relationship between two variables that tends to vary in the same direction; for instance, there should be a linear relationship between IQ score and grades in school—as the value of the first variable increases, the value of the second variable should also increase

long-term memory   Permanent information storage component of the brain

mastery experiences   Activities in which the individual has an observable effect on the environment usually evidenced by objective success or failure

mastery imagery   Use of imaginal rehearsal specifically for improving skill execution

mediation   Pertaining to one element or event occurring between two other elements or events; for example, an arbitrator is often called in to mediate between labor and management during a dispute

mental error   Performance error that occurs as a result of attending to an inappropriate internal or external cue

mnemonic device   An aid or linguistic formula designed to improve retention of information

model   A visual or graphic representation of the relationships between identifiable variables; for example, Xs and Os drawn on a coach's blackboard represent athletes' positions or movements

modified progressive relaxation training   Abbreviated version of Jacobson's original progressive relaxation program

multivariate   The study of two or more variables at the same time

need for control   Relative need to be in a decision-making or leadership role

negative reinforcement   Withdrawal or removal of an unpleasant stimulus

outcome expectations   A person's knowledge about what behavior is needed to produce a certain outcome

operant   Something, such as reinforcement, that acts on a person in a manner that then produces an effect

operant conditioning   Conditioning in which a response is followed by a reinforcing event, increasing the strength and liklihood of recurrence of that response

operational definition   A definition that specifies how something is manipulated or measured

paradigm The experimental protocol used in a particular investigation and usually drawn logically from either a theoretical or hypothetical framework

perception Process through which information is received through the senses and translated into conscious meaning in the brain

perception of causality Person's beliefs about the causes underlying outcomes, particularly whether or not the performer is the causative agent or if some external factor is the causative agent

phenomenological description Description of an event or process that is based on personal experience

phenomenology As used in this text, a scientific method based on personal, subjective experience

phenomenon Any observation, experience, or circumstance that can be described and measured scientifically

personality traits Enduring predispositions or tendencies to behave in certain ways; also called individual difference variables because these are the unique psychological characteristics that make one person different from another

positive reinforcement Application of a pleasant stimulus after the emission of a response

potential productivity Possible achievement of a sport team if it used all of its resources optimally

predictive validity Degree to which a particular test is able to forecast actual performance on an appropriate task

pride in performance approach Process of attempting to increase motivation by having athletes and coaches mutually establish limited, achievable goals

principle of contiguity Principle that reinforcement must follow a response closely in time

principle of contingency The application of reinforcement should be dependent on the enactment of a desired response

principle of stimulus generalization Principle that states that once a response has become associated with one stimulus there is a tendency for the response to transfer to new, similar stimuli

propositional network Manner in which images are stored in memory; abstract forms that contain information about relationships, relevant descriptions, and modality-specific information

proprioceptive feedback Sensory information that arises from the muscles and joints (kinesthetic feedback) or the inner ear (vestibular feedback) and provides information relative to position or movement

psyching-up strategies Techniques designed to increase arousal or motivation

psychopathy A state of psychological disorder, disease, or abnormality

psychophysiology The application of physiological methods to the understanding of individual behavior

punishment Application of an unpleasant stimulus after a response

quasi-experiment An experiment in which only a dependent variable is assessed

reciprocal relationship A mutual, equivalent, or interchangeable relationship

reinforcement approach Process of attempting to increase motivation by positively reinforcing athletes, contingent on the emission of a desired response

replica Facsimile of an original; in sport psychology an observer's matching response based on the model's original response

Ringleman effect Effect of losses in individual motivation in group situations

selective attention The process of attending to one set of cues to the exclusion of other cues

self-efficacy theory A cognitive approach to motivation which focuses on the strength of a person's conviction that he or she can successfully make a response that is required to produce a certain outcome

self-esteem   A feeling of competence or self-worth

self-fulfilling prophecy   Process whereby a person acts out in reality the expectancies held in cognition

self-instructional training   Teaching athletes the use of specific covert instructions designed to enhance attentional control and problem-solving ability

self-reinforcement   The self-generated reinforcement which a performer generates for himself or herself

self-serving bias (egocentric bias)   A self-protective or ego-protective strategy whereby people tend to take personal responsibility for success while denying similar responsibility for failure

sensory modalities   Any of the seven faculties connected with the ability of the brain and nerves to receive and react to stimuli such as sounds, sights, and smells

situational favorableness   Factor within contingency theory that addresses the question of the degree to which the group situation will allow the leader to exhibit power, influence, or control; it takes three factors into account—leader-member relationships, task structure, and position power

social approval   The motivational or achievement goal of receiving the approval of others

social learning theory   A cognitively-based theory of observational learning which emphasizes the role of symbolic coding and self-determining processes

social loafing   Decreases in individual effort or motivation in group settings

social satisfaction   Dimension of cohesion that pertains to the degree to which team membership allows persons to achieve desired goals

socio-emotional orientation   Orientation reflected by a leader who is supportive of others, concerned about interrelationships among group members, and not overly concerned about the task

sociometric cohesion   Dimension of cohesion that pertains to the degree to which group members like one another

sport mastery   The motivational or achievement goal of performing well in order to improve or perfect one's own skill regardless of the accomplishment of others

stimulus   An observable event in the environment that precedes a response

stimulus generalization   The transfer of a response to a new similar stimulus

stress inoculation   Process of gradually exposing persons to increasing amounts of stress to build an immunity to stress

structural interference   Cause of performance decreases as a result of attempting to perform two tasks simultaneously when both tasks require the use of common receptor or effector systems

subjective competitive situation   How a competitive situation is cognitively appraised by a performer

supportive approach   Process of attempting to increase motivation by providing athletes with positive reinforcements prior to actual performance

symbol   A representation of the meaning of information in memory or cognition

symbolic coding   Process of coding information so that the meaning is represented in memory; visual and verbal codes are common symbolic representations

symbolic representation theory   The first cognitively-based theory of observational learning

task-oriented   Characteristic of a leader who places highest priority on the successful completion of the task

template   A cognitive plan or mental model that is a mirror image of a motor skill or movement pattern

temporal   As used here, this term refers to an association between two variables that exists on the basis of time, as opposed to a relationship between two variables that exists as a function of space or physical location

terminal objective The end or desired objective

theory A constellation of hypothesized relationships used to describe the interrelationships between multiple variables or phenomena

theory of interpersonal compatibility Theory that incorporates the three interpersonal needs of control, inclusion, and affection to explain the relative compatibility within interpersonal relationships

tonus Degree of muscle tone or tension

trait theory A theory that views human behavior as primarily determined by stable personality characteristics

true experiment An experiment that contains at least one independent variable, one dependent variable, and a control group

uncontrollability The perception of independence between a person's own response and the consequence of that response; this perception discriminates between the learned helpless person and the mastery-oriented person

variable An entity that can be quantified; that is, it can be assigned a numerical value

verbal representational system The symbolic coding of information in linguistic or word form

vicarious reinforcement Reinforcement which the model receives after performance

Yerkes-Dodson law Proposal that there is an optimal level of arousal for best performance of a particular task; for example, simple tasks are facilitated by high arousal, whereas complex tasks are facilitated by lower arousal

REFERENCES

CHAPTER 1

Landers, D.M. (1983). Whatever happened to theory testing in sport psychology? *Journal of Sport Psychology, 5,* 135-151.

Lewin, K. (1935). *Dynamic theory of personality.* New York: McGraw-Hill.

CHAPTER 2

Bird, A.M. (1979). *The interactional-mediational paradigm: Toward theory development in personality and motor behavior.* Paper presented at the annual meeting of the North American Society for the Psychology of Sport and Physical Activity, Three-Rivers, Quebec, Canada.

Demers, G. (1983). Emotional states of high-caliber divers. *Swimming Technique,* May-July, 32-35.

Garai, J.E., & Scheinfeld, A. (1970). Sex differences in mental and behavioral traits. *Genetic Psychological Monographs, 81,*123-142.

Helmreich, R., & Spence, J.T. (1977). Sex roles and achievement. In R.W. Christina & D.M. Landers (Eds.), *Psychology of motor behavior and sport.* Champaign, IL: Human Kinetics.

Kane, J.E. (1964). Psychological correlates of physique and physical abilities. In E. Jokl & E. Simon (Eds.), *International research in sport and physical education.* Springfield, IL: Charles C Thomas.

Martens, R. (1975). The paradigmatic crisis in american sport psychology. *Sportwissenschaft, 5,* 9-24.

Martens, R. (1977). *Sport competition anxiety test.* Champaign, IL: Human Kinetics.

Martens, R. (1983). *Development of the competitive state anxiety inventory–2 (SCAT–2).* Unpublished manuscript.

Morgan, W.P. (1968). Personality characteristics of wrestlers participating in the world championships. *Journal of Sports Medicine and Physical Fitness, 8,* 212-216.

Morgan, W.P. (1980). The trait psychology controversy. *Research Quarterly for Exercise and Sport, 51,* 50-76.

Morgan, W.P., & Costill, D.L. (1972). Psychological characteristics of the marathon runner. *Journal of Sports Medicine and Physical Fitness, 12,* 42-46.

Morgan, W.P., & Johnson, R.W. (1977). Psychologic characterization of the elite wrestler: A mental health model. *Medicine and Science in Sports, 9,* 55-56.

Morgan, W.P., & Pollock, M.L. (1977). Psychologic characterization of the elite distance runner. *Annals of the New York Academy of Science, 301,* 382-403.

Nagle, F.J., Morgan, W.P., Hellickson, R.D., Serfass, R.C., & Alexander, J.F. (1975). Spotting success traits in olympic contenders. *Physician and Sportsmedicine, 3,* 31-34.

Rushall, B.S. (1970). An evaluation of the relationship between personality and physical performance categories. In G.S. Kenyon (Ed.), *Contemporary psychology of sport*. Chicago, IL: Athletic Institute.

Schurr, K.T., Ashley, M.A., & Joy, K.L. (1977). A multivariate analysis of male athlete characteristics: Sport type and success. *Multivariate Experimental Clinical Research, 3*, 53-68.

Williams, J.M. (1978). Personality characteristics of the successful female athlete. In W.F. Straub (Ed.), *Sport psychology: An analysis of athlete behavior*. Ithaca, NY: Mouvement Publications.

Zuckerman, M. (1979). Traits, states, situations, and uncertainty. *Journal of Behavioral Assessment, 1*, 43-54.

CHAPTER 3

Anderson, J.R. (1980). *Cognitive psychology and its implications*. San Francisco: W.H. Freeman.

Berlyne, D.E. (1966). Conflict and arousal. *Scientific American, 215*, 82-87.

Bird, A.M. (1973). Effects of social facilitation upon females' performance on two psychomotor tasks. *Research Quarterly, 44*, 322-330.

Bowen, H.M., Andersen, B., & Promisel, D. (1966). Studies of divers' performance during the SEALAB II project. *Human Factors, 8*, 183-199.

Carment, D.W., & Hodkins, B. (1973). Coaction and competition in India and Canada. *Journal of Cross Cultural Psychology, 4*, 459-469.

Carron, A.V. (1980). *Social psychology of sport*. Ithaca, NY: Mouvement Publications.

Cottrell, N.B. (1972). Social facilitation. In C.G. McClintock (Ed.), *Experimental social psychology*, New York: Holt, Rinehart & Winston.

Cottrell, N.B., Wack, D.L., Sekerak, G.L., & Rittle, R.H. (1968). Social facilitation of dominant responses by the presence of an audience and the mere presence of others. *Journal of Personality and Social Psychology, 9*, 245-250.

deVries, H.A. (1968). Immediate and long term effects of exercise upon resting muscle action potential. *The Journal of Sports Medicine and Physical Fitness, 8*, 1-11.

deVries, H.A. (1981). Tranquilizer effect of exercise: A critical review. *The Physician and Sportsmedicine, 11*, 45-54.

deVries, H.A., & Adams, G.M. (1972). Electromyographic comparison of single doses of exercise and meprobamate as to effects on muscular relaxation. *American Journal of Physical Medicine, 51*, 130-141.

deVries, H.A., Wiswell, R.A., Bulbulian, R., & Moritani, T. (1981). Tranquilizer effect of exercise. *American Journal of Physical Medicine, 60*, 57-66.

Duffy, E. (1957). The psychological significance of the concept of "arousal" or "activation." *Psychological Review, 64,* 265-275.

Fenz, W.D. (1964). Conflict and stress as related to physiological activation and sensory, perceptual, and cognitive functioning. *Psychological Monographs, 78,* Whole No. 585.

Fenz, W.D., & Epstein, S. (1967). Gradients of physiological arousal in parachutists as a function of an approaching jump. *Psychosomatic Medicine, 29,* 33-51.

Fenz, W.D., & Epstein, S. (1968). Specific and general inhibitory reactions associated with mastery of stress. *Journal of Experimental Psychology, 77,* 52-56.

Fenz, W.D., & Epstein, S. (1969). Stress: In the air. *Psychology Today, 3,* 27-28, 58-59.

Fenz, W.D., & Jones, G.B. (1972). Individual differences in physiologic arousal and performance in sport parachutists. *Psychosomatic Medicine, 34,* 1-8.

Fenz, W.D., Kluck, B.I., & Bankart, C.P. (1969). Effect of threat and uncertainty on mastery of stress. *Journal of Experimental Psychology, 79,* 473-479.

Fiske, D.W., & Maddi, S.R. (1961). *Functions of varied experience.* Homewood, IL: Dorsey Press.

Fitts, P.M., & Posner, M.I. (1967). *Human performance.* Belmont, CA: Brooks Cole.

Gould, D., Weinberg, R.S., & Jackson, A. (1980). Effect of mental preparation strategies on a muscular endurance task. *Journal of Sport Psychology, 2,* 329-339.

Jacobson, E. (1936). The course of relaxation in muscles of athletes. *American Journal of Psychology, 48,* 98-108.

Jacobson, E. (1938). *Progressive relaxation.* Chicago, IL: The University of Chicago Press.

Landers, D.M., and McCullagh, P.D. (1976). Social facilitation of motor performance. In J.F. Keogh (Ed.), *Exercise and sport science reviews* (Vol. 4). New York: Academic Press.

Malmo, R.B. (1959). Activation: A neuropsychological dimension. *Psychological Review, 66,* 367-386.

Martens, R. (1974). Arousal and motor performance. In J.H. Wilmore (Ed.), *Exercise and sport science reviews* (Vol. 2). New York: Academic Press.

Nideffer, R.M. (1980). Identifying and developing optimal levels of arousal in sport. Unpublished manuscript.

Oxendine, J.B. (1970). Emotional arousal and motor performance. *Quest, 13,* 23-30.

Schmidt, R.A. (1982). *Motor control and learning,* Champaign, IL: Human Kinetics.

Shelton, A.O., & Mahoney, M.J. (1978). The content and effect of "psyching-up" strategies in weight lifters. *Cognitive Therapy and Research, 2,* 275-284.

Weinberg, R.S. (1982). The relationship between mental preparation strategies and motor performance: A review and critique. *Quest, 33,* 195-213.

Weinberg, R.S., Gould, D., & Jackson, A. (1980). Cognition and motor performance: Effect of psyching-up strategies on three motor tasks. *Cognitive Therapy and Research, 4,* 239-245.

Weltman, G., & Egstrom, G.H. (1966). Perceptual narrowing in novice divers. *Human Factors, 8,* 499-506.

Zajonc, R.B. (1968). Social facilitation. In D. Cartwright & A. Zander (Eds.), *Group dynamics.* New York: Harper & Row.

CHAPTER 4

Bird, A.M., Ravizza, K.H., & Reis, J.A. (1983). Physical activity, anxiety, and attentional style. Unpublished manuscript.

Byrd, O.E. (1963). The relief of tension by exercise: A survey of medical viewpoints and practices. *The Journal of School Health, 33,* 238-239.

deVries, H.A. (1968). Immediate and long term effects of exercise upon resting muscle action potential. *The Journal of Sports Medicine and Physical Fitness, 8,* 1-11.

deVries, H.A. (1981). Tranquilizer effect of exercise: A critical review. *The Physician and Sportsmedicine, 11*, 45-54.

deVries, H.A., & Adams, G.M. (1972). Electromyographic comparison of single doses of exercise and meprobamate as to effects on muscular relaxation. *American Journal of Physical Medicine, 51*, 130-141.

deVries, H.A., Wiswell, R.A., Bulbulian, R., & Moritani, T. (1981). Tranquilizer effect of exercise. *American Journal of Physical Medicine, 60*, 57-66.

Duffy, E. (1957). The psychological significance of the concept of "arousal" or "activation." *Psychological Review, 64*, 265-275.

Easterbrook, J.A. (1959). The effect of emotion on cue utilization and the organization of behavior. *Psychological Review, 66*, 183-201.

Fenz, W.D. (1975). Coping mechanisms and performance under stress. In D.M. Landers, D.V. Harris, & R.W. Christina (Eds.), *Psychology of sport and motor behavior II*. University Park, PA: The Pennsylvania State University.

Gould, D., Horn, T., & Spreemann, J. (1983a). Competitive anxiety in junior elite wrestlers. *Journal of Sport Psychology, 5*, 58-71.

Gould, D., Horn, T., & Spreemann, J. (1983b). Sources of stress in junior elite wrestlers. *Journal of Sport Psychology, 5*, 159-171.

Gould, D., Weiss, M., & Weinberg, R. (1981). Psychological characteristics of successful and nonsuccessful big ten wrestlers. *Journal of Sport Psychology, 3*, 69-81.

Gruber, J.J., & Beauchamp, D. (1979). Relevancy of the competitive state anxiety inventory in a sport environment. *Research Quarterly, 50*, 207-214.

Hall, E.G., & Purvis, G. (1981). The relationship of anxiety to competitive bowling. In G.C. Roberts and D.M. Landers (Eds.), *Psychology of motor behavior and sport*. Champaign, IL: Human Kinetics.

Highlen, P.S., & Bennett, B.B. (1979). Psychological characteristics of successful and nonsuccessful elite wrestlers: An exploratory study. *Journal of Sport Psychology, 1*, 123-137.

Huddleston, S., & Gill, D.L. (1981). State anxiety as a function of skill level and proximity to competition. *Research Quarterly for Exercise and Sport, 52*, 31-34.

Kahneman, D. (1973). *Attention and effort*. Englewood Cliffs, NJ: Prentice Hall.

Klavora, P. (1975). Application of the Spielberger trait-state anxiety model and STAI in precompetition anxiety research. In D.M. Landers, D.V. Harris, & R.W. Christina (Eds.), *Psychology of sport and motor behavior II*. University Park, PA: The Pennsylvania State University.

Klavora, P. (1978). An attempt to derive inverted-U curves based on the relationship between anxiety and athletic performance. In D.M. Landers & R.W. Christina (Eds.), *Psychology of motor behavior and sport*. Champaign, IL: Human Kinetics.

Kroll, W. (1979). The stress in high performance athletics. In P. Klavora and J.V. Daniel (Eds.), *Coach, athlete, and the sport psychologist*. University of Toronto, Toronto, Ontario, Canada.

Landers, D.M. (1980). The arousal-performance relationship revisited. *Research Quarterly for Exercise and Sport, 51*, 77-90.

Mahoney, M.J., & Avener, M. (1977). Psychology of the elite athlete: An exploratory study. *Cognitive Therapy and Research, 1*, 135-141.

Malmo, R.B. (1959). Activation: A neuropsychological dimension. *Psychological Review, 66*, 367-386.

Martens, R. (1971). Anxiety and motor behavior: A review. *Journal of Motor Behavior, 3*, 151-179.

Martens, R. (1975). *Social psychology & physical activity*. New York: Harper & Row.

Martens, R. (1977). *Sport competition anxiety test*. Champaign, IL: Human Kinetics.

Martens, R. (1983). *Development of the competitive state anxiety inventory—2 (SCAI—2)*. Unpublished manuscript.

Martens, R., Burton, D., Rivkin, F., & Simon, J. (1980). Reliability and validity of the competitive state anxiety inventory (CSAI). In C.H. Nadeau, W.R. Halliwell, K.M. Newell & G.C. Roberts (Eds.), *Psychology of motor behavior and sport*. Champaign, IL: Human Kinetics.

Martens, R., & Landers, D.M. (1970). Motor performance under stress: A test of the inverted-U hypothesis. *Journal of Personality and Social Psychology, 16*, 29-37.

Meyers, A.W., Cooke, C.J., Cullen, J., & Liles, L. (1979). Psychological aspects of athletic competitors: A replication across sports. *Cognitive Therapy and Research, 3*, 361-366.

Morgan, W.P. (1970). Pre-match anxiety in a group of college wrestlers. *Medicine and Science in Sports, 2*, 24-27.

Morgan, W.P. (1973). Influence of acute physical activity on state anxiety. *Proceedings of the National College Physical Education Association for Men*.

Morgan, W.P. (1976). Psychological consequences of vigorous physical activity and sport. *Proceedings of the American Academy of Physical Education*.

Morgan, W.P., & Hammer, W.M. (1974). Influence of competitive wrestling upon state anxiety. *Medicine and Science in Sports, 6*, 58-61.

Morgan, W.P., & Horstman, D.H. (1976). Anxiety reduction following acute physical activity. *Medicine and Science in Sports, 8*, 62.

Morgan, W.P., Roberts, J.A., Brand, F.R., & Feinerman, A.D. (1970). Psychological effect of chronic physical activity. *Medicine and Science in Sports, 2*, 213-217.

Oxendine, J.B. (1970). Emotional arousal and motor performance. *Quest, 13*, 23-32.

Passer, M.W. (1983). Fear of failure, fear of evaluation, perceived competence, and self-esteem in competitive-trait-anxious children. *Journal of Sport Psychology, 5*, 172-188.

Passer, M.W. (1984). Competitive trait anxiety in children and adolescents. In J.M. Silva & R.S. Weinberg (Eds.), *Psychological foundations of sport and exercise*. Champaign, IL: Human Kinetics.

Passer, M.W., & Scanlan, T.K. (1980). *A sociometric analysis of popularity and leadership status among players on youth soccer teams*. Paper presented at the annual meeting of the North American Society for the Psychology of Sport and Physical Activity, Boulder, CO.

Pitts, F.N. (1969). The biochemistry of anxiety. *Scientific American, 220*, 69-75.

Pitts, F.N., & McClure, J.N. (1967). Lactate metabolism in anxiety neurosis. *New England Journal of Medicine, 277*, 1329-1336.

Scanlan, T.K., & Passer, M.W. (1977). The effects of competition trait anxiety and game win-loss on perceived threat in a natural competitive setting. In D.M. Landers & R.W. Christina (Eds.), *Psychology of motor behavior and sport*. Champaign, IL: Human Kinetics.

Scanlan, T.K., & Passer, M.W. (1979). Sources of competitive stress in young female athletes. *Journal of Sport Psychology, 1*, 151-159.

Schmidt, R.A. (1982). *Motor control and learning*. Champaign, IL: Human Kinetics.

Simon, J.A., & Martens, R. (1977). SCAT as a predictor of A-states in varying competitive situations. In D.M. Landers & R.W. Christina (Eds.), *Psychology of motor behavior and sport*. Champaign, IL: Human Kinetics.

Simon, J.A., & Martens, R. (1979). Children's anxiety in sport and nonsport evaluative activities. *Journal of Sport Psychology, 1*, 160-169.

Sontroem, R.J., & Bernardo, P. (1982). Intraindividual pregame state anxiety and basketball performance: A re-examination of the inverted-U curve. *Journal of Sport Psychology, 4*, 235-245.

Spielberger, C.D. (1966). *Anxiety and behavior*. New York: Academic Press.

Spielberger, C.D. (1973). *State-trait anxiety inventory for children: Preliminary manual*. Palo Alto, CA: Consulting Psychologists Press.

Spielberger, C.D. (1977). Anxiety: Theory and research. In B.B. Wolman (Ed.), *International encyclopedia of neurology, psychiatry, psychoanalysis and psychology*. New York: Human Sciences.

Spielberger, C.D., Gorsuch, R.L., & Lushene, R.E. (1970). *Manual for the state-trait anxiety inventory*. Palo Alto, CA: Consulting Psychologists Press.

Taylor, J.A. (1953). A personality scale of manifest anxiety. *Journal of Abnormal and Social Psychology, 48*, 285-290.

Weinberg, R.S. (1978). The effects of success and failure on the patterning of neuromuscular energy. *Journal of Motor Behavior, 10*, 53-61.

Weinberg, R.S., & Genuchi, M. (1980). Relationship between competitive trait anxiety, state anxiety, and golf performance: A field study. *Journal of Sport Psychology, 2*, 148-154.

Weinberg, R.S., & Hunt, V.V. (1976). The interrelationships between anxiety, motor performance and electromyography. *Journal of Motor Behavior, 8*, 219-224.

Weinberg, R.S., & Ragan, J. (1978). Motor performance under three levels of trait anxiety and stress. *Journal of Motor Behavior, 10*, 169-176.

CHAPTER 5

Ash, M.J., & Zellner, R.D. (1978). *Speculations on the use of biofeedback training in sport psychology*. In D.M. Landers & R.W. Christina (Eds.), *Psychology of motor behavior and sport*. Champaign, IL: Human Kinetics.

Benson, H. (1975). *The relaxation response*. New York: William Morrow.

Benson, H., Beary, J.F., & Carol, M.P. (1974). The relaxation response. *Psychiatry, 37*, 37-46.

Bernstein, D.A., & Borkovec, T.D. (1973). *Progressive relaxation: A training manual for the helping professional*. Champaign, IL: Research Press.

Borkovec, T.D. (1981). Stress management in athletics: An overview of cognitive and physiological techniques. *Motor Skills: Theory into Practice, 5*, 45-52.

Cannon, W.B. (1941). The emergency function of the adrenal medulla in pain and the major emotions. *American Journal of Physiology, 33*, 356.

Cooke, C.E., & Van Vogt, A.E. (1965). *Hypnotism handbook*. Alhambra, CA: Borden.

Daniels, F.S. (1981). *Biofeedback training and performance in rifle marksmen*. Unpublished master's thesis, Pennsylvania State University, University Park, PA.

Daniels, F.S., & Hatfield, B. (1981). Biofeedback. *Motor Skills: Theory into Practice, 5*, 69-72.

Daniels, F.S., & Landers, D.M. (1981). Biofeedback and shooting performance: A test of disregulation and systems theory, *Journal of Sport Psychology, 4*, 271-282.

DeWitt, D.J. (1980). Cognitive and biofeedback training for stress reduction with university athletes. *Journal of Sport Psychology, 2*, 288-294.

Dishman, R.K. (1980). Overview of ergogenic properties of hypnosis. *Journal of Physical Education and Recreation, 51*, 52-54.

French, S.N. (1978). Electromyographic biofeedback for tension control during gross motor skill acquisition. *Perceptual and Motor Skills, 47*, 883-889.

Girdano, D., & Everly, G. (1979). *Controlling stress and tension*. Englewood Cliffs, N.J.: Prentice-Hall.

Gorton, B.E. (1949). The physiology of hypnosis. *Psychiatric Quarterly, 23*, 457-485.

Hatfield, B., & Daniels, F.S. (1981). The use of hypnosis as a stress management technique. *Motor Skills: Theory into Practice, 5*, 62-68.

Harrison, R.P., & Feltz, D.L. (1981). Stress inoculation for athletes: Description and case example. *Motor Skills: Theory into Practice, 5*, 53-61.

Hickman, J.L. (1979). How to elicit supernormal capabilities in athletes. In P. Klavora & J.V. Daniel (Eds.), *Coach athlete, and the sport psychologist*. University of Toronto, Toronto, Ontario, Canada.

Honey, C.A. (1978). *The art and science of hypnotism*. Unpublished manuscript.

Jacobson, E. (1938). *Progressive relaxation*. Chicago: University of Chicago Press.

Lane, J.F. (1980). Improving athletic performance through visuomotor behavior rehearsal. In R.M. Suinn (Ed.), *Psychology in sports,* Minneapolis, MN: Burgess.

Layman, E.M. (1978). Meditation and sports performance. In W.F. Straub (Ed.), *Sport psychology: An analysis of athlete behavior*. Ithaca, NY: Mouvement Publications.

LeCron, L.M., & Bordeaux, J. (1947). *Hypnotism today*. North Hollywood, CA: Wilshire.

Long, B.C. Stress management for the athlete: A cognitive behavioral model. In C.H. Nadeau, W.R. Halliwell, K.M. Newell, & G.C. Roberts (Eds.), *Psychology of motor behavior and sport*. Champaign, IL: Human Kinetics.

Mandler, G., Mandler, J.M., & Uviller, E.T. (1958). Autonomic feedback: The perception of autonomic activity. *Journal of Abnormal and Social Psychology, 56,* 367-373.

Martens, R. (1977). *Sport competition anxiety test*. Champaign, IL: Human Kinetics.

Martens, R. (1983). *Development of the competitive state anxiety inventory—2 (SCAI—2)* Unpublished manuscript.

Meichenbaum, D. (1977). *Cognitive-behavior modification*. New York: Plenum.

Meichenbaum, D., & Cameron, R. (1973). Training schizophrenics to talk to themselves: A means of developing attentional controls. *Behavior Therapy, 4,* 515-534.

Meichenbaum, D., & Turk, D. (1976). The cognitive-behavioral management of anxiety, anger, and pain. In P.O. Davidson (Ed.), *The behavioral management of anxiety, depression, and pain*. New York: Brunner/Mazel.

Nideffer, R.M. (1981). *The ethics and practice of applied sport psychology*. Ithaca, NY: Mouvement Publications.

Orlick, T. (1980). *In pursuit of excellence*. Champaign, IL: Human Kinetics.

Schultz, J., & Luthe, W. (1969). *Autogenic methods* (Vol. 1), New York: Grune and Stratton.

Smith, R.E. (1980). A cognitive-affective approach to stress management training for athletes. In C.H. Nadeau, W.R. Halliwell, K.M. Newell, & G.C. Roberts (Eds.), *Psychology of motor behavior and sport*. Champaign, IL: Human Kinetics.

Smith, R.E., & Smoll, F.L. (1978). Psychological intervention and sports medicine: Stress management training and coach effectiveness training. *University of Washington Medicine, 5,* 20-24.

Suinn, R.M. (1976). Body thinking: Psychology for olympic champs. *Psychology Today, 10,* 38-43.

Suinn, R.M. (1980). Psychology and sports performance: Principles and applications. In R.M. Suinn (Ed.), *Psychology in sports*. Minneapolis, MN: Burgess.

Wilkinson, M.O., Landers, D.M., & Daniels, F.S. (1981). Breathing patterns and their influence on rifle shooting. *American Marksman, 6,* 8-9.

Ziegler, S.G., Klinzing, J., & Williamson, K. (1982) The effects of two stress management training programs on cardiorespiratory efficiency. *Journal of Sport Psychology, 4,* 280-289.

CHAPTER 6

Anderson, J.R. (1980) *Cognitive psychology*. San Francisco, CA: Freeman.

Bird, A.M., Ravizza, K.H., & Reis, J.A. (1983). *Physical activity, anxiety, and attentional style*. Unpublished manuscript.

Easterbrook, J.A. (1959). The effect of emotion on cue utilization and the organization of behavior. *Psychological Review, 66,* 183-201.

Etzel, E.J. (1979). Validation of a conceptual model characterizing attention among international rifle shooters. *Journal of Sport Psychology, 1,* 281-290.

Fitts, P.M., & Posner, M.I. (1967). *Human performance*. Belmont, CA: Brooks Cole.

Fleishman, E.A., & Rich, S. (1963). Role of kinesthetic and spacial-visual abilities in perceptual motor learning. *Journal of Experimental Psychology, 66,* 6-11.

Gardner, R.W., Holtzman, P.S., Klein, G.S., Linton, H.B., & Spence, D.P. (1959). Cognitive control: A study of individual consistencies in cognitive behavior. *Psychological Issues, 1* (4). (Monograph)

Gould, D., Weiss, M., & Weinberg, R. (1981). Psychological characteristics of successful and nonsuccessful big ten wrestlers. *Journal of Sport Psychology, 3,* 69-81.

Highlen, P.S., & Bennett, B.B. (1979). Psychological characteristics of successful and nonsuccessful elite wrestlers: An exploratory study. *Journal of Sport Psychology, 1,* 123-137.

Keele, S.W., & Hawkins, H.L. (1982). Explorations of individual differences relevant to high skill level. *Journal of Motor Behavior, 14,* 3-23.

Landers, D.M. (1982). Arousal, attention, and skilled performance: Further considerations. *Quest, 33,* 271-283.

Landers, D.M., Furst, D.M., & Daniels, F.S. (1981). *Anxiety/attention and shooting ability: Testing the predictive validity of the test of attentional and interpersonal style (TAIS).* Paper presented at the annual meeting of the North American Society for the Psychology of Sport and Physical Activity, College Park, MD.

Martin, R.H. (1983). *Effectiveness of attentional focus and basketball free-throw percentage: An attempt at prediction.* Unpublished master's project, California State University, Fullerton.

Morgan, W.P., & Pollock, M.L. (1977). Psychologic characterization of the elite distance runner. In P. Milvy (Ed.), *Annals of the New York Academy of Science, 301,* 382-403.

Nideffer, R.M. (1976). Test of attentional and interpersonal style. *Journal of Personality and Social Psychology, 34,* 394-404.

Nideffer, R.M. (1981). *The ethics and practice of applied sport psychology.* Ithaca, NY: Mouvement Publications.

Nideffer, R.M. (1982). *Self-assessment for coaches.* Unpublished manuscript.

Nideiffer, R.M., & Sharpe, R. (1978). *ACT: Attention control training.* New York: Wyden.

Reis, J.A., & Bird, A.M. (1982). Cue processing as a function of breadth of attention. *Journal of Sport Psychology, 4,* 64-72.

Sacks, M.H., Milvy, P., Perry, S.W., & Sherman, L.R. (1981). Mental status and psychological coping during a 100-mile race. In M.H. Sacks and M.L. Sachs (Eds.), *Psychology of running.* Champaign, IL: Human Kinetics.

Schmidt, R.A. (1982). *Motor control and learning.* Champaign, IL: Human Kinetics.

Schlesinger, H.S. (1954). Cognitive attitudes in relation to susceptibility to interference. *Journal of Personality, 22,* 354-374.

Silverman, J. The problem of attention in research and theory in schizophrenia. *Psychological Review, 71,* 352-379.

Turner, R.G., & Gilliland, L. (1977). Comparison of self-report and performance measures of attention. *Perceptual and Motor Skills, 45,* 409-410.

Van Schoyck, S.R., & Grasha, A.F. (1981). Attentional style variations and athletic ability: The advantages of a sports-specific test. *Journal of Sport Psychology, 3,* 149-165.

Walker, R., Nideffer, R., & Boomer, W. (1977). Diving performance as it is correlated with arousal and concentration time. *Swimming Technique,* Winter, 117-122.

Wachtel, P.L. (1967). Conceptions of broad and narrow attention. *Psychological Bulletin, 68,* 417-429.

Zuckerman, M. (1979). Traits, states, situations, and uncertainty. *Journal of Behavioral Assessment, 1,* 43-54.

CHAPTER 7

Adams, J.A. (1971). A closed-loop theory of motor learning, *Journal of Motor Behavior, 3,* 111-150.

Bandura, A. (1977). *Social learning theory.* Englewood Cliffs, NJ: Prentice-Hall.

Bandura, A., & Jeffery, R.W. (1973). Role of symbolic coding and rehearsal processes in observational learning. *Journal of Personality and Social Psychology, 26*, 122-130.

Bandura, A., Jeffery, R., and Bachicha, D.L. (1974). Analysis of memory codes and cumulative rehearsal in observational learning. *Journal of Research in Personality, 7*, 295-305.

Bandura, A., & Kupers, C.J. The transmission of patterns of self-reinforcement through modeling. *Journal of Abnormal and Social Psychology, 69*, 1-9.

Bird, A.M., & Rikli, R. (1983). Observational learning and practice variability. *Research Quarterly for Exercise and Sport, 54*, 1-4.

Bird, A.M., Ross, D., & Laguna, P.L. (1982). *Relative effectiveness of observational learning versus overt practice for learning of a timing task.* Unpublished manuscript.

Carroll, W.R., & Bandura, A. (1982). The role of visual monitoring in observational learning of action patterns: Making the unobservable observable. *Journal of Motor Behavior, 14*, 153-167.

Doody, S.G., Bird, A.M., & Ross, D. (in press). The effect of auditory and visual models on acquisition of a timing task. *Journal of Human Movement Science.*

Feltz, D.L. (1982). The effects of age and number of demonstrations on modeling of form and performance. *Research Quarterly for Exercise and Sport, 53*, 291-296.

Festinger, L.A. (1954). A theory of social comparison processes. *Human Relations, 7*, 117-140.

Fleishman, E.A., & Rich, S. (1963). Role of kinesthetic and spacial-visual abilities in perceptual motor learning. *Journal of Experimental Psychology, 66*, 6-11.

Gallwey, W.T. (1974). *The inner game of tennis.* New York: Random House.

Gerst, M.S. (1971). Symbolic coding processes in observational learning. *Journal of Personality and Social Psychology, 19*, 7-17.

Gewirtz, J.L., & Stingle, K.G. (1968). Learning of generalized imitation as the basis for identification. *Psychological Review, 75*, 374-397.

Gould, D. (1978). *The influence of motor task types on model effectiveness.* Unpublished doctoral dissertation. University of Illinois, Champaign, IL.

Gould, D., & Roberts, G.C. (1982). Modeling and motor skill acquisition. *Quest, 33*, 214-230.

Gould, D., & Weiss, M. (1981). The effects of model similarity and model talk on self-efficacy and muscular endurance. *Journal of Sport Psychology, 3*, 17-29.

Jeffery, R.W. (1976). The influence of symbolic and motor rehearsal on observational learning. *Journal of Research in Personality, 10*, 116-127.

Jeffrey, D.B. (1974). A comparison of the effects of external control and self-control on the modification and maintenance of weight. *Journal of Abnormal Psychology, 83*, 404-410.

Keele, S.W. (1977). Current status of the motor program concept. In D.M. Landers and R.W. Christina (Eds.), *Psychology of motor behavior and sport.* Champaign, IL: Human Kinetics.

Landers, D.M. (1975). Observational learning of a motor skill: Temporal spacing of demonstrations and audience presence. *Journal of Motor Behavior, 7*, 281-287.

Landers, D.M., & Landers, D.M. (1973). Teacher versus peer model: Effects of model's presence and performance level on motor behavior. *Journal of Motor Behavior, 5*, 129-140.

Marston, A.R. (1965). Imitation, self-reinforcement, and reinforcement of another person. *Journal of Personality and Social Psychology, 2*, 255-261.

Martens, R., Burwitz, L., & Zuckerman, J. (1976). Modeling effects on motor performance. *Research Quarterly, 47*, 277-291.

McGuire, W.J. (1961). Some factors influencing the effectiveness of demonstration films: Repetition of instructions, slow motion, distribution of showings, and explanatory narrations. In A.A. Lumsdaine (Ed.), *Student response in programmed instruction.* Washington, DC: National Academy of Sciences–National Research Council.

Miller, N.E., & Dollard, J. (1941). *Social learning and imitation.* New Haven, Conn.: Yale University Press.

Ross, D. (March, 1983). Personal communication.

Ross, D., Bird, A.M., Doody, S.G., & Zoeller, M. (in press). Effects of knowledge of results (KR), modeling and videotape feedback on motor performance. *Journal of Human Movement Science*.

Sarason, I.G. (1968). Verbal learning, modeling, and juvenile delinquency. *American Psychologist, 23,* 254-266.

Sarason, I.G., Pederson, A.M., & Nyman, B. (1968). Test anxiety and the observation of models. *Journal of Personality, 36,* 493-511.

Schmidt, R.A. (1975). A schema theory of discrete motor skill learning. *Psychological Review, 82,* 225-260.

Sheffield, F. (1961). Theoretical considerations in the learning of complex sequential tasks from demonstrations and practice. In A.A. Lumsdaine (Ed.), *Student response in programmed instruction.* Washington, DC: National Academy of Sciences–National Research Council.

Sheffield, F., & Maccoby, N. (1961). Summary and interpretation of research on organizational principles in constructing filmed demonstrations. In A.A. Lumsdaine (Ed.), *Student response in programmed instruction.* Washington, DC: National Academy of Sciences–National Research Council.

Thomas, J.R., Pierce, C., & Ridsdale, S. (1977). Age differences in children's ability to model motor behavior. *Research Quarterly, 48,* 592-597.

Walker, E.L., & Tarte, R.D. (1963). Memory storage as a function of arousal and time with homogeneous and heterogeneous lists. *Journal of Verbal Learning and Verbal Behavior, 2,* 113-119.

Weiss, M.R. (1983). Modeling and motor performance: A developmental perspective. *Research Quarterly for Exercise and Sport, 54,* 190-197.

Yando, R., Seitz, V., & Zigler, E. (1978). *Imitation: A developmental perspective.* New York: Wiley.

Zoeller, M. (1983). *The effects of anxiety on the observational learning of a motor skill.* Unpublished master's thesis, California State University, Fullerton.

CHAPTER 8

Anderson, J.R. (1980). *Cognitive psychology.* San Francisco, CA: Freeman.

Bandura, A. (1977). *Social learning theory.* Englewood Cliffs, NJ: Prentice-Hall.

Bandura, A., Jeffery, R., & Bachicha, D.L. (1974). Analysis of memory codes and cumulative rehearsal in observational learning. *Journal of Research in Personality, 7,* 295-305.

Carpenter, W.B. (1894) *Principles of mental physiology.* NY: Appleton.

Carroll, W.R., & Bandura, A. (1982). The role of visual monitoring in observational learning of action patterns: Making the unobservable observable. *Journal of Motor Behavior, 14,* 153-167.

Chevalier-Girard, N., & Wilberg, R.B. (1978). *The effects of image and label on the free recall of movement lists.* Paper presented at the meeting of the Canadian Society for Psychomotor Learning and Sport Psychology, Toronto, Canada.

Corbin, C.B. (1967). The effect of covert rehearsal on development of a complex motor skill. *Journal of General Psychology, 76,* 143-150.

Dunlap, J.L. (1983). *The efficacy of imagery rehearsal during performance of a motor task.* Unpublished master's thesis, California State University, Fullerton.

Epstein, M.L. (1980). The relationship of mental imagery and mental rehearsal to performance of a motor task. *Journal of Sport Psychology, 2,* 211-220.

Feltz, D.L., & Landers, D.M. (1983). The effects of mental practice on motor skill learning and performance: A meta-analysis. *Journal of Sport Psychology, 5,* 25-57.

Fitts, P.M., & Posner, M.J. (1967). *Human performance.* Belmont, CA: Brookes Cole.

Fleishman, E.A., & Rich, S. (1963). Role of kinesthetic and spacial-visual abilities in perceptual motor learning. *Journal of Experimental Psychology, 66,* 6-11.

Fosbury, D. (1974). Fosbury on flopping. *Track technique, 55,* 1749-1750.

Gallwey, W.T. (1974). *The inner game of tennis.* New York: Random House.

Gallwey, W.T., & Kriegel, B. (1977). *Inner skiing.* New York: Random House.

Hale, B.D. (1982). The effects of internal and external imagery on muscular and ocular concomitants. *Journal of Sport Psychology, 4,* 379-387.

Hale, B.D. (1981). *The effects of internal and external imagery on muscular and ocular concomitants.* Unpublished doctoral dissertation, The Pennsylvania State University, University Park.

Hall, C.R. (1980). Imagery for movement. *Journal of Human Movement Studies, 6,* 252-264.

Hall, C., & Buckolz, E. (1982-1983). Imagery and the recall of movement patterns. *Imagination, Cognition and Personality, 2,* 251-260.

Highlen, P.S., & Bennett, B.B. (1979). Psychological characteristics of successful and nonsuccessful elite wrestlers: An exploratory study. *Journal of Sport Psychology, 1,* 123-137.

Ho, L., & Shea, J.B. (1978). Levels of processing and the coding of position cues in motor short-term memory. *Journal of Motor Behavior, 10,* 113-121.

Housner, L., & Hoffman, S.J. (1981). Imagery ability in recall of distance and location information. *Journal of Motor Behavior, 13,* 207-223.

Jacobson, E. (1931). Electrical measurements of neuromuscular states during mental activities. *American Journal of Physiology, 96,* 115-121.

Keele, S.W. (1977). Current status of the motor program concept. In D.M. Landers and R.W. Christina (Eds.), *Psychology of motor behavior and sport.* Champaign, IL: Human Kinetics.

Kieras, D. (1978). Beyond pictures and words: Alternative information-processing models for imagery effects in verbal memory. *Psychological Bulletin, 85,* 532-554.

Kohl, R.M., & Roenker, D.L. (1983). Mechanism involvement during skill imagery. *Journal of Motor Behavior, 15,* 179-190.

Kohl, R.M., Roenker, D.L., Turner, P., & White, W. (1983). *The external control of skill imagery.* Paper presented at the annual meeting of the North American Society for the Psychology of Sport and Physical Activity, East Lansing, MI.

Kosslyn, S.M., & Schwartz, S.P.A. (1977). A simulation of visual imagery. *Cognitive Science, 1,* 265-298.

Lang, P.J. (1979). A bio-informational theory of emotional imagery. *Psychophysiology, 16,* 495-512.

Mackay, D.G. (1981). The problem of rehearsal or mental practice. *Journal of Motor Behavior, 13,* 274-285.

Mahoney, M.J., & Avener, M. (1977). Psychology of the elite athlete: An exploratory study. *Cognitive Therapy and Research, 1,* 135-141.

Meyers, A.W., Cooke, C.J., Cullen, J., & Liles, L. (1979). Psychological aspects of athletic competitors: A replication across sports. *Cognitive Therapy and Research, 3,* 361-366.

Minas, S.C. (1978). Mental practice of a complex perceptual-motor skill. *Journal of Human Movement Studies, 4,* 102-107.

Minas, S.C. (1980). Acquisition of a motor skill following guided mental and physical practice. *Journal of Human Movement Studies, 6,* 127-141.

Nicklaus, J. (1974). *Golf my way.* New York: Simon & Schuster.

Nicklaus, J. (1976). *Playing better golf.* New York: King Features Syndicate.

Paivio, A. (1971). *Imagery and verbal processes.* New York: Holt, Rinehart & Winston.

Paivio, A. (1973). Psychophysiological correlates of imagery. In F.J. McGuigan and R.A. Schoonover (Eds.), *The psychophysiology of thinking: Studies of covert processes.* New York: Academic Press.

Phipps, S.J., & Morehouse, C.A. (1969). Effects of mental practice on the acquisition of motor skills of varied difficulty. *Research Quarterly, 40,* 773-778.

Posner, M.I., & Keele, S.W. (1969). Attentional demands of movement. *Proceedings of the 16th Congress of Applied Psychology.* Amsterdam: Swets & Zeittinger.

Pylyshyn, Z.W. (1973). What the mind's eye tells the mind's brain: A critique of mental imagery. *Psychological Bulletin, 80,*1-22.

Rawlings, E.I., & Rawlings, I.L. (1974). Rotary pursuit tracking following mental rehearsal as a function of voluntary control of visual imagery. *Perceptual and Motor Skills, 38,* 302.

Rotella, R.J., Gansneder, B., Ojala, D., & Billing, J. (1980). Cognitions and coping strategies of elite skiers: An exploratory study of young developing athletes. *Journal of Sport Psychology, 2,* 350-354.

Ryan, E.D., & Simmons, J. (1981). Cognitive demand, imagery, and frequency of mental rehearsal as factors influencing acquisition of motor skills. *Journal of Sport Psychology, 3,* 35-45.

Schramm, V. (1967). *An investigation of the electromyographic responses obtained during mental practice.* Unpublished master's thesis, University of Wisconsin, Madison.

Schmidt, R.A. (1975). A schema theory of discrete motor skill learning. *Psychological Review, 82,* 225-260.

Schmidt, R.A. (1982). *Motor control and learning.* Champaign, IL: Human Kinetics.

Shea, J.B. (1977). Effects of labelling on motor short-term memory. *Journal of Experimental Psychology: Human Learning and Memory, 3,* 92-99.

Sheehan, P.W. (1966). Functional similarity of imaging to perceiving: Individual differences in vividness of imagery. *Perceptual and Motor Skills, 23,* 1011-1033.

Sheehan, P.W. (1967). Visual imagery and the organizational properties of perceived stimuli. *British Journal of Psychology, 58,* 247-252.

Start, K.B., & Richardson, A. (1964). Imagery and mental practice. *British Journal of Educational Psychology, 34,* 280-281.

Suinn, R.M. (1976). Body thinking: Psychology of olympic champs. *Psychology Today, 10,* 38-44.

Wrisberg, C.A., & Ragsdale, M.R. (1979). Cognitive demand and practice level: Factors in the mental rehearsal of motor skills. *Journal of Human Movement Studies, 5,* 201-208.

CHAPTER 9

Bandura, A. (1977). Self-efficacy: Toward a unifying theory of behavioral change. *Psychological Review, 84,* 191-215.

Bird, A.M., & Brame, J.M. (1979). Self vs. team attributions: A test of the "I'm o.k., but the team's so-so" phenomenon. *Research Quarterly, 49,* 260-268.

Bird, A.M., Foster, C.D., & Maruyama, G. (1980) Convergent and incremental effects of cohesion on attributions for self and team. *Journal of Sport Psychology, 2,* 181-194.

Bird, A.M., & Williams, J.M. (1980). A developmental-attributional analysis of sex-role stereotypes for sport. *Developmental Psychology, 16,* 319-322.

Borkovec, T.D. (1978). Self-efficacy: Cause or reflection of behavioral change? In S. Rachman (Ed.), *Advances in behaviour research and therapy* (Vol. 1). Oxford: Pergamon.

Connell, J.P. (1980). *A multidimensional measure of children's perceptions of control.* Unpublished master's thesis, University of Denver.

deCharms, R. (1968). *Personal causation.* New York: Academic Press.

Deci, E.L. (1971). Effects of externally mediated rewards on intrinsic motivation. *Journal of Personality and Social Psychology, 18,* 105-115.

Deci, E.L. (1972). Intrinsic motivation, extrinsic reinforcement. *Journal of Personality and Social Psychology, 22,* 113-120.

Deci, E.L. (1978). Intrinsic motivation: Theory and application. In D.M. Landers & R.W. Christina (Eds.), *Psychology of motor behavior and sport.* Champaign, IL: Human Kinetics.

Deci, E.L., & Ryan, R.M. (1980). The empirical exploration of intrinsic motivational processes. In L. Berkowitz (Ed.), *Advances in experimental social psychology* (Vol. 13). New York: Academic Press.

Dweck, C.S. (1975). The role of expectations and attributions in the alleviation of learned help-lessness. *Journal of Personality and Social Psychology, 31,* 674-685.

Dweck, C.S. (1980). Learned helplessness in sport. In C.H. Nadeau, W.R. Halliwell, K.M. Newell, & G.C. Roberts, (Eds.), *Psychology of motor behavior and sport.* Champaign, IL: Human Kinetics.

Dweck, C.S., & Reppucci, N.D. (1973). Learned helplessness and reinforcement responsibility in children. *Journal of Personality and Social Psychology, 25,* 109-116.

Feltz, D.L. (1982). Path analysis of the causal elements in Bandura's theory of self-efficacy and an anxiety-based model of avoidance behavior. *Journal of Personality and Social Psychology, 42,* 764-781.

Feltz, D.L., Landers, D.M., & Raeder, U. (1979). Enhancing self-efficacy in high-avoidance motor tasks: A comparison of modeling techniques. *Journal of Sport Psychology, 1,* 112-122.

Gilmor, T.M., & Minton, H.L. (1974). Internal versus external attributions of task performance as a function of locus of control, initial confidence and success-failure outcome. *Journal of Personality, 42,* 159-174.

Greene, D., & Lepper, M.R. (1974). Effects of extrinsic rewards on children's subsequent intrinsic interest. *Child Development, 45,* 1141-1145.

Halliwell, W.R. (1978). A reaction to Deci's paper on intrinsic motivation. In D.M. Landers & R.W. Christina (Eds.), *Psychology of motor behavior and sport.* Champaign, IL: Human Kinetics.

Harter, S. (1981). The development of competence motivation in the mastery of cognitive and physical skills: Is there still a place for joy? In G.C. Roberts & D.M. Landers (Eds.), *Psychology of motor behavior and sport.* Champaign, IL: Human Kinetics.

Heider, F. (1944). Social perception and phenomenal causality. *Psychological Review, 51,* 358-374.

Heider, F. (1958). *The psychology of interpersonal relations.* New York: Wiley & Sons.

Iso-Ahola, S.E. (1977). Immediate attributional effects of success and failure in the field: Testing some laboratory hypotheses. *European Journal of Social Psychology, 7,* 275-296.

Iso-Ahola, S.E. (1979). Sex-role stereotypes and causal attributions for success and failure in motor performance. *Research Quarterly, 50,* 630-640.

Jones, E.E., & Davis, K.E. (1965). From acts to dispositions: The attribution process in person perception. In L. Berkowitz (Ed.), *Advances in experimental social psychology* (Vol. 2). New York: Academic Press.

Kelley, H.H. (1973). The process of causal attribution. *American Psychologist, 28,* 107-128.

Kukla, A. (1972). Foundations of an attributional theory of performance. *Psychological Review, 79,* 454-470.

Lang, P.J. (1978). Self-efficacy theory: Thoughts on cognition and unification. In S. Rachman (Ed.), *Advances in behaviour research and therapy* (Vol. 1). Oxford: Pergamon.

Lefebvre, L.M. (1979). Achievement motivation and causal attribution in male and female athletes. *International Journal of Sport Psychology, 10,* 31-41.

McAuley, E. (1983). *Modeling and self-efficacy: An examination of Bandura's model of behavioral change.* Paper presented at the annual meeting of the North American Society for Psychology of Sport and Physical Activity, East Lansing, MI

McClelland, D.C., Atkinson, J.W., & Lowell, E.L. (1953). *The achievement motive.* New York: Appleton-Century-Crofts.

Rejeski, W.J., & Brawley, L.R. (1983). Attribution theory in sport: Current status and new perspectives. *Journal of Sport Psychology, 5,* 77-99.

Roberts, G.C. (1984). Toward a new theory of motivation in sport: The role of perceived ability. In J.M. Silva and R.S. Weinberg (Eds.), *Psychological foundations in sport,* Champaign, IL: Human Kinetics.

Roberts, G.C., Kleiber, D.A., & Duda, J.L. (1981). An analysis of motivation in children's sport: The role of perceived competence in participation. *Journal of Sport Psychology, 3*, 206-216.

Ryan, E.D. (1980). Attribution, intrinsic motivation, and athletics. In C.H. Nadeau, W.R. Halliwell, K.M. Newell, & G.C. Roberts (Eds.), *Psychology of motor behavior and sport*, Champaign, IL: Human Kinetics.

Scanlan, T.K., & Passer, M.W. (1980). Self-serving biases in the competitive sport setting: An attributional dilemma. *Journal of Sport Psychology, 2*, 124-136.

Seligman, M., & Maier, S. Failure to escape traumatic shock. *Journal of Experimental Psychology, 74*, 1-9.

Spink, K.S. (1978) Win-loss casual attributions of high school basketball players. *Canadian Journal of Applied Sport Sciences, 3*, 195-201.

Spink, K.S. (1980). The role of ego-involvement, objective outcome, and perceived performance in determination of causal attributions. Unpublished doctoral dissertation, University of Illinois, Urbana.

Vallerand, R.J. (1983). The effect of differential amounts of positive verbal feedback on the intrinsic motivation of male hockey players. *Journal of Sport Psychology, 5*, 100-107.

Vallerand, R.J., & Reid, G. (1984). On the causal effects of perceived competence on intrinsic motivation: A test of cognitive evaluation theory. *Journal of Sport Psychology, 6*, 94-102.

Weinberg, R.S., Gould, D., & Jackson, A. (1979). Expectations and performance: An empirical test of Bandura's self-efficacy theory. *Journal of Sport Psychology, 1*, 320-331.

Weinberg, R.S., Yukelson, D., & Jackson, A. (1980). Effect of public and private efficacy expectations on competitive performance. *Journal of Sport Psychology, 2*, 340-349.

Weiner, B. (1972). *Theories of motivation: From mechanism to cognition*. Chicago, IL: Rand McNally.

Weiner, B. (1979). A theory of motivation for some classroom experiences. *Journal of Educational Psychology, 71*, 3-25.

Weiner, B. (1981). The role of affect in sports psychology. In G.C. Roberts & D.M. Landers (Eds.), *Psychology of motor behavior and sport*. Champaign, IL: Human Kinetics.

Weiner, B., Frieze, I.H., Kukla, A., Reed, L., Rest, S., & Rosenbaum, R.M. (1971). *Perceiving the causes of success and failure*. New York: General Learning Press.

Weiner, B., & Kukla, A. (1970). An attributional analysis of achievement motivation. *Journal of Personality and Social Psychology, 15*, 1-20.

White, R. (1959). Motivation reconsidered: The concept of competence. *Psychological Review, 66*, 297-323.

Yan Lan, L., & Gill, D.L. (1984). The relationship among self-efficacy, stress responses, and a cognitive feedback manipulation. *Journal of Sport Psychology, 6*, 227-238.

CHAPTER 10

Arms, R.L., Russell, G.W., & Sandilands, M.L. (1980). Effects of viewing aggressive sports on the hostility of spectators. In R.M. Suinn (Ed.), *Psychology in sports*, Minneapolis: Burgess.

Ardrey, R. (1966). *The territorial imperative*. New York: Atheneum.

Bandura, A. (1973). *Aggression: A social learning analysis*. Englewood Cliffs, NJ: Prentice-Hall.

Bandura, A. (1977). *Social learning theory*. Englewood Cliffs, NJ: Prentice-Hall.

Bandura, A., Ross, D., & Ross, S. (1961). Transmission of aggression through imitation of aggressive models. *Journal of Abnormal and Social Psychology, 63*, 575-582.

Berkowitz, L. (1965). The concept of aggressive drive: Some additional considerations. In L. Berkowitz (Ed.), *Advances in Experimental Social Psychology, 2*, 301-329.

Berkowitz, L. (1970). Experimental investigations of hostility catharsis. *Journal of Consulting and Clinical Psychology, 35*, 1-7.

Berkowitz, L. (1978). Sports competition and aggression. In W.F. Straub (Ed.), *Sport psychology*, Ithaca, NY: Mouvement Publications.

Berkowitz, L. (1981). On the difference between internal and external reactions to legitimate and illegitimate frustrations: A demonstration. *Aggressive Behavior, 7,* 83-96.

Berkowitz, L., & LePage, A. (1967). Weapons as aggression-eliciting stimuli. *Journal of Personality and Social Psychology, 7,* 202-207.

Cavanaugh, B.M., & Silva, J.M. (1980). Spectator perceptions of fan misbehavior: An attitudinal inquiry. In C.H. Nadeau, W.R. Halliwell, K.M. Newell, & G.C. Roberts (Eds.), *Psychology of motor behavior and sport,* Champaign, IL: Human Kinetics.

Corran, R. (1980). Violence and the coach. In R.M. Suinn (Ed.), *Psychology in sports,* Minneapolis: Burgess.

Dollard, J., Miller, N., Doob, L., Mourer, O.H., & Sears, R.R. (1939). *Frustration and aggression.* New Haven, CN: Yale University Press.

Feigley, D.A. (1983). Is aggression justifiable? *Journal of Physical Education, Recreation and Dance, 54,* 63-64.

Geen, R.G., & O'Neal, E.C. (1969). Activation of cue-elicited aggression by general arousal. *Journal of Personality and Social Psychology, 11,* 289-292.

Goldstein, J.H., & Arms, R.L. (1971). Effects of observing athletic contests on hostility. *Sociometry, 34,* 83-90.

Harrell, W.A. (1980). Aggression by high school basketball players: An observational study of the effects of opponents' aggression and frustration-inducing factors. *International Journal of Sport Psychology, 11,* 290-298.

Lorenz, K. (1966). *On aggression.* New York, N.Y.: Harcourt, Brace & World.

Martens, R. (1975). *Social psychology & physical activity.* New York: Harper & Row.

Moyer, K.E. (1976). The physiology of violence. In A.C. Fisher (Ed.), *Psychology of sport,* Palo Alto, CA: Mayfield.

Novaco, R.W. (1979). The cognitive regulation of anger and stress. In P.C. Kendall & S.D. Hollon (Eds.), *Cognitive-behavioral interventions.* New York: Academic Press.

Ryan, E.D. (1970). The cathartic effect of vigorous motor activity on aggressive behavior. *Research Quarterly, 41,* 542-551.

Sherif, M., & Sherif, C.W. (1953). *Groups in harmony and tension,* New York: Harper & Row.

Silva, J.M. (1979). Changes in the affective state of guilt as a function of exhibiting proactive assertion or hostile aggression. In G.C. Roberts, & K.M. Newell (Eds.), *Psychology of motor behavior and sport,* Champaign, IL: Human Kinetics.

Silva, J.M. (1980a). Assertive and aggressive behavior in sport: A definitional clarification. In C.H. Nadeau, W.R. Halliwell, K.M. Newell, & G.C. Roberts (Eds.), *Psychology of motor behavior and sport,* Champaign, IL: Human Kinetics.

Silva, J.M. (1980b). Understanding aggressive behavior and its effects upon athletic performance. In W.F. Straub (Ed.), *Sport psychology.* Ithaca, NY: Mouvement Publications.

Smith, M.D. (1978). Hockey violence: Interring some myths. In W.F. Straub (Ed.), *Sport psychology.* Ithaca, NY: Mouvement Publications.

Thirer, J., & Rampey, M.S. (1979). Effects of abusive spectators' behavior on performance of home and visiting inter-collegiate basketball teams. *Perceptual and Motor Skills, 48,* 1047-1054.

Turner, R.H. (1970). The effects of viewing college football, basketball and wrestling on the elicited aggressive responses of male spectators. In G.S. Kenyon (Ed.), *Contemporary psychology of sport.* Chicago: Athletic Institute.

Volkamer, N. (1971). Investigations into the aggressiveness in competitive social systems. *Sportwissenschaft, 1,* 68-76.

Wankel, L.M. (1972). An examination of illegal aggression in intercollegiate hockey. In I.D. Williams, & L.M. Wankel (Eds.), *Proceedings of the fourth Canadian psychomotor learning and sport psychology symposium*. Ontario, Canada: University of Waterloo.

Zillmann, D. (1979). *Hostility and aggression*. New York: Wiley & Sons.

Zillmann, D., Johnson, R.C., & Day, K.D. (1974). Provoked and unprovoked aggressiveness in athletics. *Journal of Research in Personality, 8*, 139-152.

Zillmann, D., Katcher, A.H., & Milsvsky, B. (1972). Excitation transfer from physical exercise to subsequent aggressive behavior. *Journal of Experimental Social Psychology, 8*, 247-259.

CHAPTER 11

Bakeman, R., & Helmreich, R. (1975). Cohesiveness and performance: Covariation and causality in an undersea environment. *Journal of Experimental Social Psychology, 11*, 478-489.

Ball, J.R., & Carron, A. (1976). The influence of team cohesion and participation motivation upon performance success in intercollegiate ice hockey. *Canadian Journal of Applied Sport Sciences, 1*, 271-275.

Bird, A.M. (1977). Development of a model for predicting team performance. *Research Quarterly, 48*, 24-32.

Bird, A.M., & Brame, J.M. (1972). Self versus team attributions: A test of the "I'm OK, but the team's so-so" phenomenon. *Research Quarterly, 49*, 260-268.

Bird, A.M., Foster, C.D., & Maruyama, G. (1980). Convergent and incremental effects of cohesion on attributions for self and team. *Journal of Sport Psychology, 2*, 181-194.

Carron, A.V. (1980). *Social psychology of sport*. Ithaca, NY: Mouvement Publications.

Carron, A.V. (1982). Processes of group interaction in sport teams. *Quest, 33*, 245-270.

Carron, A.V., & Ball, J.R. (1977). Cause-effect characteristics of cohesiveness and participation motivation in intercollegiate hockey. *International Review of Sport Sociology, 12*, 49-60.

Davis, J.H. (1969). *Group performance*. Reading, MA: Addison-Wesley.

Donnelly, P. (1975). *An analysis of the relationship between organizational half-life and organizational effectiveness*. Unpublished manuscript.

Festinger, L., Schachter, S., & Back, K. (1950). *Social pressures in informal groups: A study of a housing project*. New York: Harper.

Forward, J. (1969). Group achievement motivation and individual motive to achieve success and to avoid failure. *Journal of Personality, 37*, 297-309.

Hagstrom, W.O., & Selvin, H.C. (1965). The dimensions of cohesiveness in small groups. *Sociometry, 28*, 30-43.

Ingham, A.G., Levinger, G., Graves, J., & Peckham, V. (1974). The Ringleman effect: Studies of group size and group performance. *Journal of Experimental Social Psychology, 10*, 371-384.

Jones, M.B. (1974). Regressing group on individual effectiveness. *Organizational Behavior and Human Performance, 11*, 426-451.

Landers, D.M., & Luschen, G. (1974). Team performance outcome and cohesiveness of competitive coacting groups. *International Review of Sport Sociology, 9*, 57-71.

Latane, B., Harkins, S.G., & Williams, K.D. (1980). *Many hands make light the work: Social loafing as a social disease*. Unpublished manuscript.

Latane, B., Williams, K.D., & Harkins, S.G. (1979). Many hands make light the work: The causes and consequences of social loafing. *Journal of Personality and Social Psychology, 37*, 823-832.

Lenk, H. (1969). Top performance despite internal conflict. In J.W. Loy & G.S. Kenyon (Eds.), *Sport, culture and society*. New York: Macmillan.

Marin, V. (1969). *Experience as a factor in pro-football success*. Unpublished manuscript.

Martens, R., Landers, D.M., & Loy, J. (1972). *Sport cohesiveness questionnaire*. Washington, DC: American Alliance of Health, Physical Education, and Recreation.

Martens, R., & Peterson, J.A. (1971). Group cohesiveness as a determinant of success and member satisfaction in team performance. *International Review of Sport Sociology, 6,* 49-61.

Steiner, I.D. (1972). *Group process and productivity.* New York: Academic Press.

Widmeyer, W.N., & Martens, R. (1978). When cohesion predicts performance outcome in sports. *Research Quarterly, 49,* 372-380.

Williams, J.M., & Hacker, C.M. (1982). Causal relationships among cohesion, satisfaction, and performance in women's intercollegiate field hockey teams. *Journal of Sport Psychology, 4,* 324-337.

Williams, K., Harkins, S., & Latane, B. (1981). Identifiability and social loafing: Two cheering experiments. *Journal of Personality and Social Psychology, 40,* 303-311.

Yukelson, D., Weinberg, R., & Jackson, A. (1984). A multidimensional sport cohesion instrument for intercollegiate basketball teams. *Journal of Sport Psychology, 6,* 103-117.

Zander, A. (1969). Group aspirations. In D. Cartwright & A. Zander (Eds.), *Group dynamics.* New York: Harper & Row.

Zander, A. (1975). Motivation and performance of sport groups. In D.M. Landers (Ed.), *Psychology of sport and motor behavior.* University Park, PA: Pennsylvania State University Press.

CHAPTER 12

Anderson, G.J. (1973). *The assessment of learning environments: A manual for the learning environment inventory and the my class inventory.* Atlantic Institute of Education.

Bird, A.M. (1977a). Leadership and cohesion within successful and unsuccessful teams: Perceptions of coaches and players. In D.M. Landers & R.W. Christina (Eds.), *Psychology of motor behavior and sport.* Champaign, IL: Human Kinetics.

Bird, A.M. (1977b). Development of a model for predicting team performance.*Research Quarterly, 48,* 24-32.

Carron, A.V. (1980). *Social psychology of sport.* Ithaca, NY: Mouvement Publications.

Carron, A.V., & Bennett, B.B. (1977). Compatibility in the coach-athlete dyad. *Research Quarterly, 48,* 671-679.

Carron, A.V., & Chelladurai, P. (1978). Psychological factors and athletic success: An analysis of coach-athlete interpersonal behavior. *Canadian Journal of Applied Sport Sciences, 3,* 43-50.

Case, R.W. (1984). Leadership in sport. *Journal of Physical Education, Recreation, and Dance, 55,* 15-16.

Chelladurai, P. (1984). Discrepancy between preferences and perceptions of leadership behavior and satisfaction of athletes in varying sports. *Journal of Sport Psychology, 6,* 27-41.

Chelladurai, P., & Carron, A.V. (1983). Athletic maturity and preferred leadership. *Journal of Sport Psychology, 5,* 371-380.

Chelladurai, P., & Saleh, S.D. (1980). Dimensions of leader behavior in sports: Development of a leadership scale. *Journal of Sport Psychology, 2,* 34-45.

Danielson, R.R. (1976). Contingency model of leadership effectiveness: For empirical investigation of its application to sport. *Motor learning, sport psychology, pedagogy and didatics of physical activity* (Monograph 5). Quebec City, Quebec, Canada.

Danielson, R.R., Zelhart, P.F., & Drake, C.J. (1975). Multidimensional scaling and factor analysis of coaching behavior as perceived by high school hockey players. *Research Quarterly, 46,* 323-334.

Fiedler, F.E. (1967). *A theory of leadership effectiveness.* New York: McGraw-Hill.

Fisher, A.C., Mancini, V.H., Hirsch, R.L., Proulx, T.J., & Staurowsky, E.J. (1982). Coach-athlete interactions and team climate. *Journal of Sport Psychology, 4,* 388-404.

Hersey, P., & Blanchard, K. (1979). *The family game.* Englewood Cliffs, NJ: Prentice-Hall.

Hersey, P., & Blanchard, K. (1982). *Management of organizational behavior: Utilizing human resources.* Englewood Cliffs, NJ: Prentice-Hall.

Inciong, P.A. (1974). *Leadership styles and team success.* Unpublished doctoral dissertation, University of Utah, Salt Lake City.

Korten, D.C. (1962). Situational determinants of leadership structure. *Journal of Conflict Resolution, 6,* 222-235.

Martens, R., Landers, D.M., & Loy, J. (1974). *Sport cohesiveness questionnaire.* Washington, DC: American Alliance of Health, Physical Education, and Recreation.

Percival, L. (1971). The coach from the athlete's viewpoint. In J.W. Taylor (Ed.), *Proceedings, symposium on the art and science of coaching.* Toronto, Canada: Fitness Institute.

Sage, G.H. (1978). Humanistic psychology and coaching. In W.F. Straub (Ed.), *Sport psychology: An analysis of athlete behavior.* Ithaca, NY: Mouvement Publications.

Schutz, W.C. (1966). *The interpersonal underworld* (5th ed.). Palo Alto, CA: Science & Behavior Books.

Schutz, W.C. (1967). *The FIRO scales.* Palo Alto, CA: Consulting Psychologists.

Smith, R.E., Smoll, F.L., & Curtis, B. (1978). Coaching behaviors in little league baseball. In F.L. Smoll & R.E. Smith (Eds.), *Psychological perspectives in youth sports.* Washington, DC: Hemisphere.

Smith, R.E., Smoll, F.L., & Curtis, B. (1979). Coach effectiveness training: A cognitive-behavioral approach to enhancing relationship skills in youth sport coaches. *Journal of Sport Psychology, 1,* 59-75.

Smith, R.E., Smoll, F.L., & Hunt, E. (1977). A system for the behavioral assessment of athletic coaches. *Research Quarterly, 48,* 401-407.

Yukelson, D., Weinberg, R., & Jackson, A. (1984). A multidimensional sport cohesion instrument for intercollegiate basketball teams. *Journal of Sport Psychology, 6,* 103-117.

INDEX

A

Achievement change program, 227-228

Achievement goals, 223-225

Achievement motivation, 226-229

Achievement orientation, relation of, to dropping out, 224

Affection in social relationships, 296

Aggression

Berkowitz's reformulation of, 252-253

catharsis hypothesis of, 249-250

cognitive-affective factors as sources of, 255-256

collective, 258-260

competition as source of, 253-254

excitement and arousal as sources of, 254-255

fan reaction to, 259-260

frustration as source of, 253-254

frustration-aggression displacment hypothesis of, 250-251

game-related variables and, 257-258

and gradient of stimulus generalization, 250

group performance, and coaching behavior, 245-307

guilt as factor in, 255-256

home versus away as factor in, 257

hostile, 247

instinct theory of, 248-249

instrumental, 247-248

nature of, 247-248

observation of, 258-259

performance level after, 256-257

physical fitness as factor in, 256

player-related variables in, 253-254

point spread as factor in, 257

realistic, 259

social learning theory of, 251-252

and sport, 246-267

stylized, 259

team standing as factor in, 257

theoretical explanations of, 248-253

total points as factor in, 257

versus assertive behavior, 248

Aggressive, overly, basketball player (case study), 262-264

Androgyny, 34

Anxiety; *see also* Stress

acute effects of exercise on, 103-104

arousal, and interventions in sport, 49-144

attention, and cue processing, 154

attentional focus, and tennis serve (case study), 165-166

and attentional style, 154-156

chronic effects of exercise on, 104, 105

competitive; *see* Competitive anxiety

and evaluation potential in discus performance (case study), 107-108

and exercise, relationship between, 103-105

intervention approaches for coping with, 113-114

and inverted-U hypothesis, 85-89

measurement of, 82-83

motor performance, sport, and exercise, 78-111

and motor skills, contemporary perspectives on, 84-89

physiological manifestations of, and relaxation response, 115-116

precompetitive; *see* Precompetitive anxiety

state; *see* State anxiety

stress, and motor performance errors, 86, 87

trait; *see* Trait anxiety

types of, 79-80

Anxiety level

effect of, on observational learning, 183-184

relationship of peripheral narrowing to, 88

Anxiety process, unifying model and, 83-84

Applied behavioral coaching (case study), 41-42

Applied versus basic research, 11-12

Arousal

anxiety, and interventions in sport, 49-144

cue reduction feedback to reduce (case study), 72

increased, conflict as generator of, 66-67

measurement of, and unifying model of sport behavior, 59-62

nature of, 51

Arousal—cont'd
  peripheral measures of, 60
  practice, level of, and motor performance, 67
  relation of power and control to, 64-65
  as source of aggression, 254-255
  and sport behavior, 50-77
  theoretical explanations of, conflicting, 51-59
Arousal level
  effect of self-esteem on, 67
  individual differences as mediating variable in, 59
  influence of personal characteristics on, 66-67
  of parachutists, 68-71
  social situation as mediating variable in, 59
  sport specific evidence on, 67-71
  task difficulty as mediating variable in, 58-59
  of underwater divers, 67-68
Assimilation and turnover, player, effect of, 273-274
Association versus dissociation, 158-159
Associational patterns, effect of, on observational
    learning, 178
Associative strategy, 158
A-state, changes in
  before and after season, 100-103
  of track and field participants, 100, 102
  within competitive process, 99-100
A-state reactions, basketball situations and, 100, 101
A-state scores
  A-trait, and basketball performance, relationships
      among, 92, 93
  of female collegiate basketball players, 100
  of high, moderate, and low A-trait basketball
      players, 92, 93
  of high school female basketball players, 100
  precompetitive, and basketball performance, rela-
      tionship between, 91
    of high versus low A-trait players, 90, 91, 92
Athletes
  and coach, compatibility of, 296-297
  and nonathletes, personality differences between,
    35
  preparing for imaginal rehearsal by, 205-206

A-trait basketball players
  A-state scores, and performance, relationships
      among, 92, 93
  high, moderate, and low, A-state scores of, 92, 93
  high versus low, performance of, 90, 91, 92
Attention
  anxiety, and cue processing, 154
  attentional style, and sport behavior, 146-169
  effect of, on observational learning, 178
  selective, 148
  and skill level, 149
  and unifying model, 160-162
Attention control for athletes (case study), 163-164
Attentional and cue processing demands, 65
Attentional constraints, overview of, 147-148
Attentional factors related to coaching effectiveness,
    156-162
Attentional focus
  anxiety, and tennis serve (case study), 165-166
  effective, 151
  and sport-related situations, 150
Attentional and Interpersonal Style, Test of; see Test
    of Attentional and Interpersonal Style
Attentional mechanism, 147-148
Attentional profile, effective versus ineffective, 151,
    152
Attentional scales of Test of Attentional and Interper-
    sonal Style, 151
Attentional shifts, 89, 154
Attentional style
  and anxiety, 154-156
  of coach, 159-160
  as individual difference variable, 149-152
  measurement of, 150-152
  and state anxiety, 155-156
  theoretical model of, 149-150
  and trait anxiety, 154-155
  and volleyball performance (case study), 164-165
Attribution patterns as function of gender, 229
Attribution retraining treatment, 227-228
Attribution theory of motivation, 225-230